THE PELICAN FREUD LIBRARY

VOLUME 11

ON METAPSYCHOLOGY: THE THEORY OF PSYCHOANALYSIS

BEYOND THE PLEASURE PRINCIPLE

THE EGO AND THE ID

AND OTHER WORKS

Sigmund Freud

Translated from the German
under the general editorship of James Strachey

The present volume
compiled and edited by Angela Richards

PENGUIN BOOKS

PENGUIN BOOKS

Published by the Penguin Group
27 Wrights Lane, London W8 5TZ, England
Viking Penguin Inc., 40 West 23rd Street, New York, New York 10010, USA
Penguin Books Australia Ltd, Ringwood, Victoria, Australia
Penguin Books Canada Ltd, 2801 John Street, Markham, Ontario, Canada L3R 1B4
Penguin Books (NZ) Ltd, 182–190 Wairau Road, Auckland 10, New Zealand

Penguin Books Ltd, Registered Offices: Harmondsworth, Middlesex, England

Beyond the Pleasure Principle,
The Ego and the Id
and other works

Present English translations first published in *The Standard Edition of the Complete Psychological Works of Sigmund Freud* by the Hogarth Press and the Institute of Psycho-Analysis, London, as follows:

'Formulations on the Two Principles of Mental Functioning', 'A Note on the Unconscious in Psychoanalysis', Volume XII (1958); 'On Narcissism: An Introduction', 'Papers on Metapsychology' (comprising 'Instincts and their Vicissitudes', 'Repression', 'The Unconscious', 'A Metapsychological Supplement to the Theory of Dreams', 'Mourning and Melancholia'), Volume XIV (1957); *Beyond the Pleasure Principle*, Volume XVIII (1955); *The Ego and the Id*, 'The Economic Problem of Masochism', 'A Note upon the "Mystic Writing-Pad" ', 'Negation', Volume XIX (1961); 'A Disturbance of Memory on the Acropolis', Volume XXII (1964), 'Splitting of the Ego in the Process of Defence', Volume XXII (1964).

'Sigmund Freud: A Sketch of his Life and Ideas' first published in *Two Short Accounts of Psycho-Analysis* in Pelican Books 1962

This collection, *On Metapsychology*, first published in Pelican Books 1984
5 7 9 10 8 6 4

Made and printed in Great Britain by
BPCC Hazell Books Ltd
Member of BPCC Ltd
Aylesbury, Bucks, England

Set in Bembo (Linotron)

THE PELICAN FREUD LIBRARY

General Editor:
Angela Richards (1973–82)
Albert Dickson (1982–)

VOLUME 11

ON METAPSYCHOLOGY

THE THEORY OF PSYCHOANALYSIS

Sigmund Freud

Sigmund Freud was born in 1856 in Moravia; between the ages of four and eighty-two his home was in Vienna: in 1938 Hitler's invasion of Austria forced him to seek asylum in London, where he died in the following year. His career began with several years of brilliant work on the anatomy and physiology of the nervous system. He was almost thirty when, after a period of study under Charcot in Paris, his interests first turned to psychology, and another ten years of clinical work in Vienna (at first in collaboration with Breuer, an older colleague) saw the birth of his creation, psychoanalysis. This began simply as a method of treating neurotic patients by investigating their minds, but it quickly grew into an accumulation of knowledge about the workings of the mind in general, whether sick or healthy. Freud was thus able to demonstrate the normal development of the sexual instinct in childhood and, largely on the basis of an examination of dreams, arrived at his fundamental discovery of the unconscious forces that influence our everyday thoughts and actions. Freud's life was uneventful, but his ideas have shaped not only many specialist disciplines, but the whole intellectual climate of the last half-century.

THE PELICAN FREUD LIBRARY

General Editor:
Angela Richards (1973–82)
Albert Dickson (1982–)

VOLUME 11

ON METAPSYCHOLOGY

THE THEORY OF PSYCHOANALYSIS

Sigmund Freud

Sigmund Freud was born in 1856 in Moravia; between the ages of four and eighty-two his home was in Vienna: in 1938 Hitler's invasion of Austria forced him to seek asylum in London, where he died in the following year. His career began with several years of brilliant work on the anatomy and physiology of the nervous system. He was almost thirty when, after a period of study under Charcot in Paris, his interests first turned to psychology, and another ten years of clinical work in Vienna (at first in collaboration with Breuer, an older colleague) saw the birth of his creation, psychoanalysis. This began simply as a method of treating neurotic patients by investigating their minds, but it quickly grew into an accumulation of knowledge about the workings of the mind in general, whether sick or healthy. Freud was thus able to demonstrate the normal development of the sexual instinct in childhood and, largely on the basis of an examination of dreams, arrived at his fundamental discovery of the unconscious forces that influence our everyday thoughts and actions. Freud's life was uneventful, but his ideas have shaped not only many specialist disciplines, but the whole intellectual climate of the last half-century.

CONTENTS

VOLUME 11
ON METAPSYCHOLOGY

INTRODUCTION TO THE PELICAN FREUD LIBRARY

The Pelican Freud Library is intended to meet the needs of the general reader by providing all Freud's major writings in translation together with an appropriate linking commentary. It is the first time that such an edition has been produced in paperback in the English language. It does not supplant *The Standard Edition of the Complete Psychological Works of Sigmund Freud*, translated from the German under the general editorship of James Strachey, in collaboration with Anna Freud, assisted by Alix Strachey and Alan Tyson, editorial assistant Angela Richards (Hogarth Press, 24 volumes, 1953–74). The *Standard Edition* remains the fullest and most authoritative collection published in any language. It does, however, provide a large enough selection to meet the requirements of all but the most specialist reader – in particular it aims to cater for students of sociology, anthropology, criminology, medicine, aesthetics and education, all of them fields in which Freud's ideas have established their relevance.

The texts are reprinted unabridged, with corrections, from the *Standard Edition*. The editorial commentary – introductions, footnotes, internal cross-references, bibliographies and indexes – is also based upon the *Standard Edition*, but it has been abridged and where necessary adapted to suit the less specialized scope and purposes of the *Pelican Freud Library*. Some corrections have been made and some new material added.

Selection of Material

This is not a complete edition of Freud's psychological works – still less of his works as a whole, which included important contributions to neurology and neuropathology dating from the early part of his professional life. Of the psychological writings, virtually all the major works have been included. The arrangement is by subject-matter, so that the main contributions to any particular theme will be found in one volume. Within each volume the works are, for the main part, in chronological sequence. The aim has been to cover the whole field of Freud's observations and his theory of psychoanalysis: that is to say, in the first place, the structure and dynamics of human mental activity; secondly, psychopathology and the mechanism of mental disorder; and thirdly, the application of psychoanalytic theory to wider spheres than the disorders of individuals which Freud originally, and indeed for the greater part of his life, investigated – to the psychology of groups, to social institutions and to religion, art and literature.

In his 'Sigmund Freud: A Sketch of his Life and Ideas' (p. 13 ff. below), James Strachey includes an account of Freud's discoveries as well as defining his principal theories and tracing their development.

Writings excluded from the Edition

The works that have been excluded are (1) The neurological writings and most of those very early works from the period before the idea of psychoanalysis had taken form. (2) Writings on the actual technique of treatment. These were written specifically for practitioners of psychoanalysis and for analysts in training and their interest is correspondingly specialized. Freud never in fact produced a complete text on psychoanalytic treatment and the papers on technique only deal with selected points of difficulty or theoretical interest. (3) Writings which cover the same ground as other major works which have been included; for example, since the *Library* includes the *Introductory Lectures on Psychoanalysis* and the *New Lectures*, it was decided to leave out several of the shorter expository works in which Freud surveys the whole subject. Similarly, because the *Interpretation of Dreams* is included, the shorter writings on this topic have been omitted. (4) Freud's private correspondence, much of which has now been published in translation[1]. This is not to imply that such letters are without interest or importance though they have not yet received full critical treatment. (5) The numerous short writings, such as reviews of books, prefaces to other authors' works, obituary notices and little *pièces d'occasion* – all of which lose interest to a large extent when separated from the books or occasions to which they refer and which would often demand long editorial explanations to make them comprehensible.

All of these excluded writings (with the exception of the works on neurology and the private letters) can be found in the *Standard Edition*.

Editorial Commentary

The bibliographical information, included at the beginning of the Editor's Note or Introduction to each work, gives the title of the German (or other) original, the date and place of its first publication and the position, where applicable, of the work in Freud's *Gesammelte Werke*, the most complete edition at present available of the works in German (published by S. Fischer Verlag, Frankfurt am Main). Details of the first translation of each work into English are also included, together with the *Standard Edition* reference. Other editions are listed only if they contain significant changes. (Full details of all German editions published in Freud's lifetime and of all English editions prior to the *Standard Edition* are included in the *Standard Edition*.)

The date of original publication of each work has been added to the half-title page, with the date of composition included in square brackets wherever it is different from the former date.

Further background information is given in introductory notes and in footnotes to the text. Apart from dealing with the time and circumstances of composition, these notes aim to make it possible to follow the inception and development of important psychoanalytic concepts by means of systematic cross-

1. [See the list, p. 25 *n*. below, and the details in the Bibliography, p. 467 ff.]

references. Most of these references are to other works included in the *Pelican Freud Library*. A secondary purpose is to date additions and alterations made by Freud in successive revisions of the text and in certain cases to provide the earlier versions. No attempt has been made to do this as comprehensively as in the *Standard Edition*, but variants are given whenever they indicate a definite change of view. Square brackets are used throughout to distinguish editorial additions from Freud's text and his own footnotes.

It will be clear from this account that I owe an overwhelming debt to the late James Strachey, the general editor and chief translator of the *Standard Edition*. He indeed was mainly responsible for the idea of a *Pelican Freud Library*, and for the original plan of contents. I have also had the advantage of discussions with Miss Anna Freud and the late Mrs Alix Strachey, both of whom gave advice of the greatest value. I am grateful to the late Mr Ernst Freud for his support and to the Publications Committee of the Institute of Psycho-Analysis for help in furthering preparations for this edition. In preparing the present volume, *On Metapsychology*, I have had invaluable assistance from Albert Dickson and from my husband, Dr A. D. Harris, to both of whom my thanks are due.

ANGELA RICHARDS, 1982

SIGMUND FREUD

A SKETCH OF HIS LIFE AND IDEAS

SIGMUND FREUD was born on 6 May 1856 in Freiberg, a small town in Moravia, which was at that time a part of Austria-Hungary. In an external sense the eighty-three years of his life were on the whole uneventful and call for no lengthy history.

He came of a middle-class Jewish family and was the eldest child of his father's second wife. His position in the family was a little unusual, for there were already two grown-up sons by his father's first wife. These were more than twenty years older than he was and one of them was already married, with a little boy; so that Freud was in fact born an uncle. This nephew played at least as important a part in his very earliest years as his own younger brothers and sisters, of whom seven were born after him.

His father was a wool-merchant and soon after Freud's birth found himself in increasing commercial difficulties. He therefore decided, when Freud was just three years old, to leave Freiberg, and a year later the whole family settled in Vienna, with the exception of the two elder half-brothers and their children, who established themselves instead in Manchester. At more than one stage in his life Freud played with the idea of joining them in England, but nothing was to come of this for nearly eighty years.

In Vienna during the whole of Freud's childhood the family lived in the most straitened conditions; but it is much to his father's credit that he gave invariable priority to the charge of Freud's education, for the boy was obviously intelligent and was a hard worker as well. The result was that he won a place in the 'Gymnasium' at the early age of nine, and for the last six of the eight years he spent at the school he was regularly top of his class. When at the age of seventeen he passed out of school his career was still undecided; his education so far had been of the most general kind, and, though he seemed in any case destined for the University, several faculties lay open to him.

Freud insisted more than once that at no time in his life did he feel 'any particular predilection for the career of a doctor. I was moved, rather,' he says, 'by a sort of curiosity, which was, however, directed more towards human concerns than towards natural objects.'[1] Elsewhere he writes: 'I have no knowledge of having had any craving in my early childhood to help suffering humanity . . . In my youth I felt an overpowering need to understand something of the riddles of the world in which we live and perhaps even to contribute something to their solution.'[2] And in yet another passage in which he was discussing the sociological studies of his last years: 'My interest, after making a lifelong *détour* through the natural sciences, medicine, and psychotherapy, returned to the cultural problems which had fascinated me long before, when I was a youth scarcely old enough for thinking.'[3]

What immediately determined Freud's choice of a scientific career was, so he tells us, being present just when he was leaving school at a public reading of an extremely flowery essay on 'Nature', attributed (wrongly, it seems) to Goethe. But if it was to be science, practical considerations narrowed the choice to medicine. And it was as a medical student that Freud enrolled himself at the University in the autumn of 1873 at the age of seventeen. Even so, however, he was in no hurry to obtain a medical degree. For his first year or two he attended lectures on a variety of subjects, but gradually concentrated first on biology and then on physiology. His very first piece of research was in his third year at the University, when he was deputed by the Professor of Comparative Anatomy to investigate a detail in the anatomy of the eel, which involved the dissection of some four hundred specimens. Soon afterwards he entered the Physiologi-

1. [*An Autobiographical Study* (1925*d*), near the opening of the work.]
2. ['Postscript to *The Question of Lay Analysis*' (1927*a*).]
3. ['Postcript (1935) to *An Autobiographical Study*' (1935*a*).]

cal Laboratory under Brücke, and worked there happily for six years. It was no doubt from him that he acquired the main outlines of his attitude to physical science in general. During these years Freud worked chiefly on the anatomy of the central nervous system and was already beginning to produce publications. But it was becoming obvious that no livelihood which would be sufficient to meet the needs of the large family at home was to be picked up from these laboratory studies. So at last, in 1881, he decided to take his medical degree, and a year later, most unwillingly, gave up his position under Brücke and began work in the Vienna General Hospital.

What finally determined this change in his life was something more urgent than family considerations: in June 1882 he became engaged to be married, and thenceforward all his efforts were directed towards making marriage possible. His fiancée, Martha Bernays, came of a well-known Jewish family in Hamburg, and though for the moment she was living in Vienna she was very soon obliged to return to her remote North-German home. During the four years that followed, it was only for brief visits that he could have glimpses of her, and the two lovers had to content themselves with an almost daily interchange of letters. Freud now set himself to establishing a position and a reputation in the medical world. He worked in various departments of the hospital, but soon came to concentrate on neuroanatomy and neuropathology. During this period, too, he published the first inquiry into the possible medical uses of cocaine; and it was this that suggested to Koller the drug's employment as a local anaesthetic. He soon formed two immediate plans: one of these was to obtain an appointment as *Privatdozent*, a post not unlike that of a university lecturer in England, the other was to gain a travelling bursary which would enable him to spend some time in Paris where the reigning figure was the great Charcot. Both of these aims, if they were realized, would, he felt, bring him real advantages, and in 1885, after a hard struggle, he achieved them both.

The months which Freud spent under Charcot at the Salpêtrière (the famous Paris hospital for nervous diseases) brought another change in the course of his life and this time a revolutionary one. So far his work had been concerned entirely with physical science and he was still carrying out histological studies on the brain while he was in Paris. Charcot's interests were at that period concentrated mainly on hysteria and hypnotism. In the world from which Freud came these subjects were regarded as barely respectable, but he became absorbed in them, and, though Charcot himself looked at them purely as branches of neuropathology, for Freud they meant the first beginnings of the investigation of the mind.

On his return to Vienna in the spring of 1886 Freud set up in private practice as a consultant in nervous diseases, and his long-delayed marriage followed soon afterwards. He did not, however, at once abandon all his neuropathological work: for several more years he studied in particular the cerebral palsies of children, on which he became a leading authority. At this period, too, he produced an important monograph on aphasia. But he was becoming more and more engaged in the treatment of the neuroses. After experimenting in vain with electrotherapy, he returned to hypnotic suggestion, and in 1888 visited Nancy to learn the technique used with such apparent success there by Liébeault and Bernheim. This still proved unsatisfactory and he was driven to yet another line of approach. He knew that a friend of his, Dr Josef Breuer, a Vienna consultant considerably his senior, had some ten years earlier cured a girl suffering from hysteria by a quite new procedure. He now persuaded Breuer to take up the method once more, and he himself applied it to several fresh cases with promising results. The method was based on the assumption that hysteria was the product of a psychical trauma which had been forgotten by the patient; and the treatment consisted in inducing her in a hypnotic state to recall the forgotten trauma to the accompaniment of appropriate emotions. Before very long Freud began to make changes both in the procedure and in the underlying theory; this led eventually to a breach with Breuer, and to the ultimate development by Freud of the whole system of ideas to which he soon gave the name of psychoanalysis.

From this moment onwards – from 1895, perhaps – to the very end of his life, the whole of Freud's intellectual existence revolved around this development, its far-reaching implications, and its theoretical and practical repercussions. It would, of course, be impossible to give in a few sentences any consecutive account of Freud's discoveries and ideas, but an attempt will be made presently to indicate in a disconnected fashion some of the main changes he has brought about in our habits of thought. Meanwhile we may continue to follow the course of his external life.

His domestic existence in Vienna was essentially devoid of episode: his home and his consulting rooms were in the same house from 1891 till his departure for London forty-seven years later. His happy marriage and his growing family – three sons and three daughters – provided a solid counterweight to the difficulties which, to begin with at least, surrounded his professional career. It was not only the nature of his discoveries that created prejudice against him in medical circles; just as great, perhaps, was the effect of the intense anti-semitic feeling which dominated the official world of Vienna: his appointment to a university professorship was constantly held back by political influence.

One particular feature of these early years calls for mention on account of its consequences. This was Freud's friendship with Wilhelm Fliess, a brilliant but unbalanced Berlin physician, who specialized in the ear and throat, but whose wider interests extended over human biology and the effects of periodic phenomena in vital processes. For fifteen years, from 1887 to 1902, Freud corresponded with him regularly, reported the development of his ideas, forwarded him long drafts outlining his future writings, and, most important of all, sent him an essay of some forty thousand words which has been given the name of a 'Project for a Scientific Psychology'. This essay was composed in 1895, at what might be described as the watershed of Freud's career, when he was reluctantly moving from physiology to psychology; it is an attempt to state the facts of psychology in purely neurological terms. This paper and all the rest of Freud's communications to Fliess have, by a lucky chance, survived: they throw a fascinating light on the development of Freud's ideas and show how much of the later findings of psychoanalysis were already present in his mind at this early stage.

Apart from his relations with Fliess, Freud had little outside support to begin with. He gradually gathered a few pupils round him in Vienna, but it was only after some ten years, in about 1906, that a change was inaugurated by the adhesion of a number of Swiss psychiatrists to his views. Chief among these were Bleuler, the head of the Zurich mental hospital, and his assistant Jung. This proved to be the beginning of the first spread of psychoanalysis. An international meeting of psychoanalysts gathered at Salzburg in 1908, and in 1909 Freud and Jung were invited to give a number of lectures in the United States. Freud's writings began to be translated into many languages, and groups of practising analysts sprang up all over the world. But the progress of psychoanalysis was not without its set-backs: the currents which its subject-matter stirred up in the mind ran too deep for its easy acceptance. In 1911 one of Freud's prominent Viennese supporters, Alfred Adler, broke away from him, and two or three years later Jung's differences from Freud led to their separation. Almost immediately after this came the First World War and an interruption of the international spread of psychoanalysis. Soon afterwards, too, came the gravest personal tragedies – the death of a daughter and of a favourite grandchild, and the onset of the malignant illness which was to pursue him relentlessly for the last sixteen years of his life. None of these troubles, however, brought any interruption to the development of Freud's observations and inferences. The structure of his ideas continued to expand and to find even wider applications – particularly in the sociological field. By now he had become generally recognized as a figure of world celebrity, and no honour pleased him more than his election in 1936, the year of his eightieth birthday, as a Corresponding Member of the Royal Society. It was no doubt this fame, supported by the efforts of influential admirers, including, it is said, President Roosevelt, that protected him from the worst excesses of the National

Socialists when Hitler invaded Austria in 1938, though they seized and destroyed his publications. Freud's departure from Vienna was nevertheless essential, and in June of that year, accompanied by some of his family, he made the journey to London, and it was there, a year later, on 23 September 1939, that he died.

It has become a journalistic cliché to speak of Freud as one of the revolutionary founders of modern thought and to couple his name with that of Einstein. Most people would however find it almost as hard to summarize the changes introduced by the one as by the other.

Freud's discoveries may be grouped under three headings – an instrument of research, the findings produced by the instrument, and the theoretical hypotheses inferred from the findings – though the three groups were of course mutually inter-related. Behind all of Freud's work, however, we should posit his belief in the universal validity of the law of determinism. As regards physical phenomena this belief was perhaps derived from his experience in Brücke's laboratory and so, ultimately, from the school of Helmholtz; but Freud extended the belief uncompromisingly to the field of mental phenomena, and here he may have been influenced by his teacher, the psychiatrist Meynert, and indirectly by the philosophy of Herbart.

First and foremost, Freud was the discoverer of the first instrument for the scientific examination of the human mind. Creative writers of genius had had fragmentary insight into mental processes, but no systematic method of investigation existed before Freud. It was only gradually that he perfected the instrument, since it was only gradually that the difficulties in the way of such an investigation became apparent. The forgotten trauma in Breuer's explanation of hysteria provided the earliest problem and perhaps the most fundamental of all, for it showed conclusively that there were active parts of the mind not immediately open to inspection either by an onlooker or by the subject himself. These parts of the mind were described by Freud, without regard for metaphysical or terminological disputes, as the unconscious. Their existence was equally demonstrated by the fact of post-hypnotic suggestion, where a person in a fully waking state performs an action which had been suggested to him some time earlier, though he had totally forgotten the suggestion itself. No examination of the mind could thus be considered complete unless it included this unconscious part of it in its scope. How was this to be accomplished? The obvious answer seemed to be: by means of hypnotic suggestion; and this was the instrument used by Breuer and, to begin with, by Freud. But it soon turned out to be an imperfect one, acting irregularly and uncertainly and sometimes not at all. Little by little, accordingly, Freud abandoned the use of suggestion and replaced it by an entirely fresh instrument, which was later known as 'free association'. He adopted the unheard-of plan of simply asking the person whose mind he was investigating to say whatever came into his head. This crucial decision led at once to the most startling results; even in this primitive form Freud's instrument produced fresh insight. For, though things went along swimmingly for a while, sooner or later the flow of associations dried up: the subject would not or could not think of anything more to say. There thus came to light the fact of 'resistance', of a force, separate from the subject's conscious will, which was refusing to collaborate with the investigation. Here was one basis for a very fundamental piece of theory, for a hypothesis of the mind as something dynamic, as consisting in a number of mental forces, some conscious and some unconscious, operating now in harmony now in opposition with one another.

Though these phenomena eventually turned out to be of universal occurrence, they were first observed and studied in neurotic patients, and the earlier years of Freud's work were largely concerned with discovering means by which the 'resistance' of these patients could be overcome and what lay behind it could be brought to light. The solution was only made possible by an extraordinary piece of self-observation on Freud's part – what we should now describe as his self-analysis. We are fortunate in having a contemporary first-hand description of this event in his letters to Fliess which have already been mentioned. This analysis enabled him to discover the nature of the unconscious processes at work in the mind and to understand why there is such a strong resistance to their becoming conscious; it enabled him to devise techniques for overcoming or evading the resistance in his patients; and, most important of all, it enabled him to realize the very great difference between the mode of functioning of these unconscious processes and that of our familiar conscious ones. A word may be said on each of these three points, for in fact they constitute the core of Freud's contributions to our knowledge of the mind.

The unconscious contents of the mind were found to consist wholly in the activity of conative trends – desires or wishes – which derive their energy directly from the primary physical instincts. They function quite regardless of any consideration other than that of obtaining immediate satisfaction, and are thus liable to be out of step with those more conscious elements in the mind which are concerned with adaptation to reality and the avoidance of external dangers. Since, moreover, these primitive trends are to a great extent of a sexual or of a destructive nature, they are bound to come in conflict with the more social and civilized mental forces. Investigations along this path were what led Freud to his discoveries of the long-disguised secrets of the sexual life of children and of the Oedipus complex.

In the second place, his self-analysis led him to an inquiry into the nature of dreams. These turned out to be, like neurotic symptoms, the product of a conflict and a compromise between the primary unconscious impulses and the secondary conscious ones. By analysing them into their elements it was therefore possible to infer their hidden unconscious contents; and, since dreams are common phenomena of almost universal occurrence, their interpretation turned out to be one of the most useful technical contrivances for penetrating the resistances of neurotic patients.

Finally, the painstaking examination of dreams enabled Freud to classify the remarkable differences between what he termed the primary and secondary processes of thought, between events in the unconscious and conscious regions of the mind. In the unconscious, it was found, there is no sort of organization or coordination: each separate impulse seeks satisfaction independently of all the rest; they proceed uninfluenced by one another; contradictions are completely inoperative, and the most opposite impulses flourish side by side. So, too, in the unconscious, associations of ideas proceed along lines without any regard to logic: similarities are treated as identities, negatives are equated with positives. Again, the objects to which the conative trends are attached in the unconscious are extraordinarily changeable – one may be replaced by another along a whole chain of associations that have no rational basis. Freud perceived that the intrusion into conscious thinking of mechanisms that belong properly to the primary process accounts for the oddity not only of dreams but of many other normal and pathological mental events.

It is not much of an exaggeration to say that all the later part of Freud's work lay in an immense extension and elaboration of these early ideas. They were applied to an elucidation of the mechanisms not only of the psychoneuroses and psychoses but also of such normal processes as slips of the tongue, making jokes, artistic creation, political institutions, and religions; they played a part in throwing fresh light on many applied sciences – archaeology, anthropology, criminology, education; they also served to account for the effectiveness of psychoanalytic therapy. Lastly, too, Freud erected on the basis of these elementary observations a theoretical superstructure, what he named a 'metapsychology', of more general concepts. These, however, fascinating as many people will find them, he always insisted were in the nature of provisional hypotheses. Quite late in his life, indeed, influenced by the ambiguity of the term 'unconscious' and its many conflicting uses, he proposed a new structural account of the mind in which the uncoordinated instinctual trends were called the 'id', the organized realistic part the 'ego', and the critical and moralizing function the 'super-ego' – a new account which has certainly made for a clarification of many issues.

This, then, will have given the reader an outline of the external events of Freud's life and some notion of the scope of his discoveries. Is it legitimate to ask for more? to try to penetrate a little further and to inquire what sort of person Freud was? Possibly not. But human curiosity about great men is insatiable, and if it is not gratified with true accounts it will inevitably clutch at mythological ones. In two of Freud's early books (*The Interpretation of Dreams* and *The Psychopathology of Everyday Life*) the presentation of his thesis had forced on him the necessity of bringing up an unusual amount of personal material. Nevertheless, or perhaps for that very reason, he intensely objected to any intrusion into his private life, and he was correspondingly the subject of a wealth of myths. According to the first and most naïve rumours, for instance, he was an abandoned profligate, devoted to the corruption of public morals. Later fantasies have tended in the opposite direction: he has been represented as a harsh moralist, a ruthless disciplinarian, an autocrat, egocentric and unsmiling, and an essentially unhappy man. To anyone who was acquainted with him, even slightly, both these pictures must seem equally preposterous. The second of them was no doubt partly derived from a knowledge of his physical sufferings during his last years; but partly too it may have been due to the unfortunate impression produced by some of his most widespread portraits. He disliked being photographed, at least by professional photographers, and his features on occasion expressed the fact; artists too seem always to have been overwhelmed by the necessity for representing the inventor of psychoanalysis as a ferocious and terrifying figure. Fortunately, however, alternative versions exist of a more amiable and truer kind – snapshots, for instance, taken on a holiday or with his children, such as will be found in his eldest son's memoir of his father (*Glory Reflected*, by Martin Freud [1957]). In many ways, indeed, this delightful and amusing book serves to redress the balance from more official biographies, invaluable as they are, and reveals something of Freud as he was in ordinary life. Some of these portraits show us that in his earlier days he had well-filled features, but in later life, at any rate after the First World

War and even before his illness, this was no longer so, and his features, as well as his whole figure (which was of medium height), were chiefly remarkable for the impression they gave of tense energy and alert observation. He was serious but kindly and considerate in his more formal manners, but in other circumstances could be an entertaining talker with a pleasantly ironical sense of humour. It was easy to discover his devoted fondness for his family and to recognize a man who would inspire affection. He had many miscellaneous interests – he was fond of travelling abroad, of country holidays, of mountain walks – and there were other, more engrossing subjects, art, archaeology, literature. Freud was a very well read man in many languages, not only in German. He read English and French fluently, besides having a fair knowledge of Spanish and Italian. It must be remembered, too, that though the later phases of his education were chiefly scientific (it is true that at the University he studied philosophy for a short time) at school he had learnt the classics and never lost his affection for them. We happen to have a letter written by him at the age of seventeen to a school friend.[1] In it he describes his varying success in the different papers of his school-leaving examination: in Latin a passage from Virgil, and in Greek thirty-three lines from, of all things, *Oedipus Rex*.

In short, we might regard Freud as what in England we should consider the best kind of product of a Victorian upbringing. His tastes in literature and art would obviously differ from ours, his views on ethics, though decidedly liberal, would not belong to the post-Freudian age. But we should see in him a man who lived a life of full emotion and of much suffering without embitterment. Complete honesty and directness were qualities that stood out in him, and so too did his intellectual readiness to take in and consider any fact, however new or extraordinary, that was presented to him. It was perhaps an inevitable corollary and extension of these qualities, combined with a general benevolence which a surface misanthropy failed

1. [Emil Fluss. The letter is included in the volume of Freud's correspondence (1960*a*).]

to disguise, that led to some features of a surprising kind. In spite of his subtlety of mind he was essentially unsophisticated, and there were sometimes unexpected lapses in his critical faculty – a failure, for instance, to perceive an untrustworthy authority in some subject that was off his own beat such as Egyptology or philology, and, strangest of all in someone whose powers of perception had to be experienced to be believed, an occasional blindness to defects in his acquaintances. But though it may flatter our vanity to declare that Freud was a human being of a kind like our own, that satisfaction can easily be carried too far. There must in fact have been something very extraordinary in the man who was first able to recognize a whole field of mental facts which had hitherto been excluded from normal consciousness, the man who first interpreted dreams, who first accepted the facts of infantile sexuality, who first made the distinction between the primary and secondary processes of thinking – the man who first made the unconscious mind real to us.

JAMES STRACHEY

[Those in search of further information will find it in the three-volume biography of Freud by Ernest Jones, an abridged version of which was published in Pelican in 1964 (reissued 1974), in the important volume of Freud's letters edited by his son and daughter-in-law, Ernst and Lucie Freud (1960*a*), in several further volumes of his correspondence, with Wilhelm Fliess (1950*a*), Karl Abraham (1965*a*), C. G. Jung (1974*a*), Oskar Pfister (1963*a*), Lou Andreas-Salomé (1966*a*), Edoardo Weiss (1970*a*) and Arnold Zweig (1968*a*), and above all in the many volumes of Freud's own works.]

CHRONOLOGICAL TABLE

This table traces very roughly some of the main turning-points in Freud's intellectual development and opinions. A few of the chief events in his external life are also included in it.

1856. 6 May. Birth at Freiberg in Moravia.
1860. Family settles in Vienna.
1865. Enters Gymnasium (secondary school).
1873. Enters Vienna University as medical student.
1876–82. Works under Brücke at the Institute of Physiology in Vienna.
1877. First publications: papers on anatomy and physiology.
1881. Graduates as Doctor of Medicine.
1882. Engagement to Martha Bernays.
1882–5. Works in Vienna General Hospital, concentrating on cerebral anatomy: numerous publications.
1884–7. Researches into the clinical uses of cocaine.
1885. Appointed *Privatdozent* (University Lecturer) in Neuropathology.
1885. (October)–1886 (February). Studies under Charcot at the Salpêtrière (hospital for nervous diseases) in Paris. Interest first turns to hysteria and hypnosis.
1886. Marriage to Martha Bernays. Sets up private practice in nervous diseases in Vienna.
1886–93. Continues work on neurology, especially on the cerebral palsies of children at the Kassowitz Institute in Vienna, with numerous publications. Gradual shift of interest from neurology to psychopathology.
1887. Birth of eldest child (Mathilde).
1887–1902. Friendship and correspondence with Wilhelm Fliess in Berlin. Freud's letters to him during this period, published posthumously in 1950, throw much light on the development of his views.
1887. Begins the use of hypnotic suggestion in his practice.
c. 1888. Begins to follow Breuer in using hypnosis for cathartic treatment of hysteria. Gradually drops hypnosis and substitutes free association.
1889. Visits Bernheim at Nancy to study his suggestion technique.
1889. Birth of eldest son (Martin).
1891. Monograph on Aphasia.
Birth of second son (Oliver).
1892. Birth of youngest son (Ernst).

1893. Publication of Breuer and Freud 'Preliminary Communication': exposition of trauma theory of hysteria and of cathartic treatment.
Birth of second daughter (Sophie).

1893–8. Researches and short papers on hysteria, obsessions, and anxiety.

1895. Jointly with Breuer, *Studies on Hysteria*: case histories and description by Freud of his technique, including first account of transference.

1893–6. Gradual divergence of views between Freud and Breuer. Freud introduces concepts of defence and repression and of neurosis being a result of a conflict between the ego and the libido.

1895. *Project for a Scientific Psychology*: included in Freud's letters to Fliess and first published in 1950. An abortive attempt to state psychology in neurological terms; but foreshadows much of Freud's later theories.
Birth of youngest child (Anna).

1896. Introduces the term 'psychoanalysis'.
Death of father (aged 80).

1897. Freud's self-analysis, leading to the abandonment of the trauma theory and the recognition of infantile sexuality and the Oedipus complex.

1900. *The Interpretation of Dreams*, with final chapter giving first full account of Freud's dynamic view of mental processes, of the unconscious, and of the dominance of the 'pleasure principle'.

1901. *The Psychopathology of Everyday Life*. This, together with the book on dreams, made it plain that Freud's theories applied not only to pathological states but also to normal mental life.

1902. Appointed Professor Extraordinarius.

1905. *Three Essays on the Theory of Sexuality*: tracing for the first time the course of development of the sexual instinct in human beings from infancy to maturity.

c. 1906. Jung becomes an adherent of psychoanalysis.

1908. First international meeting of psychoanalysts (at Salzburg).

1909. Freud and Jung invited to the USA to lecture.
Case history of the first analysis of a child (Little Hans, aged five): confirming inferences previously made from adult analyses, especially as to infantile sexuality and the Oedipus and castration complexes.

c. 1910. First emergence of the theory of 'narcissism'.

1911–15. Papers on the technique of psychoanalysis.

1911. Secession of Adler.
Application of psychoanalytic theories to a psychotic case: the autobiography of Dr Schreber.

1913–14. *Totem and Taboo*: application of psychoanalysis to anthropological material.

1914. Secession of Jung.
'On the History of the Psycho-Analytic Movement'. Includes a polemical section on Adler and Jung.
Writes his last major case history, of the 'Wolf Man' (not published till 1918).

1915. Writes a series of twelve 'metapsychological' papers on basic theoretical questions, of which only five have survived.
1915–17. *Introductory Lectures*: giving an extensive general account of the state of Freud's views up to the time of the First World War.
1919. Application of the theory of narcissism to the war neuroses.
1920. Death of second daughter.
Beyond the Pleasure Principle: the first explicit introduction of the concept of the 'compulsion to repeat' and of the theory of the 'death instinct'.
1921. *Group Psychology*. Beginnings of a systematic analytic study of the ego.
1923. *The Ego and the Id*. Largely revised account of the structure and functioning of the mind with the division into an id, an ego, and a super-ego.
1923. First onset of cancer.
1925. Revised views on the sexual development of women.
1926. *Inhibitions, Symptoms and Anxiety*. Revised views on the problem of anxiety.
1927. *The Future of an Illusion*. A discussion of religion: the first of a number of sociological works to which Freud devoted most of his remaining years.
1930. *Civilization and its Discontents*. This includes Freud's first extensive study of the destructive instinct (regarded as a manifestation of the 'death instinct'). Freud awarded the Goethe Prize by the City of Frankfurt.
Death of mother (aged 95).
1933. Hitler seizes power in Germany: Freud's books publicly burned in Berlin.
1934–8. *Moses and Monotheism*: the last of Freud's works to appear during his lifetime.
1936. Eightieth birthday. Election as Corresponding Member of Royal Society.
1938. Hitler's invasion of Austria. Freud leaves Vienna for London.
An Outline of Psycho-Analysis. A final, unfinished, but profound exposition of psychoanalysis.
1939. 3 September. Death in London.

JAMES STRACHEY

FORMULATIONS ON THE TWO PRINCIPLES OF MENTAL FUNCTIONING (1911)

EDITOR'S NOTE

FORMULIERUNGEN ÜBER DIE ZWEI PRINZIPIEN DES PSYCHISCHEN GESCHEHENS

(A) German Editions:

1911 *Jb. psychoanalyt. psychopath. Forsch.*, **3** (1), 1–8.
1924 *Gesammelte Schriften*, **5**, 409–17.
1943 *Gesammelte Werke*, **8**, 230–38.

(B) English Translations:
'Formulations Regarding the Two Principles in Mental Functioning'

1925 *Collected Papers*, **4**, 13–21. (Tr. M. N. Searl.)
1958 *Standard Edition*, **12**, 213–26. (Translation, with a modified title, based on that of 1925, but largely rewritten.)

The present edition is a reprint of the *Standard Edition* version, with editorial modifications.

We learn from Dr Ernest Jones that Freud began planning this paper in June 1910, and was working at it simultaneously with the Schreber case history (1911*c*). His progress at it was slow, but on 26 October he spoke on the subject before the Vienna Psycho-Analytical Society, but found the audience unresponsive, and was himself dissatisfied with his presentation. It was not until December that he actually began writing the paper. It was finished at the end of January 1911, but was not published till late in the spring, when it appeared in the same issue of the *Jahrbuch* as the Schreber case.

With this well-known paper, which is one of the classics of psychoanalysis, and with the almost contemporary third section of the Schreber case history, Freud, for the first time after an interval of more than ten years, took up once again a discussion of the general theoretical hypotheses which were implied by his clinical findings. In the meantime he had only occasionally touched on questions of psychological theory, for example in Chapter VI of his book on jokes (1905*c*), *P.F.L.*, **6**, 215 ff. His first extensive attempt at such a discussion had been in quasi-neurological terminology in his 'Project for a Scientific Psychology' of 1895, which, however, was not published in his lifetime (Freud, 1950*a*). Chapter VII of *The Interpretation of Dreams* (1900*a*) was an exposition of a very similar set of hypotheses, but this time in purely psychological terms. Much of the material in the present paper (and especially in its earlier part) is derived directly from these two sources. The work gives the impression of being in the nature of a stock-taking. It is as though Freud were bringing up for his own inspection, as it were, the fundamental hypotheses of an earlier period, and preparing them to serve as a basis for the major theoretical discussions which lay ahead in the immediate future – the paper on narcissism, for instance, and the great series of metapsychological papers.

The present exposition of his views is exceedingly condensed and is not easy to assimilate even to-day. Although we know now that Freud was saying very little in it that had not long been present in his mind, at the time of its publication it must have struck its readers as bewilderingly full of novelties. The paragraphs marked (1), for instance, on p. 37 ff., would be obscure indeed to those who could have no acquaintance either with the 'Project' or with the metapsychological papers and who would have to derive what light they could from a number of almost equally condensed and quite unsystematized passages in *The Interpretation of Dreams*. It is scarcely surprising that Freud's first audience was unresponsive.

The main theme of the work is the distinction between the regulating principles (the pleasure principle[1] and the reality prin-

1. The actual term 'pleasure principle' occurs for the first time in this paper (p. 36 below).

ciple) which respectively dominate the primary and secondary mental processes. The thesis had in fact already been stated in the 'Project'. It was again discussed in Chapter VII of *The Interpretation of Dreams* (*P.F.L.*, **4**, 718–21 and 757 ff.). But the fullest treatment was reserved for the paper on the metapsychology of dreams (1917*d* [1915]), written some three years after this one. A more detailed account of the development of Freud's views on the subject of our mental attitude towards reality will be found in the Editor's Note to that paper (see pp. 225–7 below).

Towards the end of the work a number of other related topics are opened up, the further development of which (like that of the main theme) is left over for later investigation. The whole paper was, in fact (as Freud himself remarks on p. 43 below), of a preparatory and exploratory nature, but it is not on that account of any less interest.

FORMULATIONS ON THE TWO PRINCIPLES OF MENTAL FUNCTIONING

We have long observed that every neurosis has as its result, and probably therefore as its purpose, a forcing of the patient out of real life, an alienating of him from reality.[1] Nor could a fact such as this escape the observation of Pierre Janet; he spoke of a loss of 'the function of reality' as being a special characteristic of neurotics, but without discovering the connection of this disturbance with the fundamental determinants of neurosis.[2] By introducing the process of repression into the genesis of the neuroses we have been able to gain some insight into this connection. Neurotics turn away from reality because they find it unbearable – either the whole or parts of it. The most extreme type of this turning away from reality is shown by certain cases of hallucinatory psychosis which seek to deny the particular event that occasioned the outbreak of their insanity (Griesinger).[3] But in fact every neurotic does the same with some fragment of reality.[4] And we are now confronted with the task of

1. [The idea, with the phrase 'flight into psychosis', is already to be found in Section III of Freud's first paper on 'The Neuro-Psychoses of Defence' (1894*a*). The actual phrase 'flight into illness' occurs in his paper on hysterical attacks (1909*a*), *P.F.L.*, **10**, 99 and 100 *n.* 1.]

2. Janet, 1909.

3. [W. Griesinger (1817–68) was a well-known Berlin psychiatrist of an earlier generation, much admired by Freud's teacher, Meynert. The passage alluded to in the text is no doubt the one mentioned by Freud three times in *The Interpretation of Dreams* (1900*a*), *P.F.L.*, **4**, 163, 214 and 326 *n.*, and again in Chapter VI of the book on jokes (1905*c*), ibid., **6**, 228. In this passage Griesinger (1845, 89) drew attention to the wish-fulfilling character of both psychoses and dreams.]

4. Otto Rank (1910) has recently drawn attention to a remarkably clear prevision of this causation shown in Schopenhauer's *The World as Will and Idea* [Volume II (Supplements), Chapter 32].

investigating the development of the relation of neurotics and of mankind in general to reality, and in this way of bringing the psychological significance of the real external world into the structure of our theories.

In the psychology which is founded on psychoanalysis we have become accustomed to taking as our starting-point the unconscious mental processes, with the peculiarities of which we have become acquainted through analysis. We consider these to be the older, primary processes, the residues of a phase of development in which they were the only kind of mental process. The governing purpose obeyed by these primary processes is easy to recognize; it is described as the pleasure-unpleasure principle, or more shortly the pleasure principle.[1] These processes strive towards gaining pleasure; psychical activity draws back from any event which might arouse unpleasure. (Here we have repression.) Our dreams at night and our waking tendency to tear ourselves away from distressing impressions are remnants of the dominance of this principle and proofs of its power.

I shall be returning to lines of thought which I have developed elsewhere[2] when I suggest that the state of psychical rest was originally disturbed by the peremptory demands of internal needs. When this happened, whatever was thought of (wished for) was simply presented in a hallucinatory manner, just as still happens to-day with our dream-thoughts every night.[3] It was only the non-occurrence of the expected satisfaction, the disappointment experienced, that led to the abandonment of this attempt at satisfaction by means of hallucination. Instead of it, the psychical apparatus had to decide to form a conception of the real circumstances in the external world and to endeavour to make a real alteration in them. A new principle of mental

1. [This seems to be the first appearance of the actual term 'pleasure principle'. In *The Interpretation of Dreams* it is always named the 'unpleasure principle' (e.g. *P.F.L.*, **4**, 759).]

2. In the General Section of *The Interpretation of Dreams*. [I.e. in Chapter VII. See in particular *P.F.L.*, **4**, 718–21 and 757 ff.]

3. The state of sleep is able to re-establish the likeness of mental life as it was before the recognition of reality, because a prerequisite of sleep is a deliberate rejection of reality (the wish to sleep).

functioning was thus introduced; what was presented in the mind was no longer what was agreeable but what was real, even if it happened to be disagreeable.[1] This setting-up of the *reality principle* proved to be a momentous step.

(1) In the first place, the new demands made a succession of adaptations necessary in the psychical apparatus, which, owing to our insufficient or uncertain knowledge, we can only retail very cursorily.

The increased significance of external reality heightened the importance, too, of the sense-organs that are directed towards that external world, and of the *consciousness* attached to them. Consciousness now learned to comprehend sensory qualities in addition to the qualities of pleasure and unpleasure which hitherto had alone been of interest to it. A special function was instituted which had periodically to search the external world,

1. I will try to amplify the above schematic account with some further details. It will rightly be objected that an organization which was a slave to the pleasure principle and neglected the reality of the external world could not maintain itself alive for the shortest time, so that it could not have come into existence at all. The employment of a fiction like this is, however, justified when one considers that the infant – provided one includes with it the care it receives from its mother – does almost realize a psychical system of this kind. It probably hallucinates the fulfilment of its internal needs; it betrays its unpleasure, when there is an increase of stimulus and an absence of satisfaction, by the motor discharge of screaming and beating about with its arms and legs, and it then experiences the satisfaction it has hallucinated. Later, as an older child, it learns to employ these manifestations of discharge intentionally as methods of expressing its feelings. Since the later care of children is modelled on the care of infants, the dominance of the pleasure principle can really come to an end only when a child has achieved complete psychical detachment from its parents. – A neat example of a psychical system shut off from the stimuli of the external world, and able to satisfy even its nutritional requirements autistically (to use Bleuler's term [1912]), is afforded by a bird's egg with its food supply enclosed in its shell; for it, the care provided by its mother is limited to the provision of warmth. – I shall not regard it as a correction, but as an amplification of the schematic picture under discussion, if it is insisted that a system living according to the pleasure principle must have devices to enable it to withdraw from the stimuli of reality. Such devices are merely the correlative of 'repression', which treats internal unpleasurable stimuli as if they were external – that is to say, pushes them into the external world.

in order that its data might be familiar already if an urgent internal need should arise – the function of *attention*.[1] Its activity meets the sense-impressions half way, instead of awaiting their appearance. At the same time, probably, a system of *notation* was introduced, whose task it was to lay down the results of this periodical activity of consciousness – a part of what we call *memory*.

The place of repression, which excluded from cathexis as productive of unpleasure some of the emerging ideas, was taken by an *impartial passing of judgement*,[2] which had to decide whether a given idea was true or false – that is, whether it was in agreement with reality or not – the decision being determined by making a comparison with the memory-traces of reality.

A new function was now allotted to motor discharge, which, under the dominance of the pleasure principle, had served as a means of unburdening the mental apparatus of accretions of stimuli, and which had carried out this task by sending innervations into the interior of the body (leading to expressive movements and the play of features and to manifestations of affect). Motor discharge was now employed in the appropriate alteration of reality; it was converted into *action*.

Restraint upon motor discharge (upon action), which then became necessary, was provided by means of the process of *thinking*, which was developed from the presentation of ideas. Thinking was endowed with characteristics which made it possible for the mental apparatus to tolerate an increased tension of stimulus while the process of discharge was postponed. It is essentially an experimental kind of acting, accompanied by displacement of relatively small quantities of cathexis together with less expenditure (discharge) of them.[3] For this purpose the con-

1. [Some remarks on Freud's views about attention will be found in an Editor's footnote to 'The Unconscious' (p. 196 below).]

2. [This notion, often repeated by Freud, appears as early as in the first edition of his book on jokes (1905*c*, Chapter VI; *P.F.L.*, **6**, 233 and *n*. 2) and is examined more deeply in his late paper on 'Negation' (1925*h*), p. 438 below. Cf. also 'The Unconscious' (1915*e*), p. 190 below.]

3. [This important theory had been put forward by Freud in *The Interpretation*

version of freely displaceable cathexes into 'bound' cathexes was necessary, and this was brought about by means of raising the level of the whole cathectic process. It is probable that thinking was originally unconscious, in so far as it went beyond mere ideational presentations and was directed to the relations between impressions of objects, and that it did not acquire further qualities, perceptible to consciousness, until it became bound to verbal residues.[1]

(2) A general tendency of our mental apparatus, which can be traced back to the economic principle of saving expenditure [of energy], seems to find expression in the tenacity with which we hold on to the sources of pleasure at our disposal, and in the difficulty with which we renounce them. With the introduction of the reality principle one species of thought-activity was split off; it was kept free from reality-testing and remained subordinated to the pleasure principle alone.[2] This activity is *phantasying*, which begins already in children's play, and later, continued as *day-dreaming*, abandons dependence on real objects.

(3) The replacement of the pleasure principle by the reality principle, with all the psychical consequences involved, which is here schematically condensed into a single sentence, is not in fact accomplished all at once; nor does it take place simultaneously all along the line. For while this development is going on in

---

of Dreams (1900*a*), *P.F.L.*, **4**, 758–9, and more clearly in *Jokes* (1905*c*), ibid., **6**, 251 and *n*. 2, as well as in 'Negation' (1925*h*), p. 440 and *n*. 2 below, where further references are given.]

1. [Cf. *The Interpretation of Dreams* (1900*a*), *P.F.L.*, **4**, 729–30, 771 *n*. and 779. This is further developed in Section VII of 'The Unconscious' (1915*e*), p. 208 below.]

2. In the same way, a nation whose wealth rests on the exploitation of the produce of its soil will yet set aside certain areas for reservation in their original state and for protection from the changes brought about by civilization. (E.g. Yellowstone Park.) [Cf. the discussions of phantasies in 'Creative Writers and Day-Dreaming' (1908*e*), *P.F.L.*, **14**, 129, and in 'Hysterical Phantasies and their Relation to Bisexuality' (1908*a*), *P.F.L.*, **10**, 87 ff. The term '*Realitätsprüfung*' seems to make its first appearance in this sentence.]

the ego-instincts, the sexual instincts become detached from them in a very significant way. The sexual instincts behave auto-erotically at first; they obtain their satisfaction in the subject's own body and therefore do not find themselves in the situation of frustration which was what necessitated the institution of the reality principle; and when, later on, the process of finding an object begins, it is soon interrupted by the long period of latency, which delays sexual development until puberty. These two factors – auto-erotism and the latency period – have as their result that the sexual instinct is held up in its psychical development and remains far longer under the dominance of the pleasure principle, from which in many people it is never able to withdraw.

In consequence of these conditions, a closer connection arises, on the one hand, between the sexual instinct and phantasy and, on the other hand, between the ego-instincts and the activities of consciousness. Both in healthy and in neurotic people this connection strikes us as very intimate, although the considerations of genetic psychology which have just been put forward lead us to recognize it as a *secondary* one. The continuance of auto-erotism is what makes it possible to retain for so long the easier momentary and imaginary satisfaction in relation to the sexual object in place of real satisfaction, which calls for effort and postponement. In the realm of phantasy, repression remains all-powerful; it brings about the inhibition of ideas *in statu nascendi* before they can be noticed by consciousness, if their cathexis is likely to occasion a release of unpleasure. This is the weak spot in our psychical organization; and it can be employed to bring back under the dominance of the pleasure principle thought-processes which had already become rational. An essential part of the psychical disposition to neurosis thus lies in the delay in educating the sexual instincts to pay regard to reality and, as a corollary, in the conditions which make this delay possible.

(4) Just as the pleasure-ego can do nothing but *wish*, work for a yield of pleasure, and avoid unpleasure, so the reality-ego need do nothing but strive for what is *useful* and guard itself against

damage.[1] Actually the substitution of the reality principle for the pleasure principle implies no deposing of the pleasure principle, but only a safeguarding of it. A momentary pleasure, uncertain in its results, is given up, but only in order to gain along the new path an assured pleasure at a later time. But the endopsychic impression made by this substitution has been so powerful that it is reflected in a special religious myth. The doctrine of reward in the after-life for the – voluntary or enforced – renunciation of earthly pleasures is nothing other than a mythical projection of this revolution in the mind. Following consistently along these lines, *religions* have been able to effect absolute renunciation of pleasure in this life by means of the promise of compensation in a future existence; but they have not by this means achieved a conquest of the pleasure principle. It is *science* which comes nearest to succeeding in that conquest; science too, however, offers intellectual pleasure during its work and promises practical gain in the end.

(5) *Education* can be described without more ado as an incitement to the conquest of the pleasure principle, and to its replacement by the reality principle; it seeks, that is, to lend its help to the developmental process which affects the ego. To this end it makes use of an offer of love as a reward from the educators; and it therefore fails if a spoilt child thinks that it possesses that love in any case and cannot lose it whatever happens.

(6) *Art* brings about a reconciliation between the two principles in a peculiar way. An artist is originally a man who turns away from reality because he cannot come to terms with the renunciation of instinctual satisfaction which it at first demands, and who allows his erotic and ambitious wishes full play in the life of phantasy. He finds the way back to reality, however,

1. The superiority of the reality-ego over the pleasure-ego has been aptly expressed by Bernard Shaw in these words: 'To be able to choose the line of greatest advantage instead of yielding in the direction of least resistance.' (*Man and Superman: A Comedy and a Philosophy.*) [A remark made by Don Juan towards the end of the Mozartean interlude in Act III. – A much more elaborate account of the relations between the 'pleasure-ego' and the 'reality-ego' is given in 'Instincts and their Vicissitudes' (1915*c*), pp. 132–4 below.]

from this world of phantasy by making use of special gifts to mould his phantasies into truths of a new kind, which are valued by men as precious reflections of reality. Thus in a certain fashion he actually becomes the hero, the king, the creator, or the favourite he desired to be, without following the long roundabout path of making real alterations in the external world. But he can only achieve this because other men feel the same dissatisfaction as he does with the renunciation demanded by reality, and because that dissatisfaction, which results from the replacement of the pleasure principle by the reality principle, is itself a part of reality.[1]

(7) While the ego goes through its transformation from a *pleasure-ego* into a *reality-ego*, the sexual instincts undergo the changes that lead them from their original auto-erotism through various intermediate phases to object-love in the service of procreation. If we are right in thinking that each step in these two courses of development may become the site of a disposition to later neurotic illness, it is plausible to suppose that the form taken by the subsequent illness (the *choice of neurosis*) will depend on the particular phase of the development of the ego and of the libido in which the dispositional inhibition of development has occurred. Thus unexpected significance attaches to the chronological features of the two developments (which have not yet been studied), and to possible variations in their synchronization.[2]

(8) The strangest characteristic of unconscious (repressed) processes, to which no investigator can become accustomed without the exercise of great self-discipline, is due to their entire disregard of reality-testing; they equate reality of thought with external actuality, and wishes with their fulfilment – with the event – just as happens automatically under the dominance of the ancient pleasure principle. Hence also the difficulty of dis-

1. Cf. the similar position taken by Otto Rank (1907). [See also 'Creative Writers and Day-Dreaming' (1908*e*), *P.F.L.*, **14**, 129, as well as the closing paragraph of Lecture 23 of the *Introductory Lectures* (1916–17), *P.F.L.*, **1**, 423–4.]

2. [This theme is developed in 'The Disposition to Obsessional Neurosis' (1913*i*), *P.F.L.*, **10**, 142 ff.]

tinguishing unconscious phantasies from memories which have become unconscious.[1] But one must never allow oneself to be misled into applying the standards of reality to repressed psychical structures, and on that account, perhaps, into undervaluing the importance of phantasies in the formation of symptoms on the ground that they are not actualities, or into tracing a neurotic sense of guilt back to some other source because there is no evidence that any actual crime has been committed. One is bound to employ the currency that is in use in the country one is exploring – in our case a neurotic currency. Suppose, for instance, that one is trying to solve a dream such as this. A man who had once nursed his father through a long and painful mortal illness, told me that in the months following his father's death he had repeatedly dreamt that *his father was alive once more and that he was talking to him in his usual way. But he felt it exceedingly painful that his father had really died, only without knowing it.* The only way of understanding this apparently nonsensical dream is by adding 'as the dreamer wished' or 'in consequence of his wish' after the words 'that his father had really died', and by further adding 'that he [the dreamer] wished it' to the last words. The dream-thought then runs: it was a painful memory for him that he had been obliged to wish for his father's death (as a release) while he was still alive, and how terrible it would have been if his father had had any suspicion of it! What we have here is thus the familiar case of self-reproaches after the loss of someone loved, and in this instance the self-reproach went back to the infantile significance of death-wishes against the father.[2]

The deficiencies of this short paper, which is preparatory rather than expository, will perhaps be excused only in small part if I plead that they are unavoidable. In these few remarks on the psychical consequences of adaptation to the reality principle I have been obliged to adumbrate views which I should

1. [This difficulty is discussed at length in the later part of Lecture 23 of the *Introductory Lectures* (1916–17), *P.F.L.*, **1**, 414 ff.]

2. [This dream was added to the 1911 edition of *The Interpretation of Dreams* (1900*a*), *P.F.L.*, **4**, 559–60, soon after the publication of the present paper.]

have preferred for the present to withhold and whose justification will certainly require no small effort. But I hope it will not escape the notice of the benevolent reader how in these pages too the dominance of the reality principle is beginning.

A NOTE ON THE UNCONSCIOUS IN PSYCHOANALYSIS
(1912)

EDITOR'S NOTE

A NOTE ON THE UNCONSCIOUS IN PSYCHOANALYSIS

(A) English Editions:

'A Note on the Unconscious in Psycho-Analysis'

1912 *Proceedings* of the Society for Psychical Research, **26** (Part 66), 312–18.

1925 *Collected Papers*, **4**, 22–9.

1958 *Standard Edition*, **12**, 255–66. (A reprint of the 1912 text, with editorial annotations.)

(B) German Translation:

'Einige Bemerkungen über den Begriff des Unbewussten in der Psychoanalyse'

1913 *Int. Z. ärztl. Psychoanal.*, **1** (2), 117–23.

1924 *Gesammelte Schriften*, **5**, 433–42.

1943 *Gesammelte Werke*, **8**, 430–39.

The present edition is a corrected reprint of the *Standard Edition* version, with some editorial changes and additions.

In 1912 Freud was invited by the Society for Psychical Research of London to contribute to a 'Special Medical Part' of its *Proceedings*, and the present paper was the result. It was written by Freud in English, but was revised, it seems, in England before its publication in November 1912. A German version of the paper appeared in the March 1913 issue of the *Zeitschrift*. There was nothing on the face of it to show that this was not also written by Freud himself. But we learn from Dr Jones (1955,

352) that it was in fact a translation of Freud's English paper made by one of his chief followers, Hanns Sachs. Lastly it must be added that when the paper was reprinted in Volume IV of the *Collected Papers* in 1925, it was subjected to a further slight 'secondary revision' which brought the terminology up to date.

As a result of all this we are left without any completely reliable text of the paper. No doubt both the revision and the translation were excellently carried out; and probably Freud himself went through both of them. Nevertheless we must necessarily remain in uncertainty where there is a question of Freud's precise choice of terms. To take an example of one difficulty. The term 'conception' is used repeatedly in paragraphs 2 to 5. We should be inclined to suppose that Freud had in mind the German word '*Vorstellung*' which is usually rendered in this edition by the English 'idea'. And in fact '*Vorstellung*' is the word used in the corresponding places in the German translation. At the end of the seventh paragraph and in the eighth the word 'idea' appears in the English text, and the corresponding word in the German is '*Idee*'. But in the tenth and eleventh paragraphs, where we once more find the English 'idea', the German rendering is almost everywhere '*Gedanke*' (which we usually translate 'thought'), but in one place '*Vorstellung*'.

In the circumstances we have thought the wisest course is simply to reprint the original English version, exactly as it appeared in the original S.P.R. *Proceedings*, with occasional footnotes where the terminology calls for comment.

Our reason for regretting this textual uncertainty will be understood when it is remembered that this is among the most important of Freud's theoretical papers. Here for the first time he gave a long and reasoned account of the grounds for his hypothesis of unconscious mental processes and set out the various ways in which he used the term 'unconscious'. The paper is in fact a study for the major work on the same subject which he was to write some three years later (1915*e*); see below, p. 161 ff.). Like the earlier paper 'On the Two Principles of Mental Functioning' (1911*b*), p. 31 ff. above, and Section III of the Schreber analysis (1911*c*), *P.F.L.*, **9**, p. 196 ff., the present one is evidence of Freud's renewed concern with psychological theory.

The discussion of the ambiguities inherent in the word 'unconscious' is of particular interest, with the distinction between its three uses – the 'descriptive', the 'dynamic' and the 'systematic'. The present account is both more elaborate and clearer than the much shorter one given in Section II of the great paper (p. 174 ff. below). For there only two uses are differentiated, the 'descriptive' and the 'systematic'; and no plain distinction appears to be made between the latter and the 'dynamic' – the term which in the present paper is applied to the *repressed* unconscious. In two later discussions of the same topic, in Chapter I of *The Ego and the Id* (1923*b*), p. 351 ff. below, and in Lecture 31 of the *New Introductory Lectures* (1933*a*), Freud returned to the triple distinction made here; and the third use of the term, the 'systematic' (touched upon only slightly at the end of the present paper), was then seen to be a step towards the structural division of the mind into 'id', 'ego' and 'super-ego', which was so greatly to clarify the whole situation.

A NOTE ON THE UNCONSCIOUS IN PSYCHOANALYSIS

I WISH to expound in a few words and as plainly as possible what the term 'unconscious' has come to mean in Psychoanalysis and in Psychoanalysis alone.

A conception – or any other psychical[1] element – which is now *present* to my consciousness may become *absent* the next moment, and may become *present again*, after an interval, unchanged, and, as we say, from memory, not as a result of a fresh perception by our senses. It is this fact which we are accustomed to account for by the supposition that during the interval the conception has been present in our mind, although *latent* in consciousness. In what shape it may have existed while present in the mind and latent in consciousness we have no means of guessing.

At this very point we may be prepared to meet with the philosophical objection that the latent conception did not exist as an object of psychology, but as a physical disposition for the recurrence of the same psychical phenomenon, i.e. of the said conception. But we may reply that this is a theory far overstepping the domain of psychology proper; that it simply begs the question by asserting 'conscious' to be an identical term with 'psychical', and that it is clearly at fault in denying psychology the right to account for its most common facts, such as memory, by its own means.

Now let us call 'conscious' the conception which is present to our consciousness and of which we are aware, and let this be the only meaning of the term 'conscious'. As for latent conceptions, if we have any reason to suppose that they exist in the

1. [In the 1925 English version, throughout the paper, 'psychical' was altered to 'mental'.]

mind – as we had in the case of memory – let them be denoted by the term 'unconscious'.

Thus an unconscious conception is one of which we are not aware, but the existence of which we are nevertheless ready to admit on account of other proofs or signs.

This might be considered an uninteresting piece of descriptive or classificatory work if no experience appealed to our judgement other than the facts of memory, or the cases of association by unconscious links. The well-known experiment, however, of the 'post-hypnotic suggestion' teaches us to insist upon the importance of the distinction between *conscious* and *unconscious* and seems to increase its value.

In this experiment, as performed by Bernheim, a person is put into a hypnotic state and is subsequently aroused. While he was in the hypnotic state, under the influence of the physician, he was ordered to execute a certain action at a certain fixed moment after his awakening, say half an hour later. He awakes, and seems fully conscious and in his ordinary condition; he has no recollection of his hypnotic state, and yet at the prearranged moment there rushes into his mind the impulse to do such and such a thing, and he does it consciously, though not knowing why. It seems impossible to give any other description of the phenomenon than to say that the order had been present in the mind of the person *in a condition of latency*, or had been present *unconsciously*, until the given moment came, and then had become conscious. But not the whole of it emerged into consciousness: only the conception of the act to be executed. All the other ideas associated with this conception – the order, the influence of the physician, the recollection of the hypnotic state, remained unconscious even then.

But we have more to learn from such an experiment. We are led from the purely descriptive to a *dynamic* view of the phenomenon. The idea of the action ordered in hypnosis not only became an object of consciousness at a certain moment, but the more striking aspect of the fact is that this idea grew *active*: it was translated into action as soon as consciousness became aware of its presence. The real stimulus to the action being the order of the physician, it is hard not to concede that the idea of the physician's order became active too. Yet this last idea did not reveal itself to consciousness, as did its outcome, the idea of the action; it remained unconscious, and so it was *active and unconscious* at the same time.

A post-hypnotic suggestion is a laboratory production, an artificial fact. But if we adopt the theory of hysterical phenomena first put forward by P. Janet and elaborated by Breuer and myself, we shall not be at a loss for plenty of natural facts showing the psychological character of the post-hypnotic suggestion even more clearly and distinctly.

The mind of the hysterical patient is full of active yet unconscious ideas; all her symptoms proceed from such ideas. It is in fact the most striking character of the hysterical mind to be ruled by them. If the hysterical woman vomits, she may do so from the idea of being pregnant. She has, however, no knowledge of this idea, although it can easily be detected in her mind, and made conscious to her, by one of the technical procedures of psychoanalysis. If she is executing the jerks and movements constituting her 'fit', she does not even consciously represent to herself the intended actions, and she may perceive those actions with the detached feelings of an onlooker. Nevertheless analysis will show that she was acting her part in the dramatic reproduction of some incident in her life, the memory of which was unconsciously active during the attack. The same preponderance of active unconscious ideas is revealed by analysis as the essential fact in the psychology of all other forms of neurosis.

We learn therefore by the analysis of neurotic phenomena that a latent or unconscious idea is not necessarily a weak one, and that the presence of such an idea in the mind admits of indirect proofs of the most cogent kind, which are equivalent to the direct proof furnished by consciousness. We feel justified in making our classification agree with this addition to our knowledge by introducing a fundamental distinction between different kinds of latent or unconscious ideas. We were accustomed to think that every latent idea was so because it was weak and that it grew conscious as soon as it became strong. We have now gained the conviction that there are some latent ideas which do not penetrate into consciousness, however strong they may have become. Therefore we may call the latent ideas of the first type *foreconscious*,[1] while we reserve the term *unconscious* (proper) for the latter type which we came to study in the neuroses. The term *unconscious*, which was used in the purely descriptive sense before, now comes to imply something more. It designates not only latent ideas in general, but especially ideas with a certain dynamic character, ideas keeping apart from consciousness in spite of their intensity and activity.

Before continuing my exposition I will refer to two objections which are likely to be raised at this point. The first of these may be stated thus: instead of subscribing to the hypothesis of unconscious ideas of which we know nothing, we had better assume that consciousness can be split up, so that certain ideas or other psychical acts may constitute a consciousness apart, which has become detached and estranged from the bulk of conscious psychical activity. Well-known pathological cases like that of Dr Azam[2] seem to go far to show that the splitting up of consciousness is no fanciful imagination.

I venture to urge against this theory that it is a gratuitous assumption, based on the abuse of the word 'conscious'. We have no right to extend the meaning of this word so far as to make it include a consciousness of which its owner himself is not aware. If philosophers find difficulty in accepting the existence of unconscious ideas, the existence of an unconscious consciousness seems to me even more objectionable. The cases described as splitting of consciousness, like Dr Azam's, might better be denoted as shifting of consciousness, – that function – or whatever it be – oscillating between two different psychi-

1. [In the 1925 English version, throughout the paper, 'foreconscious' was altered to 'preconscious', which has, of course, become the regular translation of the German '*vorbewusst*'.]

2. [The reference is to the case of Félida X., a striking example of alternating or double personality and probably the first of its kind to be investigated and recorded in detail. The case was first described by E. Azam of Bordeaux. (See Azam, 1876 and 1887.)]

cal complexes which become conscious and unconscious in alternation.

The other objection that may probably be raised would be that we apply to normal psychology conclusions which are drawn chiefly from the study of pathological conditions. We are enabled to answer it by another fact, the knowledge of which we owe to psychoanalysis. Certain deficiencies of function of most frequent occurrence among healthy people, e.g. *lapsus linguae*, errors in memory and speech, forgetting of names, etc., may easily be shown to depend on the action of strong unconscious ideas in the same way as neurotic symptoms. We shall meet with another still more convincing argument at a later stage of this discussion.

By the differentiation of foreconscious and unconscious ideas, we are led on to leave the field of classification and to form an opinion about functional and dynamical relations in psychical action. We have found a *foreconscious activity* passing into consciousness with no difficulty, and an *unconscious activity* which remains so and seems to be cut off from consciousness.

Now we do not know whether these two modes of psychical activity are identical or essentially divergent from their beginning, but we may ask why they should become different in the course of psychical action. To this last question psychoanalysis gives a clear and unhesitating answer. It is by no means impossible for the product of unconscious activity to pierce into consciousness, but a certain amount of exertion is needed for this task. When we try to do it in ourselves, we become aware of a distinct feeling of *repulsion*[1] which must be overcome, and when we produce it in a patient we get the most unquestionable signs of what we call his *resistance* to it. So we learn that the unconscious idea is excluded from consciousness by living forces which oppose themselves to its reception, while they do not object to other ideas, the foreconscious ones. Psychoanalysis leaves no room for doubt that the repulsion from unconscious

1. [In the German translation the word 'repulsion', here and lower down, is rendered by '*Abwehr*', of which the usual English version is 'defence' or 'fending off'.]

ideas is only provoked by the tendencies embodied in their contents. The next and most probable theory which can be formulated at this stage of our knowledge is the following. Unconsciousness is a regular and inevitable phase in the processes constituting our psychical activity; every psychical act begins as an unconscious one, and it may either remain so or go on developing into consciousness, according as it meets with resistance or not. The distinction between foreconscious and unconscious activity is not a primary one, but comes to be established after repulsion has sprung up. Only then the difference between foreconscious ideas, which can appear in consciousness and reappear at any moment, and unconscious ideas which cannot do so gains a theoretical as well as a practical value. A rough but not inadequate analogy to this supposed relation of conscious to unconscious activity might be drawn from the field of ordinary photography. The first stage of the photograph is the 'negative'; every photographic picture has to pass through the 'negative process', and some of these negatives which have held good in examination are admitted to the 'positive process' ending in the picture.

But the distinction between foreconscious and unconscious activity, and the recognition of the barrier which keeps them asunder, is not the last or the most important result of the psychoanalytic investigation of psychical life. There is one psychical product to be met with in the most normal persons, which yet presents a very striking analogy to the wildest productions of insanity, and was no more intelligible to philosophers than insanity itself. I refer to dreams. Psychoanalysis is founded upon the analysis of dreams; the interpretation of dreams is the most complete piece of work the young science has done up to the present. One of the most common types of dream-formation may be described as follows: a train of thoughts has been aroused by the working of the mind in the daytime, and retained some of its activity, escaping from the general inhibition of interests which introduces sleep and constitutes the psychical preparation for sleeping. During the night this train of thoughts succeeds in finding connections with one of the unconscious tendencies present ever since his childhood in the mind of the dreamer, but ordinarily *repressed* and excluded from his conscious life. By the borrowed force of this unconscious help, the thoughts, the residue of the day's work,[1] now become active again, and emerge into consciousness in the shape of the dream. Now three things have happened:

(1) The thoughts have undergone a change, a disguise and a distortion, which represents the part of the unconscious helpmate.

(2) The thoughts have occupied consciousness at a time when they ought not.

(3) Some part of the unconscious, which could not otherwise have done so, has emerged into consciousness.

We have learnt the art of finding out the 'residual thoughts', the *latent thoughts of the dream*,[2] and, by comparing them with the apparent[3] *dream*, we are able to form a judgement on the changes they underwent and the manner in which these were brought about.

The latent thoughts of the dream differ in no respect from the products of our regular conscious activity; they deserve the name of foreconscious thoughts, and may indeed have been conscious at some moment of waking life. But by entering into connection with the unconscious tendencies during the night they have become assimilated to the latter, degraded as it were to the condition of unconscious thoughts, and subjected to the laws by which unconscious activity is governed. And here is the opportunity to learn what we could not have guessed from speculation, or from another source of empirical information – that the laws of unconscious activity differ widely from those of the conscious. We gather in detail what the peculiarities of the *Unconscious* are, and we may hope to learn still more about them by a profounder investigation of the processes of dream-formation.

1. [In the 1925 English version the word 'mental' was inserted before 'work'.]

2. [In the German translation the last nine words are replaced by: 'the "day's residues", and the *latent dream-thoughts*, . . .'.]

3. [This word was altered to 'manifest' in the 1925 English version.]

This inquiry is not yet half finished, and an exposition of the results obtained hitherto is scarcely possible without entering into the most intricate problems of dream-analysis. But I would not break off this discussion without indicating the change and progress in our comprehension of the Unconscious which are due to our psychoanalytic study of dreams.

Unconsciousness seemed to us at first only an enigmatical characteristic of a definite psychical act. Now it means more for us. It is a sign that this act partakes of the nature of a certain psychical category known to us by other and more important characters[1] and that it belongs to a system of psychical activity which is deserving of our fullest attention. The index-value of the unconscious has far outgrown its importance as a property. The system revealed by the sign that the single acts forming parts of it are unconscious we designate by the name 'The Unconscious', for want of a better and less ambiguous term. In German, I propose to denote this system by the letters *Ubw*, an abbreviation of the German word 'Unbewusst'.[2] And this is the third and most significant sense which the term 'unconscious' has acquired in psychoanalysis.

1. [This was altered to 'features' in the 1925 English version.]
2. [The equivalent English abbreviation is, of course, '*Ucs.*'.]

ON NARCISSISM: AN INTRODUCTION
(1914)

EDITOR'S NOTE

ZUR EINFÜHRUNG DES NARZISSMUS

(A) German Editions:

1914 *Jb. Psychoanal.*, **6**, 1–24.
1924 Leipzig, Vienna and Zurich: Internationaler Psycho-analytischer Verlag. Pp. 35.
1925 *Gesammelte Schriften*, **6**, 155–87.
1946 *Gesammelte Werke*, **10**, 138–70.

(B) English Translations:
'On Narcissism: an Introduction'

1925 *Collected Papers*, **4**, 30–59. (Tr. C. M. Baines.)
1957 *Standard Edition*, **14**, 67–102. (Translation based on that of 1925.)

The present edition is a corrected reprint of the *Standard Edition* version, with editorial modifications.

The idea of writing the present paper emerges in Freud's letters for the first time in June 1913, and he finished a first draft of it during a holiday in Rome, in the third week of September of the same year. It was not until the end of February 1914 that he started on the final version and it was completed a month later.

The title of this paper would have been more literally translated 'On the Introduction of the Concept of Narcissism'. Freud had been using the term for many years previously. We learn from Ernest Jones (1955, 304) that at a meeting of the Vienna Psycho-Analytical Society on 10 November 1909 Freud had declared that narcissism was a necessary intermediate stage between auto-erotism and object-love. At about the same time he was preparing the second edition of the *Three Essays on the Theory of Sexuality* (1905*d*) for the press (the preface is dated 'December 1909'), and it seems probable that the first public mention of the new term is to be found in a footnote added to that edition (*P.F.L.*, **7**, 56 *n.*) – assuming, that is to say, that the new edition appeared in the early part of 1910. For at the end of May in the same year Freud's book on *Leonardo* (1910*c*) appeared, in which there is a considerably longer reference to narcissism (middle of Section III). A paper on the subject by Rank, mentioned by Freud at the beginning of the present study, was published in 1911, and other references by Freud himself soon followed; e.g. in Section III of the Schreber analysis (1911*c*), *P.F.L.*, **9**, 196, and in *Totem and Taboo* (1912–13), Section III (3), ibid., **13**, 146–8.

The paper is among the most important of Freud's writings and may be regarded as one of the pivots in the evolution of his views. It sums up his earlier discussions on the subject of narcissism and considers the place taken by narcissism in sexual development; but it goes far beyond this. For it enters into the deeper problems of the relations between the ego and external objects, and it draws the new distinction between 'ego-libido' and 'object-libido'. Furthermore – most important of all, perhaps – it introduces the concepts of the 'ego ideal' and of the self-observing agency related to it, which were the basis of what was ultimately to be described as the 'super-ego' in *The Ego and the Id* (1923*b*). And in addition to all this, at two points in the paper – at the end of the first section and at the beginning of the third – it trenches upon the controversies with Adler and Jung which were the principal theme of the 'History of the Psycho-Analytic Movement' (1914*d*) written more or less simultaneously with the present work during the early months of 1914. Indeed, one of Freud's motives in writing this paper was, no doubt, to show that the concept of narcissism offers an alternative to Jung's non-sexual 'libido' and to Adler's 'masculine protest'.

These are far from being the only topics raised in the paper, and it is therefore scarcely surprising that it should have an unusual appearance of being over-compressed – of its framework bursting from the quantity of material it contains. Freud himself seems to have felt something of the kind. Ernest Jones tells us (1955, 340) that 'he was very dissatisfied with the result' and wrote to Abraham: 'The "Narcissism" had a difficult labour and bears all the marks of a corresponding deformation.'

However this may be, the paper is one which demands and repays prolonged study; and it was the starting-point of many later lines of thought. Some of these, for instance, were pursued further in 'Mourning and Melancholia' (1917*e* [1915]), p. 247 ff. below, and in Chapters VIII and XI of *Group Psychology* (1921*c*). The subject of narcissism, it may be added, occupies the greater part of Lecture 26 of the *Introductory Lectures* (1916–17), *P.F.L.*, **1**, 461 ff. The further development of the fresh views on the structure of the mind which are already beginning to become apparent in the present paper led Freud later to a re-assessment of some of the statements he makes here, especially as regards the functioning of the ego. In this connection it must be pointed out that the meaning which Freud attached to '*das Ich*' (almost invariably translated by 'the ego' in this edition) underwent a gradual modification. At first he used the term without any great precision, as we might speak of 'the self'; but in his latest writings he gave it a very much more definite and narrow meaning. The present paper occupies a transitional point in this development. The whole topic will be found discussed more fully in the Editor's Introduction to *The Ego and the Id* (1923*b*), p. 345 below.

ON NARCISSISM: AN INTRODUCTION

I

THE term narcissism is derived from clinical description and was chosen by Paul Näcke[1] in 1899 to denote the attitude of a person who treats his own body in the same way in which the body of a sexual object is ordinarily treated – who looks at it, that is to say, strokes it and fondles it till he obtains complete satisfaction through these activities. Developed to this degree, narcissism has the significance of a perversion that has absorbed the whole of the subject's sexual life, and it will consequently exhibit the characteristics which we expect to meet with in the study of all perversions.

Psychoanalytic observers were subsequently struck by the fact that individual features of the narcissistic attitude are found in many people who suffer from other disorders – for instance, as Sadger has pointed out, in homosexuals – and finally it seemed probable that an allocation of the libido such as deserved to be described as narcissism might be present far more extensively, and that it might claim a place in the regular course of human sexual development.[2] Difficulties in psychoanalytic work upon neurotics led to the same supposition, for it seemed as though

1. [In a footnote added by Freud in 1920 to his *Three Essays* (1905*d*, *P.F.L.*, **7**, 140 *n*. 2) he said that he was wrong in stating in the present paper that the term 'narcissism' was introduced by Näcke and that he should have attributed it to Havelock Ellis. Ellis himself, however, subsequently (1927) wrote a short paper in which he corrected Freud's correction and argued that the priority should in fact be divided between himself and Näcke, explaining that the term 'narcissus-like' had been used by him in 1898 as a description of a psychological attitude, and that Näcke in 1899 had introduced the term '*Narcismus*' to describe a sexual perversion. The German word used by Freud is '*Narzissmus*'. In his paper on Schreber (1911*c*), *P.F.L.*, **9**, 198 *n*. 1, he defends this form of the word on the ground of euphony against the possibly more correct '*Narzissismus*'.]

2. Otto Rank (1911).

this kind of narcissistic attitude in them constituted one of the limits to their susceptibility to influence. Narcissism in this sense would not be a perversion, but the libidinal complement to the egoism of the instinct of self-preservation, a measure of which may justifiably be attributed to every living creature.

A pressing motive for occupying ourselves with the conception of a primary and normal narcissism arose when the attempt was made to subsume what we know of dementia praecox (Kraepelin) or schizophrenia (Bleuler) under the hypothesis of the libido theory. Patients of this kind, whom I have proposed to term paraphrenics,[1] display two fundamental characteristics: megalomania and diversion of their interest from the external world – from people and things. In consequence of the latter change, they become inaccessible to the influence of psychoanalysis and cannot be cured by our efforts. But the paraphrenic's turning away from the external world needs to be more precisely characterized. A patient suffering from hysteria or obsessional neurosis has also, as far as his illness extends, given up his relation to reality. But analysis shows that he has by no means broken off his erotic relations to people and things. He still retains them in phantasy; i.e he has, on the one hand, substituted for real objects imaginary ones from his memory, or has mixed the latter with the former; and on the other hand, he has renounced the initiation of motor activities for the attainment of his aims in connection with those objects. Only to this condition of the libido may we legitimately apply the term 'introversion' of the libido which is used by Jung indiscriminately.[2] It is otherwise with the paraphrenic. He seems really to have withdrawn his libido from people and things in the external world, without replacing them by others in phantasy. When he *does* so replace them, the process seems to be a secondary one and to be part of an attempt at recovery, designed to lead the libido back to objects.[3]

1. [For a discussion of Freud's use of this term, see a long Editor's footnote near the end of Section III of the Schreber analysis (1911*c*), *P.F.L.*, **9**, 215 *n.* 2.]

2. [Cf. a footnote in 'The Dynamics of Transference' (1912*b*.]

3. In connection with this see my discussion of the 'end of the world' in

The question arises: What happens to the libido which has been withdrawn from external objects in schizophrenia? The megalomania characteristic of these states points the way. This megalomania has no doubt come into being at the expense of object-libido. The libido that has been withdrawn from the external world has been directed to the ego and thus gives rise to an attitude which may be called narcissism. But the megalomania itself is no new creation; on the contrary, it is, as we know, a magnification and plainer manifestation of a condition which had already existed previously. This leads us to look upon the narcissism which arises through the drawing in of object-cathexes as a secondary one, superimposed upon a primary narcissism that is obscured by a number of different influences.

Let me insist that I am not proposing here to explain or penetrate further into the problem of schizophrenia, but that I am merely putting together what has already been said elsewhere,[1] in order to justify the introduction of the concept of narcissism. This extension of the libido theory – in my opinion, a legitimate one – receives reinforcement from a third quarter, namely, from our observations and views on the mental life of children and primitive peoples. In the latter we find characteristics which, if they occurred singly, might be put down to megalomania: an over-estimation of the power of their wishes and mental acts, the 'omnipotence of thoughts', a belief in the thaumaturgic force of words, and a technique for dealing with the external world – 'magic' – which appears to be a logical application of these grandiose premisses.[2] In the children of to-day, whose development is much more obscure to us, we expect to find an exactly analogous attitude towards the external world.[3] Thus we

---

[Section III of] the analysis of Senatspräsident Schreber [1911*c*; *P.F.L.*, **9**, 207–11]; also Abraham, 1908. [See also below, pp. 79–80.]

1. [See, in particular, the works referred to in the last footnote. On pp. 79–80 below, Freud in fact penetrates further into the problem.]

2. Cf. the passages in my *Totem and Taboo* (1912–13) which deal with this subject. [*P.F.L.*, **13**, 141–8.]

3. Cf. Ferenczi (1913*a*).

form the idea of there being an original libidinal cathexis of the ego, from which some is later given off to objects, but which fundamentally persists and is related to the object-cathexes much as the body of an amoeba is related to the pseudopodia which it puts out.[1] In our researches, taking, as they did, neurotic symptoms for their starting-point, this part of the allocation of libido necessarily remained hidden from us at the outset. All that we noticed were the emanations of this libido – the object-cathexes, which can be sent out and drawn back again. We see also, broadly speaking, an antithesis between ego-libido and object-libido.[2] The more of the one is employed, the more the other becomes depleted. The highest phase of development of which object-libido is capable is seen in the state of being in love, when the subject seems to give up his own personality in favour of an object-cathexis; while we have the opposite condition in the paranoic's phantasy (or self-perception) of the 'end of the world'.[3] Finally, as regards the differentiation of psychical energies, we are led to the conclusion that to begin with, during the state of narcissism, they exist together and that our analysis is too coarse to distinguish between them; not until there is object-cathexis is it possible to discriminate a sexual energy – the libido – from an energy of the ego-instincts.[4]

Before going any further I must touch on two questions which lead us to the heart of the difficulties of our subject. In the first place, what is the relation of the narcissism of which we are now speaking to auto-erotism, which we have described

1. [Freud used this and similar analogies more than once again, e.g. in Lecture 26 of his *Introductory Lectures* (1916–17), *P.F.L.*, **1**, 465–6 and 470. He later revised some of the views expressed here. See the end of the Editor's Note, p. 63 above.]

2. [This distinction is drawn here by Freud for the first time.]

3. [See footnote 3, pp. 66–7 above.] There are two mechanisms of this 'end of the world' idea: in the one case, the whole libidinal cathexis flows off to the loved object; in the other, it all flows back into the ego.

4. [Some account of the development of Freud's views on the instincts will be found in the Editor's Note to 'Instincts and their Vicissitudes', below, p. 108 ff.]

as an early state of the libido?[1] Secondly, if we grant the ego a primary cathexis of libido, why is there any necessity for further distinguishing a sexual libido from a non-sexual energy of the ego-instincts? Would not the postulation of a single kind of psychical energy save us all the difficulties of differentiating an energy of the ego-instincts from ego-libido, and ego-libido from object-libido?[2]

As regards the first question, I may point out that we are bound to suppose that a unity comparable to the ego cannot exist in the individual from the start; the ego has to be developed. The auto-erotic instincts, however, are there from the very first; so there must be something added to auto-erotism – a new psychical action – in order to bring about narcissism.

To be asked to give a definite answer to the second question must occasion perceptible uneasiness in every psychoanalyst. One dislikes the thought of abandoning observation for barren theoretical controversy, but nevertheless one must not shirk an attempt at clarification. It is true that notions such as that of an ego-libido, an energy of the ego-instincts, and so on, are neither particularly easy to grasp, nor sufficiently rich in content; a speculative theory of the relations in question would begin by seeking to obtain a sharply defined concept as its basis. But I am of opinion that that is just the difference between a speculative theory and a science erected on empirical interpretation. The latter will not envy speculation its privilege of having a smooth, logically unassailable foundation, but will gladly content itself with nebulous, scarcely imaginable basic concepts, which it hopes to apprehend more clearly in the course of its development, or which it is even prepared to replace by others. For these ideas are not the foundation of science, upon which everything rests: that foundation is observation alone. They are not the bottom but the top of the whole structure, and they can be replaced and discarded without damaging it. The same thing is happening in our day in the science of physics, the basic notions of which as

1. [See the second of Freud's *Three Essays* (1905*d*), *P.F.L.*, **7**, 97–9.]

2. [Cf. a remark on this passage in the Editor's Note to 'Instincts and their Vicissitudes', p. 111 below.]

regards matter, centres of force, attraction, etc., are scarcely less debatable than the corresponding notions in psychoanalysis.[1]

The value of the concepts 'ego-libido' and 'object-libido' lies in the fact that they are derived from the study of the intimate characteristics of neurotic and psychotic processes. A differentiation of libido into a kind which is proper to the ego and one which is attached to objects is an unavoidable corollary to an original hypothesis which distinguished between sexual instincts and ego-instincts. At any rate, analysis of the pure transference neuroses (hysteria and obsessional neurosis) compelled me to make this distinction and I only know that all attempts to account for these phenomena by other means have been completely unsuccessful.

In the total absence of any theory of the instincts which would help us to find our bearings, we may be permitted, or rather, it is incumbent upon us, to start off by working out some hypothesis to its logical conclusion, until it either breaks down or is confirmed. There are various points in favour of the hypothesis of there having been from the first a separation between sexual instincts and others, ego-instincts, besides the serviceability of such a hypothesis in the analysis of the transference neuroses. I admit that this latter consideration alone would not be unambiguous, for it might be a question of an indifferent psychical energy[2] which only becomes libido through the act of cathecting an object. But, in the first place, the distinction made in this concept corresponds to the common, popular distinction between hunger and love. In the second place, there are *biological* considerations in its favour. The individual does actually carry on a twofold existence: one to serve his own purposes and the other as a link in a chain, which he serves against his will, or at least involuntarily. The individual himself

1. [This line of thought was expanded by Freud in the opening passage of his paper on 'Instincts and their Vicissitudes' (1915*c*), below, pp. 113–14.]

2. [This notion reappears in *The Ego and the Id* (1923*b*), pp. 384–5 below, where the German word '*indifferent*' is, however (in the uncorrected printings of that volume), wrongly translated 'neutral'.]

regards sexuality as one of his own ends; whereas from another point of view he is an appendage to his germ-plasm, at whose disposal he puts his energies in return for a bonus of pleasure. He is the mortal vehicle of a (possibly) immortal substance – like the inheritor of an entailed property, who is only the temporary holder of an estate which survives him. The separation of the sexual instincts from the ego-instincts would simply reflect this twofold function of the individual.[1] Thirdly, we must recollect that all our provisional ideas in psychology will presumably some day be based on an organic substructure. This makes it probable that it is special substances and chemical processes which perform the operations of sexuality and provide for the extension of individual life into that of the species.[2] We are taking this probability into account in replacing the special chemical substances by special psychical forces.

I try in general to keep psychology clear from everything that is different in nature from it, even biological lines of thought. For that very reason I should like at this point expressly to admit that the hypothesis of separate ego-instincts and sexual instincts (that is to say, the libido theory) rests scarcely at all upon a psychological basis, but derives its principal support from biology. But I shall be consistent enough [with my general rule] to drop this hypothesis if psychoanalytic work should itself produce some other, more serviceable hypothesis about the instincts. So far, this has not happened. It may turn out that, most basically and on the longest view, sexual energy – libido – is only the product of a differentiation in the energy at work generally in the mind. But such an assertion has no relevance. It relates to matters which are so remote from the problems of our observation, and of which we have so little cognizance, that it is as idle to dispute it as to affirm it; this primal identity may well have as little to do with our analytic interests as the primal kin-

1. [The psychological bearing of Weismann's germ-plasm theory was discussed by Freud at much greater length in Chapter VI of *Beyond the Pleasure Principle* (1920*g*), p. 318 below.]

2. [See below, footnote 3, p. 122.]

ship of all the races of mankind has to do with the proof of kinship required in order to establish a legal right of inheritance. All these speculations take us nowhere. Since we cannot wait for another science to present us with the final conclusions on the theory of the instincts, it is far more to the purpose that we should try to see what light may be thrown upon this basic problem of biology by a synthesis of the *psychological* phenomena. Let us face the possibility of error; but do not let us be deterred from pursuing the logical implications of the hypothesis we first adopted[1] of an antithesis between ego-instincts and sexual instincts (a hypothesis to which we were forcibly led by analysis of the transference neuroses), and from seeing whether it turns out to be without contradictions and fruitful, and whether it can be applied to other disorders as well, such as schizophrenia.

It would, of course, be a different matter if it were proved that the libido theory has already come to grief in the attempt to explain the latter disease. This has been asserted by C. G. Jung (1912) and it is on that account that I have been obliged to enter upon this last discussion, which I would gladly have been spared. I should have preferred to follow to its end the course embarked upon in the analysis of the Schreber case without any discussion of its premisses. But Jung's assertion is, to say the least of it, premature. The grounds he gives for it are scanty. In the first place, he appeals to an admission of my own that I myself have been obliged, owing to the difficulties of the Schreber analysis, to extend the concept of libido (that is, to give up its sexual content) and to identify libido with psychical interest in general. Ferenczi (1913*b*), in an exhaustive criticism of Jung's work, has already said all that is necessary in correction of this erroneous interpretation. I can only corroborate his criticism and repeat that I have never made any such retractation of the libido theory. Another argument of Jung's, namely, that we cannot suppose that the withdrawal of the libido is in itself enough to

1. ['*Ersterwählte*' ('first selected') in the editions before 1924. The later editions read '*ersterwähnte*' ('first mentioned'), which seems to make less good sense and may be a misprint.]

bring about the loss of the normal function of reality,[1] is no argument but a dictum. It 'begs the question',[2] and saves discussion; for whether and how this is possible was precisely the point that should have been under investigation. In his next major work, Jung (1913 [339–40]) just misses the solution I had long since indicated: 'At the same time', he writes, 'there is this to be further taken into consideration (a point to which, incidentally, Freud refers in his work on the Schreber case [1911*c*]) – that the introversion of the *libido sexualis* leads to a cathexis of the "ego", and that it may possibly be this that produces the result of a loss of reality. It is indeed a tempting possibility to explain the psychology of the loss of reality in this fashion.' But Jung does not enter much further into a discussion of this possibility. A few lines later he dismisses it with the remark that this determinant 'would result in the psychology of an ascetic anchorite, not in a dementia praecox'. How little this inapt analogy can help us to decide the question may be learnt from the consideration that an anchorite of this kind, who, 'tries to eradicate every trace of sexual interest' (but only in the popular sense of the word 'sexual'), does not even necessarily display any pathogenic allocation of the libido. He may have diverted his sexual interest from human beings entirely, and yet may have sublimated it into a heightened interest in the divine, in nature, or in the animal kingdom, without his libido having undergone an introversion on to his phantasies or a return to his ego. This analogy would seem to rule out in advance the possibility of differentiating between interest emanating from erotic sources and from others. Let us remember, further, that the researches of the Swiss school, however valuable, have elucidated only two features in the picture of dementia praecox – the presence in it of complexes known to us both in healthy and neurotic subjects, and the similarity of the phantasies that occur in it to popular myths – but that they have not been able to throw any further light on the mechanism of the

1. [The phrase is from Janet (1909): '*La fonction du réel*'. See the opening sentences of Freud, 1911*b*, p. 35 above.]

2. [In English in the original.]

disease. We may repudiate Jung's assertion, then, that the libido theory has come to grief in the attempt to explain dementia praecox, and that it is therefore disposed of for the other neuroses as well.

II

Certain special difficulties seem to me to lie in the way of a direct study of narcissism. Our chief means of access to it will probably remain the analysis of the paraphrenias. Just as the transference neuroses have enabled us to trace the libidinal instinctual impulses, so dementia praecox and paranoia will give us an insight into the psychology of the ego. Once more, in order to arrive at an understanding of what seems so simple in normal phenomena, we shall have to turn to the field of pathology with its distortions and exaggerations. At the same time, other means of approach remain open to us, by which we may obtain a better knowledge of narcissism. These I shall now discuss in the following order: the study of organic disease, of hypochondria and of the erotic life of the sexes.

In estimating the influence of organic disease upon the distribution of libido, I follow a suggestion made to me orally by Sándor Ferenczi. It is universally known, and we take it as a matter of course, that a person who is tormented by organic pain and discomfort gives up his interest in the things of the external world, in so far as they do not concern his suffering. Closer observation teaches us that he also withdraws *libidinal* interest from his love-objects: so long as he suffers, he ceases to love. The commonplace nature of this fact is no reason why we should be deterred from translating it into terms of the libido theory. We should then say: the sick man withdraws his libidinal cathexes back upon his own ego, and sends them out again when he recovers. 'Concentrated is his soul', says Wilhelm Busch of the poet suffering from toothache, 'in his molar's narrow hole.'[1] Here libido and ego-interest share the same fate and are once

1. [Einzig in der engen Höhle
Des Backenzahnes weilt die Seele.
Balduin Bählamm, Chapter VIII.]

more indistinguishable from each other. The familiar egoism of the sick person covers both. We find it so natural because we are certain that in the same situation we should behave in just the same way. The way in which a lover's feelings, however strong, are banished by bodily ailments, and suddenly replaced by complete indifference, is a theme which has been exploited by comic writers to an appropriate extent.

The condition of sleep, too, resembles illness in implying a narcissistic withdrawal of the positions of the libido on to the subject's own self, or, more precisely, on to the single wish to sleep. The egoism of dreams fits very well into this context. [Cf. below, p. 230.] In both states we have, if nothing else, examples of changes in the distribution of libido that are consequent upon an alteration of the ego.

Hypochondria, like organic disease, manifests itself in distressing and painful bodily sensations, and it has the same effect as organic disease on the distribution of libido. The hypochondriac withdraws both interest and libido – the latter specially markedly – from the objects of the external world and concentrates both of them upon the organ that is engaging his attention. A difference between hypochondria and organic disease now becomes evident: in the latter, the distressing sensations are based upon demonstrable [organic] changes; in the former, this is not so. But it would be entirely in keeping with our general conception of the processes of neurosis if we decided to say that hypochondria must be right: organic changes must be supposed to be present in it, too.

But what could these changes be? We will let ourselves be guided at this point by our experience, which shows that bodily sensations of an unpleasurable nature, comparable to those of hypochondria, occur in the other neuroses as well. I have said before that I am inclined to class hypochondria with neurasthenia and anxiety-neurosis as a third 'actual' neurosis.[1] It would

1. [This seems to have been first hinted at in a footnote near the end of Section II of the Schreber case (1911*c*), *P.F.L.*, **9**, 193 *n.* 2. Freud returned to the subject

probably not be going too far to suppose that in the case of the other neuroses a small amount of hypochondria was regularly formed at the same time as well. We have the best example of this, I think, in anxiety neurosis with its superstructure of hysteria. Now the familiar prototype of an organ that is painfully tender, that is in some way changed and that is yet not diseased in the ordinary sense, is the genital organ in its states of excitation. In that condition it becomes congested with blood, swollen and humected, and is the seat of a multiplicity of sensations. Let us now, taking any part of the body, describe its activity of sending sexually exciting stimuli to the mind as its 'erotogenicity', and let us further reflect that the considerations on which our theory of sexuality was based have long accustomed us to the notion that certain other parts of the body – the 'erotogenic' zones – may act as substitutes for the genitals and behave analogously to them.[1] We have then only one more step to take. We can decide to regard erotogenicity as a general characteristic of all organs and may then speak of an increase or decrease of it in a particular part of the body. For every such change in the erotogenicity of the organs there might then be a parallel change of libidinal cathexis in the ego. Such factors would constitute what we believe to underlie hypochondria and what may have the same effect upon the distribution of libido as is produced by a material illness of the organs.

We see that, if we follow up this line of thought, we come up against the problem not only of hypochondria, but of the other 'actual' neuroses – neurasthenia and anxiety neurosis. Let us therefore stop at this point. It is not within the scope of a purely psychological inquiry to penetrate so far behind the frontiers of physiological research. I will merely mention that from this point of view we may suspect that the relation of hypo-

later towards the end of Lecture 24 of the *Introductory Lectures* (1916–17), *P.F.L.*, **1**, 437–8. At a much earlier period, he had already approached the question of the relation between hypochondria and the other 'actual' neuroses. See Section 1 (2) of his first paper on anxiety neurosis (1895*b* [1894]), *P.F.L.*, **10**, 38.]

1. [Cf. *Three Essays* (1905*d*), *P.F.L.*, **7**, 99–100.]

chondria to paraphrenia is similar to that of the other 'actual' neuroses to hysteria and obsessional neurosis: we may suspect, that is, that it is dependent on ego-libido just as the others are on object-libido, and that hypochondriacal anxiety is the counterpart, as coming from ego-libido, to neurotic anxiety. Further, since we are already familiar with the idea that the mechanism of falling ill and of the formation of symptoms in the transference neuroses – the path from introversion to regression – is to be linked to a damming-up of object-libido,[1] we may come to closer quarters with the idea of a damming-up of ego-libido as well and may bring this idea into relation with the phenomena of hypochondria and paraphrenia.

At this point, our curiosity will of course raise the question why this damming-up of libido in the ego should have to be experienced as unpleasurable. I shall content myself with the answer that unpleasure is always the expression of a higher degree of tension, and that therefore what is happening is that a quantity in the field of material events is being transformed here as elsewhere into the psychical quality of unpleasure. Nevertheless it may be that what is decisive for the generation of unpleasure is not the absolute magnitude of the material event, but rather some particular function of that absolute magnitude.[2] Here we may even venture to touch on the question of what makes it necessary at all for our mental life to pass beyond the limits of narcissism and to attach the libido to objects.[3] The answer which would follow from our line of thought would once more be that this necessity arises when the cathexis of the ego with libido exceeds a certain amount. A strong egoism is a protection against falling ill, but in the last resort we must begin to love in order not to fall ill, and we are bound to fall ill if, in consequence of frustration, we are unable to love. This

1. Cf. [the opening pages of] 'Types of Onset of Neurosis' (1912*c*) [*P.F.L.*, **10**, 119 ff.]

2. [This whole question is discussed much more fully in 'Instincts and their Vicissitudes' (1915*c*), below, p. 115 ff.]

3. [A much more elaborate discussion of this problem too will be found in 'Instincts and their Vicissitudes' (1915*c*), p. 131 ff. below.]

follows somewhat on the lines of Heine's picture of the psychogenesis of the Creation:

> Krankheit ist wohl der letzte Grund
> Des ganzen Schöpferdrangs gewesen;
> Erschaffend konnte ich genesen,
> Erschaffend wurde ich gesund.[1]

We have recognized our mental apparatus as being first and foremost a device designed for mastering excitations which would otherwise be felt as distressing or would have pathogenic effects. Working them over in the mind helps remarkably towards an internal draining away of excitations which are incapable of direct discharge outwards, or for which such a discharge is for the moment undesirable. In the first instance, however, it is a matter of indifference whether this internal process of working-over is carried out upon real or imaginary objects. The difference does not appear till later – if the turning of the libido on to unreal objects (introversion) has led to its being dammed up. In paraphrenics, megalomania allows of a similar internal working-over of libido which has returned to the ego; perhaps it is only when the megalomania fails that the damming-up of libido in the ego becomes pathogenic and starts the process of recovery which gives us the impression of being a disease.

I shall try here to penetrate a little further into the mechanism of paraphrenia and shall bring together those views which already seem to me to deserve consideration. The difference between paraphrenic affections and the transference neuroses appears to me to lie in the circumstance that, in the former, the libido that is liberated by frustration does not remain attached to objects in phantasy, but withdraws on to the ego. Megalomania would accordingly correspond to the psychical mastering of this latter amount of libido, and would thus be the counterpart of the introversion on to phantasies that is found in the transference neuroses; a failure of this psychical function gives

1. [God is imagined as saying: 'Illness was no doubt the final cause of the whole urge to create. By creating, I could recover; by creating, I became healthy.' *Neue Gedichte*, 'Schöpfungslieder VII'.]

rise to the hypochondria of paraphrenia and this is homologous to the anxiety of the transference neuroses. We know that this anxiety can be resolved by further psychical working-over, i.e. by conversion, reaction-formation or the construction of protections (phobias). The corresponding process in paraphrenics is an attempt at restoration, to which the striking manifestations of the disease are due. Since paraphrenia frequently, if not usually, brings about only a *partial* detachment of the libido from objects, we can distinguish three groups of phenomena in the clinical picture: (1) those representing what remains of a normal state or of neurosis (residual phenomena); (2) those representing the morbid process (detachment of libido from its objects and, further, megalomania, hypochondria, affective disturbance and every kind of regression); (3) those representing restoration, in which the libido is once more attached to objects, after the manner of a hysteria (in dementia praecox or paraphrenia proper), or of an obsessional neurosis (in paranoia). This fresh libidinal cathexis differs from the primary one in that it starts from another level and under other conditions.[1] The difference between the transference neuroses brought about in the case of this fresh kind of libidinal cathexis and the corresponding formations where the ego is normal should be able to afford us the deepest insight into the structure of our mental apparatus.

A third way in which we may approach the study of narcissism is by observing the erotic life of human beings, with its many kinds of differentiation in man and woman. Just as object-libido at first concealed ego-libido from our observation, so too in connection with the object-choice of infants (and of growing children) what we first noticed was that they derived their sexual objects from their experiences of satisfaction. The first auto-erotic sexual satisfactions are experienced in connection with vital functions which serve the purpose of self-preservation. The sexual instincts are at the outset attached to the satisfaction of

1. [See some further remarks on this at the end of the paper on 'The Unconscious' (pp. 209–10 below).]

the ego-instincts; only later do they become independent of these, and even then we have an indication of that original attachment in the fact that the persons who are concerned with a child's feeding, care, and protection become his earliest sexual objects: that is to say, in the first instance his mother or a substitute for her. Side by side, however, with this type and source of object-choice, which may be called the 'anaclitic' or 'attachment' type,[1] psychoanalytic research has revealed a second type, which we were not prepared for finding. We have discovered, especially clearly in people whose libidinal development has suffered some disturbance, such as perverts and homosexuals, that in their later choice of love-objects they have taken as a model not their mother but their own selves. They are plainly seeking *themselves* as a love-object, and are exhibiting a type of object-choice which must be termed 'narcissistic'. In this observation we have the strongest of the reasons which have led us to adopt the hypothesis of narcissism.

We have, however, not concluded that human beings are divided into two sharply differentiated groups, according as their object-choice conforms to the anaclitic or to the narcissistic type; we assume rather that both kinds of object-choice are open to each individual, though he may show a preference for one or the other. We say that a human being has originally two sexual objects – himself and the woman who nurses him – and in doing

1. ['*Anlehnungstypus*.' Literally, 'leaning-on type'. The term has been rendered in English as the 'anaclitic type' by analogy with the grammatical term 'enclitic', used of particles which cannot be the first word in a sentence, but must be appended to, or must lean up against, a more important one, e.g. the Latin '*enim*' or the Greek 'δέ'. This seems to be the first published appearance of the actual term '*Anlehnungstypus*'. The idea that a child arrives at its first sexual object on the basis of its nutritional instinct is to be found in the first edition of the *Three Essays* (1905*d*), *P.F.L.*, **7**, 144; but the two or three explicit mentions in that work of the 'anaclitic type' were not added to it until the 1915 edition. The term '*angelehnte*' ('attached') is used in a similar sense near the beginning of Section III of the Schreber case history (1911*c*), *P.F.L.*, **9**, 198 and *n*. 3, but the underlying hypothesis is not stated there. – It should be noted that the 'attachment' (or '*Anlehnung*') indicated by the term is that of the sexual instincts to the ego-instincts, not of the child to its mother.]

so we are postulating a primary narcissism in everyone, which may in some cases manifest itself in a dominating fashion in his object-choice.

A comparison of the male and female sexes then shows that there are fundamental differences between them in respect of their type of object-choice, although these differences are of course not universal. Complete object-love of the attachment type is, properly speaking, characteristic of the male. It displays the marked sexual overvaluation which is doubtless derived from the child's original narcissism and thus corresponds to a transference of that narcissism to the sexual object. This sexual overvaluation is the origin of the peculiar state of being in love, a state suggestive of a neurotic compulsion, which is thus traceable to an impoverishment of the ego as regards libido in favour of the love-object.[1] A different course is followed in the type of female most frequently met with, which is probably the purest and truest one. With the onset of puberty the maturing of the female sexual organs, which up till then have been in a condition of latency, seems to bring about an intensification of the original narcissism, and this is unfavourable to the development of a true object-choice with its accompanying sexual overvaluation. Women, especially if they grow up with good looks, develop a certain self-contentment which compensates them for the social restrictions that are imposed upon them in their choice of object. Strictly speaking, it is only themselves that such women love with an intensity comparable to that of the man's love for them. Nor does their need lie in the direction of loving, but of being loved; and the man who fulfils this condition is the one who finds favour with them. The importance of this type of woman for the erotic life of mankind is to be rated very high. Such women have the greatest fascination for men, not only for aesthetic reasons, since as a rule they are the most beautiful, but also because of a combination of interesting psychological factors. For it seems very evident that another person's narcissism has a great attraction for those who have renounced part of their

1. [Freud returned to this in a discussion of being in love in Chapter VIII of his *Group Psychology* (1921*c*), *P.F.L.*, **12**, 142 ff.]

own narcissism and are in search of object-love. The charm of a child lies to a great extent in his narcissism, his self-contentment and inaccessibility, just as does the charm of certain animals which seem not to concern themselves about us, such as cats and the large beasts of prey. Indeed, even great criminals and humorists, as they are represented in literature, compel our interest by the narcissistic consistency with which they manage to keep away from their ego anything that would diminish it. It is as if we envied them for maintaining a blissful state of mind – an unassailable libidinal position which we ourselves have since abandoned. The great charm of narcissistic women has, however, its reverse side; a large part of the lover's dissatisfaction, of his doubts of the woman's love, of his complaints of her enigmatic nature, has its root in this incongruity between the types of object-choice.

Perhaps it is not out of place here to give an assurance that this description of the feminine form of erotic life is not due to any tendentious desire on my part to depreciate women. Apart from the fact that tendentiousness is quite alien to me, I know that these different lines of development correspond to the differentiation of functions in a highly complicated biological whole; further, I am ready to admit that there are quite a number of women who love according to the masculine type and who also develop the sexual overvaluation proper to that type.

Even for narcissistic women, whose attitude towards men remains cool, there is a road which leads to complete object-love. In the child which they bear, a part of their own body confronts them like an extraneous object, to which, starting out from their narcissism, they can then give complete object-love. There are other women, again, who do not have to wait for a child in order to take the step in development from (secondary) narcissism to object-love. Before puberty they feel masculine and develop some way along masculine lines; after this trend has been cut short on their reaching female maturity, they still retain the capacity of longing for a masculine ideal – an ideal which is in fact a survival of the boyish nature that they themselves once possessed.[1]

What I have so far said by way of indication may be concluded by a short summary of the paths leading to the choice of an object.

A person may love:–

(1) According to the narcissistic type:
- (*a*) what he himself is (i.e. himself),
- (*b*) what he himself was,
- (*c*) what he himself would like to be,
- (*d*) someone who was once part of himself.

(2) According to the anaclitic (attachment) type:
- (*a*) the woman who feeds him,
- (*b*) the man who protects him,

and the succession of substitutes who take their place. The inclusion of case (*c*) of the first type cannot be justified till a later stage of this discussion. [P. 96.]

The significance of narcissistic object-choice for homosexuality in men must be considered in another connection.[2]

The primary narcissism of children which we have assumed, and which forms one of the postulates of our theories of the libido, is less easy to grasp by direct observation than to confirm by inference from elsewhere. If we look at the attitude of affectionate parents towards their children, we have to recognize that it is a revival and reproduction of their own narcissism, which they have long since abandoned. The trustworthy pointer constituted by overvaluation, which we have already recognized as a narcissistic stigma in the case of object-choice, dominates, as

1. [Freud developed his views on female sexuality in a number of later papers: on a case of female homosexuality (1920*a*), *P.F.L.*, **9**, 371–400, on the effects of the anatomical distinction between the sexes (1925*j*), ibid., **7**, 331–43, on the sexuality of women (1931*b*), ibid., **7**, 371–92, and in Lecture 33 of his *New Introductory Lectures* (1933*a*), ibid., **2**, 145–69.]

2. [Freud had already raised this point in Section III of his study on Leonardo (1910*c*), *P.F.L.*, **14**, 190 ff.]

we all know, their emotional attitude. Thus they are under a compulsion to ascribe every perfection to the child – which sober observation would find no occasion to do – and to conceal and forget all his shortcomings. (Incidentally, the denial of sexuality in children is connected with this.) Moreover, they are inclined to suspend in the child's favour the operation of all the cultural acquisitions which their own narcissism has been forced to respect, and to renew on his behalf the claims to privileges which were long ago given up by themselves. The child shall have a better time than his parents; he shall not be subject to the necessities which they have recognized as paramount in life. Illness, death, renunciation of enjoyment, restrictions on his own will, shall not touch him; the laws of nature and of society shall be abrogated in his favour; he shall once more really be the centre and core of creation – 'His Majesty the Baby',[1] as we once fancied ourselves. The child shall fulfil those wishful dreams of the parents which they never carried out – the boy shall become a great man and a hero in his father's place, and the girl shall marry a prince as a tardy compensation for her mother. At the most touchy point in the narcissistic system, the immortality of the ego, which is so hard pressed by reality, security is achieved by taking refuge in the child. Parental love, which is so moving and at bottom so childish, is nothing but the parents' narcissism born again, which, transformed into object-love, unmistakably reveals its former nature.

1. [In English in the original. Perhaps a reference to a well-known Royal Academy picture of the Edwardian age, which bore that title and showed two London policemen holding up the crowded traffic to allow a nursery-maid to wheel a perambulator across the street. – 'His Majesty the Ego' appears in Freud's earlier paper on 'Creative Writers and Day-Dreaming' (1908*e*), *P.F.L.*, **14**, 138.]

Denial of child sexuality

Parental love narcissism

III

The disturbances to which a child's original narcissism is exposed, the reactions with which he seeks to protect himself from them and the paths into which he is forced in doing so – these are themes which I propose to leave on one side, as an important field of work which still awaits exploration. The most significant portion of it, however, can be singled out in the shape of the 'castration complex' (in boys, anxiety about the penis – in girls, envy for the penis) and treated in connection with the effect of early deterrence from sexual activity. Psychoanalytic research ordinarily enables us to trace the vicissitudes undergone by the libidinal instincts when these, isolated from the ego-instincts, are placed in opposition to them; but in the particular field of the castration complex, it allows us to infer the existence of an epoch and a psychical situation in which the two groups of instincts, still operating in unison and inseparably mingled, make their appearance as narcissistic interests. It is from this context that Adler [1910] has derived his concept of the 'masculine protest', which he has elevated almost to the position of the sole motive force in the formation of character and neurosis alike and which he bases not on a narcissistic, and therefore still a libidinal, trend, but on a social valuation. Psychoanalytic research has from the very beginning recognized the existence and importance of the 'masculine protest', but it has regarded it, in opposition to Adler, as narcissistic in nature and derived from the castration complex. The 'masculine protest' is concerned in the formation of character, into the genesis of which it enters along with many other factors, but it is completely unsuited for explaining the problems of the neuroses, with regard to which Adler takes account of nothing but the manner in which they serve the ego-instincts. I find it quite impossible to place the genesis of neurosis upon the narrow basis of the castration complex, however powerfully it may come to the fore in men among their resistances to the cure of a neurosis. Incidentally, I know of cases of neurosis in which the 'masculine protest', or, as we regard it, the castration complex, plays no pathogenic part, and even fails to appear at all.[1]

Observation of normal adults shows that their former megalomania has been damped down and that the psychical characteristics from which we inferred their infantile narcissism have been effaced. What has become of their ego-libido? Are we to suppose that the whole amount of it has passed into object-cathexes? Such a possibility is plainly contrary to the whole trend of our argument; but we may find a hint at another answer to the question in the psychology of repression.

We have learnt that libidinal instinctual impulses undergo the vicissitude of pathogenic repression if they come into conflict with the subject's cultural and ethical ideas. By this we never mean that the individual in question has a merely intellectual knowledge of the existence of such ideas; we always mean that he recognizes them as a standard for himself and submits to the claims they make on him. Repression, we have said, proceeds from the ego; we might say with greater precision that it proceeds from the self-respect of the ego. The same impressions, experiences, impulses and desires that one man indulges or at least works over consciously will be rejected with the utmost indignation by another, or even stifled before they enter consciousness.[2] The difference between the two, which contains the

1. [In a letter dated 30 September 1926, replying to a question from Dr Edoardo Weiss (who has kindly brought it to our attention), Freud wrote: 'Your question, in connection with my assertion in my paper on Narcissism, as to whether there are neuroses in which the castration complex plays no part, puts me in an embarrassing position. I no longer recollect what it was I had in mind at the time. Today, it is true, I could not name any neurosis in which this complex is not to be met with, and in any case I should not have written the sentence today. But we know so little of the whole subject that I should prefer not to give a final decision either way.' (1970*a* [1919–35].) – A further criticism of Adler's views on the 'masculine protest' will be found in the 'History of the Psycho-Analytic Movement' (1914*d*) and, in more detail, in ' "A Child is Being Beaten" ' (1919*e*), *P.F.L.*, **10**, 189–92.]

2. [Cf. some remarks in the paper on repression (1915*d*), below, p. 150.]

conditioning factor of repression, can easily be expressed in terms which enable it to be explained by the libido theory. We can say that the one man has set up an *ideal* in himself by which he measures his actual ego, while the other has formed no such ideal. For the ego the formation of an ideal would be the conditioning factor of repression.[1]

This ideal ego is now the target of the self-love which was enjoyed in childhood by the actual ego. The subject's narcissism makes its appearance displaced on to this new ideal ego, which, like the infantile ego, finds itself possessed of every perfection that is of value. As always where the libido is concerned, man has here again shown himself incapable of giving up a satisfaction he had once enjoyed. He is not willing to forgo the narcissistic perfection of his childhood; and when, as he grows up, he is disturbed by the admonitions of others and by the awakening of his own critical judgement, so that he can no longer retain that perfection, he seeks to recover it in the new form of an ego ideal. What he projects before him as his ideal is the substitute for the lost narcissism of his childhood in which he was his own ideal.[2]

We are naturally led to examine the relation between this forming of an ideal and sublimation. Sublimation is a process that concerns object-libido and consists in the instinct's directing itself towards an aim other than, and remote from, that of sexual satisfaction; in this process the accent falls upon deflection from sexuality. Idealization is a process that concerns the *object*; by it that object, without any alteration in its nature, is aggrandized and exalted in the subject's mind. Idealization is possible in the sphere of ego-libido as well as in that of object-libido. For example, the sexual overvaluation of an object is an idealization of it. In so far as sublimation describes something that has to do

1. [Cf. a footnote to Chapter XI of *Group Psychology* (1921*c*), as follows: 'Trotter [1916] traces repression back to the herd instinct. It is a translation of this into another form of expression rather than a contradiction when I say in my paper on narcissism that "for the ego the formation of an ideal would be the conditioning factor of repression".' (*P.F.L.*, **12**, 164 n.)]

2. [In the editions previous to 1924 this read: '. . . is only the substitute . . .']

with the instinct and idealization something to do with the object, the two concepts are to be distinguished from each other.[1]

The formation of an ego ideal is often confused with the sublimation of instinct, to the detriment of our understanding of the facts. A man who has exchanged his narcissism for homage to a high ego ideal has not necessarily on that account succeeded in sublimating his libidinal instincts. It is true that the ego ideal demands such sublimation, but it cannot enforce it; sublimation remains a special process which may be prompted by the ideal but the execution of which is entirely independent of any such prompting. It is precisely in neurotics that we find the highest differences of potential between the development of their ego ideal and the amount of sublimation of their primitive libidinal instincts; and in general it is far harder to convince an idealist of the inexpedient location of his libido than a plain man whose pretensions have remained more moderate. Further, the formation of an ego ideal and sublimation are quite differently related to the causation of neurosis. As we have learnt, the formation of an ideal heightens the demands of the ego and is the most powerful factor favouring repression; sublimation is a way out, a way by which those demands can be met *without* involving repression.[2]

It would not surprise us if we were to find a special psychical agency which performs the task of seeing that narcissistic satisfaction from the ego ideal is ensured and which, with this end in view, constantly watches the actual ego and measures it by that ideal.[3] If such an agency does exist, we cannot possibly come upon it as a *discovery* – we can only *recognize* it; for we may

1. [Freud recurs to the topic of idealization in Chapter VIII of his *Group Psychology* (1921*c*), *P.F.L.*, **12**, 143.]

2. [The possible connection between sublimation and the transformation of sexual object-libido into narcissistic libido is discussed by Freud towards the beginning of Chapter III of *The Ego and the Id* (1923*b*), p. 369 below.]

3. [It was from a combination of this agency and the ego ideal that Freud was later to evolve the super-ego. Cf. *Group Psychology* (1921*c*), *P.F.L.*, **12**, 161 ff., and *The Ego and the Id* (1923*b*), p. 367 ff. below.]

reflect that what we call our 'conscience' has the required characteristics. Recognition of this agency enables us to understand the so-called 'delusions of being noticed' or more correctly, of being *watched*, which are such striking symptoms in the paranoid diseases and which may also occur as an isolated form of illness, or intercalated in a transference neurosis. Patients of this sort complain that all their thoughts are known and their actions watched and supervised; they are informed of the functioning of this agency by voices which characteristically speak to them in the third person ('Now she's thinking of that again', 'now he's going out'). This complaint is justified; it describes the truth. A power of this kind, watching, discovering and criticizing all our intentions, does really exist. Indeed, it exists in every one of us in normal life.

Delusions of being watched present this power in a regressive form, thus revealing its genesis and the reason why the patient is in revolt against it. For what prompted the subject to form an ego ideal, on whose behalf his conscience acts as watchman, arose from the critical influence of his parents (conveyed to him by the medium of the voice), to whom were added, as time went on, those who trained and taught him and the innumerable and indefinable host of all the other people in his environment – his fellow-men – and public opinion.

In this way large amounts of libido of an essentially homosexual kind are drawn into the formation of the narcissistic ego ideal and find outlet and satisfaction in maintaining it. The institution of conscience was at bottom an embodiment, first of parental criticism, and subsequently of that of society – a process which is repeated in what takes place when a tendency towards repression develops out of a prohibition or obstacle that came in the first instance from without. The voices, as well as the undefined multitude, are brought into the foreground again by the disease, and so the evolution of conscience is reproduced regressively. But the revolt against this 'censoring agency' arises out of the subject's desire (in accordance with the fundamental character of his illness) to liberate himself from all these influences, beginning with the parental one, and out of his withdrawal of homosexual libido from them. His conscience then confronts him in a regressive form as a hostile influence from without.

The complaints made by paranoics also show that at bottom the self-criticism of conscience coincides with the self-observation on which it is based. Thus the activity of the mind which has taken over the function of conscience has also placed itself at the service of internal research, which furnishes philosophy with the material for its intellectual operations. This may have some bearing on the characteristic tendency of paranoics to construct speculative systems.[1]

It will certainly be of importance to us if evidence of the activity of this critically observing agency – which becomes heightened into conscience and philosophic introspection – can be found in other fields as well. I will mention here what Herbert Silberer has called the 'functional phenomenon', one of the few indisputably valuable additions to the theory of dreams. Silberer, as we know, has shown that in states between sleeping and waking we can directly observe the translation of thoughts into visual images, but that in these circumstances we frequently have a representation, not of a thought-content, but of the actual state (willingness, fatigue, etc.) of the person who is struggling against sleep. Similarly, he has shown that the conclusions of some dreams or some divisions in their content merely signify the dreamer's own perception of his sleeping and waking. Silberer has thus demonstrated the part played by observation – in the sense of the paranoic's delusions of being watched – in the formation of dreams. This part is not a constant one. Probably the reason why I overlooked it is because it does not play any great part in my own dreams; in persons who are gifted

1. I should like to add to this, merely by way of suggestion, that the developing and strengthening of this observing agency might contain within it the subsequent genesis of (subjective) memory and the time-factor, the latter of which has no application to unconscious processes. [For some further light on these two points see 'The Unconscious', pp. 191 and 192–3 below.]

philosophically and accustomed to introspection it may become very evident.[1]

We may here recall that we have found that the formation of dreams takes place under the dominance of a censorship which compels distortion of the dream-thoughts. We did not, however, picture this censorship as a special power, but chose the term to designate one side of the repressive trends that govern the ego, namely the side which is turned towards the dream-thoughts. If we enter further into the structure of the ego, we may recognize in the ego ideal and in the dynamic utterances of conscience the *dream-censor*[2] as well. If this censor is to some extent on the alert even during sleep, we can understand how it is that its suggested activity of self-observation and self-criticism – with such thoughts as, 'now he is too sleepy to think', 'now he is waking up' – makes a contribution to the content of the dream.[3]

At this point we may attempt some discussion of the self-regarding attitude in normal people and in neurotics.

In the first place self-regard appears to us to be an expression of the size of the ego; what the various elements are which go to determine that size is irrelevant. Everything a person possesses or achieves, every remnant of the primitive feeling of

1. [See Silberer (1909 and 1912). In 1914 – the year in which he wrote the present paper – Freud added a much longer discussion of this phenomenon to *The Interpretation of Dreams* (*P.F.L.*, **4**, 645–9).]

2. [Here and at the beginning of the next sentence, as well as below on p. 95, Freud makes use of the personal form, '*Zensor*', instead of his almost universal '*Zensur*' ('censorship'). Cf. a footnote to the passage in *The Interpretation of Dreams*, referred to in the last footnote (ibid., **4**, 648 *n*. 2). The distinction between the two words is clearly brought out in a sentence near the end of Lecture 26 of the *Introductory Lectures* (1916–17): 'We know the self-observing agency as the ego-censor, the conscience; it is this that exercises the dream-censorship during the night.' Ibid., **1**, 479.]

3. I cannot here determine whether the differentiation of the censoring agency from the rest of the ego is capable of forming the basis of the philosophic distinction between consciousness and self-consciousness.

omnipotence which his experience has confirmed, helps to increase his self-regard.

Applying our distinction between sexual and ego-instincts, we must recognize that self-regard has a specially intimate dependence on narcissistic libido. Here we are supported by two fundamental facts: that in paraphrenics self-regard is increased, while in the transference neuroses it is diminished; and that in love-relations not being loved lowers the self-regarding feelings, while being loved raises them. As we have indicated, the aim and the satisfaction in a narcissistic object-choice is to be loved.[1]

Further, it is easy to observe that libidinal object-cathexis does not raise self-regard. The effect of dependence upon the loved object is to lower that feeling: a person in love is humble. A person who loves has, so to speak, forfeited a part of his narcissism, and it can only be replaced by his being loved. In all these respects self-regard seems to remain related to the narcissistic element in love.

The realization of impotence, of one's own inability to love, in consequence of mental or physical disorder, has an exceedingly lowering effect upon self-regard. Here, in my judgement, we must look for one of the sources of the feelings of inferiority which are experienced by patients suffering from the transference neuroses and which they are so ready to report. The main source of these feelings is, however, the impoverishment of the ego, due to the extraordinarily large libidinal cathexes which have been withdrawn from it – due, that is to say, to the injury sustained by the ego through sexual trends which are no longer subject to control.

Adler [1907] is right in maintaining that when a person with an active mental life recognizes an inferiority in one of his organs, it acts as a spur and calls out a higher level of performance in him through overcompensation. But it would be altogether an exaggeration if, following Adler's example, we sought to attribute every successful achievement to this factor of an

1. [This subject is enlarged on by Freud in Chapter VIII of his *Group Psychology* (1921*c*), *P.F.L.*, **12**, 143 ff.]

original inferiority of an organ. Not all artists are handicapped with bad eyesight, nor were all orators originally stammerers. And there are plenty of instances of excellent achievements springing from *superior* organic endowment. In the aetiology of neuroses organic inferiority and imperfect development play an insignificant part – much the same as that played by currently active perceptual material in the formation of dreams. Neuroses make use of such inferiorities as a pretext, just as they do of every other suitable factor. We may be tempted to believe a neurotic woman patient when she tells us that it was inevitable she should fall ill, since she is ugly, deformed or lacking in charm, so that no one could love her; but the very next neurotic will teach us better – for she persists in her neurosis and in her aversion to sexuality, although she seems more desirable, and is more desired, than the average woman. The majority of hysterical women are among the attractive and even beautiful representatives of their sex, while, on the other hand, the frequency of ugliness, organic defects and infirmities in the lower classes of society does not increase the incidence of neurotic illness among them.

The relations of self-regard to erotism – that is, to libidinal object-cathexes – may be expressed concisely in the following way. Two cases must be distinguished, according to whether the erotic cathexes are ego-syntonic, or, on the contrary, have suffered repression. In the former case (where the use made of the libido is *ego-syntonic*), love is assessed like any other activity of the ego. Loving in itself, in so far as it involves longing and deprivation, lowers self-regard; whereas being loved, having one's love returned, and possessing the loved object, raises it once more. When libido is repressed, the erotic cathexis is felt as a severe depletion of the ego, the satisfaction of love is impossible, and the re-enrichment of the ego can be effected only by a withdrawal of libido from its objects. The return of the object-libido to the ego and its transformation into narcissism represents,[1] as it were, a happy love once more; and, on

1. ['*Darstellt.*' In the first edition only: '*herstellt*', 'establishes'.]

the other hand, it is also true that a real happy love corresponds to the primal condition in which object-libido and ego-libido cannot be distinguished.

The importance and extensiveness of the topic must be my justification for adding a few more remarks which are somewhat loosely strung together.

The development of the ego consists in a departure from primary narcissism and gives rise to a vigorous attempt to recover that state. This departure is brought about by means of the displacement of libido on to an ego ideal imposed from without; and satisfaction is brought about from fulfilling this ideal.

At the same time the ego has sent out the libidinal object-cathexes. It becomes impoverished in favour of these cathexes, just as it does in favour of the ego ideal, and it enriches itself once more from its satisfactions in respect of the object, just as it does by fulfilling its ideal.

One part of self-regard is primary – the residue of infantile narcissism; another part arises out of the omnipotence which is corroborated by experience (the fulfilment of the ego ideal), whilst a third part proceeds from the satisfaction of object-libido.

The ego ideal has imposed severe conditions upon the satisfaction of libido through objects; for it causes some of them to be rejected by means of its censor,[1] as being incompatible. Where no such ideal has been formed, the sexual trend in question makes its appearance unchanged in the personality in the form of a perversion. To be their own ideal once more, in regard to sexual no less than other trends, as they were in childhood – this is what people strive to attain as their happiness.

Being in love consists in a flowing-over of ego-libido on to the object. It has the power to remove repressions and re-instate perversions. It exalts the sexual object into a sexual ideal. Since, with the object type (or attachment type), being in love occurs in virtue of the fulfilment of infantile conditions for loving, we

1. [See footnote 2, p. 92.]

may say that whatever fulfils that condition is idealized.

The sexual ideal may enter into an interesting auxiliary relation to the ego ideal. It may be used for substitutive satisfaction where narcissistic satisfaction encounters real hindrances. In that case a person will love in conformity with the narcissistic type of object choice, will love what he once was and no longer is, or else what possesses the excellences which he never had at all (cf. (*c*) [p. 84]). The formula parallel to the one there stated runs thus: what possesses the excellence which the ego lacks for making it an ideal, is loved. This expedient is of special importance for the neurotic, who, on account of his excessive object-cathexes, is impoverished in his ego and is incapable of fulfilling his ego ideal. He then seeks a way back to narcissism from his prodigal expenditure of libido upon objects, by choosing a sexual ideal after the narcissistic type which possesses the excellences to which he cannot attain. This is the cure by love, which he generally prefers to cure by analysis. Indeed, he cannot believe in any other mechanism of cure; he usually brings expectations of this sort with him to the treatment and directs them towards the person of the physician. The patient's incapacity for love, resulting from his extensive repressions, naturally stands in the way of a therapeutic plan of this kind. An unintended result is often met with when, by means of the treatment, he has been partially freed from his repressions: he withdraws from further treatment in order to choose a love-object, leaving his cure to be continued by a life with someone he loves. We might be satisfied with this result, if it did not bring with it all the dangers of a crippling dependence upon his helper in need.

The ego ideal opens up an important avenue for the understanding of group psychology. In addition to its individual side, this ideal has a social side; it is also the common ideal of a family, a class or a nation. It binds not only a person's narcissistic libido, but also a considerable amount of his homosexual libido,[1] which is in this way turned back into the ego. The want of satisfaction

1. [The importance of homosexuality in the structure of groups had been hinted at in *Totem and Taboo* (1912–13), and was again referred to in *Group Psychology* (1921*c*). Cf. *P.F.L.*, **13**, 205; ibid., **12**, 156*n*., and 176.

which arises from the non-fulfilment of this ideal liberates homosexual libido, and this is transformed into a sense of guilt (social anxiety). Originally this sense of guilt was a fear of punishment by the parents, or, more correctly, the fear of losing their love; later the parents are replaced by an indefinite number of fellow-men. The frequent causation of paranoia by an injury to the ego, by a frustration of satisfaction within the sphere of the ego ideal, is thus made more intelligible, as is the convergence of ideal-formation and sublimation in the ego ideal, as well as the involution of sublimations and the possible transformation of ideals in paraphrenic disorders.

PAPERS ON METAPSYCHOLOGY
[1915]

PAPERS ON METAPSYCHOLOGY

EDITOR'S INTRODUCTION

FREUD published his first extended account of his views on psychological theory in the seventh chapter of *The Interpretation of Dreams* (1900*a*), *P.F.L.*, **4**, 652 ff., which incorporated, in a transmuted form, much of the substance of his earlier, unpublished 'Project' (1950*a* [1895]). Apart from occasional short discussions, such as the one in Chapter VI of his book on jokes (1905*c*), *P.F.L.*, **6**, 215 ff., ten years passed before he again began to enter deeply into theoretical problems. An exploratory paper on 'The Two Principles of Mental Functioning' (1911*b*), p. 35 above, was followed by other more or less tentative approaches – in Part III of his Schreber analysis (1911*c*), *P.F.L.*, **9**, 196 ff., in his English paper on the unconscious (1912*g*), p. 50 above, and in the long discussion of narcissism (1914*c*), p. 65 above. Finally, in the spring and summer of 1915, he once more undertook a full-length and systematic exposition of his psychological theories.

The five papers which follow form an interconnected series. As we learn from a footnote to the fourth of them (p. 229), they are part of a collection which Freud had originally planned to publish in book form under the title *Zur Vorbereitung einer Metapsychologie* (*Preliminaries to a Metapsychology*).[1] He adds that the intention of the series was to provide a stable theoretical foundation for psychoanalysis.

Though the first three of these papers were published in 1915

1. In *G. S.*, **5** (1924), 432, the paper written by Freud for the Society for Psychical Research (1912*g*), p. 50 above, is included under the rubric 'Papers on Metapsychology' along with the present five papers. It did not, however, form part of the original collection.

and the last two in 1917, we learn from Dr Ernest Jones (1955, 208) that they were in fact all written in a period of some seven weeks between 15 March and 4 May 1915. We also learn from Dr Jones (ibid., 209) that seven more papers were added to the series during the following three months, the whole collection of twelve being completed by 9 August. These further seven papers, however, were never published by Freud and it seems probable that at some later date he destroyed them, for no trace of them has been found and indeed their very existence was unknown or forgotten until Dr Jones came to examine Freud's letters. At the time he was writing them in 1915 he kept his correspondents (Abraham, Ferenczi and Jones) informed of his progress; but there seems to be only a single reference to them afterwards, in a letter to Abraham in November 1917. This was written shortly before the time of publication of the last two papers to appear, and it seems to imply that the seven others were still in existence then and that he still intended to publish them, though he felt that an opportune moment had not yet arrived. (Cf. Freud, 1965*a*.)[1]

1. The original existence of these papers is confirmed by several passages in Freud's correspondence. For instance, in a letter to J. J. Putnam of 8 July 1915 he writes: 'I myself am using the break in my work [due to the War] at this time to finish off a book containing a collection of twelve psychological essays.' (Freud, 1960*a*.) Also in another, of 30 July 1915, to Lou Andreas-Salomé: 'Fruit of the present time will probably take the form of a book consisting of 12 essays beginning with the one on instincts and their vicissitudes . . . The book is finished except for the necessary revision caused by the arranging and fitting in of the individual essays.' In a further letter to Lou Andreas-Salomé of 25 May 1916: 'My book containing 12 essays of this kind cannot be published before the end of the war, and who knows *how* long after that ardently longed-for date.' Freud also mentions the existence of the 'twelve' essays and his intention of publishing them after the War in a letter of 17 December 1915 to Ludwig Binswanger (Freud, 1955*f*). – The assumption that Freud ultimately rejected the last seven papers as unsatisfactory is strongly borne out by an exchange with Lou Andreas-Salomé. In a letter of 18 March 1919 she asks: 'Where is your Metapsychology, now that the published chapters have been included in the IVth volume of the "N1" [*S.K.S.N.*]? Where are the remaining ones, which were already finished?' Freud replies (2 April): 'Where is my Metapsychology? In the first place it remains unwritten. Working-over material systematically is not possible for me; the fragmentary nature of my observations and the sporadic character

We are told the subjects with which five of the last seven papers dealt: Consciousness, Anxiety, Conversion Hysteria, Obsessional Neurosis and the Transference Neuroses in General; and we can detect possible references to them in the surviving papers. We can even guess the subjects which the two unspecified papers may have discussed – namely, Sublimation and Projection[1] (or Paranoia) – for there are fairly plain allusions to these. The collection of twelve papers would thus have been a comprehensive one, dealing with the underlying processes in most of the principal neuroses and psychoses (conversion hysteria, anxiety hysteria, obsessional neurosis, manic-depressive insanity and paranoia) as well as in dreams, with the mental mechanisms of repression, sublimation, introjection and projection, and with the two mental systems of consciousness and the unconscious.

It is difficult to exaggerate our loss from the disappearance of these papers. There was a unique conjunction of favourable factors at the time at which Freud wrote them. His previous major theoretical work (the seventh chapter of *The Interpretation of Dreams*) had been written fifteen years before, at a relatively early stage of his psychological studies. Now, however, he had some twenty-five years of psychoanalytic experience behind him on which to base his theoretical constructions, while he remained at the summit of his intellectual powers. And it was at this time that the accidental circumstance of the shrinking of his practice owing to the outbreak of the first World War gave him the necessary leisure for five months in which to carry

of my ideas will not permit it. If, however, I should live another ten years, remain capable of work during that time, not starve, not be killed, not be too deeply taken up with the misery of my family or of those around me – a little much in the way of conditions – then I promise to produce further contributions to it. A first one in this line will be contained in an essay "Beyond the Pleasure Principle" . . .' (Cf. Freud, 1966*a*.)

1. In part III of the Schreber analysis (1911*c*), *P.F.L.*, **9**, 204–5, 205 *n.* 2, and 210, Freud discussed the mechanism of projection, but professed himself dissatisfied and promised to consider it more fully in a later work. This he seems never to have done, unless it was in one of these missing papers.

through his attempt. We may try to console ourselves, no doubt, with the reflection that much of the contents of the lost papers must have found its way into Freud's later writings. But we would give a great deal to possess connected discussions on such questions as consciousness or sublimation in place of the scattered and relatively meagre allusions with which we have in fact to rest satisfied.

In view of the special importance of this series of papers, the closeness of their reasoning and the occasional abstruseness of the topics with which they deal, particular efforts have been made to render them with accuracy. The translation has throughout (and especially where there are doubtful passages) been kept as close as possible to the German, even at the risk of its reading stiffly. (Such un-English terms, for instance, as 'the repressed' and 'the mental' have been freely used.) Although the version published in 1925 has been taken as a basis, what follows is in effect an entirely new one. It has also seemed reasonable to include more than the usual quantity of introductory material, to annotate the text very freely, and in particular to give ample references to other parts of Freud's writings which may throw light on any obscurities. A list of the more important of his theoretical works will be found in an appendix (pp. 465–6 below).

INSTINCTS AND THEIR VICISSITUDES
(1915)

EDITOR'S NOTE

TRIEBE UND TRIEBSCHICKSALE

(A) German Editions:

1915 *Int. Z. ärztl. Psychoanal.*, **3** (2), 84–100.
1924 *Gesammelte Schriften*, **5**, 443–65.
1946 *Gesammelte Werke*, **10**, 210–32.

(B) English Translations:
'Instincts and their Vicissitudes'

1925 *Collected Papers*, **4**, 69–83. (Tr. C. M. Baines.)
1957 *Standard Edition*, **14**, 109–40. (Translation, based on that of 1925, but largely rewritten.)

The present edition is a reprint of the *Standard Edition* version, with editorial modifications.

Freud began writing this paper on 15 March 1915; it and the following one ('Repression') had been completed by 4 April.

It should be remarked by way of preface that here (and throughout the *Pelican Freud Library*) we have followed the *Standard Edition* rendering of the German word '*Trieb*' by the English 'instinct'. The choice of this English equivalent rather than such possible alternatives as 'drive' or 'urge' is discussed in the General Preface to the first volume of the *Standard Edition* (**1**, xxiv–xxvi). The word 'instinct' is in any case not used here in the sense which seems at the moment to be the most current among biologists. But Freud shows in the course of this paper the meaning which he attaches to the word so translated. Incidentally, on p. 200 below, in the paper on 'The Unconscious', he himself uses the German word '*Instinkt*', though possibly in a rather different sense.[1]

There is, however, an ambiguity in Freud's use of the term '*Trieb*' ('instinct') and '*Triebrepräsentanz*' ('instinctual representative') to which, for the sake of clearer understanding, attention must be drawn. On p. 118 below he describes an instinct as 'a concept on the frontier between the mental and the somatic, . . . the psychical representative[2] of the stimuli originating from within the organism and reaching the mind'. He had twice before given descriptions in almost the same words. Some years earlier, towards the end of Section III of his discussion of the case of Schreber (1911*c*), *P.F.L.*, **9**, 213, he wrote of instinct as 'the concept on the frontier between the somatic and the mental . . ., the psychical repesentative of organic forces'. And again, in a passage probably written a few months before the present paper and added to the third edition (published in 1915, but with a preface dated 'October 1914') of his *Three Essays* (1905*d*), *P.F.L.*, **7**, 83, he wrote of instinct as 'the psychical representative of an endosomatic, continuously flowing source of stimulation . . . The concept of instinct is thus one of those lying on the frontier between the mental and the physical'. These three accounts seem to make it plain that Freud was drawing no distinction between an instinct and its 'psychical representative'. He was apparently regarding the instinct itself as the psychical representative of somatic forces. If now, however, we turn to the later papers in this series, we seem to find him drawing a very sharp distinction between the instinct and its psychical representative. This is perhaps shown most clearly in a passage in 'The Unconscious' (p. 179 below): 'An instinct can never become an object of consciousness – only the idea [*Vorstellung*] that represents the instinct can. Even in the unconscious, more-

1. As applied to animals. It is so used in half a dozen other places in his writings.

2. The German word here and in the Schreber quotation is '*Repräsentant*', a particularly formal word used mainly in legal or constitutional language. In all the other quotations which follow, as well as almost invariably later, Freud writes '*Repräsentanz*', which is a more abstract form.

over, an instinct cannot be represented otherwise than by an idea. . . . When we nevertheless speak of an unconscious instinctual impulse or of a repressed instinctual impulse . . . we can only mean an instinctual impulse the ideational representative of which is unconscious.' This same view appears in many other passages. For instance, in 'Repression' (p. 147 below) Freud speaks of 'the psychical (ideational) representative of the instinct' and goes on: '. . . the representative in question persists unaltered and the instinct remains attached to it'; and again, in the same paper (p. 152), he writes of an instinctual representative as 'an idea or group of ideas which is cathected with a definite quota of psychical energy (libido or interest) coming from an instinct', and proceeds to say that 'besides the idea, some other element representing the instinct has to be taken into account'. In this second group of quotations, therefore, the instinct is no longer regarded as being the psychical representative of somatic impulses but rather as itself being something non-psychical. Both of these apparently differing views of the nature of an instinct are to be found elsewhere in Freud's later writings, though the second predominates. It may be, however, that the contradiction is more apparent than real, and that its solution lies precisely in the ambiguity of the concept itself – a frontier-concept between the physical and the mental.

In a number of passages Freud expressed his dissatisfaction with the state of psychological knowledge about the instincts. Not long before, for instance, in his paper on narcissism (1914*c*, p. 70 above), he had complained of 'the total absence of any theory of the instincts which would help us to find our bearings'. Later, too, in *Beyond the Pleasure Principle* (1920*g*), p. 306 below, he wrote of the instincts as 'at once the most important and the most obscure element of psychological research'. The present paper is a relatively early attempt to deal with the subject comprehensively. Its many successors corrected and supplemented it at a number of points, but it nevertheless holds the field as the clearest account of what Freud understood by the instincts and of the way in which he thought they operated. Subsequent reflection, it is true, led him to alter his views on their classification as well as on their deeper determinants; but this paper is an indispensable basis for understanding the developments that were to follow.

The course of Freud's changing views on the classification of the instincts may perhaps be appropriately summarized here. It is a surprising fact that the instincts make their explicit appearance at a comparatively late point in the sequence of his writings. The word 'instinct' is scarcely to be found in the works of the Breuer period or in the Fliess correspondence or even in *The Interpretation of Dreams* (1900*a*). Not until the *Three Essays* (1905*d*) is the 'sexual instinct' freely mentioned as such; the 'instinctual impulses',[1] which were to become one of Freud's commonest terms, seem not to appear till the paper on 'Obsessive Actions and Religious Practices' (1907*b*). But this is mainly no more than a *verbal* point: the instincts were of course there under other names. Their place was taken to a great extent by such things as 'excitations', 'affective ideas', 'wishful impulses', 'endogenous stimuli', and so on. For instance, a distinction is drawn below (p. 114) between a 'stimulus', which operates as a force giving a single impact, and an 'instinct', which always operates as a constant one. This precise distinction had been drawn by Freud twenty years earlier in almost identical words except that instead of 'stimulus' and 'instinct' he spoke of 'exogenous' and 'endogenous excitations'.[2] Similarly, Freud points out below (p. 115) that the primitive organism cannot take evasive action against instinctual needs as it can against external stimuli. In this case too he had anticipated the idea twenty years before, though once again the term used was 'endogenous stimuli'. This second passage, in Section 1 of Part I of the 'Project' (1950*a* [1895]), goes on to say that these endogenous stimuli 'have their origin in the cells of the body and give rise to the major needs: hunger, respiration and sexuality', but nowhere here is the actual word 'instinct' to be found.

The conflict which underlies the psychoneuroses was at this early period sometimes described as being between 'the ego' and

1. '*Triebregungen.*'

2. See the end of Section III of Freud's first paper on anxiety neurosis (1895*b*), *P.F.L.*, **10**, 59–60.

'sexuality'; and though the term 'libido' was often used, the concept was of a manifestation of 'somatic sexual tension', which in its turn was regarded as a chemical event. Only in the *Three Essays* (1905*d*) was libido explicitly established as an expression of the sexual instinct. The other party to the conflict, 'the ego', remained undefined for much longer. It was chiefly discussed in connection with its functions – in particular 'repression', 'resistance' and 'reality-testing' – but (apart from a very early attempt in Section 14 of Part I of the 'Project') little was said either of its structure or dynamics.[1] The 'self-preservative' instincts had scarcely ever been referred to, except indirectly in connection with the theory that the libido had attached itself to them in the earlier phases of its development;[2] and there seemed no obvious reason for connecting them with the part played by the ego as the repressive agent in neurotic conflicts. Then, with apparent suddenness, in a short paper on psychogenic disturbance of vision (1910*i*, *P.F.L.*, **10**, 109 ff.), Freud introduced the term 'ego-instincts' and identified these on the one hand with the self-preservative instincts and on the other with the repressive function. From this time forward the conflict was regularly represented as being between two sets of instincts – the libido and the ego-instincts.

The introduction of the concept of 'narcissism', however, raised a complication. In his paper on that theory (1914*c*), Freud advanced the notion of 'ego-libido' (or 'narcissistic libido') which cathects the ego, as contrasted with 'object-libido' which cathects objects (p. 68 above). A passage in that paper (loc. cit.) as well as a remark in the present one (p. 121) show that he was already feeling uneasy as to whether his 'dualistic' classification of the instincts would hold. It is true that in the Schreber analysis (1911*c*) he insisted on the difference between 'ego-cathexes' and 'libido' and between 'interest emanating from erotic sources' and 'interest in general' – a distinction which reappears in the rejoin-

1. Cf. the end of the Editor's Note to the paper on Narcissism (p. 63 above), and a discussion of 'reality-testing' in the Editor's Note to 'A Metapsychological Supplement to the Theory of Dreams' (p. 226 below).

2. See, for instance, a passage in the *Three Essays*, *P.F.L.*, **7**, 97–8, where, however, the explicit mention of self-preservation was added in 1915.

der to Jung in the paper on narcissism (pp. 72–4 above). The term 'interest' is used again in the present paper (p. 133); and in Lecture 26 of the *Introductory Lectures* (1916–17) 'ego-interest' or simply 'interest' is regularly contrasted with 'libido'. Nevertheless, the exact nature of these non-libidinal instincts was obscure. The turning-point in Freud's classification of the instincts was reached in *Beyond the Pleasure Principle* (1920*g*). In Chapter VI of that work he frankly recognized the difficulty of the position that had been reached, and explicitly declared that 'narcissistic libido was of course a manifestation of the force of the sexual instinct' and that 'it had necessarily to be identified with the "self-preservative instincts".' (See below, p. 325 ff.) He still held, however, that there were ego-instincts and object-instincts other than libidinal ones; and it was here that, still adhering to a dualistic view, he introduced his hypothesis of the death instinct. An account of the development of his views on the classification of the instincts up to that point was given in the long footnote at the end of Chapter VI of *Beyond the Pleasure Principle* (see below, pp. 334–5), and a further discussion of the subject, in the light of his newly completed picture of the structure of the mind, occupied Chapter IV of *The Ego and the Id* (1923*b*), p. 380 below. He traversed the whole ground once again in much detail in Chapter VI of *Civilization and its Discontents* (1930*a*), and he there for the first time gave especial consideration to the aggressive and destructive instincts. He had earlier paid little attention to these except where (as in sadism and masochism) they were fused with libidinal elements; but he now discussed them in their pure form and explained them as derivatives of the death instinct. A still later review of the subject will be found in the second half of Lecture 32 of the *New Introductory Lectures* (1933*a*) and a final summary in Chapter II of the posthumous *Outline of Psycho-Analysis* (1940*a* [1938]).[1]

1. The Editor's Introduction to *Civilization and its Discontents* (1930*a*) describes in detail the development of Freud's views on this subject. Some remarks on the destructive instinct and the possibility of its sublimation are contained in two letters of Freud's to Princess Marie Bonaparte of 27 May and 17 June 1937. They are printed in Appendix A (Nos. 33 and 34) of the third volume of Ernest Jones's biography (1957).

INSTINCTS AND THEIR VICISSITUDES

We have often heard it maintained that sciences should be built up on clear and sharply defined basic concepts. In actual fact no science, not even the most exact, begins with such definitions. The true beginning of scientific activity consists rather in describing phenomena and then in proceeding to group, classify and correlate them. Even at the stage of description it is not possible to avoid applying certain abstract ideas to the material in hand, ideas derived from somewhere or other but certainly not from the new observations alone. Such ideas – which will later become the basic concepts of the science – are still more indispensable as the material is further worked over. They must at first necessarily possess some degree of indefiniteness; there can be no question of any clear delimitation of their content. So long as they remain in this condition, we come to an understanding about their meaning by making repeated references to the material of observation from which they appear to have been derived, but upon which, in fact, they have been imposed. Thus, strictly speaking, they are in the nature of conventions – although everything depends on their not being arbitrarily chosen but determined by their having significant relations to the empirical material, relations that we seem to sense before we can clearly recognize and demonstrate them. It is only after more thorough investigation of the field of observation that we are able to formulate its basic scientific concepts with increased precision, and progressively so to modify them that they become serviceable and consistent over a wide area. Then, indeed, the time may have come to confine them in definitions. The advance of knowledge, however, does not tolerate any rigidity even in definitions. Physics furnishes an excellent illustration of the way in which even 'basic concepts' that have been established in the form of definitions are constantly being altered in their content.[1]

A conventional basic concept of this kind, which at the moment is still somewhat obscure but which is indispensable to us in psychology, is that of an 'instinct'.[2] Let us try to give a content to it by approaching it from different angles.

First, from the angle of *physiology*. This has given us the concept of a 'stimulus' and the pattern of the reflex arc, according to which a stimulus applied to living tissue (nervous substance) *from* the outside is discharged by action *to* the outside. This action is expedient in so far as it withdraws the stimulated substance from the influence of the stimulus, removes it out of its range of operation.

What is the relation of 'instinct' to 'stimulus'? There is nothing to prevent our subsuming the concept of 'instinct' under that of 'stimulus' and saying that an instinct is a stimulus applied to the mind. But we are immediately set on our guard against *equating* instinct and mental stimulus. There are obviously other stimuli to the mind besides those of an instinctual kind, stimuli which behave far more like physiological ones. For example, when a strong light falls on the eye, it is not an instinctual stimulus; it *is* one, however, when a dryness of the mucous membrane of the pharynx or an irritation of the mucous membrane of the stomach makes itself felt.[3]

We have now obtained the material necessary for distinguishing between instinctual stimuli and other (physiological) stimuli that operate on the mind. In the first place, an instinctual stimulus does not arise from the external world but from within the organism itself. For this reason it operates differently upon the mind and different actions are necessary in order to remove it. Further, all that is essential in a stimulus is covered if we assume that it operates with a single impact, so that it can be disposed

1. [A similar line of thought had been developed in the paper on narcissism (1914*c*, pp. 69–70 above).]

2. ['*Trieb*' in the original. See Editor's Note, p. 108.]

3. Assuming, of course, that these internal processes are the organic basis of the respective needs of thirst and hunger.

of by a single expedient action. A typical instance of this is motor flight from the source of stimulation. These impacts may, of course, be repeated and summated, but that makes no difference to our notion of the process and to the conditions for the removal of the stimulus. An instinct, on the other hand, never operates as a force giving a *momentary* impact but always as a *constant* one. Moreover, since it impinges not from without but from within the organism, no flight can avail against it. A better term for an instinctual stimulus is a 'need'. What does away with a need is 'satisfaction'. This can be attained only by an appropriate ('adequate') alteration of the internal source of stimulation.

Let us imagine ourselves in the situation of an almost entirely helpless living organism, as yet unorientated in the world, which is receiving stimuli in its nervous substance.[1] This organism will very soon be in a position to make a first distinction and a first orientation. On the one hand, it will be aware of stimuli which can be avoided by muscular action (flight); these it ascribes to an external world. On the other hand, it will also be aware of stimuli against which such action is of no avail and whose character of constant pressure persists in spite of it; these stimuli are the signs of an internal world, the evidence of instinctual needs. The perceptual substance of the living organism will thus have found in the efficacy of its muscular activity a basis for distinguishing between an 'outside' and an 'inside'.[2]

1. [The hypothesis which follows concerning the behaviour of a primitive living organism, and the postulation of a fundamental 'principle of constancy', had been stated in similar terms in some of the very earliest of Freud's psychological works. See, for instance, Chapter VII, Sections C and E, of *The Interpretation of Dreams* (1900*a*), *P.F.L.*, **4**, 701 ff. and 745 ff. But it had been expressed still earlier in *neurological* terms in his posthumously published 'Project' of 1895 (1950*a*, Part I, Section 1), as well as, more briefly, in his lecture on the Breuer and Freud 'Preliminary Communication' (1893*h*) and in the penultimate paragraph of his French paper on hysterical paralyses (1893*c*). Freud returned to the hypothesis once more, in Chapters I and IV of *Beyond the Pleasure Principle* (1920*g*), pp. 275 ff. and 297 ff. below; and reconsidered it in 'The Economic Problem of Masochism' (1924*c*), p. 413 below. Cf. footnote, pp. 117–18 below.]

2. [See further below, p. 131 ff. Freud dealt with the subject later in his paper on 'Negation' (1925*h*), p. 439 ff. below, and in Chapter I of *Civilization and its Discontents* (1930*a*), *P.F.L.*, **12**, 254–5.]

We thus arrive at the essential nature of instincts in the first place by considering their main characteristics – their origin in sources of stimulation within the organism and their appearance as a constant force – and from this we deduce one of their further features, namely, that no actions of flight avail against them. In the course of this discussion, however, we cannot fail to be struck by something that obliges us to make a further admission. In order to guide us in dealing with the field of psychological phenomena, we do not merely apply certain conventions to our empirical material as basic *concepts*; we also make use of a number of complicated *postulates*. We have already alluded to the most important of these, and all we need now do is to state it expressly. This postulate is of a biological nature, and makes use of the concept of 'purpose' (or perhaps of expediency) and runs as follows: the nervous system is an apparatus which has the function of getting rid of the stimuli that reach it, or of reducing them to the lowest possible level; or which, if it were feasible, would maintain itself in an altogether unstimulated condition.[1] Let us for the present not take exception to the indefiniteness of this idea and let us assign to the nervous system the task – speaking in general terms – of *mastering stimuli*. We then see how greatly the simple pattern of the physiological reflex is complicated by the introduction of instincts. External stimuli impose only the single task of withdrawing from them; this is accomplished by muscular movements, one of which eventually achieves that aim and thereafter, being the expedient movement, becomes a hereditary disposition. Instinctual stimuli, which originate from within the organism, cannot be dealt with by this mechanism. Thus they make far higher demands on the nervous system and cause it to undertake involved and interconnected activities by which the external world is so changed as to afford satisfaction to the internal source of stimulation. Above all, they oblige the nervous system to renounce its ideal intention of keeping off stimuli, for they maintain an incessant and unavoidable afflux of stimulation. We may therefore well con-

1. [This is the 'principle of constancy'. See footnote 1 above, p. 115.]

clude that instincts and not external stimuli are the true motive forces behind the advances that have led the nervous system, with its unlimited capacities, to its present high level of development. There is naturally nothing to prevent our supposing that the instincts themselves are, at least in part, precipitates of the effects of external stimulation, which in the course of phylogenesis have brought about the modifications in the living substance.

When we further find that the activity of even the most highly developed mental apparatus is subject to the pleasure principle, i.e. is automatically regulated by feelings belonging to the pleasure-unpleasure series, we can hardly reject the further hypothesis that these feelings reflect the manner in which the process of mastering stimuli takes place – certainly in the sense that unpleasurable feelings are connected with an increase and pleasurable feelings with a decrease of stimulus. We will, however, carefully preserve this assumption in its present highly indefinite form, until we succeed, if that is possible, in discovering what sort of relation exists between pleasure and unpleasure, on the one hand, and fluctuations in the amounts of stimulus affecting mental life, on the other. It is certain that many very various relations of this kind, and not very simple ones, are possible.[1]

1. [It will be seen that two principles are here involved. One of these is the 'principle of constancy' (see above, p. 116, and footnote 1, p. 115). It is stated again in *Beyond the Pleasure Principle*, 1920*g*, Chapter I (p. 277 below), as follows: 'The mental apparatus endeavours to keep the quantity of excitation present in it as low as possible or at least to keep it constant.' For this principle Freud, in the same work (ibid., 329), adopted the term 'Nirvana principle'. The second principle involved is the 'pleasure principle', stated at the beginning of the paragraph to which this note is appended. It, too, is restated in *Beyond the Pleasure Principle* (ibid., 275): 'The course taken by mental events is automatically regulated by the pleasure principle . . . [That course] takes a direction such that its final outcome coincides with . . . an avoidance of unpleasure or a production of pleasure.' Freud seems to have assumed to begin with that these two principles were closely correlated and even identical. Thus, in his 'Project' of 1895 (Freud, 1950*a*, Part I, Section 8) he writes: 'Since we have certain knowledge of a trend in physical life towards *avoiding unpleasure*, we are tempted to identify that trend with the primary trend towards inertia [i.e. towards avoiding excitation].' A

If now we apply ourselves to considering mental life from a *biological* point of view, an 'instinct' appears to us as a concept on the frontier between the mental and the somatic, as the psychical representative of the stimuli originating from within the organism and reaching the mind, as a measure of the demand made upon the mind for work in consequence of its connection with the body.[1]

We are now in a position to discuss certain terms which are used in reference to the concept of an instinct – for example, its 'pressure', its 'aim', its 'object' and its 'source'.

By the pressure [*Drang*] of an instinct we understand its motor factor, the amount of force or the measure of the demand for work which it represents. The characteristic of exercising pressure is common to all instincts; it is in fact their very essence. Every instinct is a piece of activity; if we speak loosely of passive instincts, we can only mean instincts whose *aim* is passive.[2]

similar view is taken in Chapter VII (E) of *The Interpretation of Dreams* (1900*a*), *P.F.L.*, **4**, 757. In the passage in the text above, however, a doubt appears to be expressed as to the completeness of the correlation between the two principles. This doubt is carried farther in *Beyond the Pleasure Principle* (pp. 276 and 337 below) and is discussed at some length in 'The Economic Problem of Masochism' (1924*c*), p. 413 ff. below. Freud there argues that the two principles cannot be identical, since there are unquestionably states of increasing tension which are pleasurable (e.g. sexual excitement), and he goes on to suggest (what had already been hinted at in the two passages in *Beyond the Pleasure Principle* just referred to) that the pleasurable or unpleasurable quality of a state may be related to a *temporal* characteristic (or rhythm) of the changes in the quantity of excitation present. He concludes that in any case the two principles must not be regarded as identical: the pleasure principle is a *modification* of the Nirvana principle. The Nirvana principle, he maintains, is to be attributed to the 'death instinct', and its modification into the pleasure principle is due to the influence of the 'life instinct' or libido.]

1. [See the discussion in the Editor's Introduction, p. 107 ff. This last point also appears in the 1915 addition to the *Three Essays* (1905*d*), *P.F.L.*, **7**, 82–3 and 82 *n.* 2, and in Chapter II of the *Outline* (1940*a*).]

2. [Some remarks on the active nature of instincts will be found in a footnote added in 1915 to Section 4 of the third of Freud's *Three Essays* (1905*d*), *P.F.L.*, **7**, 141 *n.* 1. – A criticism of Adler for misunderstanding this 'pressing' characteristic of instincts appears at the end of the second Section of Part III of the 'Little Hans' analysis (1909*b*), *P.F.L.*, **8**, 296–7.]

The aim [*Ziel*] of an instinct is in every instance satisfaction, which can only be obtained by removing the state of stimulation at the source of the instinct. But although the ultimate aim of each instinct remains unchangeable, there may yet be different paths leading to the same ultimate aim; so that an instinct may be found to have various nearer or intermediate aims, which are combined or interchanged with one another. Experience permits us also to speak of instincts which are 'inhibited in their aim', in the case of processes which are allowed to make some advance towards instinctual satisfaction but are then inhibited or deflected. We may suppose that even processes of this kind involve a partial satisfaction.

The object [*Objekt*] of an instinct is the thing in regard to which or through which the instinct is able to achieve its aim. It is what is most variable about an instinct and is not originally connected with it, but becomes assigned to it only in consequence of being peculiarly fitted to make satisfaction possible. The object is not necessarily something extraneous: it may equally well be a part of the subject's own body. It may be changed any number of times in the course of the vicissitudes which the instinct undergoes during its existence; and highly important parts are played by this displacement of instinct. It may happen that the same object serves for the satisfaction of several instincts simultaneously, a phenomenon which Adler [1908] has called a 'confluence' of instincts [*Triebverschränkung*].[1] A particularly close attachment of the instinct to its object is distinguished by the term 'fixation'. This frequently occurs at very early periods of the development of an instinct and puts an end to its mobility through its intense opposition to detachment.[2]

By the source [*Quelle*] of an instinct is meant the somatic process which occurs in an organ or part of the body and whose stimulus is represented in mental life by an instinct. We do not know whether this process is invariably of a chemical nature or whether it may also correspond to the release of other, e.g.

1. [Two instances of this are given by Freud in the analysis of 'Little Hans' (1909*b*), *P.F.L.*, **8**, 265 and 284.]

2. [Cf. below, p. 147.]

mechanical, forces. The study of the sources of instincts lies outside the scope of psychology. Although instincts are wholly determined by their origin in a somatic source, in mental life we know them only by their aims. An exact knowledge of the sources of an instinct is not invariably necessary for purposes of psychological investigation; sometimes its source may be inferred from its aim.

Are we to suppose that the different instincts which originate in the body and operate on the mind are also distinguished by different *qualities*, and that that is why they behave in qualitatively different ways in mental life? This supposition does not seem to be justified; we are much more likely to find the simpler assumption sufficient – that the instincts are all qualitatively alike and owe the effect they make only to the amount of excitation they carry, or perhaps, in addition, to certain functions of that quantity. What distinguishes from one another the mental effects produced by the various instincts may be traced to the difference in their sources. In any event, it is only in a later connection that we shall be able to make plain what the problem of the quality of instincts signifies.[1]

What instincts should we suppose there are, and how many? There is obviously a wide opportunity here for arbitrary choice. No objection can be made to anyone's employing the concept of an instinct of play or of destruction or of gregariousness, when the subject-matter demands it and the limitations of psychological analysis allow of it. Nevertheless, we should not neglect to ask ourselves whether instinctual motives like these, which are so highly specialized on the one hand, do not admit of further dissection in accordance with the *sources* of the instinct, so that only primal instincts – those which cannot be further dissected – can lay claim to importance.

I have proposed that two groups of such primal instincts should be distinguished: the *ego*, or *self-preservative*, instincts and the *sexual* instincts. But this supposition has not the status of a

1. [It is not clear what 'later connection' Freud had in mind.]

necessary postulate, as has, for instance, our assumption about the biological purpose of the mental apparatus [p. 116]; it is merely a working hypothesis, to be retained only so long as it proves useful, and it will make little difference to the results of our work of description and classification if it is replaced by another. The occasion for this hypothesis arose in the course of the evolution of psychoanalysis, which was first employed upon the psychoneuroses, or, more precisely, upon the group described as 'transference neuroses' (hysteria and obsessional neurosis); these showed that at the root of all such affections there is to be found a conflict between the claims of sexuality and those of the ego. It is always possible that an exhaustive study of the other neurotic affections (especially of the narcissistic psychoneuroses, the schizophrenias) may oblige us to alter this formula and to make a different classification of the primal instincts. But for the present we do not know of any such formula, nor have we met with any argument unfavourable to drawing this contrast between sexual and ego-instincts.[1]

I am altogether doubtful whether any decisive pointers for the differentiation and classification of the instincts can be arrived at on the basis of working over the psychological material. This working-over seems rather itself to call for the application to the material of definite assumptions concerning instinctual life, and it would be a desirable thing if those assumptions could be taken from some other branch of knowledge and carried over to psychology. The contribution which biology has to make here certainly does not run counter to the distinction between sexual and ego-instincts. Biology teaches that sexuality is not to be put on a par with other functions of the individual; for its purposes go beyond the individual and have as their content the production of new individuals – that is, the preservation of the species. It shows, further, that two views, seemingly equally well-founded, may be taken of the relation between the ego and sexuality. On the one view, the individual is the principal thing,

1. [See the Editor's Note, p. 111.]

sexuality is one of its activities and sexual satisfaction one of its needs; while on the other view the individual is a temporary and transient appendage to the quasi-immortal germ-plasm, which is entrusted to him by the process of generation.[1] The hypothesis that the sexual function differs from other bodily processes in virtue of a special chemistry is, I understand, also a postulate of the Ehrlich[2] school of biological research.[3]

Since a study of instinctual life from the direction of consciousness presents almost insuperable difficulties, the principal source of our knowledge remains the psychoanalytic investigation of mental disturbances. Psychoanalysis, however, in consequence of the course taken by its development, has hitherto been able to give us information of a fairly satisfactory nature only about the *sexual* instincts; for it is precisely that group which alone can be observed in isolation, as it were, in the psychoneuroses. With the extension of psychoanalysis to the other neurotic affections, we shall no doubt find a basis for our knowledge of the ego-instincts as well, though it would be rash to expect equally favourable conditions for observation in this further field of research.

This much can be said by way of a general characterization of the sexual instincts. They are numerous, emanate from a great variety of organic sources, act in the first instance independently of one another and only achieve a more or less complete synthesis at a late stage. The aim which each of them strives for is

1. [See footnote 1, p. 71 above. The same point is made near the beginning of Lecture 26 of the *Introductory Lectures* (1916–17), *P.F.L.*, **1**, 463. Cf. also Chapter VI of *Beyond the Pleasure Principle* (1920*g*), p. 318 ff. below.]

2. [Paul Ehrlich (1854–1915), a German medical scientist of great distinction, was an advocate of 'chemical thinking' in medicine and biology. His pioneering work in chemotherapy at the Royal Institute for Experimental Therapy at Frankfurt am Main gained him the Nobel Prize for Physiology and Medicine in 1908.]

3. [This hypothesis had already been announced by Freud in the first edition of his *Three Essays* (1905*d*), *P.F.L.*, **7**, 137 *n*. But he had held it for at least ten years previously. See, for instance, Draft I in the Fliess correspondence (1950*a*), probably written in 1895.]

the attainment of 'organ-pleasure';[1] only when synthesis is achieved do they enter the service of the reproductive function and thereupon become generally recognizable as sexual instincts. At their first appearance they are attached to the instincts of self-preservation, from which they only gradually become separated; in their choice of object, too, they follow the paths that are indicated to them by the ego-instincts.[2] A portion of them remains associated with the ego-instincts throughout life and furnishes them with libidinal components, which in normal functioning easily escape notice and are revealed clearly only by the onset of illness.[3] They are distinguished by possessing the capacity to act vicariously for one another to a wide extent and by being able to change their objects readily. In consequence of the latter properties they are capable of functions which are far removed from their original purposive actions – capable, that is, of 'sublimation'.

Our inquiry into the various vicissitudes which instincts undergo in the process of development and in the course of life must be confined to the sexual instincts, which are the more familiar to us. Observation shows us that an instinct may undergo the following vicissitudes:–

Reversal into its opposite.
Turning round upon the subject's own self.
Repression.
Sublimation.

Since I do not intend to treat of sublimation here[4] and since

1. ['Organ-pleasure' (i.e. pleasure attached to one particular bodily organ) seems to be used here for the first time by Freud. The term is discussed at greater length in the early part of Lecture 21 of the *Introductory Lectures* (1916–17), *P.F.L.*, **1**, 366–7 and 371. The underlying idea, of course, goes back much earlier. See, for instance, the opening passage of the third of the *Three Essays* (1905*d*), *P.F.L.*, **7**, 127 ff.]

2. [Cf. 'On Narcissism', pp. 80–81 above.]

3. [Ibid., p. 75 f. above]

4. [Sublimation had already been touched upon in the paper on narcissism (pp. 88 ff.); but it seems possible that it formed the subject of one of the lost metapsychological papers. (See Editor's Introduction, p. 103.)]

repression requires a special chapter to itself [cf. next paper, p. 145], it only remains for us to describe and discuss the two first points. Bearing in mind that there are motive forces which work against an instinct's being carried through in an unmodified form, we may also regard these vicissitudes as modes of *defence* against the instincts.

Reversal of an instinct into its opposite resolves on closer examination into two different processes: a *change* from *activity to passivity*, and a *reversal of its content*. The two processes, being different in their nature, must be treated separately.

Examples of the first process are met with in the two pairs of opposites: sadism–masochism and scopophilia–exhibitionism. The reversal affects only the *aims* of the instincts. The active aim (to torture, to look at) is replaced by the passive aim (to be tortured, to be looked at). Reversal of *content* is found in the single instance of the transformation of love into hate.

The turning round of an instinct upon the subject's own self is made plausible by the reflection that masochism is actually sadism turned round upon the subject's own ego, and that exhibitionism includes looking at his own body. Analytic observation, indeed, leaves us in no doubt that the masochist shares in the enjoyment of the assault upon himself, and that the exhibitionist shares in the enjoyment of [the sight of] his exposure. The essence of the process is thus the change of the *object*, while the aim remains unchanged. We cannot fail to notice, however, that in these examples the turning round upon the subject's self and the transformation from activity to passivity converge or coincide.

To elucidate the situation, a more thorough investigation is essential.

In the case of the pair of opposites sadism–masochism, the process may be represented as follows:

(*a*) Sadism consists in the exercise of violence or power upon some other person as object.

(*b*) This object is given up and replaced by the subject's self. With the turning round upon the self the change from an active to a passive instinctual aim is also effected.

(*c*) An extraneous person is once more sought as object; this person, in consequence of the alteration which has taken place in the instinctual aim, has to take over the role of the subject.[1]

Case (*c*) is what is commonly termed masochism. Here, too, satisfaction follows along the path of the original sadism, the passive ego placing itself back in phantasy in its first role, which has now in fact been taken over by the extraneous subject.[2] Whether there is, besides this, a more direct masochistic satisfaction is highly doubtful. A primary masochism, not derived from sadism in the manner I have described, seems not to be met with.[3] That it is not superfluous to assume the existence of stage (*b*) is to be seen from the behaviour of the sadistic instinct in obsessional neurosis. There there is a turning round upon the subject's self *without* an attitude of passivity towards another person: the change has only got as far as stage (*b*). The desire to torture has turned into self-torture and self-punishment, not into masochism. The active voice is changed, not into the passive, but into the reflexive, middle voice.[4]

Our view of sadism is further prejudiced by the circumstance that this instinct, side by side with its general aim (or perhaps, rather, within it), seems to strive towards the accomplishment of a quite special aim – not only to humiliate and master, but, in addition, to inflict pains. Psychoanalysis would appear to show that the infliction of pain plays no part among the original purposive actions of the instinct. A sadistic child takes no account of whether or not he inflicts pains, nor does he intend

1. [Though the general sense of these passages is clear, there may be some confusion in the use of the word 'subject'. As a rule 'subject' and 'object' are used respectively for the person in whom an instinct (or other state of mind) originates, and the person or thing to which it is directed. Here, however, 'subject' seems to be used for the person who plays the active part in the relationship – the agent. The word is more obviously used in this sense in the parallel passage on p. 127 and elsewhere below.]

2. [See last footnote.]

3. [*Footnote added* 1924:] In later works (cf. 'The Economic Problem of Masochism', 1924*c*) [p. 413 ff. below] relating to problems of instinctual life I have expressed an opposite view.

4. [The allusion here is to the voices of the Greek verb.]

to do so. But when once the transformation into masochism has taken place, the pains are very well fitted to provide a passive masochistic aim; for we have every reason to believe that sensations of pain, like other unpleasurable sensations, trench upon sexual excitation and produce a pleasurable condition, for the sake of which the subject will even willingly experience the unpleasure of pain.[1] When once feeling pains has become a masochistic aim, the sadistic aim of *causing* pains can arise also, retrogressively; for while these pains are being inflicted on other people, they are enjoyed masochistically by the subject through his identification of himself with the suffering object. In both cases, of course, it is not the pain itself which is enjoyed, but the accompanying sexual excitation – so that this can be done especially conveniently from the sadistic position. The enjoyment of pain would thus be an aim which was originally masochistic, but which can only become an instinctual aim in someone who was originally sadistic.

For the sake of completeness I may add that feelings of pity cannot be described as a result of a transformation of instinct occurring in sadism, but necessitate the notion of a *reaction-formation* against that instinct. (For the difference, see later.)[2]

Rather different and simpler findings are afforded by the investigation of another pair of opposites – the instincts whose respective aim is to look and to display oneself (scopophilia and exhibitionism, in the language of the perversions). Here again we may postulate the same stages as in the previous instance:–

1. [See a passage near the end of the second of the *Three Essays* (1905*d*), *P.F.L.*, **7**, 123 and *n.* 1.]

2. [It is not clear to what passage this refers, unless it was in a missing paper on sublimation. There is in fact some discussion of the subject in 'Thoughts for the Times on War and Death' (1915*b*), *P.F.L.*, **12**, 68. In a footnote added in 1915 (the year in which the present paper was written) to the *Three Essays* (1905*d*), Freud insists that sublimation and reaction-formation are to be regarded as distinct processes (*P.F.L.*, **7**, 94 *n.* 2). – The German word for 'pity' is '*Mitleid*', literally 'suffering with', 'compassion'. Another view of the origin of the feeling is expressed in the 'Wolf Man' analysis (1918*b*), ibid., **9**, 327, which was actually written, in all probability, at the end of 1914, a few months earlier than the present paper.]

(*a*) Looking as an *activity* directed towards an extraneous object. (*b*) Giving up of the object and turning of the scopophilic instinct towards a part of the subject's own body; with this, transformation to passivity and setting up of a new aim – that of being looked at. (*c*) Introduction of a new subject[1] to whom one displays oneself in order to be looked at by him. Here, too, it can hardly be doubted that the active aim appears before the passive, that looking precedes being looked at. But there is an important divergence from what happens in the case of sadism, in that we can recognize in the case of the scopophilic instinct a yet earlier stage than that described as (*a*). For the beginning of its activity the scopophilic instinct is auto-erotic: it has indeed an object, but that object is part of the subject's own body. It is only later that the instinct is led, by a process of comparison, to exchange this object for an analogous part of someone else's body – stage (*a*). This preliminary stage is interesting because it is the source of *both* the situations represented in the resulting pair of opposites, the one or the other according to which element in the original situation is changed. The following might serve as a diagrammatic picture of the scopophilic instinct:–

(α)	Oneself looking at a sexual organ	=	A sexual organ being looked at by oneself
(β)	Oneself looking at an extraneous object (active scopophilia)	(γ)	An object which is oneself or part of oneself being looked at by an extraneous person (exhibitionism)

A preliminary stage of this kind is absent in sadism, which from the outset is directed upon an extraneous object, although it might not be altogether unreasonable to construct such a stage out of the child's efforts to gain control over his own limbs.[2]

With regard to both the instincts which we have just taken as examples, it should be remarked that their transformation by a reversal from activity to passivity and by a turning round upon

1. [I.e. agent; see footnote 1, p. 125.]
2. [*Footnote added* 1924;] Cf. footnote 3, p. 125.

the subject never in fact involves the whole quota of the instinctual impulse. The earlier active direction of the instinct persists to some degree side by side with its later passive direction, even when the process of its transformation has been very extensive. The only correct statement to make about the scopophilic instinct would be that all the stages of its development, its auto-erotic, preliminary stage as well as its final active or passive form, co-exist alongside one another; and the truth of this becomes obvious if we base our opinion, not on the actions to which the instinct leads, but on the mechanism of its satisfaction. Perhaps, however, it is permissible to look at the matter and represent it in yet another way. We can divide the life of each instinct into a series of separate successive waves, each of which is homogeneous during whatever period of time it may last, and whose relation to one another is comparable to that of successive eruptions of lava. We can then perhaps picture the first, original eruption of the instinct as proceeding in an unchanged form and undergoing no development at all. The next wave would be modified from the outset – being turned, for instance, from active to passive – and would then, with this new characteristic, be added to the earlier wave, and so on. If we were then to take a survey of the instinctual impulse from its beginning up to a given point, the succession of waves which we have described would inevitably present the picture of a definite development of the instinct.

The fact that, at this[1] later period of development of an instinctual impulse, its (passive) opposite may be observed alongside of it deserves to be marked by the very apt term introduced by Bleuler – 'ambivalence'.[2]

1. ['*Jener*'. In the first edition only, '*jeder*', 'every'.]

2. [The term 'ambivalence', coined by Bleuler (1910, and 1911, 43 and 305), seems not to have been used by him in this sense. He distinguished three kinds of ambivalence: (1) emotional, i.e. oscillation between love and hate, (2) volitional, i.e. inability to decide on an action, and (3) intellectual, i.e. belief in contradictory propositions. Freud generally uses the term in the first of these senses. See, for instance, the first occasion on which he seems to have adopted it, near the end of his paper on 'The Dynamics of Transference' (1912*b*), and later in the present paper (pp. 130 and 137). The passage in the text is one of the few in

This reference to the developmental history of instincts and the permanence of their intermediate stages should make the development of instincts fairly intelligible to us. Experience shows that the amount of demonstrable ambivalence varies greatly between individuals, groups and races. Marked instinctual ambivalence in a human being living at the present day may be regarded as an archaic inheritance, for we have reason to suppose that the part played in instinctual life by the active impulses in their unmodified form was greater in primaeval times than it is on an average to-day.[1]

We have become accustomed to call the early phase of the development of the ego, during which its sexual instincts find auto-erotic satisfaction, 'narcissism', without at once entering on any discussion of the relation between auto-erotism and narcissism. It follows that the preliminary stage of the scopophilic instinct, in which the subject's own body is the object of the scopophilia, must be classed under narcissism, and that we must describe it as a narcissistic formation. The active scopophilic instinct develops from this, by leaving narcissism behind. The passive scopophilic instinct, on the contrary, holds fast to the narcissistic object. Similarly the transformation of sadism into masochism implies a return to the narcissistic object. And in both these cases [i.e. in passive scopophilia and masochism] the narcissistic *subject* is, through identification, replaced by another, extraneous ego. If we take into account our constructed preliminary narcissistic stage of sadism, we shall be approaching a more general realization – namely, that the instinctual vicissitudes which consist in the instinct's being turned round upon the subject's own ego and undergoing reversal from activity to passivity are dependent on the narcissistic organization of the ego and bear the stamp of that phase. They perhaps correspond to the attempts at defence which at higher stages of the devel-

---

which he has applied the term to activity and passivity. For another instance of this exceptional use see a passage in Section III of the 'Wolf Man' case history (1918*b*), *P.F.L.*, **9**, 256.]

1. [See *Totem and Taboo* (1912–13, *P.F.L.*, **12**, 123.]

opment of the ego are effected by other means. [See above, p. 124.]

At this point we may call to mind that so far we have considered only two pairs of opposite instincts: sadism–masochism and scopophilia–exhibitionism. These are the best-known sexual instincts that appear in an ambivalent manner. The other components of the later sexual function are not yet sufficiently accessible to analysis for us to be able to discuss them in a similar way. In general we can assert of them that their activities are *auto-erotic*; that is to say, their object is negligible in comparison with the organ which is their source, and as a rule coincides with that organ. The object of the scopophilic instinct, however, though it too is in the first instance a part of the subject's own body, is not the eye itself; and in sadism the organic source, which is probably the muscular apparatus with its capacity for action, points unequivocally at an object other than itself, even though that object is part of the subject's own body. In the auto-erotic instincts, the part played by the organic source is so decisive that, according to a plausible suggestion of Federn (1913) and Jekels (1913), the form and function of the organ determine the activity or passivity of the instinctual aim.

The change of the *content* [cf. p. 124] of an instinct into its opposite is observed in a single instance only – the *transformation of love into hate.*[1] Since it is particularly common to find both these directed simultaneously towards the same object, their co-existence furnishes the most important example of ambivalence of feeling. [See p. 128 *n.* 2.]

The case of love and hate acquires a special interest from the circumstance that it refuses to be fitted into our scheme of the instincts. It is impossible to doubt that there is the most intimate relation between these two opposite feelings and sexual life, but we are naturally unwilling to think of love as being some kind of special component instinct of sexuality in the same way as the others we have been discussing. We should prefer to regard

1. [In the German editions previous to 1924 this reads 'the transformation of *love and hate*'.]

loving as the expression of the *whole* sexual current of feeling; but this idea does not clear up our difficulties, and we cannot see what meaning to attach to an opposite content of this current.

Loving admits not merely of one, but of three opposites. In addition to the antithesis 'loving–hating', there is the other one of 'loving–being loved'; and, in addition to these, loving and hating taken together are the opposite of the condition of unconcern or indifference. The second of these three antitheses, loving–being loved, corresponds exactly to the transformation from activity to passivity and may be traced to an underlying situation in the same way as in the case of the scopophilic instinct. This situation is that of *loving oneself*, which we regard as the characteristic feature of narcissism. Then, according as the object or the subject is replaced by an extraneous one, what results is the active aim of loving or the passive one of being loved – the latter remaining near to narcissism.

Perhaps we shall come to a better understanding of the several opposites of loving if we reflect that our mental life as a whole is governed by *three polarities*, the antitheses

Subject (ego)–Object (external world),
Pleasure–Unpleasure, and
Active–Passive.

The antithesis ego–non-ego (external), i.e. subject-object, is, as we have already said [p. 115], thrust upon the individual organism at an early stage, by the experience that it can silence *external* stimuli by means of muscular action but is defenceless against *instinctual* stimuli. This antithesis remains, above all, sovereign in our intellectual activity and creates for research the basic situation which no efforts can alter. The polarity of pleasure–unpleasure is attached to a scale of feelings, whose paramount importance in determining our actions (our will) has already been emphasized [p. 117]. The antithesis active-passive must not be confused with the antithesis ego-subject–external world-object. The relation of the ego to the external world is passive in so far as it receives stimuli from it and active when it reacts to these. It is forced by its instincts into a quite special degree of activity towards the external world, so that we might bring out the essential point if we say that the ego-subject is passive in respect of external stimuli but active through its own instincts. The antithesis active–passive coalesces later with the antithesis masculine–feminine, which, until this has taken place, has no psychological meaning. The coupling of activity with masculinity and of passivity with femininity meets us, indeed, as a biological fact; but it is by no means so invariably complete and exclusive as we are inclined to assume.[1]

The three polarities of the mind are connected with one another in various highly significant ways. There is a primal psychical situation in which two of them coincide. Originally, at the very beginning of mental life, the ego is cathected with instincts and is to some extent capable of satisfying them on itself. We call this condition 'narcissism' and this way of obtaining satisfaction 'auto-erotic'.[2] At this time the external world is

1. [This question is discussed at much greater length in a footnote added in 1915 (the year in which the present paper was written) to the third of Freud's *Three Essays* (1905*d*), *P.F.L.*, **7**, 141 and *n.* 1. – See also p. 78 above.]

2. Some of the sexual instincts are, as we know, capable of this auto-erotic satisfaction, and so are adapted to being the vehicle for the development under the dominance of the pleasure principle [from the original 'reality-ego' into the 'pleasure-ego'] which we are about to describe [in the next paragraphs of the text]. Those sexual instincts which from the outset require an object, and the needs of the ego-instincts, which are never capable of auto-erotic satisfaction, naturally disturb this state [of primal narcissism] and so pave the way for an advance from it. Indeed, the primal narcissistic state would not be able to follow the development [that is to be described] if it were not for the fact that every individual passes through a period during which he is helpless and has to be looked after and during which his pressing needs are satisfied by an external agency and are thus prevented from becoming greater. – [This very condensed footnote might have been easier to understand if it had been placed two or three paragraphs further on. It may perhaps be expanded as follows. In his paper on the 'Two Principles of Mental Functioning' (1911*b*), p. 42 above, Freud had introduced the idea of the transformation of an early 'pleasure-ego' into a 'reality-ego'. In the passage which follows in the text above, he argues that there is in fact a still earlier *original* 'reality-ego'. This original 'reality-ego', instead of proceeding directly into the *final* 'reality-ego', is replaced, under the dominating influence of the pleasure principle, by a 'pleasure-ego'. The footnote enumerates those factors, on the one hand, which would favour this latter turn of events,

not cathected with interest (in a general sense) and is indifferent for purposes of satisfaction. During this period, therefore, the ego-subject coincides with what is pleasurable and the external world with what is indifferent (or possibly unpleasurable, as being a source of stimulation). If for the moment we define loving as the relation of the ego to its sources of pleasure, the situation in which the ego loves itself only and is indifferent to the external world illustrates the first of the opposites which we found to 'loving'.[1]

In so far as the ego is auto-erotic, it has no need of the external world, but, in consequence of experiences undergone by the instincts of self-preservation, it acquires objects from that world, and, in spite of everything, it cannot avoid feeling internal instinctual stimuli for a time as unpleasurable. Under the dominance of the pleasure principle a further development now takes place in the ego. In so far as the objects which are presented to it are sources of pleasure, it takes them into itself, 'introjects' them (to use Ferenczi's [1909] term[2]); and, on the other hand, it expels whatever within itself becomes a cause of unpleasure. (See below [pp. 187–8 and 231], the mechanism of projection.)

Thus the original 'reality-ego', which distinguished internal

---

and those factors, on the other hand, which would work against it. The existence of auto-erotic libidinal instincts would encourage the diversion to a 'pleasure-ego', while the *non*-auto-erotic libidinal instincts and the self-preservative instincts would be likely instead to bring about a direct transition to the final adult 'reality-ego'. This latter result would, he remarks, in fact come about, if it were not that parental care of the helpless infant satisfies this second set of instincts, artificially prolongs the primary state of narcissism, and so helps to make the establishment of the 'pleasure-ego' possible.]

1. [On p. 131 Freud enumerates the opposites of loving in the following order: (1) hating, (2) being loved and (3) indifference. In the present passage, and below on pp. 134 and 137–8, he adopts a different order: (1) indifference, (2) hating and (3) being loved. It seems probable that in this second arrangement he gives indifference the first place as being the first to appear in the course of development.]

2. [This seems to be the first occasion on which Freud himself used the term. Cf. the footnote on pp. 249–50 below.]

and external by means of a sound objective criterion,[1] changes into a purified 'pleasure-ego', which places the characteristic of pleasure above all others. For the pleasure-ego the external world is divided into a part that is pleasurable, which it has incorporated into itself, and a remainder that is extraneous to it. It has separated off a part of its own self, which it projects into the external world and feels as hostile. After this new arrangement, the two polarities coincide once more: the ego-subject coincides with pleasure, and the external world with unpleasure (with what was earlier indifference).

When, during the stage of primary narcissism, the object makes its appearance, the second opposite to loving, namely hating, also attains its development.[2]

As we have seen, the object is brought to the ego from the external world in the first instance by the instincts of self-preservation; and it cannot be denied that hating, too, originally characterized the relation of the ego to the alien external world with the stimuli it introduces. Indifference falls into place as a special case of hate or dislike, after having first appeared as their forerunner. At the very beginning, it seems, the external world, objects, and what is hated are identical. If later on an object turns out to be a source of pleasure, it is loved, but it is also incorporated into the ego; so that for the purified pleasure-ego once again objects coincide with what is extraneous and hated.

Now, however, we may note that just as the pair of opposites love–indifference reflects the polarity ego–external world, so the second antithesis love–hate[2] reproduces the polarity pleasure–unpleasure, which is linked to the first polarity. When the purely narcissistic stage has given place to the object-stage, pleasure and unpleasure signify relations of the ego to the object. If the object becomes a source of pleasurable feelings, a motor urge is set up which seeks to bring the object closer to the ego and to incorporate it into the ego. We then speak of the

1. [See above, p. 115 and footnote 2. The 'reality-ego' and the 'pleasure-ego' had already been introduced in the paper on the two principles of mental functioning (1911*b*), p. 40 above.]

2. [See footnote 1, p. 133.]

'attraction' exercised by the pleasure-giving object, and say that we 'love' that object. Conversely, if the object is a source of unpleasurable feelings, there is an urge which endeavours to increase the distance between the object and the ego and to repeat in relation to the object the original attempt at flight from the external world with its emission of stimuli. We feel the 'repulsion' of the object, and hate it; this hate can afterwards be intensified to the point of an aggressive inclination against the object – an intention to destroy it.

We might at a pinch say of an instinct that it 'loves' the objects towards which it strives for purposes of satisfaction; but to say that an instinct 'hates' an object strikes us as odd. Thus we become aware that the attitudes[1] of love and hate cannot be made use of for the relations of *instincts* to their objects, but are reserved for the relations of the *total ego* to objects. But if we consider linguistic usage, which is certainly not without significance, we shall see that there is a further limitation to the meaning of love and hate. We do not say of objects which serve the interests of self-preservation that we *love* them; we emphasize the fact that we *need* them, and perhaps express an additional, different kind of relation to them by using words that denote a much reduced degree of love – such as, for example, 'being fond of', 'liking' or 'finding agreeable'.

Thus the word 'to love' moves further and further into the sphere of the pure pleasure-relation of the ego to the object and finally becomes fixed to sexual objects in the narrower sense and to those which satisfy the needs of sublimated sexual instincts. The distinction between the ego-instincts and the sexual instincts which we have imposed upon our psychology is thus seen to be in conformity with the spirit of our language. The fact that we are not in the habit of saying of a single sexual instinct that it loves its object, but regard the relation of the ego

1. [German '*Beziehungen*', literally 'relations'. In the first edition this word is printed '*Bezeichnungen*', 'descriptions' or 'terms' – which seems to make better sense. The word 'relations' in the later part of the sentence stands for '*Relationen*' in the German text.]

to its sexual object as the most appropriate case in which to employ the word 'love' – this fact teaches us that the word can only begin to be applied in this relation after there has been a synthesis of all the component instincts of sexuality under the primacy of the genitals and in the service of the reproductive function.

It is noteworthy that in the use of the word 'hate' no such intimate connection with sexual pleasure and the sexual function appears. The relation of *unpleasure* seems to be the sole decisive one. The ego hates, abhors and pursues with intent to destroy all objects which are a source of unpleasurable feeling for it, without taking into account whether they mean a frustration of sexual satisfaction or of the satisfaction of self-preservative needs. Indeed, it may be asserted that the true prototypes of the relation of hate are derived not from sexual life, but from the ego's struggle to preserve and maintain itself.

So we see that love and hate, which present themselves to us as complete opposites in their content, do not after all stand in any simple relation to each other. They did not arise from the cleavage of any originally common entity, but sprang from different sources, and had each its own development before the influence of the pleasure–unpleasure relation made them into opposites.

It now remains for us to put together what we know of the genesis of love and hate. Love is derived from the capacity of the ego to satisfy some of its instinctual impulses auto-erotically by obtaining organ-pleasure. It is originally narcissistic, then passes over on to objects, which have been incorporated into the extended ego, and expresses the motor efforts of the ego towards these objects as sources of pleasure. It becomes intimately linked with the activity of the later sexual instincts and, when these have been completely synthesized, coincides with the sexual impulsion as a whole. Preliminary stages of love emerge as provisional sexual aims while the sexual instincts are passing through their complicated development. As the first of these aims we recognize the phase of *incorporating* or *devouring* – a type of love which is consistent with abolishing the object's separate existence and which may therefore be described as ambivalent.[1] At the higher stage of the pregenital sadistic-anal organization,[2] the striving for the object appears in the form of an urge for mastery, to which injury or annihilation of the object is a matter of indifference. Love in this form and at this preliminary stage is hardly to be distinguished from hate in its attitude towards the object. Not until the genital organization is established does love become the opposite of hate.

Hate, as a relation to objects, is older than love. It derives from the narcissistic ego's primordial repudiation of the external world with its outpouring of stimuli. As an expression of the reaction of unpleasure evoked by objects, it always remains in an intimate relation with the self-preservative instincts; so that sexual and ego-instincts can readily develop an antithesis which repeats that of love and hate. When the ego-instincts dominate the sexual function, as is the case at the stage of the sadistic-anal organization, they impart the qualities of hate to the instinctual aim as well.

The history of the origins and relations of love makes us understand how it is that love so frequently manifests itself as 'ambivalent' – i.e. as accompanied by impulses of hate against the same object.[3] The hate which is admixed with the love is in part derived from the preliminary stages of loving which have not been wholly surmounted; it is also in part based on reactions of repudiation by the ego-instincts, which, in view of the frequent conflicts between the interests of the ego and those of love, can find grounds in real and contemporary motives. In both cases, therefore, the admixed hate has as its source the self-preservative instincts. If a love-relation with a given object is broken off, hate not infrequently emerges in its place, so that we get the impression of a transformation of love into hate. This

1. [Freud's first published account of the oral stage was given in a paragraph added to the third (1915) edition of his *Three Essays*, *P.F.L.*, **7**, 116–17. The preface to that edition is dated 'October 1914' – some months before the present paper was written. See also below, p. 258 ff.]

2. [See 'The Disposition to Obsessional Neurosis' (1913*i*), *P.F.L.*, **10**, 134 ff.]

3. [See footnote 2, p. 128.]

account of what happens leads on to the view that the hate, which has its real motives, is here reinforced by a regression of the love to the sadistic preliminary stage; so that the hate acquires an erotic character and the continuity of a love-relation is ensured.

The third antithesis of loving, the transformation of loving into being loved,[1] corresponds to the operation of the polarity of activity and passivity, and is to be judged in the same way as the cases of scopophilia and sadism.[2]

We may sum up by saying that the essential feature in the vicissitudes undergone by instincts lies in *the subjection of the instinctual impulses to the influences of the three great polarities that dominate mental life.* Of these three polarities we might describe that of activity–passivity as the *biological*, that of ego–external world as the *real*, and finally that of pleasure–unpleasure as the *economic* polarity.

The instinctual vicissitude of *repression* will form the subject of an inquiry which follows [in the next paper].

1. See footnote 1, p. 133.]

2. [The relation between love and hate was further discussed by Freud, in the light of his hypothesis of a death instinct, in Chapter IV of *The Ego and the Id* (1923*b*), p. 380 ff. below.]

REPRESSION
(1915)

EDITOR'S NOTE

DIE VERDRÄNGUNG

(A) German Editions:

1915 *Int. Z. ärztl. Psychoanal.*, **3** (3), 129–38.
1924 *Gesammelte Schriften*, **5**, 466–79.
1946 *Gesammelte Werke*, **10**, 248–61.

(B) English Translations:
'Repression'

1925 *Collected Papers*, **4**, 84–97. (Tr. C. M. Baines.)
1957 *Standard Edition*, **14**, 141–58. (Translation, based on that of 1925, but very largely rewritten.)

The present edition is a reprint of the *Standard Edition* version, with some editorial modifications.

In his 'History of the Psycho-Analytic Movement' (1914*d*), Freud declared that 'the theory of repression is the corner-stone on which the whole structure of psychoanalysis rests'; and in the present essay, together with Section IV of the paper on 'The Unconscious' which follows it (p. 183 ff.), he gave his most elaborate formulation of that theory.

The concept of repression goes back historically to the very beginnings of psychoanalysis. The first published reference to it was in the Breuer and Freud 'Preliminary Communication' of 1893 (*P.F.L.*, **3**, 61 and *n.* 1). The term '*Verdrängung*' had been used by the early nineteenth-century psychologist Herbart and may possibly have come to Freud's knowledge through his teacher Meynert, who had been an admirer of Herbart.[1] But, as Freud himself insisted in the passage of the 'History' already quoted, 'the theory of repression quite certainly came to me independently of any other source'. 'It was a novelty', he wrote in his *Autobiographical Study* (1925*d*), 'and nothing like it had ever before been recognized in mental life.' There are several accounts in Freud's writings of how the discovery came about: for instance, in the *Studies on Hysteria* (1895*d*), *P.F.L.*, **3**, 351–3, and again in the 'History'. All these accounts are alike in emphasizing the fact that the concept of repression was inevitably suggested by the clinical phenomenon of resistance, which in turn was brought to light by a technical innovation – namely, the abandonment of hypnosis in the cathartic treatment of hysteria.

It will be noticed that in the account given in the *Studies* the term actually used to describe the process is not 'repression' but 'defence'. At this early period the two terms were used by Freud indifferently, almost as equivalents, though 'defence' was perhaps the commoner. Soon, however, as he remarked in his paper on sexuality in the neuroses (1906*a*), *P.F.L.*, **10**, 77, 'repression' began to be used quite generally in place of 'defence'. Thus, for instance, in the 'Rat Man' case history (1909*d*) Freud discussed the mechanism of 'repression' in obsessional neurosis – i.e. the displacement of the emotional cathexis from the objectionable idea, as contrasted with the complete expulsion of the idea from consciousness in hysteria – and spoke of 'two kinds of repression' (*P.F.L.*, **9**, 76–7). It is, indeed, in this wider sense that the term is used in the present paper, as is shown by the discussion towards the end of it on the different mechanisms of repression in the various forms of psychoneurosis. It seems pretty clear, however, that the form of repression which Freud had chiefly in mind here was that which occurs in hysteria; and much later on, in Chapter XI, Section A (*c*), of *Inhibitions, Symptoms and Anxiety* (1926*d*), *P.F.L.*, **10**, 322 ff., he proposed to restrict the term 'repression' to this one particular mechanism and to revive

1. See below, p. 162. A full discussion of this will be found in the first volume of Ernest Jones's biography (1953, 407 ff.).

'defence' as 'a general designation for all the techniques which the ego makes use of in conflicts which may lead to a neurosis'. The importance of making this distinction was later illustrated by him in Section V of 'Analysis Terminable and Interminable' (1937*c*).

The special problem of the nature of the motive force which puts repression into operation was one which was a constant source of concern to Freud, though it is scarcely touched on in the present paper. In particular there was the question of the relation between repression and sex, and to this Freud in his early days gave fluctuating replies, as may be seen at many points in the Fliess correspondence (1950*a*). Subsequently, however, he firmly rejected any attempt at 'sexualizing' repression. A full discussion of this question (with particular reference to the views of Adler) will be found in the last section of '"A Child is Being Beaten"' (1919*e*), *P.F.L.*, **10**, 189 ff. Later still, in *Inhibitions, Symptoms and Anxiety* (1926*d*), especially in Chapter IV, and in the earlier part of Lecture 32 of the *New Introductory Lectures* (1933*a*), he threw fresh light on the subject by arguing that anxiety was not, as he had previously held and as he states below, for instance on pp. 153 and 155, a *consequence* of repression but was one of the chief motive forces leading to it.[1]

1. The distinction between repression and the 'disavowal' or 'denial' ('*Verleugnung*') by the ego of external reality or some part of it was first discussed by Freud at length in his paper on 'Fetishism' (1927*e*), *P.F.L.*, **7**, 353 and *n*. 1. See also p. 227 below.

REPRESSION

ONE of the vicissitudes an instinctual impulse may undergo is to meet with resistances which seek to make it inoperative. Under certain conditions, which we shall presently investigate more closely, the impulse then passes into the state of 'repression' ['*Verdrängung*']. If what was in question was the operation of an external stimulus, the appropriate method to adopt would obviously be flight; with an instinct, flight is of no avail, for the ego cannot escape from itself. At some later period, rejection based on judgement (*condemnation*) will be found to be a good method to adopt against an instinctual impulse. Repression is a preliminary stage of condemnation, something between flight and condemnation; it is a concept which could not have been formulated before the time of psychoanalytic studies.

It is not easy in theory to deduce the possibility of such a thing as repression. Why should an instinctual impulse undergo a vicissitude like this? A necessary condition of its happening must clearly be that the instinct's attainment of its aim should produce unpleasure instead of pleasure. But we cannot well imagine such a contingency. There are no such instincts: satisfaction of an instinct is always pleasurable. We should have to assume certain peculiar circumstances, some sort of process by which the pleasure of satisfaction is changed into unpleasure.

In order the better to delimit repression, let us discuss some other instinctual situations. It may happen that an external stimulus becomes internalized – for example, by eating into and destroying some bodily organ – so that a new source of constant excitation and increase of tension arises. The stimulus thereby acquires a far-reaching similarity to an instinct. We know that a case of this sort is experienced by us as *pain*. The aim of this pseudo-instinct, however, is simply the cessation of the change in the organ and of the unpleasure accompanying it. There is no other direct pleasure to be attained by cessation of pain. Further, pain is imperative; the only things to which it can yield are removal by some toxic agent or the influence of mental distraction.

The case of pain is too obscure to give us any help in our purpose.[1] Let us take the case in which an instinctual stimulus such as hunger remains unsatisfied. It then becomes imperative and can be allayed by nothing but the action that satisfies it;[2] it keeps up a constant tension of need. Nothing in the nature of a repression seems in this case to come remotely into question.

Thus repression certainly does not arise in cases where the tension produced by lack of satisfaction of an instinctual impulse is raised to an unbearable degree. The methods of defence which are open to the organism against that situation must be discussed in another connection.[3]

Let us rather confine ourselves to clinical experience, as we meet with it in psychoanalytic practice. We then learn that the satisfaction of an instinct which is under repression would be quite possible, and further, that in every instance such a satisfaction would be pleasurable in itself; but it would be irreconcilable with other claims and intentions. It would, therefore, cause pleasure in one place and unpleasure in another. It has consequently become a condition for repression that the motive force of unpleasure shall have acquired more strength than the pleasure obtained from satisfaction. Psychoanalytic observation of the transference neuroses, moreover, leads us to conclude that repression is not a defensive mechanism which is present from the very beginning, and that it cannot arise until a sharp cleavage

1. [Pain and the organism's method of dealing with it are discussed in Chapter IV of *Beyond the Pleasure Principle* (1920*g*), p. 301 ff. below. The subject is already raised in Part I, Section 6, of the 'Project' (1950*a* [1895]), and in the closing paragraphs of *Inhibitions, Symptoms and Anxiety* (1926*d*), *P.F.L.*, **10**, 331–3.]

2. [In the 'Project' (1950*a* [1895]), Part I, Section 1, this is termed the 'specific action'.]

3. [It is not clear what 'other connection' Freud had in mind.]

has occurred between conscious and unconscious mental activity – that *the essence of repression lies simply in turning something away, and keeping it at a distance, from the conscious.*[1] This view of repression would be made more complete by assuming that, before the mental organization reaches this stage, the task of fending off instinctual impulses is dealt with by the other vicissitudes which instincts may undergo – e.g. reversal into the opposite or turning round upon the subject's own self [cf. pp. 123–4].

It seems to us now that, in view of the very great extent to which repression and what is unconscious are correlated, we must defer probing more deeply into the nature of repression until we have learnt more about the structure of the succession of psychical agencies and about the differentiation between what is unconscious and conscious. [See the following paper, p. 183 ff.] Till then, all we can do is to put together in a purely descriptive fashion a few characteristics of repression that have been observed clinically, even though we run the risk of having to repeat unchanged much that has been said elsewhere.

We have reason to assume that there is a *primal repression*, a first phase of repression, which consists in the psychical (ideational) representative of the instinct[2] being denied entrance into the conscious. With this a *fixation* is established; the representative in question persists unaltered from then onwards and the instinct remains attached to it. This is due to the properties of unconscious processes of which we shall speak later [p. 191].

The second stage of repression, *repression proper*, affects mental derivatives of the repressed representative, or such trains of thought as, originating elsewhere, have come into associative connection with it. On account of this association, these ideas experience the same fate as what was primally repressed. Repression proper, therefore, is actually an after-pressure.[3]

1. [A modification of this formula will be found below on pp. 208–9.]

2. [See the Editor's Note to the previous paper, p. 107 ff.]

3. ['*Nachdrängen.*' Freud uses the same term in his account of the process in the Schreber analysis (see next footnote), and also in his paper on 'The Unconscious' (see below, pp 183 and 184). But, on alluding to the point more than twenty years later in the third section of 'Analysis Terminable and Interminable' (1937*c*), he uses the word '*Nachverdrängung*' ('after-repression').]

Moreover, it is a mistake to emphasize only the repulsion which operates from the direction of the conscious upon what is to be repressed; quite as important is the attraction exercised by what was primally repressed upon everything with which it can establish a connection. Probably the trend towards repression would fail in its purpose if these two forces did not co-operate, if there were not something previously repressed ready to receive what is repelled by the conscious.[1]

Under the influence of the study of the psychoneuroses, which brings before us the important effects of repression, we are inclined to overvalue their psychological bearing and to forget too readily that repression does not hinder the instinctual representative from continuing to exist in the unconscious, from organizing itself further, putting out derivatives and establishing connections. Repression in fact interferes only with the relation of the instinctual representative to *one* psychical system, namely, to that of the conscious.

Psychoanalysis is able to show us other things as well which are important for understanding the effects of repression in the psychoneuroses. It shows us, for instance, that the instinctual representative develops with less interference and more profusely if it is withdrawn by repression from conscious influence. It proliferates in the dark, as it were, and takes on extreme forms of expression, which when they are translated and presented to the neurotic are not only bound to seem alien to him, but frighten him by giving him the picture of an extraordinary and dangerous strength of instinct. This deceptive strength of instinct is the result of an uninhibited development in phantasy and of the damming-up consequent on frustrated satisfaction. The fact that this last result is bound up with repression points

1. [The account of the two stages of repression given in the last two paragraphs had been anticipated by Freud four years earlier (though in a somewhat different form) in the third section of the Schreber analysis (1911*c*), *P.F.L.*, **9**, 205–6, and in a letter to Ferenczi of 6 December 1910 (Jones, 1955, 499). See also the footnote added in 1914 to *The Interpretation of Dreams* (1900*a*), ibid., **4**, 698 *n*. 2.]

the direction in which the true significance of repression has to be looked for.

Reverting once more, however, to the opposite aspect of repression, let us make it clear that it is not even correct to suppose that repression withholds from the conscious *all* the derivatives of what was primally repressed.[1] If these derivatives have become sufficiently far removed from the repressed representative, whether owing to the adoption of distortions or by reason of the number of intermediate links inserted, they have free access to the conscious. It is as though the resistance of the conscious against them was a function of their distance from what was originally repressed. In carrying out the technique of psychoanalysis, we continually require the patient to produce such derivatives of the repressed as, in consequence either of their remoteness or of their distortion, can pass the censorship of the conscious. Indeed, the associations which we require him to give without being influenced by any conscious purposive idea and without any criticism, and from which we reconstitute a conscious translation of the repressed representative – these associations are nothing else than remote and distorted derivatives of this kind. During this process we observe that the patient can go on spinning a thread of such associations, till he is brought up against some thought, the relation of which to what is repressed becomes so obvious that he is compelled to repeat his attempt at repression. Neurotic symptoms, too, must have fulfilled this same condition, for they are derivatives of the repressed, which has, by their means, finally won the access to consciousness which was previously denied to it.[2]

We can lay down no general rule as to what degree of distortion and remoteness is necessary before the resistance on the

1. [What follows in this paragraph is discussed at greater length in Section VI of 'The Unconscious' (below, p. 194 ff.).]

2. [In the German editions before 1924 the latter part of this sentence read: 'Welches sich . . . den ihm versagten Zugang vom Bewusstsein endlich erkämpft hat'. This was translated formerly 'which has finally . . . wrested from consciousness the right of way previously denied it'. In the German editions from 1924 onwards the word '*vom*' was corrected to '*zum*', thus altering the sense to that given in the text above.]

part of the conscious is removed. A delicate balancing is here taking place, the play of which is hidden from us; its mode of operation, however, enables us to infer that it is a question of calling a halt when the cathexis of the unconscious reaches a certain intensity – an intensity beyond which the unconscious would break through to satisfaction. Repression acts, therefore, in a *highly individual* manner. Each single derivative of the repressed may have its own special vicissitude; a little more or a little less distortion alters the whole outcome. In this connection we can understand how it is that the objects to which men give most preference, their ideals, proceed from the same perceptions and experiences as the objects which they most abhor, and that they were originally only distinguished from one another through slight modifications. [Cf. p. 87.] Indeed, as we found in tracing the origin of the fetish,[1] it is possible for the original instinctual representative to be split in two, one part undergoing repression, while the remainder, precisely on account of this intimate connection, undergoes idealization.

The same result as follows from an increase or a decrease in the degree of distortion may also be achieved at the other end of the apparatus, so to speak, by a modification in the condition for the production of pleasure and unpleasure. Special techniques have been evolved, with the purpose of bringing about such changes in the play of mental forces that what would otherwise give rise to unpleasure may on this occasion result in pleasure; and, whenever a technical device of this sort comes into operation, the repression of an instinctual representative which would otherwise be repudiated is lifted. These techniques have till now only been studied in any detail in jokes.[2] As a rule the repression is only temporarily lifted and is promptly reinstated.

Observations like this, however, enable us to note some further characteristics of repression. Not only is it, as we have just shown, *individual* in its operation, but it is also exceedingly

1. [Cf. Section 2 (A) of the first of Freud's *Three Essays* (1905*d*), *P.F.L.*, **7**, 65–8 and footnotes.]

2. [See the second chapter of Freud's book on jokes (1905*c*), *P.F.L.*, **6**, 47 ff.]

mobile. The process of repression is not to be regarded as an event which takes place *once*, the results of which are permanent, as when some living thing has been killed and from that time onward is dead; repression demands a persistent expenditure of force, and if this were to cease the success of the repression would be jeopardized, so that a fresh act of repression would be necessary. We may suppose that the repressed exercises a continuous pressure in the direction of the conscious, so that this pressure must be balanced by an unceasing counter-pressure.[1] Thus the maintenance of a repression involves an uninterrupted expenditure of force, while its removal results in a saving from an economic point of view. The mobility of repression, incidentally, also finds expression in the psychical characteristics of the state of sleep, which alone renders possible the formation of dreams.[2] With a return to waking life the repressive cathexes which have been drawn in are once more sent out.

Finally, we must not forget that after all we have said very little about an instinctual impulse when we have established that it is repressed. Without prejudice to its repression, such an impulse may be in widely different states. It may be inactive, i.e. only very slightly cathected with psychical energy; or it may be cathected in varying degrees, and so enabled to be active. True, its activation will not result in a direct lifting of the repression, but it will set in motion all the processes which end in a penetration by the impulse into consciousness along circuitous paths. With unrepressed derivatives of the unconscious the fate of a particular idea is often decided by the degree of its activity or cathexis. It is an everyday occurrence that such a derivative remains unrepressed so long as it represents only a small amount of energy, although its content would be calculated to give rise to a conflict with what is dominant in consciousness. The quantitative factor proves decisive for this conflict: as soon as the basically obnoxious idea exceeds a certain degree of strength, the conflict becomes a real one, and it is precisely this activation

1. [This is discussed further on p. 183 f. below.]

2. [Cf. *The Interpretation of Dreams* (1900*a*), Chap. VII (C), *P.F.L.*, **4**, 721–2. See also below, pp. 232–3.]

that leads to repression. So that, where repression is concerned, an increase of energic cathexis operates in the same sense as an approach to the unconscious, while a decrease of that cathexis operates in the same sense as remoteness from the unconscious or distortion. We see that the repressive trends may find a substitute for repression in a weakening of what is distasteful.

In our discussion so far we have dealt with the repression of an instinctual representative, and by the latter we have understood an idea[1] or group of ideas which is cathected with a definite quota of psychical energy (libido or interest) coming from an instinct. Clinical observation now obliges us to divide up what we have hitherto regarded as a single entity; for it shows us that besides the idea, some other element representing the instinct has to be taken into account, and that this other element undergoes vicissitudes of repression which may be quite different from those undergone by the idea. For this other element of the psychical representative the term *quota of affect* has been generally adopted.[2] It corresponds to the instinct in so far as the latter has become detached from the idea and finds expression, proportionate to its quantity, in processes which are sensed as affects. From this point on, in describing a case of repression, we shall have to follow up separately what, as the result of repression, becomes of the *idea*, and what becomes of the instinctual energy linked to it.

We should be glad to be able to say something general about the vicissitudes of both; and having taken our bearings a little we shall in fact be able to do so. The general vicissitude which overtakes the *idea* that represents the instinct can hardly be anything else than that it should vanish from the conscious if it was previously conscious, or that it should be held back from consciousness if it was about to become conscious. The difference is not important; it amounts to much the same thing as the difference between my ordering an undesirable guest out of my

1. [‘*Vorstellung*.’ See footnote 2, p. 176.]
2. [‘*Affektbetrag*.’ This term dates back to the Breuer period. Cf., for instance, the last paragraphs of Freud's paper, 1894*a*, and the Editor's Appendix to it.]

drawing-room (or out of my front hall), and my refusing, after recognizing him, to let him cross my threshold at all.[1] The *quantitative* factor of the instinctual representative has three possible vicissitudes, as we can see from a cursory survey of the observations made by psychoanalysis: either the instinct is altogether suppressed, so that no trace of it is found, or it appears as an affect which is in some way or other qualitatively coloured, or it is changed into anxiety.[2] The two latter possibilities set us the task of taking into account, as a further instinctual vicissitude, the *transformation* into *affects*, and especially into *anxiety*, of the psychical energies of *instincts*.

We recall the fact that the motive and purpose of repression was nothing else than the avoidance of unpleasure. It follows that the vicissitude of the quota of affect belonging to the representative is far more important than the vicissitude of the idea, and this fact is decisive for our assessment of the process of repression. If a repression does not succeed in preventing feelings of unpleasure or anxiety from arising, we may say that it has failed, even though it may have achieved its purpose as far as the ideational portion is concerned. Repressions that have failed will of course have more claim on our interest than any that may have been successful; for the latter will for the most part escape our examination.

We must now try to obtain some insight into the *mechanism* of the process of repression. In particular we want to know whether there is a single mechanism only, or more than one, and whether perhaps each of the psychoneuroses is distinguished

1. This simile, which is thus applicable to the process of repression, may also be extended to a characteristic of it which has been mentioned earlier: I have merely to add that I must set a permanent guard over the door which I have forbidden this guest to enter, since he would otherwise burst it open. (See above [p. 151].) [The simile had been elaborated by Freud in the second of his *Five Lectures* (1910*a*).]

2. [Freud's altered views on this last point were stated by him in *Inhibitions, Symptoms and Anxiety* (1926*d*), especially at the end of Chapter IV and in Chapter XI, Section A (*b*); *P.F.L.*, **10**, 263–4 and 320 ff.]

by a mechanism of repression peculiar to it. At the outset of this enquiry, however, we are met by complications. The mechanism of a repression becomes accessible to us only by our deducing that mechanism from the *outcome* of the repression. Confining our observations to the effect of repression on the ideational portion of the representative, we discover that as a rule it creates a *substitutive formation*. What is the mechanism by which such a substitute is formed? Or should we distinguish several mechanisms here as well? Further, we know that repression leaves *symptoms* behind it. May we then suppose that the forming of substitutes and the forming of symptoms coincide, and, if this is so on the whole, is the mechanism of forming symptoms the same as that of repression? The general probability would seem to be that the two are widely different, and that it is not the repression itself which produces substitutive formations and symptoms, but that these latter are indications of a *return of the repressed*[1] and owe their existence to quite other processes. It would also seem advisable to examine the mechanisms by which substitutes and symptoms are formed before considering the mechanisms of repression.

Obviously this is no subject for further speculation. The place of speculation must be taken by a careful analysis of the results of repression observable in the different neuroses. I must, however, suggest that we should postpone this task, too, until we have formed reliable conceptions of the relation of the conscious to the unconscious.[2] But, in order that the present discussion may not be entirely unfruitful, I will say in advance that (1) the mechanism of repression does not in fact coincide with the mechanism or mechanisms of forming substitutes, (2) there are a great many different mechanisms of forming substitutes and (3) the mechanisms of repression have at least this one thing in

1. [The concept of a 'return of the repressed' is a very early one in Freud's writings. It appears already in Section II of his second paper on 'The Neuro-Psychoses of Defence' (1896*b*), as well as in the still earlier draft of that paper sent to Fliess on 1 January 1896 (1950*a*, Draft K).]

2. [Freud takes up the task in Section IV of his paper on 'The Unconscious', below, p. 183 ff.]

common: a *withdrawal of the cathexis of energy* (or of *libido*, where we are dealing with sexual instincts).

Further, restricting myself to the three best-known forms of psychoneurosis, I will show by means of some examples how the concepts here introduced find application to the study of repression. From the field of *anxiety hysteria* I will choose a well-analysed example of an animal phobia.[1] The instinctual impulse subjected to repression here is a libidinal attitude towards the father, coupled with fear of him. After repression, this impulse vanishes out of consciousness: the father does not appear in it as an object of libido. As a substitute for him we find in a corresponding place some animal which is more or less fitted to be an object of anxiety. The formation of the substitute for the ideational portion [of the instinctual representative] has come about by *displacement* along a chain of connections which is determined in a particular way. The quantitative portion has not vanished, but has been transformed into anxiety. The result is fear of a wolf, instead of a demand for love from the father. The categories here employed are of course not enough to supply an adequate explanation of even the simplest case of psychoneurosis: there are always other considerations to be taken into account.

A repression such as occurs in an animal phobia must be described as radically unsuccessful. All that it has done is to remove and replace the idea; it has failed altogether in sparing unpleasure. And for this reason, too, the work of the neurosis does not cease. It proceeds to a second phase, in order to attain its immediate and more important purpose. What follows is an attempt at flight – the formation of the *phobia proper*, of a number of avoidances which are intended to prevent a release of the anxiety. More specialized investigation enables us to understand the mechanism by which the phobia achieves its aim. [See p. 185 ff. below.]

We are obliged to take quite another view of the process of

1. [This is, of course, a reference to the case history of the 'Wolf Man' (1918*b*), *P.F.L.*, **9**, 233 ff., which, though it was not published till three years after the present paper, had already been completed in essentials.]

repression when we consider the picture of a true *conversion hysteria*. Here the salient point is that it is possible to bring about a total disappearance of the quota of affect. When this is so, the patient displays towards his symptoms what Charcot called '*la belle indifférence des hystériques*'.[1] In other cases this suppression is not so completely successful: some distressing sensations may attach to the symptoms themselves, or it may prove impossible to prevent some release of anxiety, which in turn sets to work the mechanism of forming a phobia. The ideational content of the instinctual representative is completely withdrawn from consciousness; as a substitute – and at the same time as a symptom – we have an over-strong innervation (in typical cases, a somatic one), sometimes of a sensory, sometimes of a motor character, either as an excitation or an inhibition. The over-innervated area proves on a closer view to be a part of the repressed instinctual representative itself – a part which, as though by a process of *condensation*, has drawn the whole cathexis on to itself. These remarks do not of course bring to light the whole mechanism of a conversion hysteria; in especial the factor of *regression*, which will be considered in another connection, has also to be taken into account.[2] In so far as repression in [conversion] hysteria is made possible only by the extensive formation of substitutes, it may be judged to be entirely unsuccessful; as regards dealing with the quota of affect, however, which is the true task of repression, it generally signifies a total success. In conversion hysteria the process of repression is completed with the formation of the symptom and does not, as in anxiety hysteria, need to continue to a second phase – or rather, strictly speaking, to continue endlessly.

A totally different picture of repression is shown, once more, in the third disorder which we shall consider for the purposes of our illustration – in *obsessional neurosis*. Here we are at first in doubt what it is that we have to regard as the instinctual

1. [Freud has already quoted this in *Studies on Hysteria* (1895*d*), *P.F.L.*, **3**, 202.]

2. [This is perhaps a reference to the missing metapsychological paper on conversion hysteria. See Editor's Introduction, p. 103.]

representative that is subjected to repression – whether it is a libidinal or a hostile trend. This uncertainty arises because obsessional neurosis has as its basis a regression owing to which a sadistic trend has been substituted for an affectionate one. It is this hostile impulse against someone who is loved which is subjected to repression. The effect at an early stage of the work of repression is quite different from what it is at a later one. At first the repression is completely successful; the ideational content is rejected and the affect made to disappear. As a substitutive formation there arises an alteration of the ego in the shape of an increased conscientiousness, and this can hardly be called a symptom. Here, substitute and symptom do not coincide. From this we learn something, too, about the mechanism of repression. In this instance, as in all others, repression has brought about a withdrawal of libido; but here it has made use of *reaction-formation* for this purpose, by intensifying an opposite. Thus in this case the formation of a substitute has the same mechanism as repression and at bottom coincides with it, while chronologically, as well as conceptually, it is distinct from the formation of a symptom. It is very probable that the whole process is made possible by the ambivalent relationship into which the sadistic impulsion that has to be repressed has been introduced.

But the repression, which was at first successful, does not hold firm; in the further course of things its failure becomes increasingly marked. The ambivalence which has enabled repression through reaction-formation to take place is also the point at which the repressed succeeds in returning. The vanished affect comes back in its transformed shape as social anxiety, moral anxiety and unlimited self-reproaches; the rejected idea is replaced by a *substitute by displacement*, often a displacement on to something very small or indifferent.[1] A tendency to a complete re-establishment of the repressed idea is as a rule unmistakably present. The failure in the repression of the quantitative, affective factor brings into play the same mechanism of flight, by means of avoidance and prohibitions, as we have seen at

1. [Cf. Section II (*c*) of the 'Rat Man' analysis, *P.F.L.*, **9**, 121.]

work in the formation of hysterical phobias. The rejection of the *idea* from the conscious is, however, obstinately maintained, because it entails abstention from action, a motor fettering of the impulsion. Thus in obsessional neurosis the work of repression is prolonged in a sterile and interminable struggle.

The short series of comparisons presented here may easily convince us that more comprehensive investigations are necessary before we can hope thoroughly to understand the processes connected with repression and the formation of neurotic symptoms. The extraordinary intricacy of all the factors to be taken into consideration leaves only one way of presenting them open to us. We must select first one and then another point of view, and follow it up through the material as long as the application of it seems to yield results. Each separate treatment of the subject will be incomplete in itself, and there cannot fail to be obscurities where it touches upon material that has not yet been treated; but we may hope that a final synthesis will lead to a proper understanding.

THE UNCONSCIOUS
(1915)

EDITOR'S NOTE

DAS UNBEWUSSTE

(A) German Editions:

1915 *Int. Z. ärztl. Psychoanal.*, **3** (4), 189–203 and (5), 257–69.
1924 *Gesammelte Schriften*, **5**, 480–519.
1946 *Gesammelte Werke*, **10**, 264–303.

(B) English Translations:
'The Unconscious'

1925 *Collected Papers*, **4**, 98–136. (Tr. C. M. Baines.)
1957 *Standard Edition*, **14**, 159–215. (Translation, based on that of 1925, but very largely rewritten.)

The present edition is a reprint of the *Standard Edition* version, with some editorial modifications.

This paper seems to have taken less than three weeks to write – from 4 April to 23 April 1915. It was published in the *Internationale Zeitschrift* later in the same year in two instalments, the first containing Sections I–IV, and the second Sections V–VII.

If the series of 'Papers on Metapsychology' may perhaps be regarded as the most important of all Freud's theoretical writings, there can be no doubt that the present essay on 'The Unconscious' is the culmination of that series.

The concept of there being unconscious mental processes is of course one that is fundamental to psychoanalytic theory. Freud was never tired of insisting upon the arguments in support of it and combating the objections to it. Indeed, the very last unfinished scrap of his theoretical writing, the fragment written by him in 1938 to which he gave the English title 'Some Elementary Lessons in Psycho-Analysis' (1940*b*), is a fresh vindication of that concept.

It should be made clear at once, however, that Freud's interest in the assumption was never a philosophical one – though, no doubt, philosophical problems inevitably lay just round the corner. His interest was a *practical* one. He found that without making that assumption he was unable to explain or even to describe a large variety of phenomena which he came across. By making it, on the other hand, he found the way open to an immensely fertile region of fresh knowledge.

In his early days and in his nearest environment there can have been no great resistance to the idea. His immediate teachers – Meynert, for instance[1] – in so far as they were interested in psychology, were governed chiefly by the views of J. F. Herbart (1776–1841), and it seems that a text-book embodying the Herbartian principles was in use at Freud's secondary school (Jones, 1953, 409 f.) A recognition of the existence of unconscious mental processes played an essential part in Herbart's system. In spite of this, however, Freud did not immediately adopt the hypothesis in the earliest stages of his psychopathological researches. He seems from the first, it is true, to have felt the force of the argument on which stress is laid in the opening pages of the present paper – the argument, that is, that to restrict mental events to those that are conscious and to intersperse them with purely physical, neural events 'disrupts psychical continuities' and introduces unintelligible gaps into the chain of observed phenomena. But there were two ways in which this difficulty could be met. We might disregard the physical events and adopt the hypothesis that the gaps are filled with unconscious mental ones; but, on the other hand, we might disregard the conscious mental events and construct a purely physical chain, without any breaks in it, which would cover all the facts of observation. To Freud, whose early scientific career had been

1. The possible influence on Freud in this respect of the physiologist Hering is discussed below in Appendix A (p. 211).

entirely concerned with physiology, this second possibility was at first irresistibly attractive. The attraction was no doubt strengthened by the views of Hughlings Jackson, of whose work he showed his admiration in his monograph on aphasia (1891*b*), a relevant passage from which will be found below in Appendix B (p. 213). The neurological method of describing psychopathological phenomena was accordingly the one which Freud began by adopting, and all his writings of the Breuer period are professedly based on that method. He became intellectually fascinated by the possibility of constructing a 'psychology' out of purely neurological ingredients, and devoted many months in the year 1895 to accomplishing the feat. Thus on 27 April of that year (Freud, 1950*a*, Letter 23) he wrote to Fliess: 'I am so deep in the "Psychology for Neurologists" that it quite consumes me, till I have to break off really overworked. I have never been so intensely preoccupied by anything. And will anything come of it? I hope so, but the going is hard and slow.' Something *did* come of it many months later – the torso which we know as the 'Project for a Scientific Psychology', despatched to Fliess in September and October 1895. This astonishing production purports to describe and explain the whole range of human behaviour, normal and pathological, by means of a complicated manipulation of two material entities – the neurone and 'quantity in a condition of flow', an unspecified physical or chemical energy. The need for postulating any unconscious mental processes was in this way entirely avoided: the chain of physical events was unbroken and complete.

There were no doubt many reasons why the 'Project' was never finished and why the whole line of thought behind it was before long abandoned. But the principal reason was that Freud the neurologist was being overtaken and displaced by Freud the psychologist: it became more and more obvious that even the elaborate machinery of the neuronal systems was far too cumbersome and coarse to deal with the subtleties which were being brought to light by 'psychological analysis' and which could only be accounted for in the language of mental processes. A displacement of Freud's interest had in fact been very gradually taking place. Already at the time of the publication of the *Aphasia* his treatment of the case of Frau Emmy von N. lay two or three years behind him, and her case history was written more than a year before the 'Project'. It is in a footnote to that case history (*P.F.L.*, **3**, 134 *n.* 2) that his first published use of the term 'the unconscious' is to be found; and though the *ostensible* theory underlying his share in the *Studies on Hysteria* (1895*d*) might be a neurological one, psychology, and with it the necessity for unconscious mental processes, was steadily creeping in. Indeed, the whole basis of the repression theory of hysteria, and of the cathartic method of treatment, cried out for a psychological explanation, and it was only by the most contorted efforts that they had been accounted for neurologically in Part II of the 'Project'.[1] A few years later, in *The Interpretation of Dreams* (1900*a*), a strange transformation had occurred: not only had the neurological account of psychology completely disappeared, but much of what Freud had written in the 'Project' in terms of the nervous system now turned out to be valid and far more intelligible when translated into mental terms. The unconscious was established once and for all.

But, it must be repeated, what Freud established was no mere metaphysical entity. What he did in Chapter VII of *The Interpretation of Dreams* was, as it were, to clothe the metaphysical entity in flesh and blood. He showed for the first time what the unconscious was like, how it worked, how it differed from other parts of the mind, and what were its reciprocal relations with them. It was to these discoveries that he returned, amplifying and deepening them, in the paper which follows.

At an earlier stage, however, it had become evident that the term 'unconscious' was an ambiguous one. Three years previously, in the paper which he wrote in English for the Society for Psychical Research (1912*g*), and which is in many ways a preliminary to the present paper, he had carefully investigated these ambiguities, and had differentiated between the 'descrip-

1. Oddly enough it was Breuer, in his theoretical contribution to the *Studies*, who was the first to make a reasoned defence of unconscious ideas (*P.F.L.*, **3**, 300 f.).

tive', 'dynamic' and 'systematic' uses of the word. He repeats the distinctions in Section II of this paper (p. 174 ff.), though in a slightly different form; and he came back to them again in Chapter I of *The Ego and the Id* (1923*b*) and, at even greater length, in Lecture 31 of the *New Introductory Lectures* (1933*a*). The untidy way in which the contrast between 'conscious' and 'unconscious' fits the differences between the various systems of the mind is already stated clearly below (pp. 196–7); but the whole position was only brought into perspective when in *The Ego and the Id* Freud introduced a new structural picture of the mind. In spite, however, of the unsatisfactory operation of the criterion 'conscious or unconscious?', Freud always insisted (as he does in two places here, pp. 174 and 196, and again both in *The Ego and the Id* and in the *New Introductory Lectures*) that that criterion 'is in the last resort our one beacon-light in the darkness of depth psychology'.[1]

1. The closing words of Chapter I of *The Ego and the Id*. – For English readers, it must be observed, there is a further ambiguity in the word 'unconscious' which is scarcely present in the German. The German words '*bewusst*' and '*unbewusst*' have the grammatical form of passive participles, and their usual sense is something like 'consciously known' and 'not consciously known'. The English 'conscious', though it *can* be used in the same way, is also used, and perhaps more commonly, in an *active* sense: 'he was conscious of the sound' and 'he lay there unconscious'. The German terms do not often have this active meaning, and it is important to bear in mind that 'conscious' is in general to be understood in a passive sense in what follows. The German word '*Bewusstsein*', on the other hand (which is here translated 'consciousness'), *does* have an active sense. Thus, for instance, on page 175 Freud speaks of a psychical act becoming 'an object of consciousness'; again, in the last paragraph of the first section of the paper (page 173) he speaks of 'the perception [of mental processes] by means of consciousness'; and in general, when he uses such phrases as 'our consciousness', he is referring to our consciousness *of* something. When he wishes to speak of a mental state's consciousness in the *passive* sense, he uses the word '*Bewusstheit*', which is translated here 'the attribute of being conscious', 'the fact of being conscious' or simply 'being conscious' – where the English 'conscious' is, as almost always in these papers, to be taken in the passive sense.

THE UNCONSCIOUS

We have learnt from psychoanalysis that the essence of the process of repression lies, not in putting an end to, in annihilating, the idea which represents an instinct, but in preventing it from becoming conscious. When this happens we say of the idea that it is in a state of being 'unconscious',[1] and we can produce good evidence to show that even when it is unconscious it can produce effects, even including some which finally reach consciousness. Everything that is repressed must remain unconscious; but let us state at the very outset that the repressed does not cover everything that is unconscious. The unconscious has the wider compass: the repressed is a part of the unconscious.

How are we to arrive at a knowledge of the unconscious? It is of course only as something conscious that we know it, after it has undergone transformation or translation into something conscious. Psychoanalytic work shows us every day that translation of this kind is possible. In order that this should come about, the person under analysis must overcome certain resistances – the same resistances as those which, earlier, made the material concerned into something repressed by rejecting it from the conscious.

I. Justification for the Concept of the Unconscious

Our right to assume the existence of something mental that is unconscious and to employ that assumption for the purposes of scientific work is disputed in many quarters. To this we can

1. [See Editor's Note, p. 165 footnote.]

reply that our assumption of the unconscious is *necessary* and *legitimate*, and that we possess numerous *proofs* of its existence.

It is *necessary* because the data of consciousness have a very large number of gaps in them; both in healthy and in sick people psychical acts often occur which can be explained only by presupposing other acts, of which, nevertheless, consciousness affords no evidence. These not only include parapraxes and dreams in healthy people, and everything described as a psychical symptom or an obsession in the sick; our most personal daily experience acquaints us with ideas that come into our head we do not know from where, and with intellectual conclusions arrived at we do not know how. All these conscious acts remain disconnected and unintelligible if we insist upon claiming that every mental act that occurs in us must also necessarily be experienced by us through consciousness; on the other hand, they fall into a demonstrable connection if we interpolate between them the unconscious acts which we have inferred. A gain in meaning is a perfectly justifiable ground for going beyond the limits of direct experience. When, in addition, it turns out that the assumption of there being an unconscious enables us to construct a successful procedure by which we can exert an effective influence upon the course of conscious processes, this success will have given us an incontrovertible proof of the existence of what we have assumed. This being so, we must adopt the position that to require that whatever goes on in the mind must also be known to consciousness is to make an untenable claim.

We can go further and argue, in support of there being an unconscious psychical state, that at any given moment consciousness includes only a small content, so that the greater part of what we call conscious knowledge must in any case be for very considerable periods of time in a state of latency, that is to say, of being psychically unconscious. When all our latent memories are taken into consideration it becomes totally incomprehensible how the existence of the unconscious can be denied. But here we encounter the objection that these latent recollections can no longer be described as psychical, but that they correspond to residues of somatic processes from which what is psychical can once more arise. The obvious answer to this is that a latent memory is, on the contrary, an unquestionable residuum of a *psychical* process. But it is more important to realize clearly that this objection is based on the equation – not, it is true, explicitly stated but taken as axiomatic – of what is conscious with what is mental. This equation is either a *petitio principii* which begs the question whether everything that is psychical is also necessarily conscious; or else it is a matter of convention, of nomenclature. In this latter case it is, of course, like any other convention, not open to refutation. The question remains, however, whether the convention is so expedient that we are bound to adopt it. To this we may reply that the conventional equation of the psychical with the conscious is totally inexpedient. It disrupts psychical continuities, plunges us into the insoluble difficulties of psycho-physical parallelism,[1] is open to the reproach that for no obvious reason it over-estimates the part played by consciousness, and that it forces us prematurely to abandon the field of psychological research without being able to offer us any compensation from other fields.

It is clear in any case that this question – whether the latent states of mental life, whose existence is undeniable, are to be conceived of as conscious mental states or as physical ones – threatens to resolve itself into a verbal dispute. We shall therefore be better advised to focus our attention on what we know with certainty of the nature of these debatable states. As far as their physical characteristics are concerned, they are totally inaccessible to us: no physiological concept or chemical process can give us any notion of their nature. On the other hand, we know for certain that they have abundant points of contact with conscious mental processes; with the help of a certain amount of work they can be transformed into, or replaced by, conscious mental processes, and all the categories which we employ to describe conscious mental acts, such as ideas, purposes, resol-

1. [Freud seems himself at one time to have been inclined to accept this theory, as is suggested by a passage in his book on aphasia (1891*b*, 56 ff.). This will be found translated below in Appendix B. (p. 213).]

utions and so on, can be applied to them. Indeed, we are obliged to say of some of these latent states that the only respect in which they differ from conscious ones is precisely in the absence of consciousness. Thus we shall not hesitate to treat them as objects of psychological research, and to deal with them in the most intimate connection with conscious mental acts.

The stubborn denial of a psychical character to latent mental acts is accounted for by the circumstance that most of the phenomena concerned have not been the subject of study outside psychoanalysis. Anyone who is ignorant of pathological facts, who regards the parapraxes of normal people as accidental, and who is content with the old saw that dreams are froth ['*Träume sind Schäume*'][1] has only to ignore a few more problems of the psychology of consciousness in order to spare himself any need to assume an unconscious mental activity. Incidentally, even before the time of psychoanalysis, hypnotic experiments, and especially post-hypnotic suggestion, had tangibly demonstrated the existence and mode of operation of the mental unconscious.[2]

The assumption of an unconscious is, moreover, a perfectly *legitimate* one, inasmuch as in postulating it we are not departing a single step from our customary and generally accepted mode of thinking. Consciousness makes each of us aware only of his own states of mind; that other people, too, possess a consciousness is an inference which we draw by analogy from their observable utterances and actions, in order to make this behaviour of theirs intelligible to us. (It would no doubt be psychologically more correct to put it in this way: that without any special reflection we attribute to everyone else our own constitution and therefore our consciousness as well, and that this identification is a *sine qua non* of our understanding.) This inference (or this identification) was formerly extended by the ego to other human beings, to animals, plants, inanimate objects and

1. [Cf. *The Interpretation of Dreams* (1900*a*), *P.F.L.*, **4**, 212.]

2. [In his very last discussion of the subject, in the unfinished fragment 'Some Elementary Lessons in Psycho-Analysis' (1940*b*), Freud entered at some length into the evidence afforded by post-hypnotic suggestion.]

to the world at large, and proved serviceable so long as their similarity to the individual ego was overwhelmingly great; but it became more untrustworthy in proportion as the difference between the ego and these 'others' widened. Today, our critical judgement is already in doubt on the question of consciousness in animals; we refuse to admit it in plants and we regard the assumption of its existence in inanimate matter as mysticism. But even where the original inclination to identification has withstood criticism – that is, when the 'others' are our fellow-men – the assumption of a consciousness in them rests upon an inference and cannot share the immediate certainty which we have of our own consciousness.

Psychoanalysis demands nothing more than that we should apply this process of inference to ourselves also – a proceeding to which, it is true, we are not constitutionally inclined. If we do this, we must say: all the acts and manifestations which I notice in myself and do not know how to link up with the rest of my mental life must be judged as if they belonged to someone else: they are to be explained by a mental life ascribed to this other person. Furthermore, experience shows that we understand very well how to interpret in other people (that is, how to fit into their chain of mental events) the same acts which we refuse to acknowledge as being mental in ourselves. Here some special hindrance evidently deflects our investigations from our own self and prevents our obtaining a true knowledge of it.

This process of inference, when applied to oneself in spite of internal opposition, does not, however, lead to the disclosure of an unconscious; it leads logically to the assumption of another, second consciousness which is united in one's self with the consciousness one knows. But at this point, certain criticisms may fairly be made. In the first place, a consciousness of which its own possessor knows nothing is something very different from a consciousness belonging to another person, and it is questionable whether such a consciousness, lacking, as it does, its most important characteristic, deserves any discussion at all. Those who have resisted the assumption of an unconscious *psychical* are not likely to be ready to exchange it for an unconscious *consciousness*. In the second place, analysis shows that the different latent mental processes inferred by us enjoy a high degree of mutual independence, as though they had no connection with one another, and knew nothing of one another. We must be prepared, if so, to assume the existence in us not only of a second consciousness, but of a third, fourth, perhaps of an unlimited number of states of consciousness, all unknown to us and to one another. In the third place – and this is the most weighty argument of all – we have to take into account the fact that analytic investigation reveals some of these latent processes as having characteristics and peculiarities which seem alien to us, or even incredible, and which run directly counter to the attributes of consciousness with which we are familiar. Thus we have grounds for modifying our inference about ourselves and saying that what is proved is not the existence of a second consciousness in us, but the existence of psychical acts which lack consciousness. We shall also be right in rejecting the term 'subconsciousness' as incorrect and misleading.[1] The well-known cases of '*double conscience*'[2] (splitting of consciousness) prove nothing against our view. We may most aptly describe them as cases of a splitting of the mental activities into two groups, and say that the same consciousness turns to one or the other of these groups alternately.

In psychoanalysis there is no choice for us but to assert that mental processes are in themselves unconscious, and to liken the perception of them by means of consciousness to the perception of the external world by means of the sense-organs.[3] We can even hope to gain fresh knowledge from the comparison. The

1. [In some of his very early writings, Freud himself used the term 'subconscious', e.g. in his French paper on hysterical paralyses (1893*c*) and in *Studies on Hysteria* (1895), *P.F.L.*, **3**, 126 *n*. But he disrecommends the term as early as in *The Interpretation of Dreams* (1900*a*), ibid., **4**, 776. He alludes to the point again in Lecture 19 of the *Introductory Lectures* (1916–17), ibid., **1**, 338 and *n*. 1, and argues it a little more fully near the end of Chapter II of *The Question of Lay Analysis* (1926*e*).]

2. [The French term for 'dual consciousness'.]

3. [This idea had already been dealt with at some length in Chapter VII (F) of *The Interpretation of Dreams* (1900*a*), *P.F.L.*, **4**, 776–8.]

psychoanalytic assumption of unconscious mental activity appears to us, on the one hand, as a further expansion of the primitive animism which caused us to see copies of our own consciousness all around us, and, on the other hand, as an extension of the corrections undertaken by Kant of our views on external perception. Just as Kant warned us not to overlook the fact that our perceptions are subjectively conditioned and must not be regarded as identical with what is perceived though unknowable, so psychoanalysis warns us not to equate perceptions by means of consciousness with the unconscious mental processes which are their object. Like the physical, the psychical is not necessarily in reality what it appears to us to be. We shall be glad to learn, however, that the correction of internal perception will turn out not to offer such great difficulties as the correction of external perception – that internal objects are less unknowable than the external world.

II. Various Meanings of 'the Unconscious' – The Topographical Point of View

Before going any further, let us state the important, though inconvenient, fact that the attribute of being unconscious is only one feature that is found in the psychical and is by no means sufficient fully to characterize it. There are psychical acts of very varying value which yet agree in possessing the characteristic of being unconscious. The unconscious comprises, on the one hand, acts which are merely latent, temporarily unconscious, but which differ in no other respect from conscious ones and, on the other hand, processes such as repressed ones, which if they were to become conscious would be bound to stand out in the crudest contrast to the rest of the conscious processes. It would put an end to all misunderstandings if, from now on, in describing the various kinds of psychical acts we were to disregard the question of whether they were conscious or unconscious, and were to classify and correlate them only according to their relation to instincts and aims, according to their composition and according to which of the hierarchy of psychical systems they belong to. This, however, is for various reasons impracticable, so that we cannot escape the ambiguity of using the words 'conscious' and 'unconscious' sometimes in a descriptive and sometimes in a systematic sense, in which latter they signify inclusion in particular systems and possession of certain characteristics. We might attempt to avoid confusion by giving the psychical systems which we have distinguished certain arbitrarily chosen names which have no reference to the attribute of being conscious. Only we should first have to specify what the grounds are on which we distinguish the systems, and in doing this we should not be able to evade the attribute of being conscious, seeing that it forms the point of departure for all our investigations.[1] Perhaps we may look for some assistance from the proposal to employ, at any rate in writing, the abbreviation

1. [Freud recurs to this below on p. 196.]

Cs. for consciousness and *Ucs.* for what is unconscious, when we are using the two words in the systematic sense.[1]

Proceeding now to an account of the positive findings of psychoanalysis, we may say that in general a psychical act goes through two phases as regards its state, between which is interposed a kind of testing (*censorship*). In the first phase the psychical act is unconscious and belongs to the system *Ucs.*; if, on testing, it is rejected by the censorship, it is not allowed to pass into the second phase; it is then said to be 'repressed' and must remain unconscious. If, however, it passes this testing, it enters the second phase and thenceforth belongs to the second system, which we will call the system *Cs.* But the fact that it belongs to that system does not yet unequivocally determine its relation to consciousness. It is not yet conscious, but it is certainly *capable of becoming conscious* (to use Breuer's expression)[2] – that is, it can now, given certain conditions, become an object of consciousness without any special resistance. In consideration of this capacity for becoming conscious we also call the system *Cs.* the 'preconscious'. If it should turn out that a certain censorship also plays a part in determining whether the preconscious becomes conscious, we shall discriminate more sharply between the systems *Pcs.* and *Cs.* [Cf. p. 196 f.] For the present let it suffice us to bear in mind that the system *Pcs.* shares the characteristics of the system *Cs.* and that the rigorous censorship exercises its office at the point of transition from the *Ucs.* to the *Pcs.* (or *Cs.*).

By accepting the existence of these two (or three) psychical systems, psychoanalysis has departed a step further from the descriptive 'psychology of consciousness' and has raised new problems and acquired a new content. Up till now, it has differed from that psychology mainly by reason of its *dynamic* view of mental processes; now in addition it seems to take account of psychical *topography* as well, and to indicate in respect of any given mental act within what system or between what systems

1. [Freud had already introduced these abbreviations in *The Interpretation of Dreams* (1900*a*), *P.F.L.*, **4**, 689 ff.]

2. [See *Studies on Hysteria*, Breuer and Freud (1895), *P.F.L.*, **3**, 304.]

it takes place. On account of this attempt, too, it has been given the name of 'depth-psychology'.[1] We shall hear that it can be further enriched by taking yet another point of view into account. [Cf. p. 184.]

If we are to take the topography of mental acts seriously we must direct our interest to a doubt which arises at this point. When a psychical act (let us confine ourselves here to one which is in the nature of an idea[2]) is transposed from the system *Ucs.* into the system *Cs.* (or *Pcs.*), are we to suppose that this transposition involves a fresh record – as it were, a second registration – of the idea in question, which may thus be situated as well in a fresh psychical locality, and alongside of which the original unconscious registration continues to exist?[3] Or are we rather to believe that the transposition consists in a change in the state of the idea, a change involving the same material and occurring in the same locality? This question may appear abstruse, but it must be raised if we wish to form a more definite conception of psychical topography, of the dimension of depth in the mind. It is a difficult one because it goes beyond pure psychology and touches on the relations of the mental apparatus to anatomy. We know that in the very roughest sense such relations exist. Research has given irrefutable proof that mental activity is bound up with the function of the brain as it is with no other organ. We are taken a step further – we do not know how much – by the discovery of the unequal importance of the different parts of the brain and their special relations to particular parts of the body and to particular mental activities. But every attempt to go on from there to discover a localization of mental

1. [By Bleuler (1914). See the 'History of the Psycho-Analytic Movement' (1914*d*).]

2. [The German word here is '*Vorstellung*', which covers the English terms 'idea', 'image' and 'presentation'.]

3. [The conception of an idea being present in the mind in more than one 'registration' was first put forward by Freud in a letter to Fliess of 6 December 1896 (Freud, 1950*a*, Letter 52). It is used in connection with the theory of memory in Chapter VII (Section B) of *The Interpretation of Dreams* (1900*a*), *P.F.L.*, **4**, 688; and it is alluded to again in Section F of the same chapter (ibid., 770) in an argument which foreshadows the present one.]

processes, every endeavour to think of ideas as stored up in nerve-cells and of excitations as migrating along nerve-fibres, has miscarried completely.[1] The same fate would await any theory which attempted to recognize, let us say, the anatomical position of the system *Cs.* – conscious mental activity – as being in the cortex, and to localize the unconscious processes in the subcortical parts of the brain.[2] There is a hiatus here which at present cannot be filled, nor is it one of the tasks of psychology to fill it. Our psychical topography has *for the present* nothing to do with anatomy; it has reference not to anatomical localities, but to regions in the mental apparatus, wherever they may be situated in the body.

In this respect, then, our work is untrammelled and may proceed according to its own requirements. It will, however, be useful to remind ourselves that as things stand our hypotheses set out to be no more than graphic illustrations. The first of the two possibilities which we considered – namely, that the *Cs.* phase of an ideal implies a fresh registration of it, which is situated in another place – is doubtless the cruder but also the more convenient. The second hypothesis – that of a merely *functional* change of state – is *a priori* more probable, but it is less plastic, less easy to manipulate. With the first, or topographical, hypothesis is bound up that of a topographical separation of the systems *Ucs.* and *Cs.* and also the possibility that an idea may exist simultaneously in two places in the mental apparatus – indeed, that if it is not inhibited by the censorship, it regularly advances from the one position to the other, possibly without losing its first location or registration.

This view may seem odd, but it can be supported by observations from psychoanalytic practice. If we communicate to a patient some idea which he has at one time repressed but which we have discovered in him, our telling him makes at first no change in his mental condition. Above all, it does not remove

1. [Freud had himself been much concerned with the question of the localization of cerebral functions in his work on aphasia (1891*b*).]

2. [Freud had insisted on this as early as in his preface to his translation of Bernheim's *De la suggestion* (Freud, 1888–9).]

the repression nor undo its effects, as might perhaps be expected from the fact that the previously unconscious idea has now become conscious. On the contrary, all that we shall achieve at first will be a fresh rejection of the repressed idea. But now the patient has in actual fact the same idea in two forms in different places in his mental apparatus: first, he has the conscious memory of the auditory trace of the idea, conveyed in what we told him; and secondly, he also has – as we know for certain – the unconscious memory of his experience as it was in its earlier form.[1] Actually there is no lifting of the repression until the conscious idea, after the resistances have been overcome, has entered into connection with the unconscious memory-trace. It is only through the making conscious of the latter itself that success is achieved. On superficial consideration this would seem to show that conscious and unconscious ideas are distinct registrations, topographically separated, of the same content. But a moment's reflection shows that the identity of the information given to the patient with his repressed memory is only apparent. To have heard something and to have experienced something are in their psychological nature two quite different things, even though the content of both is the same.

So for the moment we are not in a position to decide between the two possibilities that we have discussed. Perhaps later on we shall come upon factors which may turn the balance in favour of one or the other. Perhaps we shall make the discovery that our question was inadequately framed and that the difference between an unconscious and a conscious idea has to be defined in quite another way.[2]

1. [The topographical picture of the distinction between conscious and unconscious ideas is presented in Freud's discussion of the case of 'Little Hans' (1909*b*), *P.F.L.*, **8**, 278–9, and at greater length in the closing paragraphs of his technical paper 'On Beginning the Treatment' (1913*c*).]

2. [This argument is taken up again on p. 207.]

III. Unconscious Feelings

We have limited the foregoing discussion to ideas; we may now raise a new question, the answer to which is bound to contribute to the elucidation of our theoretical views. We have said that there are conscious and unconscious ideas; but are there also unconscious instinctual impulses, emotions and feelings, or is it in this instance meaningless to form combinations of the kind?

I am in fact of the opinion that the antithesis of conscious and unconscious is not applicable to instincts. An instinct can never become an object of consciousness – only the idea that represents the instinct can. Even in the unconscious, moreover, an instinct cannot be represented otherwise than by an idea. If the instinct did not attach itself to an idea or manifest itself as an affective state, we could know nothing about it. When we nevertheless speak of an unconscious instinctual impulse or of a repressed instinctual impulse, the looseness of phraseology is a harmless one. We can only mean an instinctual impulse the ideational representative of which is unconscious, for nothing else comes into consideration.[1]

We should expect the answer to the question about unconscious feelings, emotions and affects to be just as easily given. It is surely of the essence of an emotion that we should be aware of it, i.e. that it should become known to consciousness. Thus the possibility of the attribute of unconsciousness would be completely excluded as far as emotions, feelings and affects are concerned. But in psychoanalytic practice we are accustomed to speak of unconscious love, hate, anger, etc., and find it impossible to avoid even the strange conjunction, 'unconscious consciousness of guilt',[2] or a paradoxical 'unconscious anxiety'. Is

1. [Cf. the Editor's Note to 'Instincts and their Vicissitudes', p. 107 ff. above.]

2. [German '*Schuldbewusstsein*', a common equivalent for '*Schuldgefühl*', 'sense of guilt'.]

there more meaning in the use of these terms than there is in speaking of 'unconscious instincts'?

The two cases are in fact not on all fours. In the first place, it may happen that an affective or emotional impulse is perceived but misconstrued. Owing to the repression of its proper representative it has been forced to become connected with another idea, and is now regarded by consciousness as the manifestation of that idea. If we restore the true connection, we call the original affective impulse an 'unconscious' one. Yet its affect was never unconscious; all that had happened was that its *idea* had undergone repression. In general, the use of the terms 'unconscious affect' and 'unconscious emotion' has reference to the vicissitudes undergone, in consequence of repression, by the quantitative factor in the instinctual impulse. We know that three such vicissitudes are possible:[1] either the affect remains, wholly or in part, as it is; or it is transformed into a qualitatively different quota of affect, above all into anxiety; or it is suppressed, i.e. it is prevented from developing at all. (These possibilities may perhaps be studied even more easily in the dream-work than in neuroses.[2]) We know, too, that to suppress the development of affect is the true aim of repression and that its work is incomplete if this aim is not achieved. In every instance where repression has succeeded in inhibiting the development of affects, we term those affects (which we restore when we undo the work of repression) 'unconscious'. Thus it cannot be denied that the use of the terms in question is consistent; but in comparison with unconscious ideas there is the important difference that unconscious ideas continue to exist after repression as actual structures in the system *Ucs.*, whereas all that corresponds in that system to unconscious affects is a potential beginning which is prevented from developing. Strictly speaking, then, and although no fault can be found with the linguistic usage, there are no unconscious affects as there are unconscious ideas. But there may very well be in the system *Ucs.* affective

1. Cf. the preceding paper on 'Repression' [p. 153].

2. [The main discussion of affects in *The Interpretation of Dreams* (1900*a*) will be found in Section H of Chapter VI, *P.F.L.*, **4**, 595 ff.]

structures which, like others, become conscious. The whole difference arises from the fact that ideas are cathexes – basically of memory-traces – whilst affects and emotions correspond to processes of discharge, the final manifestations of which are perceived as feelings. In the present state of our knowledge of affects and emotions we cannot express this difference more clearly.[1]

It is of especial interest to us to have established the fact that repression can succeed in inhibiting an instinctual impulse from being turned into a manifestation of affect. This shows us that the system *Cs.* normally controls affectivity as well as access to motility; and it enhances the importance of repression, since it shows that repression results not only in withholding things from consciousness, but also in preventing the development of affect and the setting-off of muscular activity. Conversely, too, we may say that as long as the system *Cs.* controls affectivity and motility, the mental condition of the person in question is spoken of as normal. Nevertheless, there is an unmistakable difference in the relation of the controlling system to the two contiguous processes of discharge.[2] Whereas the control by the *Cs.* over voluntary motility is firmly rooted, regularly withstands the onslaught of neurosis and only breaks down in psychosis, control by the *Cs.* over the development of affects is less secure. Even within the limits of normal life we can recognize that a constant struggle for primacy over affectivity goes on between the two systems *Cs.* and *Ucs.*, that certain spheres of influence are marked off from one another and that intermixtures between the operative forces occur.

The importance of the system *Cs.* (*Pcs.*)[3] as regards access to

1. [This question is discussed again in Chapter II of *The Ego and the Id* (1923*b*), p. 357 ff. below. The nature of affects is more clearly discussed in Lecture 25 of the *Introductory Lectures* (1916–17), *P.F.L.*, **1**, 440 ff., and also in Chapter VIII of *Inhibitions, Symptoms and Anxiety* (1926*d*), ibid., **10**, 288–90.]

2. Affectivity manifests itself essentially in motor (secretory and vasomotor) discharge resulting in an (internal) alteration of the subject's own body without reference to the external world; motility, in actions designed to effect changes in the external world.

3. [In the 1915 edition only, '(*Pcs.*)' does not occur.]

the release of affect and to action enables us also to understand the part played by substitutive ideas in determining the form taken by illness. It is possible for the development of affect to proceed directly from the system *Ucs.*; in that case the affect always has the character of anxiety, for which all 'repressed' affects are exchanged. Often, however, the instinctual impulse has to wait until it has found a substitutive idea in the system *Cs.* The development of affect can then proceed from this conscious substitute, and the nature of that substitute determines the qualitative character of the affect. We have asserted [p. 152] that in repression a severance takes place between the affect and the idea to which it belongs, and that each then undergoes its separate vicissitudes. Descriptively, this is incontrovertible; in actuality, however, the affect does not as a rule arise till the break-through to a new representation in the system *Cs.* has been successfully achieved.

IV. Topography and Dynamics of Repression

We have arrived at the conclusion that repression is essentially a process affecting ideas on the border between the systems *Ucs.* and *Pcs.* (*Cs.*), and we can now make a fresh attempt to describe the process in greater detail.

It must be a matter of a *withdrawal* of cathexis; but the question is, in which system does the withdrawal take place and to which system does the cathexis that is withdrawn belong? The repressed idea remains capable of action in the *Ucs.*, and it must therefore have retained its cathexis. What has been withdrawn must be something else. [Cf. p. 207, below.] Let us take the case of repression proper ('after-pressure') [p. 147], as it affects an idea which is preconscious or even actually conscious. Here repression can only consist in withdrawing from the idea the (pre)conscious cathexis which belongs to the system *Pcs.* The idea then either remains uncathected, or receives cathexis from the *Ucs.*, or retains the *Ucs.* cathexis which it already had. Thus there is a withdrawal of the preconscious cathexis, retention of the unconscious cathexis, or replacement of the preconscious cathexis by an unconscious one. We notice, moreover, that we have based these reflections (as it were, without meaning to) on the assumption that the transition from the system *Ucs.* to the system next to it is not effected through the making of a new registration but through a change in its state, an alteration in its cathexis. The functional hypothesis has here easily defeated the topographical one. [See above, pp. 176–7.]

But this process of withdrawal of libido[1] is not adequate to make another characteristic of repression comprehensible to us. It is not clear why the idea which has remained cathected or has received cathexis from the *Ucs.* should not, in virtue of its cathexis, renew the attempt to penetrate into the system *Pcs.* If it could do so, the withdrawal of libido from it would have to be repeated, and the same performance would go on endlessly;

1. [For the use of 'libido' here see four paragraphs lower down.]

but the outcome would not be repression. So, too, when it comes to describing *primal* repression, the mechanism just discussed of withdrawal of preconscious cathexis would fail to meet the case; for here we are dealing with an unconscious idea which has as yet received *no* cathexis from the *Pcs.* and therefore cannot have that cathexis withdrawn from it.

What we require, therefore, is another process which maintains the repression in the first case [i.e. the case of after-pressure] and, in the second [i.e. that of primal repression], ensures its being established as well as continued. This other process can only be found in the assumption of an *anticathexis*, by means of which the system *Pcs.* protects itself from the pressure upon it of the unconscious idea. We shall see from clinical examples how such an anticathexis, operating in the system *Pcs.*, manifests itself. It is this which represents the permanent expenditure [of energy] of a primal repression, and which also guarantees the permanence of that repression. Anticathexis is the sole mechanism of primal repression; in the case of repression proper ('after-pressure') there is in addition withdrawal of the *Pcs.* cathexis. It is very possible that it is precisely the cathexis which is withdrawn from the idea that is used for anticathexis.

We see how we have gradually been led into adopting a third point of view in our account of psychical phenomena. Besides the dynamic and the topographical points of view [pp. 175–6], we have adopted the *economic* one. This endeavours to follow out the vicissitudes of amounts of excitation and to arrive at least at some *relative* estimate of their magnitude.

It will not be unreasonable to give a special name to this whole way of regarding our subject-matter, for it is the consummation of psychoanalytic research. I propose that when we have succeeded in describing a psychical process in its dynamic, topographical and economic aspects, we should speak of it as a *metapsychological*[1] presentation. We must say at once that in the

1. [Freud had first used this term some twenty years earlier in a letter to Fliess of 13 February 1896. (Freud, 1950*a*, Letter 41.) He had only used it once before in his *published* works: in the *Psychopathology of Everyday Life* (1901*b*), Chapter XII (C), *P.F.L.*, **5**, 321–2.]

present state of our knowledge there are only a few points at which we shall succeed in this.

Let us make a tentative effort to give a metapsychological description of the process of repression in the three transference neuroses which are familiar to us. Here we may replace 'cathexis' by 'libido',[1] because, as we know, it is the vicissitudes of *sexual* instincts with which we shall be dealing.

In anxiety hysteria a first phase of the process is frequently overlooked, and may perhaps be in fact missed out; on careful observation, however, it can be clearly discerned. It consists in anxiety appearing without the subject knowing what he is afraid of. We must suppose that there was present in the *Ucs.* some love-impulse demanding to be transposed into the system *Pcs.*; but the cathexis directed to it from the latter system has drawn back from the impulse (as though in an attempt at flight) and the unconscious libidinal cathexis of the rejected idea has been discharged in the form of anxiety.

On the occasion of a repetition (if there should be one) of this process, a first step is taken in the direction of mastering the unwelcome development of anxiety.[2] The [*Pcs.*] cathexis that has taken flight attaches itself to a substitutive idea which, on the one hand, is connected by association with the rejected idea, and, on the other, has escaped repression by reason of its remoteness from that idea. This substitutive idea – a 'substitute by displacement' [p. 155] – permits the still uninhibitable development of anxiety to be rationalized. It now plays the part of an anticathexis for the system *Cs.* (*Pcs.*),[3] by securing it against an emergence in the *Cs.* of the repressed idea. On the other hand it is, or acts as if it were, the point of departure for the release of the anxiety-affect, which has now really become quite uninhibitable. Clinical observation shows, for instance, that a child suffering from an animal phobia experiences anxiety under two kinds of conditions: in the first place, when his repressed love-

1. [Freud had already done this four paragraphs earlier.]
2. [This is the 'second phase' of the process.]
3. [In the 1915 edition only '(*Pcs.*)' does not occur.]

impulse becomes intensified, and, in the second, when he perceives the animal he is afraid of. The substitutive idea acts in the one instance as a point at which there is a passage across from the system *Ucs.* to the system *Cs.*, and, in the other instance, as a self-sufficing source for the release of anxiety. The extending dominance of the system *Cs.* usually manifests itself in the fact that the first of these two modes of excitation of the substitutive idea gives place more and more to the second. The child may perhaps end by behaving as though he had no predilection whatever towards his father but had become quite free from him, and as though his fear of the animal was a real fear – except that this fear of the animal, fed as such a fear is from an unconscious instinctual source, proves obdurate and exaggerated in the face of all influences brought to bear from the system *Cs.*, and thereby betrays its derivation from the system *Ucs.* – In the second phase of anxiety hysteria, therefore, the anticathexis from the system *Cs.* has led to substitutive-formation.

Soon the same mechanism finds a fresh application. The process of repression, as we know, is not yet completed, and it finds a further aim in the task of inhibiting the development of the anxiety which arises from the substitute.[1] This is achieved by the whole of the associated environment of the substitutive idea being cathected with special intensity, so that it can display a high degree of sensibility to excitation. Excitation of any point in this outer structure must inevitably, on account of its connection with the substitutive idea, give rise to a slight development of anxiety; and this is now used as a signal to inhibit, by means of a fresh flight on the part of the [*Pcs.*] cathexis, the further progress of the development of anxiety.[2] The further away the sensitive and vigilant anticathexes are situated from the feared substitute, the more precisely can the mechanism function

1. [The 'third phase'.]

2. [The notion of a small release of unpleasure acting as a 'signal' to prevent a much larger release is already to be found in Freud's 1895 'Project' (1950*a*, Part II, Section 6) and in *The Interpretation of Dreams* (1900*a*), *P.F.L.*, **4**, 762. The idea is, of course, developed much further in *Inhibitions, Symptoms and Anxiety* (1926*d*), e.g. in Chapter XI, Section A (*b*), ibid., **10**, 320–22.]

which is designed to isolate the substitutive idea and to protect it from fresh excitations. These precautions naturally only guard against excitations which approach the substitutive idea from outside, through perception; they never guard against instinctual excitation, which reaches the substitutive idea from the direction of its link with the repressed idea. Thus the precautions do not begin to operate till the substitute has satisfactorily taken over representation of the repressed, and they can never operate with complete reliability. With each increase of instinctual excitation the protecting rampart round the substitutive idea must be shifted a little further outwards. The whole construction, which is set up in an analogous way in the other neuroses, is termed a *phobia*. The flight from a conscious cathexis of the substitutive idea is manifested in the avoidances, renunciations and prohibitions by which we recognize anxiety hysteria.

Surveying the whole process, we may say that the third phase repeats the work of the second on an ampler scale. The system *Cs.* now protects itself against the activation of the substitutive idea by an anticathexis of its environment, just as previously it had secured itself against the emergence of the repressed idea by a cathexis of the substitutive idea. In this way the formation of substitutes by displacement has been further continued. We must also add that the system *Cs.* had earlier only one small area at which the repressed instinctual impulse could break through, namely, the substitutive idea; but that ultimately this *enclave* of unconscious influence extends to the whole phobic outer structure. Further, we may lay stress on the interesting consideration that by means of the whole defensive mechanism thus set in action a projection outward of the instinctual danger has been achieved. The ego behaves as if the danger of a development of anxiety threatened it not from the direction of an instinctual impulse but from the direction of a perception, and it is thus enabled to react against this external danger with the attempts at flight represented by phobic avoidances. In this process repression is successful in one particular: the release of anxiety can to some extent be dammed up, but only at a heavy sacrifice of personal freedom. Attempts at flight from the demands of instinct are, however, in general useless, and, in spite of everything, the result of phobic flight remains unsatisfactory.

A great deal of what we have found in anxiety hysteria also holds good for the other two neuroses, so that we can confine our discussion to their points of difference and to the part played by anticathexis. In conversion hysteria the instinctual cathexis of the repressed idea is changed into the innervation of the symptom. How far and in what circumstances the unconscious idea is drained empty by this discharge into innervation, so that it can relinquish its pressure upon the system *Cs.* – these and similar questions had better be reserved for a special investigation of hysteria.[1] In conversion hysteria the part played by the anticathexis proceeding from the system *Cs.* (*Pcs.*)[2] is clear and becomes manifest in the formation of the symptom. It is the anticathexis that decides upon what portion of the instinctual representative the whole cathexis of the latter is able to be concentrated. The portion thus selected to be a symptom fulfils the condition of expressing the wishful aim of the instinctual impulse no less than the defensive or punitive efforts of the system *Cs.*; thus it becomes hypercathected, and it is maintained from both directions like the substitutive idea in anxiety hysteria. From this circumstance we may conclude without hesitation that the amount of energy expended by the system *Cs.* on repression need not be so great as the cathectic energy of the symptom; for the strength of the repression is measured by the amount of anticathexis expended, whereas the symptom is supported not only by this anticathexis but also by the instinctual cathexis from the system *Ucs.* which is condensed in the symptom.

As regards obsessional neurosis, we need only add to the observations brought forward in the preceding paper [p. 156 f.] that it is here that the anticathexis from the system *Cs.* comes most noticeably into the foreground. It is this which, organized

1. [Probably a reference to the missing metapsychological paper on conversion hysteria. (See Editor's Introduction, p. 103.) – Freud had already touched on the question in *Studies on Hysteria* (1895*d*), *P.F.L.*, **3**, 237–8.]

2. [In the 1915 edition only, '(*Pcs.*)' does not occur.]

as a reaction-formation, brings about the first repression, and which is later the point at which the repressed idea breaks through. We may venture the supposition that it is because of the predominance of the anticathexis and the absence of discharge that the work of repression seems far less successful in anxiety hysteria and in obsessional neurosis than in conversion hysteria.[1]

1. [The topics in the present section were reconsidered by Freud in *Inhibitions, Symptoms and Anxiety* (1926*d*). See especially *P.F.L.*, **10**, 281 ff., 299 and *n.* 2, and 303–4.]

V. The Special Characteristics of the System *Ucs.*

The distinction we have made between the two psychical systems receives fresh significance when we observe that processes in the one system, the *Ucs.*, show characteristics which are not met with again in the system immediately above it.

The nucleus of the *Ucs.* consists of instinctual representatives which seek to discharge their cathexis; that is to say, it consists of wishful impulses. These instinctual impulses are co-ordinate with one another, exist side by side without being influenced by one another, and are exempt from mutual contradiction. When two wishful impulses whose aims must appear to us incompatible become simultaneously active, the two impulses do not diminish each other or cancel each other out, but combine to form an intermediate aim, a compromise.

There are in this system no negation, no doubt, no degrees of certainty: all this is only introduced by the work of the censorship between the *Ucs.* and the *Pcs.* Negation is a substitute, at a higher level, for repression.[1] In the *Ucs.* there are only contents, cathected with greater or lesser strength.

The cathectic intensities [in the *Ucs.*] are much more mobile. By the process of *displacement* one idea may surrender to another its whole quota of cathexis; by the process of *condensation* it may appropriate the whole cathexis of several other ideas. I have proposed to regard these two processes as distinguishing marks of the so-called *primary psychical process*. In the system *Pcs.* the *secondary process*[2] is dominant. When a primary process is allowed

1. [Cf. the similar statement in 'Formulations on the Two Principles of Mental Functioning' (1911*b*), p. 38 above, and the references given in footnote 2.]

2. Cf. the discussion in Chapter VII of *The Interpretation of Dreams* (1900*a*) [Section E, *P.F.L.*, **4**, 745 ff.], based on ideas developed by Breuer in *Studies on Hysteria* (Breuer and Freud, 1895). [A comment on Freud's attribution of these hypotheses to Breuer will be found in the Editor's Introduction to the latter work (ibid., **3**,44) and in a footnote to the same volume (ibid., 269).]

to take its course in connection with elements belonging to the system *Pcs.*, it appears 'comic' and excites laughter.[1]

The processes of the system *Ucs.* are *timeless*; i.e. they are not ordered temporally, are not altered by the passage of time; they have no reference to time at all. Reference to time is bound up, once again, with the work of the system *Cs.*[2]

The *Ucs.* processes pay just as little regard to *reality*. They are subject to the pleasure principle; their fate depends only on how strong they are and on whether they fulfil the demands of the pleasure-unpleasure regulation.[3]

To sum up: *exemption from mutual contradiction, primary process* (mobility of cathexes), *timelessness*, and *replacement of external by psychical reality* – these are the characteristics which we may expect to find in processes belonging to the system *Ucs.*[4]

1. [Freud had expressed this idea in very similar words in Chapter VII (E) of *The Interpretation of Dreams* (1900*a*), ibid., **4**, 765–6. The point is dealt with more fully in his book on jokes (1905*c*), especially in the second and third Sections of Chapter VII, ibid., **6**, 260 ff.]

2. [In the 1915 edition only, this read '*Pcs.*' – Mentions of the 'timelessness' of the unconscious will be found scattered throughout 'Freud' writings. The earliest is perhaps a sentence dating from 1897 (Freud, 1950*a*, Draft M) in which he declares that 'disregard of the characteristic of time is no doubt an essential distinction between activity in the preconscious and unconscious'. See also a hint in 'The Aetiology of Hysteria' (1896*c*). The point is indirectly alluded to in *The Interpretation of Dreams* (1900*a*), *P.F.L.*, **4**, 733–4, but the first explicit published mention of it seems to have been in a footnote added in 1907 to *The Psychopathology of Everyday Life* (1901*b*), ibid., **5**, 339 *n.* 1. Another passing allusion occurs in a footnote to the paper on narcissism (p. 91 above). Freud returned to the question more than once in his later writings: particularly in *Beyond the Pleasure Principle* (1920*g*), p. 299 below, and in Lecture 31 of the *New Introductory Lectures* (1933*a*), *P.F.L.*, **2**, 106.]

3. [Cf. Section 8 of 'The Two Principles of Mental Functioning' (1911*b*), pp. 42–3 above. 'Reality-testing' is dealt with at some length in the next paper (p. 239 ff. below).]

4. We are reserving for a different context the mention of another notable privilege of the *Ucs.* [Freud clarified this in a letter to Groddeck of 5 June 1917: 'In my essay on the *Ucs.* which you mention you will find an inconspicuous note: "We are reserving for a different context the mention of another notable privilege of the *Ucs.*" I will divulge to you what this note refers to: the assertion that the unconscious act exerts on somatic processes an influence of intense plastic power which the conscious act can never do.' (Freud, 1960*a*.)]

Unconscious processes only become cognizable by us under the conditions of dreaming and of neurosis – that is to say, when processes of the higher, *Pcs.*, system are set back to an earlier stage by being lowered (by regression). In themselves they cannot be cognized, indeed are even incapable of carrying on their existence; for the system *Ucs.* is at a very early moment overlaid by the *Pcs.* which has taken over access to consciousness and to motility. Discharge from the system *Ucs.* passes into somatic innervation that leads to development of affect; but even this path of discharge is, as we have seen [p. 180 f.], contested by the *Pcs.* By itself, the system *Ucs.* would not in normal conditions be able to bring about any expedient muscular acts, with the exception of those already organized as reflexes.

The full significance of the characteristics of the system *Ucs.* described above could only be appreciated by us if we were to contrast and compare them with those of the system *Pcs.* But this would take us so far afield that I propose that we should once more call a halt and not undertake the comparison of the two till we can do so in connection with our discussion of the higher system.[1] Only the most pressing points of all will be mentioned at this stage.

The processes of the system *Pcs.* display – no matter whether they are already conscious or only capable of becoming conscious – an inhibition of the tendency of cathected ideas towards discharge. When a process passes from one idea to another, the first idea retains a part of its cathexis and only a small portion undergoes displacement. Displacements and condensations such as happen in the primary process are excluded or very much restricted. This circumstance caused Breuer to assume the existence of two different states of cathectic energy in mental life: one in which the energy is tonically 'bound' and the other in which it is freely mobile and presses towards discharge.[2] In my opinion this distinction represents the deepest insight we have gained up to the present into the nature of nervous energy, and I do not see how we can avoid making it. A metapsychological

1. [A probable reference to the lost paper on consciousness.].
2. [Cf. footnote 2, on p. 190.]

presentation would most urgently call for further discussion at this point, though perhaps that would be too daring an undertaking as yet.

Further, it devolves upon the system *Pcs.* to make communication possible between the different ideational contents so that they can influence one another, to give them an order in time,[1] and to set up a censorship or several censorships; 'reality-testing' too, and the reality principle, are in its province. Conscious memory, moreover, seems to depend wholly on the *Pcs.*[2] This should be clearly distinguished from the memory-traces in which the experiences of the *Ucs.* are fixed, and probably corresponds to a special registration such as we proposed (but later rejected) to account for the relation of conscious to unconscious ideas [p. 176 ff.]. In this connection, also, we shall find means for putting an end to our oscillations in regard to the naming of the higher system – which we have hitherto spoken of indifferently, sometimes as the *Pcs.* and sometimes as the *Cs.*

Nor will it be out of place here to utter a warning against any over-hasty generalization of what we have brought to light concerning the distribution of the various mental functions between the two systems. We are describing the state of affairs as it appears in the adult human being, in whom the system *Ucs.* operates, strictly speaking, only as a preliminary stage of the higher organization. The question of what the content and connections of that system are during the development of the individual, and of what significance it possesses in animals – these are points on which no conclusion can be deduced from our description: they must be investigated independently.[3] Moreover, in human beings we must be prepared to find possible pathological conditions under which the two systems alter, or even exchange, both their content and their characteristics.

1. [There is a hint at the mechanism by which the *Pcs.* effects this in the penultimate paragraph of Freud's paper on the 'Mystic Writing-Pad' (1925*a*), pp. 433–4 below.]

2. [Cf. above, p. 91 *n.* – In the 1915 edition only, this read '*Cs*'.]

3. [One of the very few remarks made by Freud on the metapsychology of animals will be found at the end of Chapter I of his *Outline of Psycho-Analysis* (1940*a*).]

VI. Communication between the Two Systems

It would nevertheless be wrong to imagine that the *Ucs.* remains at rest while the whole work of the mind is performed by the *Pcs.* – that the *Ucs.* is something finished with, a vestigial organ, a residuum from the process of development. It is wrong also to suppose that communication between the two systems is confined to the act of repression, with the *Pcs.* casting everything that seems disturbing to it into the abyss of the *Ucs.* On the contrary, the *Ucs.* is alive and capable of development and maintains a number of other relations with the *Pcs.*, amongst them that of co-operation. In brief, it must be said that the *Ucs.* is continued into what are known as derivatives,[1] that it is accessible to the impressions of life, that it constantly influences the *Pcs.*, and is even, for its part, subjected to influences from the *Pcs.*

Study of the derivatives of the *Ucs.* will completely disappoint our expectations of a schematically clear-cut distinction between the two psychical systems. This will no doubt give rise to dissatisfaction with our results and will probably be used to cast doubts on the value of the way in which we have divided up the psychical processes. Our answer is, however, that we have no other aim but that of translating into theory the results of observation, and we deny that there is any obligation on us to achieve at our first attempt a well-rounded theory which will commend itself by its simplicity. We shall defend the complications of our theory so long as we find that they meet the results of observation, and we shall not abandon our expectations of being led in the end by those very complications to the discovery of a state of affairs which, while simple in itself, can account for all the complications of reality.

Among the derivatives of the *Ucs.* instinctual impulses, of the sort we have described, there are some which unite in them-

1. [See 'Repression', p. 149.]

selves characters of an opposite kind. On the one hand, they are highly organized, free from self-contradiction, have made use of every acquisition of the system *Cs.* and would hardly be distinguished in our judgement from the formations of that system. On the other hand they are unconscious and are incapable of becoming conscious. Thus *qualitatively* they belong to the system *Pcs.*, but *factually* to the *Ucs.* Their origin is what decides their fate. We may compare them with individuals of mixed race who, taken all round, resemble white men, but who betray their coloured descent by some striking feature or other, and on that account are excluded from society and enjoy none of the privileges of white people. Of such a nature are those phantasies of normal people as well as of neurotics which we have recognized as preliminary stages in the formation both of dreams and of symptoms and which, in spite of their high degree of organization, remain repressed and therefore cannot become conscious.[1] They draw near to consciousness and remain undisturbed so long as they do not have an intense cathexis, but as soon as they exceed a certain height of cathexis they are thrust back. Substitutive formations, too, are highly organized derivatives of the *Ucs.* of this kind; but these succeed in breaking through into consciousness, when circumstances are favourable – for example, if they happen to join forces with an anticathexis from the *Pcs.*

When, elsewhere,[2] we come to examine more closely the preconditions for becoming conscious, we shall be able to find a solution of some of the difficulties that arise at this juncture. Here it seems a good plan to look at things from the angle of consciousness, in contrast to our previous approach, which was upwards from the *Ucs.* To consciousness the whole sum of psychical processes presents itself as the realm of the preconscious. A very great part of this preconscious originates in the unconscious, has the character of its derivatives and is subjected to a censorship before it can become conscious. Another part of

1. [This question is elaborated in a footnote added in 1920 to Section 5 of the third of Freud's *Three Essays* (1905*d*), *P.F.L.*, **7**, 149 *n.* 1.]

2. [Another probable reference to the lost paper on consciousness.]

the *Pcs.* is capable of becoming conscious without any censorship. Here we come upon a contradiction of an earlier assumption. In discussing the subject of repression we were obliged to place the censorship which is decisive for becoming conscious between the systems *Ucs.* and *Pcs.* [p. 175]. Now it becomes probable that there is a censorship between the *Pcs.* and the *Cs.*[1] Nevertheless we shall do well not to regard this complication as a difficulty, but to assume that to every transition from one system to that immediately above it (that is, every advance to a higher stage of psychical organization) there corresponds a new censorship. This, it may be remarked, does away with the assumption of a continuous laying down of new registrations [p. 176].

The reason for all these difficulties is to be found in the circumstance that the attribute of being conscious, which is the only characteristic of psychical processes that is directly presented to us, is in no way suited to serve as a criterion for the differentiation of systems. [Cf. p. 174 above.] Apart from the fact that the conscious is not always conscious but also at times latent, observation has shown that much that shares the characteristics of the system *Pcs.* does not become conscious; and we learn in addition that the act of becoming conscious is dependent on the attention of the *Pcs.* being turned in certain directions.[2]

1. [See p. 175. The point had already been raised by Freud in Chapter VII (F) of *The Interpretation of Dreams* (1900*a*), *P.F.L.*, **4**, 775–6 and 779. It is discussed at greater length below, pp. 197–8.]

2. [Literally: 'we learn in addition that becoming conscious is restricted by certain directions of its attention.' The 'its' almost certainly refers to the *Pcs.* This rather obscure sentence would probably be clearer if we possessed the lost paper on consciousness. The gap here is particularly tantalizing, as it seems likely that the reference is to a discussion of the function of 'attention' – a subject on which Freud's later writings throw very little light. There are two or three passages in *The Interpretation of Dreams* (1900*a*) which seem relevant in this connection: 'The excitatory processes occurring in [the preconscious] can enter consciousness without further impediment provided that certain other conditions are fulfilled: for instance . . . that the function which can only be described as "attention" is distributed in a particular way' (*P.F.L.*, **4**, 690). 'Becoming conscious is connected with the application of a particular psychical function, that of attention' (ibid., 751). 'The system *Pcs.* not merely bars access to consciousness, it also

Hence consciousness stands in no simple relation either to the different systems or to repression. The truth is that it is not only the psychically repressed that remains alien to consciousness, but also some of the impulses which dominate our ego – something, therefore, that forms the strongest functional antithesis to the repressed. The more we seek to win our way to a metapsychological view of mental life, the more we must learn to emancipate ourselves from the importance of the symptom of 'being conscious'.[1]

So long as we still cling to this belief we see our generalizations regularly broken through by exceptions. On the one hand we find that derivatives of the *Ucs.*[2] become conscious as substitutive formations and symptoms – generally, it is true, after having undergone great distortion as compared with the unconscious, though often retaining many characteristics which call for repression. On the other hand, we find that many preconscious formations remain unconscious, though we should have expected that, from their nature, they might very well have become conscious. Probably in the latter case the stronger attraction of the *Ucs.* is asserting itself. We are led to look for the more important distinction as lying, not between the conscious and the preconscious, but between the preconscious and the unconscious. The *Ucs.* is turned back on the frontier of the

. . . has at its disposal for distribution a mobile cathectic energy, a part of which is familiar to us in the form of attention' (ibid., 776). In contrast to the paucity of allusions to the subject in Freud's later writings, the 'Project' of 1895 treats of attention at great length and regards it as one of the principal forces at work in the mental apparatus (Freud, 1950*a*, especially Section 1 of Part III). He there (as well as in his paper on 'The Two Principles of Mental Functioning', 1911*b*, see p. 39 above) relates it in particular to the function of 'reality-testing'. See the Editor's Note to 'A Metapsychological Supplement to the Theory of Dreams' (below, p. 226), where the relation of attention to the system *Pcpt.* is considered.]

1. [The complication discussed in this paragraph was reinforced by Freud at the end of Chapter I of *The Ego and the Id* (1923*b*), p. 356 below, and in the following chapter he propounded his new structural picture of the mind, which so greatly simplified his whole description of its workings.]

2. [All the German editions read '*Vbw*' (*Pcs.*). It seems probable that this is a misprint for '*Ubw*' (*Ucs.*). This is confirmed by an inspection of the MS.]

Pcs. by the censorship, but derivatives of the *Ucs.* can circumvent this censorship, achieve a high degree of organization and reach a certain intensity of cathexis in the *Pcs.* When, however, this intensity is exceeded and they try to force themselves into consciousness, they are recognized as derivatives of the *Ucs.* and are repressed afresh at the new frontier of censorship, between the *Pcs.* and the *Cs.* Thus the first of these censorships is exercised against the *Ucs.* itself, and the second against its *Pcs.* derivatives. One might suppose that in the course of individual development the censorship had taken a step forward.

In psychoanalytic treatment the existence of the second censorship, located between the systems *Pcs.* and *Cs.*, is proved beyond question. We require the patient to form numerous derivatives of the *Ucs.*, we make him pledge himself to overcome the objections of the censorship to these preconscious formations becoming conscious, and by overthrowing *this* censorship, we open up the way to abrogating the repression accomplished by the *earlier* one. To this let us add that the existence of the censorship between the *Pcs.* and the *Cs.* teaches us that becoming conscious is no mere act of perception, but is probably also a *hypercathexis* [cf. below, p. 207], a further advance in the psychical organization.

Let us turn to the communications between the *Ucs.* and the other systems, less in order to establish anything new than in order to avoid omitting what is most prominent. At the roots of instinctual activity the systems communicate with one another most extensively. One portion of the processes which are there excited passes through the *Ucs.*, as through a preparatory stage, and reaches the highest psychical development in the *Cs.*; another portion is retained as *Ucs.* But the *Ucs.* is also affected by experiences originating from external perception. Normally all the paths from perception to the *Ucs.* remain open, and only those leading on from the *Ucs.* are subject to blocking by repression.

It is a very remarkable thing that the *Ucs.* of one human being can react upon that of another, without passing through the *Cs.* This deserves closer investigation, especially with a view to finding out whether preconscious activity can be excluded as playing a part in it; but, descriptively speaking, the fact is incontestable.[1]

The content of the system *Pcs.* (or *Cs.*) is derived partly from instinctual life (through the medium of the *Ucs.*), and partly from perception. It is doubtful how far the processes of this system can exert a direct influence on the *Ucs.*; examination of pathological cases often reveals an almost incredible independence and lack of susceptibility to influence on the part of the *Ucs.* A complete divergence of their trends; a total severance of the two systems, is what above all characterizes a condition of illness. Nevertheless, psychoanalytic treatment is based upon an influencing of the *Ucs.* from the direction of the *Cs.*, and at any rate shows that this, though a laborious task, is not impossible. The derivatives of the *Ucs.* which act as intermediaries between the two systems open the way, as we have already said [p. 198], towards accomplishing this. But we may safely assume that a spontaneously effected alteration in the *Ucs.* from the direction of the *Cs.* is a difficult and slow process.

Co-operation between a preconscious and an unconscious impulse, even when the latter is intensely repressed, may come about if there is a situation in which the unconscious impulse can act in the same sense as one of the dominant trends. The repression is removed in this instance, and the repressed activity is admitted as a reinforcement of the one intended by the ego. The unconscious becomes ego-syntonic in respect of this single conjunction without any change taking place in its repression apart from this. In this co-operation the influence of the *Ucs.* is unmistakable: the reinforced tendencies reveal themselves as being nevertheless different from the normal; they make specially perfect functioning possible, and they manifest a resistance in the face of opposition which is similar to that offered, for instance, by obsessional symptoms.

The content of the *Ucs.* may be compared with an aboriginal population in the mind. If inherited mental formations exist in

1. [Cf. an example of this in Freud (1913*i*), *P.F.L.*, **10**, 136–8.]

the human being – something analogous to instinct[1] in animals – these constitute the nucleus of the *Ucs.* Later there is added to them what is discarded during childhood development as unserviceable; and this need not differ in its nature from what is inherited. A sharp and final division between the content of the two systems does not, as a rule, take place till puberty.

1. [The German word here is '*Instinkt*', not the usual '*Trieb*'. (See Editor's Note to 'Instincts and their Vicissitudes', p. 107 above.) – The question of the inheritance of mental formations was to be discussed by Freud soon afterwards in Lecture 23 of his *Introductory Lectures* (1916–17), *P.F.L.*, **1**, 407–9, and in his 'Wolf Man' case history (1918*b*), *P.F.L.*, **9**, 337.]

VII. Assessment of the Unconscious

What we have put together in the preceding discussions is probably as much as we can say about the *Ucs.* so long as we only draw upon our knowledge of dream-life and the transference neuroses. It is certainly not much, and at some points it gives an impression of obscurity and confusion; and above all it offers us no possibility of co-ordinating or subsuming the *Ucs.* into any context with which we are already familiar. It is only the analysis of one of the affections which we call narcissistic psychoneuroses that promises to furnish us with conceptions through which the enigmatic *Ucs.* will be brought more within our reach and, as it were, made tangible.

Since the publication of a work by Abraham (1908) – which that conscientious author has attributed to my instigation – we have tried to base our characterization of Kraepelin's 'dementia praecox' (Bleuler's 'schizophrenia') on its position with reference to the antithesis between ego and object. In the transference neuroses (anxiety hysteria, conversion hysteria and obsessional neurosis) there was nothing to give special prominence to this antithesis. We knew, indeed, that frustration in regard to the object brings on the outbreak of the neurosis and that the neurosis involves a renunciation of the real object; we knew too that the libido that is withdrawn from the real object reverts first to a phantasied object and then to one that had been repressed (introversion).[1] But in these disorders object-cathexis in general is retained with great energy, and more detailed examination of the process of repression has obliged us to assume that object-cathexis persists in the system *Ucs.* in spite of – or rather in consequence of – repression. [Cf. p. 148.] Indeed, the capacity for transference, of which we make use for therapeutic purposes in these affections, presupposes an unimpaired object-cathexis.

1. [The process is described in detail in Section (*a*) of Freud's paper on 'Types of Onset of Neurosis' (1912*c*), *P.F.L.*, **10**, 119–21.]

In the case of schizophrenia, on the other hand, we have been driven to the assumption that after the process of repression the libido that has been withdrawn does not seek a new object, but retreats into the ego; that is to say, that here the object-cathexes are given up and a primitive objectless condition of narcissism is re-established. The incapacity of these patients for transference (so far as the pathological process extends), their consequent inaccessibility to therapeutic efforts, their characteristic repudiation of the external world, the appearance of signs of a hypercathexis of their own ego, the final outcome in complete apathy – all these clinical features seem to agree excellently with the assumption that their object-cathexes have been given up. As regards the relation of the two psychical systems to each other, all observers have been struck by the fact that in schizophrenia a great deal is expressed as being conscious which in the transference neuroses can only be shown to be present in the *Ucs.* by psychoanalysis. But to begin with we were not able to establish any intelligible connection between the ego-object relation and the relationships of consciousness.

What we are seeking seems to present itself in the following unexpected way. In schizophrenics we observe – especially in the initial stages, which are so instructive – a number of changes in *speech*, some of which deserve to be regarded from a particular point of view. The patient often devotes peculiar care to his way of expressing himself, which becomes 'stilted' and 'precious'. The construction of his sentences undergoes a peculiar disorganization, making them so incomprehensible to us that his remarks seem nonsensical. Some reference to bodily organs or innervations is often given prominence in the content of these remarks. To this may be added the fact that in such symptoms of schizophrenia as are comparable with the substitutive formations of hysteria or obsessional neurosis, the relation between the substitute and the repressed material nevertheless displays peculiarities which would surprise us in these two forms of neurosis.

Dr Victor Tausk of Vienna has placed at my disposal some observations that he has made in the initial stages of schizophrenia in a female patient, which are particularly valuable in that the patient was ready to explain her utterances herself.[1] I will take two of his examples to illustrate the view I wish to put forward, and I have no doubt that every observer could easily produce plenty of such material.

A patient of Tausk's, a girl who was brought to the clinic after a quarrel with her lover, complained that *her eyes were not right, they were twisted*. This she herself explained by bringing forward a series of reproaches against her lover in coherent language. 'She could not understand him at all, he looked different every time; he was a hypocrite, an eye-twister,[2] he had twisted her eyes; now she had twisted eyes; they were not her eyes any more; now she saw the world with different eyes.'

The patient's comments on her unintelligible remark have the value of an analysis, for they contain the equivalent of the remark expressed in a generally comprehensible form. They throw light at the same time on the meaning and the genesis of schizophrenic word-formation. I agree with Tausk in stressing in this example the point that the patient's relation to a bodily organ (the eye) has arrogated to itself the representation of the whole content [of her thoughts]. Here the schizophrenic utterance exhibits a hypochondriac trait: it has become '*organ-speech*'.[3]

A second communication by the same patient was as follows: 'She was standing in church. Suddenly she felt a jerk; she had to *change her position, as though somebody was putting her into a position, as though she was being put in a certain position.*'

Now came the analysis of this through a fresh series of reproaches against her lover. 'He was common, he had made her common, too, though she was naturally refined. He had made her like himself by making her think that he was superior to her; now she had become like him, because she thought she would be better if she were like him. He had *given a false*

1. [A paper referring to the same patient was later published by Tausk (1919).]
2. [The German '*Augenverdreher*' has the figurative meaning of 'deceiver'.]
3. [Cf. Freud's discussion of hypochondria in his paper on narcissism (1914*c*), above, p. 76 ff.]

impression of his position; now she was just like him' (by identification), 'he had *put her in a false position*'.

The physical movement of 'changing her position', Tausk remarks, depicted the words 'putting her in a false position' and her identification with her lover. I would call attention once more to the fact that the whole train of thought is dominated by the element which has for its content a bodily innervation (or, rather, the sensation of it). Furthermore, a hysterical woman would, in the first example, have *in fact* convulsively twisted her eyes, and, in the second, have given actual jerks, instead of having the *impulse* to do so or the *sensation* of doing so: and in neither example would she have any accompanying conscious thoughts, nor would she have been able to express any such thoughts afterwards.

These two observations, then, argue in favour of what we have called hypochondriacal speech or 'organ-speech'. But, what seems to us more important, they also point to something else, of which we have innumerable instances (for example, in the cases collected in Bleuler's monograph [1911]) and which may be reduced to a definite formula. In schizophrenia *words* are subjected to the same process as that which makes the dream-images out of latent dream-thoughts – to what we have called the *primary psychical process*. They undergo condensation, and by means of displacement transfer their cathexes to one another in their entirety. The process may go so far that a single word, if it is specially suitable on account of its numerous connections, takes over the representation of a whole train of thought.[1] The works of Bleuler, Jung and their pupils offer a quantity of material which particularly supports this assertion.[2]

Before we draw any conclusion from impressions such as these, let us consider further the distinctions between the for-

1. [*The Interpretation of Dreams* (1900*a*) Chapter VII (E), *P.F.L.*, **4**, 753–5.]

2. The dream-work, too, occasionally treats words like things, and so creates very similar 'schizophrenic' utterances or neologisms. [See *The Interpretation of Dreams* (1900*a*), Chapter VI (A), ibid., **4**, 403 ff. A distinction between what happens in dreams and in schizophrenia is drawn, however, in 'A Metapsychological Supplement to the Theory of Dreams', pp. 236–7 below.]

mation of substitutes in schizophrenia on the one hand, and in hysteria and obsessional neurosis on the other – subtle distinctions which nevertheless make a strange impression. A patient whom I have at present under observation has allowed himself to be withdrawn from all the interests of life on account of a bad condition of the skin of his face. He declares that he has blackheads and deep holes in his face which everyone notices. Analysis shows that he is playing out his castration complex upon his skin. At first he worked at these blackheads remorselessly; and it gave him great satisfaction to squeeze them out, because, as he said, something spurted out when he did so. Then he began to think that a deep cavity appeared wherever he had got rid of a blackhead, and he reproached himself most vehemently with having ruined his skin for ever by 'constantly fiddling about with his hand'. Pressing out the content of the blackheads is clearly to him a substitute for masturbation. The cavity which then appears owing to his fault is the female genital, i.e. the fulfilment of the threat of castration (or the phantasy representing that threat) provoked by his masturbating. This substitutive formation has, in spite of its hypochondriacal character, considerable resemblance to a hysterical conversion; and yet we have a feeling that something different must be going on here, that a substitutive formation such as this cannot be attributed to hysteria, even before we can say in what the difference consists. A tiny little cavity such as a pore of the skin would hardly be used by a hysteric as a symbol for the vagina, which he is otherwise ready to compare with every imaginable object that encloses a hollow space. Besides, we should expect the multiplicity of these little cavities to prevent him from using them as a substitute for the female genital. The same applies to the case of a young patient reported by Tausk some years ago to the Vienna Psycho-Analytical Society. This patient behaved in other respects exactly as though he were suffering from an obsessional neurosis; he took hours to wash and dress, and so on. It was noticeable, however, that he was able to give the meaning of his inhibitions without any resistance. In putting on his stockings, for instance, he was disturbed by the idea that he must pull apart the stitches in the knitting, i.e. the holes, and to him every hole was a symbol of the female genital aperture. This again is a thing which we cannot attribute to an obsessional neurotic. Reitler (1913) observed a patient of the latter sort, who also suffered from having to take a long time over putting on his stockings; this man, after overcoming his resistances, found as the explanation that his foot symbolized a penis, that putting on the stocking stood for a masturbatory act, and that he had to keep on pulling the stocking on and off, partly in order to complete the picture of masturbation, and partly in order to undo that act.

If we ask ourselves what it is that gives the character of strangeness to the substitutive formation and the symptom in schizophrenia, we eventually come to realize that it is the predominance of what has to do with words over what has to do with things. As far as the thing goes, there is only a very slight similarity between squeezing out a blackhead and an emission from the penis, and still less similarity between the innumerable shallow pores of the skin and the vagina; but in the former case there is, in both instances, a 'spurting out', while in the latter the cynical saying, 'a hole is a hole', is true verbally. What has dictated the substitution is not the resemblance between the things denoted but the sameness of the words used to express them. Where the two – word and thing – do not coincide, the formation of substitutes in schizophrenia deviates from that in the transference neuroses.

If now we put this finding alongside the hypothesis that in schizophrenia object-cathexes are given up, we shall be obliged to modify the hypothesis by adding that the cathexis of the *word*-presentations of objects is retained. What we have permissibly called the conscious presentation[1] of the object can now be split

1. ['*Vorstellung*.' This word has as a rule been translated above by 'idea'. (See above, p. 176 *n.* 2.) From this point till the end of the paper, '*Vorstellung*' is uniformly translated by 'presentation', as are the cognate terms 'word-presentation' and 'thing-presentation'. For other references to these terms, cf. 'Mourning and Melancholia' (1917*e*), p. 265 below, Chapter VI (A) of *The Interpretation of Dreams* (1900*a*), *P.F.L.*, **4**, 403, and Chapter IV of the book on jokes

up into the presentation of the *word* and the presentation of the *thing*; the latter consists in the cathexis, if not of the direct memory-images of the thing, at least of remoter memory-traces derived from these. We now seem to know all at once what the difference is between a conscious and an unconscious presentation [see p. 178]. The two are not, as we supposed, different registrations of the same content in different psychical localities, nor yet different functional states of cathexis in the same locality; but the conscious presentation comprises the presentation of the thing plus the presentation of the word belonging to it, while the unconscious presentation is the presentation of the thing alone. The system *Ucs.* contains the thing-cathexes of the objects, the first and true object-cathexes; the system *Pcs.* comes about by this thing-presentation being hypercathected through being linked with the word-presentations corresponding to it. It is these hypercathexes, we may suppose, that bring about a higher psychical organization and make it possible for the primary process to be succeeded by the secondary process which is dominant in the *Pcs.* Now, too, we are in a position to state precisely what it is that repression denies to the rejected presentation in the transference neuroses [p. 183]: what it denies to the presentation is translation into words which shall remain attached to the object. A presentation which is not put into words, or a psychical act which is not hypercathected, remains thereafter in the *Ucs.* in a state of repression.

I should like to point out at what an early date we already possessed the insight which to-day enables us to understand one of the most striking characteristics of schizophrenia. In the last few pages of *The Interpretation of Dreams*, which was published in 1900, the view was developed that thought-processes, i.e. those acts of cathexis which are comparatively remote from perception, are in themselves without quality and unconscious, and

(1905*c*), ibid., 6, 167–8. – The distinction between 'word-presentations' and 'thing-presentations' no doubt derives from Freud's studies on the aphasias, and the matter was discussed at some length in his monograph on the subject (1891*b*), though in somewhat different terminology. The relevant passage in that work has been translated below in Appendix C (p. 216).]

that they attain their capacity to become conscious only through being linked with the residues of perceptions of *words*.[1] But word-presentations, for their part too, are derived from sense-perceptions, in the same way as thing-presentations are; the question might therefore be raised why presentations of objects cannot become conscious through the medium of their *own* perceptual residues. Probably, however, thought proceeds in systems so far remote from the original perceptual residues that they have no longer retained anything of the qualities of those residues, and, in order to become conscious, need to be reinforced by new qualities. Moreover, by being linked with words, cathexes can be provided with quality even when they represent only *relations* between presentations of objects and are thus unable to derive any quality from perceptions. Such relations, which become comprehensible only through words, form a major part of our thought-processes. As we can see, being linked with word-presentations is not yet the same thing as becoming conscious, but only makes it possible to become so; it is therefore characteristic of the system *Pcs.* and of that system alone.[2] With these discussions, however, we have evidently departed from our subject proper and find ourselves plunged into problems concerning the preconscious and the conscious, which for good reasons we are reserving for separate treatment.[3]

As regards schizophrenia, which we only touch on here so far as seems indispensable for a general understanding of the *Ucs.*, a doubt must occur to us whether the process here termed repression has anything at all in common with the repression which takes place in the transference neuroses. The formula that repression is a process which occurs between the systems *Ucs.*

1. [*The Interpretation of Dreams* (1900*a*), *P.F.L.*, **4**, 778–9. See also ibid., 729–30. This hypothesis had in fact been put forward (though not published) by Freud even earlier, in his 'Project' of 1895 (1950*a*, towards the beginning of Section 1 of Part III). It had also been mentioned by him more recently, in his paper on 'The Two Principles of Mental Functioning' (1911*b*), see p. 39 above.]

2. [Freud took up this subject again at the beginning of Chapter II of *The Ego and the Id* (1923*b*), see p. 358 below.]

3. [This seems likely to be another reference to the unpublished paper on consciousness. See, however, below, p. 240.]

and *Pcs.* (or *Cs.*), and results in keeping something at a distance from consciousness [p. 147], must in any event be modified, in order that it may also be able to include the case of dementia praecox and other narcissistic affections. But the ego's attempt at flight, which expresses itself in the withdrawal of the conscious cathexis, nevertheless remains a factor common [to the two classes of neurosis]. The most superficial reflection shows us how much more radically and profoundly this attempt at flight, this flight of the ego, is put into operation in the narcissistic neuroses.

If, in schizophrenia, this flight consists in withdrawal of instinctual cathexis from the points which represent the *unconscious* presentation of the object, it may seem strange that the part of the presentation of this object which belongs to the system *Pcs.* – namely, the word-presentations corresponding to it – should, on the contrary, receive a more intense cathexis. We might rather expect that the word-presentation, being the preconscious part, would have to sustain the first impact of repression and that it would be totally uncathectable after repression had proceeded as far as the unconscious thing-presentations. This, it is true, is difficult to understand. It turns out that the cathexis of the word-presentation is not part of the act of repression, but represents the first of the attempts at recovery or cure which so conspicuously dominate the clinical picture of schizophrenia.[1] These endeavours are directed towards regaining the lost object, and it may well be that to achieve this purpose they set off on a path that leads to the object *via* the verbal part of it, but then find themselves obliged to be content with words instead of things. It is a general truth that our mental activity moves in two opposite directions: either it starts from the instincts and passes through the system *Ucs.* to conscious thought-activity; or, beginning with an instigation from outside, it passes through the system *Cs.* and *Pcs.* till it reaches the *Ucs.* cathexes of the ego and objects. This second path must, in spite of the repression which has taken place, remain traversable,

1. [See Part III of Freud's Schreber analysis (1911*c*), *P.F.L.*, **9**, 209–10 and 216. – A further schizophrenic attempt at recovery is mentioned below, p. 238.]

and it lies open to some extent to the endeavours made by the neurosis to regain its objects. When we think in abstractions there is a danger that we may neglect the relations of words to unconscious thing-presentations, and it must be confessed that the expression and content of our philosophizing then begins to acquire an unwelcome resemblance to the mode of operation of schizophrenics.[1] We may, on the other hand, attempt a characterization of the schizophrenic's mode of thought by saying that he treats concrete things as though they were abstract.

If we have made a true assessment of the nature of the *Ucs.* and have correctly defined the difference between an unconscious and a preconscious presentation, then our researches will inevitably bring us back from many other points to this same piece of insight.

1. [Freud had already made this point at the end of the second essay in *Totem and Taboo* (1912–13), *P.F.L.*, **13**, 130.]

APPENDIX A

FREUD AND EWALD HERING

AMONG Freud's seniors in Vienna was the physiologist Ewald Hering (1834–1918), who, as we learn from Dr Jones (1953, 244), offered the young man a post as his assistant at Prague; this was probably while Freud was still working at Brücke's Physiological Institute, most likely in 1882; Hering went to Prague as Professor Ordinarius in 1870. An episode some forty years later seems to suggest, as Ernst Kris (1956) pointed out, that Hering's influence may have contributed to Freud's views on the unconscious. (Cf. above, p. 162.)[1] In 1880 Samuel Butler published his *Unconscious Memory*. This included a translation of a lecture delivered by Hering in 1870, 'Über das Gedächtnis als eine allgemeine Funktion der organisierten Materie' ('On Memory as a Universal Function of Organized Matter'), with which Butler found himself in general agreement. A book with the title *The Unconscious*, by Israel Levine, was published in England in 1923; and a German translation of it by Anna Freud appeared in 1926. One section of it, however (Part I, Section 13), which deals with Samuel Butler, was translated by Freud himself. The author, Levine, though he mentioned Hering's lecture, was more concerned with Butler than with Hering, and in that connection (on page 34 of the German translation) Freud added a footnote as follows:–

'German readers, familiar with this lecture of Hering's and regarding it as a masterpiece, would not, of course, be inclined to bring into the foreground the considerations based on it by Butler. Moreover, some pertinent remarks are to be found in

1. [In *Beyond the Pleasure Principle* (1920*g*), another reference to Ewald Hering suggests that his ideas may also have contributed to Freud's theory of the dualistic classification of the instincts. See below, p. 322.]

Hering which allow psychology the right to assume the existence of unconscious mental activity: "Who could hope to disentangle the fabric of our inner life with its thousandfold complexities, if we were willing to pursue its threads only so far as they traverse consciousness? . . . Chains such as these of unconscious material nerve-processes, which end in a link accompanied by a conscious perception, have been described as 'unconscious trains of ideas' and 'unconscious inferences'; and from the standpoint of psychology this can be justified. For the mind would often slip through the fingers of psychology, if psychology refused to keep a hold on the mind's unconscious states." [Hering, 1870, 11 and 13.]'

APPENDIX B

PSYCHO-PHYSICAL PARALLELISM

[It has been pointed out above (p. 163) that Freud's earlier views on the relation between the mind and the nervous system were greatly influenced by Hughlings Jackson. This is particularly shown by the following passage extracted from his monograph on aphasia (1891*b*, 56–8). It is especially instructive to compare the last sentences on the subject of latent memories with Freud's later position. In order to preserve a uniform terminology, a new translation has been made.]

After this digression we return to the consideration of aphasia. We may recall that on the basis of Meynert's teachings the theory has grown up that the speech apparatus consists of distinct cortical centres in whose cells the word-presentations are contained, these centres being separated by a functionless cortical region, and linked together by white fibres (associative fasciculi). The question may at once be raised whether a hypothesis of this kind, which encloses presentations in nerve cells, can possibly be correct and permissible. I think not.

The tendency of earlier periods in medicine was to localize whole mental faculties, as they are defined by psychological nomenclature, in certain regions of the brain. By contrast, therefore, it was bound to seem a great advance when Wernicke declared that only the simplest psychical elements, the different sensory presentations, could legitimately be localized – localized at the central termination of the peripheral nerve which has received the impression. But shall we not be making the same mistake in principle, whether what we are trying to localize is a complicated concept, a whole mental activity, or a psychical element? Is it justifiable to take a nerve fibre, which for the whole length of its course has been a purely physiological structure and has been subject to purely physiological modifications, and to plunge its end into the sphere of the mind and to fit this end out with a presentation or a mnemic image? If 'will', 'intelligence', and so on, are recognized as being psychological technical terms to which very complicated states of affairs correspond in the physiological world, can we feel any more sure that a 'simple sensory presentation' is anything other than a technical term of the same kind?

It is probable that the chain of physiological events in the nervous system does not stand in a causal connection with the psychical events. The physiological events do not cease as soon as the psychical ones begin; on the contrary, the physiological chain continues. What happens is simply that, after a certain point of time, each (or some) of its links has a psychical phenomenon corresponding to it. Accordingly, the psychical is a process parallel to the physiological – 'a dependent concomitant'.[1]

I know quite well that I cannot accuse the people whose views I am here disputing of having executed this jump and change in their scientific angle of approach [i.e. from the physiological to the psychological] without consideration. They obviously mean nothing else than that the physiological modification of the nerve fibres which accompanies sensory excitation produces another modification in the central nerve cell, and that this latter modification becomes the physiological correlate of the 'presentation'. Since they can say a great deal more about presentations than about the modifications, of which no physiological characterization whatever has yet been reached and which are unknown, they make use of the elliptical statement that the presentation is localized in the nerve cell. This way of putting matters, however, at once leads to a confusion between the two things, which need have no resemblance to each other. In psychology a simple presentation is something elementary for us, which we can sharply distinguish from its connections with other presentations. This leads us to suppose that the physio-

1. [In English in the original. The phrase is from Hughlings Jackson.]

logical correlate of the presentation – i.e. the modification that originates from the excited nerve fibre with its termination at the centre – is something simple too, which can be localized at a particular point. To draw a parallel of this kind is of course entirely unjustifiable; the characteristics of the modification must be established on their own account and independently of their psychological counterpart.[1]

What, then, is the physiological correlate of a simple presentation or of the same presentation when it recurs? Clearly nothing static, but something in the nature of a process. This process admits of localization. It starts from a particular point in the cortex and spreads from there over the whole cortex or along certain tracts. When this process is completed, it leaves a modification behind in the cortex that has been affected by it – the possibility of remembering. It is highly doubtful whether there is anything psychical that corresponds to this modification either. Our consciousness shows nothing of a sort to justify, from the psychical point of view, the name of a 'latent mnemic image'. But whenever the same state of the cortex is provoked again, the psychical aspect comes into being once more as a mnemic image

1. Hughlings Jackson has given the most emphatic warning against confusions of this kind between the physical and the psychical in the process of speech: 'In all our studies of diseases of the nervous system we must be on our guard against the fallacy that what are physical states in lower centres fine away into psychical states in higher centres; that, for example, vibrations of sensory nerves become sensations, or that somehow or another an idea produces a movement.' (1878, 306.)

APPENDIX C

WORDS AND THINGS

[The final section of Freud's paper on 'The Unconscious' seems to have roots in his early monograph on aphasia (1891*b*). It may be of interest, therefore, to reproduce here a passage from that work which, though not particularly easy to follow in itself, nevertheless throws light on the assumptions that underlay some of Freud's later views. The passage has the further incidental interest of presenting Freud in the very unusual position of talking in the technical language of the 'academic' psychology of the later nineteenth century. The passage here quoted follows after a train of destructive and constructive anatomical and physiological argument which has led Freud to a hypothetical scheme of neurological functioning which he describes as the 'speech apparatus'. It must be noted, however, that there is an important and perhaps confusing difference between the terminology Freud uses here and in 'The Unconscious'. What he here calls the 'object-presentation' is what in 'The Unconscious' he calls the 'thing-presentation'; while what in 'The Unconscious' he calls the 'object-presentation' denotes a complex made up of the combined 'thing-presentation' and 'word-presentation' – a complex which has no name given to it in the *Aphasia* passage. The translation has been made specially for this occasion, since, for terminological reasons, the published one was not entirely adapted to the present purpose. As in the last section of 'The Unconscious', we have here always used the word 'presentation' to render the German '*Vorstellung*', while 'image' stands for the German '*Bild*'. The passage runs from p. 74 to p. 81 of the original German edition.]

I now propose to consider what hypotheses are required to

explain disturbances of speech on the basis of a speech apparatus constructed in this manner – in other words, what the study of disturbance of speech teaches us about the function of this apparatus. In doing so I shall keep the psychological and anatomical sides of the question as separate as possible.

From the point of view of psychology the unit of the function of speech is the 'word', a complex presentation, which proves to be a combination put together from auditory, visual and kinaesthetic elements. We owe our knowledge of this combination to pathology, which shows us that in organic lesions of the apparatus of speech a disintegration of speech takes place along the lines on which the combination is put together. We shall thus expect to find that the absence of one of these elements of the word-presentation will prove to be the most important indication for enabling us to arrive at a localization of the disease. Four components of the word-presentation are usually distinguished: the 'sound-image', the 'visual letter-image', the 'motor speech-image' and the 'motor writing-image'. This combination, however, turns out to be more complicated when one enters into the probable process of association that takes place in each of the various activities of speech:–

(1) We learn to *speak* by associating a 'sound-image of a word' with a 'sense of the innervation of a word'.[1] After we have spoken, we are also in possession of a 'motor speech-presentation' (centripetal sensations from the organs of speech); so that, in a motor respect, the 'word' is doubly determined for us. Of the two determining elements the first – the innervatory word-presentation – seems to have the least value from a psychological point of view; indeed its appearance at all as a psychical factor may be disputed. In addition to this, after speaking, we receive a 'sound-image' of the spoken word. So long as we have

1. ['It was once supposed that actively initiated movements involved a peculiar sort of sensation connected directly with the discharge of nervous impulses from the motor areas of the brain to the muscles . . . The existence of this "innervation-sense", or sense of energy put forth, is now generally denied.' Stout (1938, 258). This last remark is confirmed by Freud a few lines lower down.]

not developed our power of speech very far, this second sound-image need not be the same as the first one, but only associated with it.[1] At this stage of speech-development – that of early childhood – we make use of a language constructed by ourselves. We behave in this like motor aphasics, for we associate a variety of extraneous verbal sounds with a single one produced by ourselves.

(2) We learn to speak the language of other people by endeavouring to make the sound-image produced by ourselves as like as possible to the one which gave rise to our speech-innervation. We learn in this way to 'repeat' – to 'say after' another person. When we juxtapose words in connected speech, we hold back the innervation of the next word till the sound-image or the motor speech-presentation (or both) of the preceding word has reached us. The security of our speech is thus overdetermined,[2] and can easily stand the loss of one or other of the determining factors. On the other hand, a loss of the correction exercised by the second sound-image and by the motor speech-image explains some of the peculiarities of paraphasia, both physiological and pathological.

(3) We learn to *spell* by linking the visual images of the letters with new sound-images, which, for their part, must remind us of verbal sounds which we already know. We at once 'repeat' the sound-image that denotes the letter; so that letters, too, are seen to be determined by two sound-images which coincide, and two motor presentations which correspond to each other.

(4) We learn to *read* by linking up in accordance with certain rules the succession of innervatory and motor word-presentations which we receive when we speak separate letters, so that new motor word-presentations arise. As soon as we have spoken these new word-presentations aloud, we discover from

1 [The second sound-image is the sound-image of the word spoken by ourselves, and the first one is that of the word we are imitating (the sound-image mentioned at the beginning of the paragraph).]

2. [In German '*überbestimmt*'. The synonymous term '*überdeterminiert*' is the one used so frequently in Freud's later writings to express the notion of multiple causation. Cf. *P.F.L.*, **3**, 289–90 *n.*]

their sound-images that the two motor images and sound-images which we have received in this way have long been familiar to us and are identical with the images used in speaking. We then associate the meaning which was attached to the primary verbal sounds with the speech-images which have been acquired by spelling. We now read with understanding. If what was spoken primarily was a dialect and not a literary language, the motor and sound-images of the words acquired through spelling have to be super-associated with the old images; thus we have to learn a new language – a task which is facilitated by the similarity between the dialect and the literary language.

It will be seen from this description of learning to read that it is a very complicated process, in which the course of the associations must repeatedly move backwards and forwards. We shall also be prepared to find that disturbances of reading in aphasia are bound to occur in a great variety of ways. The only thing that decisively indicates a lesion in the *visual* element of reading is a disturbance in the reading of *separate letters*. The *combination* of letters into a word takes place during transmission to the speech-tract and will thus be abolished in *motor* aphasia. An *understanding* of what is read is arrived at only through the medium of the sound-images produced by the words that have been spoken, or through the medium of the motor word-images that arose in speaking. It is therefore seen to be a function that is extinguished not only where there are motor lesions, but also where there are *acoustic* ones. Understanding what is read is further seen to be a function independent of the actual performance of reading. Anyone can discover from self-observation that there are several kinds of reading, in some of which we do without an understanding of what is read. When I am reading proofs with a view to paying special attention to the visual images of the letters and other typographical signs, the sense of what I read escapes me so completely that I have to read the proofs through again specially, if I want to correct the style. When, on the other hand, I am reading a book that interests me, a novel, for instance, I overlook all the misprints; and it may happen that the names of the characters in it leave only a confused impression on my mind – a recollection, perhaps, that they are long or short, or contain some unusual letter, such as an 'x' or a 'z'. When I have to read aloud, and have to pay particular attention to the sound-images of my words and the intervals between them, I am once more in danger of concerning myself too little with the meaning of the words; and as soon as I get tired I read in such a way that, though other people can still understand what I am reading, I myself no longer know what I have read. These are phenomena of divided attention, which arise precisely here because an understanding of what is read only comes about in such a very circuitous way. If the process of reading itself offers difficulties, there is no longer any question of understanding. This is made clear by analogy with our behaviour when we are learning to read; and we must be careful not to regard the absence of understanding as evidence of the interruption of a tract. Reading aloud is not to be regarded as a process in any way different from reading to oneself, apart from the fact that it helps to divert attention from the sensory part of the process of reading.

(5) We learn to *write* by reproducing the visual images of the letters by means of innervatory images of the hand, till the same or similar visual images appear. As a rule, the writing images are only similar to, and super-associated with, the reading images, since what we learn to read is *print* and what we learn to write is *hand-writing*. Writing proves to be a comparatively simple process and one that is not so easily disturbed as reading.

(6) It is to be assumed that later on, too, we carry out these different functions of speech along the same associative paths as those along which we learnt them. At this later stage, abbreviations and substitutions may occur, but it is not always easy to say what their nature is. Their importance is diminished by the consideration that in cases of organic lesion the apparatus of speech will probably be damaged to some extent as a whole and be compelled to return to the modes of association which are primary, well-established and lengthier. As regards reading, the 'visual word-image' undoubtedly makes its influence felt with

practised readers, so that individual words (particularly proper names) can be read even without spelling them.

A word is thus a complex presentation consisting of the images enumerated above; or, to put it in another way, there corresponds to the word a complicated associative process into which the elements of visual, acoustic and kinaesthetic origin enumerated above enter together.

A word, however, acquires its *meaning* by being linked to an 'object-presentation',[1] at all events if we restrict ourselves to a consideration of substantives. The object-presentation itself is once again a complex of associations made up of the greatest variety of visual, acoustic, tactile, kinaesthetic and other presentations. Philosophy tells us that an object-presentation consists in nothing more than this – that the appearance of there being a 'thing' to whose various 'attributes' these sense-impressions

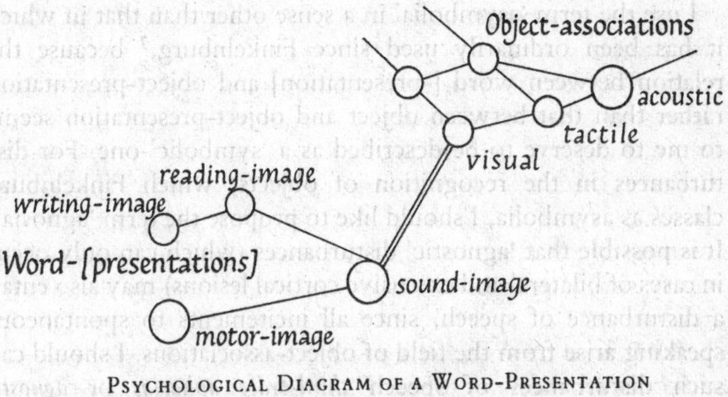

PSYCHOLOGICAL DIAGRAM OF A WORD-PRESENTATION

The word-presentation is shown as a closed complex of presentations, whereas the object-presentation is shown as an open one. The word-presentation is not linked to the object-presentation by *all* its constituent elements, but only by its sound-image. Among the object-associations, it is the visual ones which stand for the object, in the same kind of way as the sound-image stands for the word. The connections linking the sound-image of the word with object-associations other than the visual ones are not indicated.

1. [The 'thing-presentation' of the paper on 'The Unconscious' (p. 206 ff.).]

bear witness is merely due to the fact that, in enumerating the sense-impressions which we have received from an object, we also assume the possibility of there being a large number of further impressions in the same chain of associations (J. S. Mill).[1] The object-presentation is thus seen to be one which is not closed and almost one which cannot be closed, while the word-presentation is seen to be something closed, even though capable of extension.

The pathology of disorders of speech leads us to assert that *the word-presentation is linked at its sensory end (by its sound-images) with the object-presentation*. We thus arrive at the existence of two classes of disturbance of speech: (1) A first-order aphasia, *verbal aphasia*, in which only the associations between the separate elements of the word-presentation are disturbed; and (2) a second-order aphasia, *asymbolic aphasia*, in which the association between the word-presentation and the object-presentation is disturbed.

I use the term 'asymbolia' in a sense other than that in which it has been ordinarily used since Finkelnburg,[2] because the relation between word [-presentation] and object-presentation rather than that between object and object-presentation seems to me to deserve to be described as a 'symbolic' one. For disturbances in the recognition of objects, which Finkelnburg classes as asymbolia, I should like to propose the term 'agnosia'. It is possible that 'agnostic' disturbances (which can only occur in cases of bilateral and extensive cortical lesions) may also entail a disturbance of speech, since all incitements to spontaneous speaking arise from the field of object-associations. I should call such disturbances of speech *third-order aphasias* or *agnostic aphasias*. Clinical observation has in fact brought to our knowledge a few cases which require to be viewed in this way. . . .

1. Cf. J. S. Mill, *A System of Logic* (1843), **1**, Book I, Chapter III, also *An Examination of Sir William Hamilton's Philosophy* (1865).

2. Quoted by Spamer (1876). [The term was introduced by Finkelnburg (1870).]

A METAPSYCHOLOGICAL SUPPLEMENT TO THE THEORY OF DREAMS
(1917 [1915])

EDITOR'S NOTE

METAPSYCHOLOGISCHE ERGÄNZUNG ZUR TRAUMLEHRE

(A) German Editions:

1917 *Int. Z. ärztl. Psychoanal.*, **4** (6), 277–87.
1924 *Gesammelte Schriften*, **5**, 520–34.
1946 *Gesammelte Werke*, **10**, 412–26.

(B) English Translations:

'Metapsychological Supplement to the Theory of Dreams'

1925 *Collected Papers*, **4**, 137–51. (Tr. C. M. Baines.)
1957 *Standard Edition*, **14**, 217–35. (Translation, based on that of 1925, but very largely rewritten.)

The present edition is a reprint of the *Standard Edition* version, with some editorial modifications.

This paper, together with the next one ('Mourning and Melancholia'), seems to have been written over a period of eleven days between 23 April and 4 May 1915. It was not published until two years later. As its title implies, it is essentially an application of Freud's newly-stated theoretical scheme to the hypotheses put forward in Chapter VII of *The Interpretation of Dreams* (1900*a*). But it resolves itself largely into a discussion of the effects produced by the state of sleep on the different 'systems' of the mind. And this discussion in turn is mainly concentrated on the problem of hallucination and on an investigation of how it is that in our normal state we are able to distinguish between phantasy and reality.

Freud had been occupied by this problem from early times.

Much space was devoted to it in his 'Project' of 1895 (Freud, 1950*a*, especially in Part I, Sections 15 and 16, and in Part III, Section 1). And the solution he proposed for it there, though stated in a different terminology, visibly resembles the one put forward in the present paper. It included two main lines of thought. Freud argued that the 'primary psychical processes' do not by themselves make any distinction between an idea and a perception; they require, in the first place, to be inhibited by the 'secondary psychical processes', and these can only come into operation where there is an 'ego' with a large enough store of cathexis to provide the energy necessary to put the inhibition into effect. The aim of the inhibition is to give time for 'indications of reality' to arrive from the perceptual apparatus. But, in the second place, besides this inhibiting and delaying function, the ego is also responsible for directing cathexes of 'attention' (see above, p. 196 and footnote 2) on to the external world, without which the indications of reality could not be observed.

In *The Interpretation of Dreams* (1900*a*), *P.F.L.*, **4**, 720 ff. and 757 ff., the function of inhibition and delay was again insisted upon as an essential factor in the process of judging whether things are real or not and was once more attributed to the 'secondary process', though the ego was no longer mentioned as such. Freud's next serious discussion of the subject was in his paper on 'The Two Principles of Mental Functioning' (1911*b*), p. 39 above, where for the first time he used the actual term 'reality-testing'. Here again the delaying feature of the process was emphasized, but the function of attention now came in for further notice. It was described as a periodic examination of the external world and was related particularly to the sense organs and to consciousness. This last side of the problem, the part played by the systems *Pcpt.* and *Cs.*, is the one which is chiefly discussed in the paper which follows.

But Freud's interest in the subject was by no means exhausted by the present discussion. In *Group Psychology* (1921*c*), for instance, he attributed the work of reality-testing to the ego ideal – an attribution which, however, he withdrew very soon afterwards, in a footnote at the beginning of Chapter III of *The Ego and the Id* (1923*b*); see p. 367 below. And now for the first time since the early days of the 'Project' reality-testing was definitely ascribed to the ego. In a still later and particularly interesting discussion of the subject in the paper on 'Negation' (1925*h*), reality-testing was shown to depend on the ego's close genetic relation with the instruments of sense perception (cf. pp. 440–41 below). In that paper, too (as well as at the end of the almost contemporary paper on the 'Mystic Writing-Pad', 1925*a*), there were further references to the ego's habit of sending out periodic exploratory cathexes into the external world – evidently an allusion in different terms to what had originally been described as 'attention'. (Cf. pp. 441 and 433 below.) But in 'Negation' Freud carried his analysis of reality-testing further, and traced the whole course of its development back to the individual's earliest object-relations.

Freud's increasing interest in ego-psychology in his later years led him to a closer examination of the relations of the ego to the external world. In two short papers (1924*b* and 1924*e*) published soon after *The Ego and the Id* he discussed the distinction between the ego's relation to reality in neuroses and psychoses. (Cf. *P.F.L.*, **10**, 213 ff. and 221 ff.) And in a paper on 'Fetishism' (1927*e*) he gave his first detailed account of a method of defence by the ego – '*Verleugnung*' ('disavowal' or 'denial') – which had not previously been clearly differentiated from repression and which described the ego's reaction to an intolerable external reality (ibid., **7**, 352 ff.). This theme was developed still further in some of Freud's very latest writings, particularly in Chapter VIII of the posthumous *Outline of Psycho-Analysis* (1940*a* [1938]).

A METAPSYCHOLOGICAL SUPPLEMENT TO THE THEORY OF DREAMS[1]

WE SHALL discover in various connections how much our enquiries benefit if certain states and phenomena which may be regarded as *normal prototypes* of pathological affections are brought up for purposes of comparison. Among these we may include such affective states as grief and being in love, as well as the state of sleep and the phenomenon of dreaming.

We are not in the habit of devoting much thought to the fact that every night human beings lay aside the wrappings in which they have enveloped their skin, as well as anything which they may use as a supplement to their bodily organs (so far as they have succeeded in making good those organs' deficiencies by substitutes), for instance, their spectacles, their false hair and teeth, and so on. We may add that when they go to sleep they carry out an entirely analogous undressing of their minds and lay aside most of their psychical acquisitions. Thus on both counts they approach remarkably close to the situation in which they began life. Somatically, sleep is a reactivation of intra-uterine existence, fulfilling as it does the conditions of repose, warmth and exclusion of stimulus; indeed, in sleep many people resume the foetal posture. The psychical state of a sleeping person is characterized by an almost complete withdrawal from the surrounding world and a cessation of all interest in it.

1. This paper and the following one are derived from a collection which I originally intended to publish in book form under the title 'Zur Vorbereitung einer Metapsychologie' ['Preliminaries to a Metapsychology']. They follow on some papers which were printed in Volume III of the *Internationale Zeitschrift für ärztliche Psychoanalyse* ('Instincts and their Vicissitudes', 'Repression' and 'The Unconscious' [included in this volume]). The intention of the series is to clarify and carry deeper the theoretical assumptions on which a psychoanalytic system could be founded. [See p. 101.]

In investigating psychoneurotic states, we find ourselves led to emphasize in each of them what are known as *temporal regressions*, i.e. the amount of developmental recession peculiar to it. We distinguish two such regressions – one affecting the development of the ego and the other that of the libido. In the state of sleep, the latter is carried to the point of restoring primitive narcissism, while the former goes back to the stage of hallucinatory satisfaction of wishes. [Cf. below, p. 235.]

It is, of course, the study of dreams which has taught us what we know of the psychical characteristics of the state of sleep. It is true that dreams only show us the dreamer in so far as he is *not* sleeping; nevertheless they are bound to reveal at the same time characteristics of sleep itself. We have come to know from observation some peculiarities of dreams which we could not at first understand, but which we can now fit into the picture without difficulty. Thus, we know that dreams are completely egoistic[1] and that the person who plays the chief part in their scenes is always to be recognized as the dreamer. This is now easily to be accounted for by the narcissism of the state of sleep. Narcissism and egoism, indeed, coincide; the word 'narcissism' is only intended to emphasize the fact that egoism is a libidinal phenomenon as well; or, to put it in another way, narcissism may be described as the libidinal complement of egoism.[2] The 'diagnostic' capacity of dreams – a phenomenon which is generally acknowledged, but regarded as puzzling – becomes equally comprehensible, too. In dreams, incipient physical disease is often detected earlier and more clearly than in waking life, and all the current bodily sensations assume gigantic proportions.[3] This magnification is hypochondriacal in character; it is conditional upon the withdrawal of all psychical cathexes from the external world back on to the ego, and it makes poss-

1. [Cf. *The Interpretation of Dreams*, Chapter V (D), *P.F.L.*, **4**, 370 ff. See, however, the addition made in 1925 to a footnote, ibid., 373 *n*. 2.]

2. [A longer discussion of the relation between narcissism and egoism will be found in Lecture 26 of Freud's *Introductory Lectures* (1916–17), ibid., **1**, 461 ff.]

3. [Cf. *The Interpretation of Dreams*, ibid., **4**, 59 and 95–6.]

ible early recognition of bodily changes which in waking life would still for a time have remained unobserved.

A dream tells us that something was going on which tended to interrupt sleep, and it enables us to understand in what way it has been possible to fend off this interruption. The final outcome is that the sleeper has dreamt and is able to go on sleeping; the internal demand which was striving to occupy him has been replaced by an external experience, whose demand has been disposed of. A dream is, therefore, among other things, a *projection*: an externalization of an internal process. We may recall that we have already met with projection elsewhere among the means adopted for defence. The mechanism of a hysterical phobia, too, culminates in the fact that the subject is able to protect himself by attempts at flight against an external danger which has taken the place of an internal instinctual claim.[1] We will, however, defer the full treatment of projection till we come to analyse the narcissistic disorder in which this mechanism plays the most striking part.[2]

In what way, however, can a case arise in which the intention to sleep meets with an interruption? The interruption may proceed from an internal excitation or from an external stimulus. Let us first consider the more obscure and more interesting case of interruption from within. Observation shows that dreams are instigated by residues from the previous day – thought-cathexes which have not submitted to the general withdrawal of cathexes, but have retained in spite of it a certain amount of libidinal or other interest.[3] Thus the narcissism of sleep has from the outset had to admit an exception at this point, and it is here that the formation of dreams takes its start. In analysis we make the acquaintance of these 'day's residues' in the shape of latent dream-thoughts; and, both by reason of their nature and of the whole situation, we must regard them as preconscious ideas, as belonging to the system *Pcs.*

1. [See the paper on 'The Unconscious', above, p. 185 ff.]
2. [A possible reference to a missing paper on paranoia (p. 103).]
3. [For this and the following paragraph see *The Interpretation of Dreams*, *P.F.L.*, **4**, 705–7.]

We cannot proceed any further in explaining the formation of dreams till we have overcome certain difficulties. The narcissism of the state of sleep implies a withdrawal of cathexis from all ideas of objects, from both the unconscious and the preconscious portions of those ideas. If, then, certain day's residues have retained their cathexis, we hesitate to suppose that they have acquired at night so much energy as to compel notice on the part of consciousness; we should be more inclined to suppose that the cathexis they have retained is far weaker than that which they possessed during the day. Here analysis saves us further speculation, for it shows that these day's residues must receive a reinforcement which has its source in unconscious instinctual impulses if they are to figure as constructors of dreams. This hypothesis presents no immediate difficulties, for we have every reason to suppose that in sleep the censorship between the *Pcs.* and the *Ucs.* is greatly reduced, so that communication between the two systems is made easier.[1]

But there is another doubt, which we must not pass over in silence. If the narcissistic state of sleep has resulted in a drawing-in of all the cathexes of the systems *Ucs.* and *Pcs.*, then there can no longer be any possibility of the preconscious day's residues being reinforced by unconscious instinctual impulses, seeing that these themselves have surrendered their cathexes to the ego. Here the theory of dream-formation ends up in a contradiction, unless we can rescue it by introducing a modification into our assumption about the narcissism of sleep.

A restrictive modification of this kind is, as we shall discover later,[2] necessary in the theory of dementia praecox as well. This must be to the effect that the repressed portion of the system *Ucs.* does not comply with the wish to sleep that comes from the ego, that it retains its cathexis in whole or in part, and that in general, in consequence of repression, it has acquired a certain measure of independence of the ego. Accordingly, too, some amount of the expenditure on repression (*anticathexis*) would have to be maintained throughout the night, in order to meet

1. [Ibid., **4**, 672–3.]
2. [It is not clear what this refers to.]

the instinctual danger – though the inaccessibility of all paths leading to a release of affect and to motility may considerably diminish the height of the anticathexis that is necessary.[1] Thus we should picture the situation which leads to the formation of dreams as follows. The wish to sleep endeavours to draw in all the cathexes sent out by the ego and to establish an absolute narcissism. This can only partly succeed, for what is repressed in the system *Ucs.* does not obey the wish to sleep. A part of the anticathexes has therefore to be maintained, and the censorship between the *Ucs.* and the *Pcs.* must remain, even if not at its full strength. So far as the dominance of the ego extends, all the systems are emptied of cathexes. The stronger the *Ucs.* instinctual cathexes are, the more unstable is sleep. We are acquainted, too, with the extreme case where the ego gives up the wish to sleep, because it feels unable to inhibit the repressed impulses set free during sleep – in other words, where it renounces sleep because of its fear of its dreams.[2]

Later on we shall learn[3] to recognize the momentous nature of this hypothesis regarding the unruliness of repressed impulses. For the present let us follow out the situation which occurs in dream-formation.

The possibility mentioned above [p. 231] – that some of the preconscious thoughts of the day may also prove resistant and retain a part of their cathexis – must be recognized as a second breach in narcissism.[4] At bottom, the two cases may be identical. The resistance of the day's residues may originate in a link with unconscious impulses which is already in existence during waking life; or the process may be somewhat less simple, and the day's residues which have not been wholly emptied of cathexis may establish a connection with the repressed material only after the state of sleep has set in, thanks to the easing of communication between the *Pcs.* and the *Ucs.* In both cases there follows the same decisive step in dream-formation: the pre-

1. [Ibid., **4**, 721–2. See also above, p. 151.]
2. [Ibid., **4**, 736 f.]
3. [The reference is again not clear.]
4. [The first being the 'unruliness of repressed impulses'.]

conscious dream-wish is formed, which *gives expression to the unconscious impulse in the material of the preconscious day's residues.* This dream-wish must be sharply distinguished from the day's residues; it need not have existed in waking life and it may already display the irrational character possessed by everything that is unconscious when we translate it into the conscious. Again, the dream-wish must not be confused with the wishful impulses which may have been present, though they certainly need not necessarily be present, amongst the preconscious (latent) dream-thoughts. If, however, there *were* any such preconscious wishes, the dream-wish associates itself with them, as a most effective reinforcement of them.

We have now to consider the further vicissitudes undergone by this wishful impulse, which in its essence represents an unconscious instinctual demand and which has been formed in the *Pcs.* as a dream-wish (a wish-fulfilling phantasy). Reflection tells us that this wishful impulse may be dealt with along three different paths. It may follow the path that would be normal in waking life, by pressing from the *Pcs.* to consciousness; or it may bypass the *Cs.* and find direct motor discharge; or it may take the unexpected path which observation enables us in fact to trace. In the first case, it would become a *delusion* having as content the fulfilment of the wish; but in the state of sleep this never happens. With our scanty knowledge of the metapsychological conditions of mental processes, we may perhaps take this fact as a hint that a complete emptying of a system renders it little susceptible to instigation. The second case, that of direct motor discharge, should be excluded by the same principle;[1] for access

1. [The 'principle of the insusceptibility to excitation of uncathected systems' (below, p. 242 *n.* 3) seems to be alluded to in one or two passages in Freud's later writings, e.g. in *Beyond the Pleasure Principle* (1920*g*), p. 302 below, and near the end of the paper on the 'Mystic Writing-Pad' (1925*a*), pp. 433–4 below. But the principle is already foreshadowed in neurological terms in Freud's 1895 'Project' (1950*a*). In Part I, Section 11, of that work he lays it down that 'a quantity passes more easily from a neurone to a cathected neurone than to an uncathected one'. And in Section 20 he actually applies this hypothesis to the very problem of motor discharge in dreams which is the subject of the present passage. He writes: 'Dreams are devoid of motor discharge and, for the most part,

to motility normally lies yet another step beyond the censorship of consciousness. But we do meet with exceptional instances in which this happens, in the form of *somnambulism*. We do not know what conditions make this possible, or why it does not happen more often. What actually happens in dream-formation is a very remarkable and quite unforeseen turn of events. The process, begun in the *Pcs.* and reinforced by the *Ucs.*, pursues a backward course, through the *Ucs.* to perception, which is pressing upon consciousness. This *regression* is the third phase of dream-formation. For the sake of clarity, we will repeat the two earlier ones: the reinforcement of the *Pcs.* day's residues by the *Ucs.*, and the setting up of the dream-wish.

We call this kind of regression a *topographical* one, to distinguish it from the previously mentioned [p. 230] *temporal* or developmental regression.[1] The two do not necessarily always coincide, but they do so in the particular example before us. The reversal of the course of the excitation from the *Pcs.* through the *Ucs.* to perception is at the same time a return to the early stage of hallucinatory wish-fulfilment.

We have already in *The Interpretation of Dreams* [*P.F.L.*, **4**, 692 ff.] described the way in which the regression of the preconscious day's residues takes place in dream-formation. In this process thoughts are transformed into images, mainly of a visual sort; that is to say, word-presentations are taken back to the thing-presentations which correspond to them, as if, in general, the process were dominated by considerations of *representability* [ibid., **4**, 698–9]. When regression has been completed, a number of cathexes are left over in the system *Ucs.* – cathexes of

of motor elements. We are paralysed in dreams. The easiest explanation of this characteristic is the absence of spinal pre-cathexis . . . Since the neurones are uncathected, the motor excitation cannot pass over the barriers . . .' A few paragraphs later on he discusses the 'retrogressive' nature of the hallucinatory characteristic of dreams, as he does in the later part of the present passage.]

1. [Cf. a paragraph added in 1914 to Chapter VII of *The Interpretation of Dreams* (1900*a*), *P.F.L.*, **4**, 699 (in which three kinds of regression are distinguished), and another discussion of regression near the beginning of Lecture 22 of the *Introductory Lectures* (1916–17), ibid., **1**, 385–7. See also Appendix A to the 'Project' (1950*a*).]

memories of *things*. The primary psychical process is brought to bear on these memories, till, by condensation of them and displacement between their respective cathexes, it has shaped the manifest dream-content. Only where the word-presentations occurring in the day's residues are recent and current residues of *perceptions*, and not the expression of *thoughts*, are they themselves treated like thing-presentations, and subjected to the influence of condensation and displacement. Hence the rule laid down in *The Interpretation of Dreams* [ibid., **4**, 545 ff.], and since confirmed beyond all doubt, that words and speeches in the dream-content are not freshly formed, but are modelled on speeches from the day preceding the dream (or on some other recent impressions, such as something that has been read). It is very noteworthy how little the dream-work keeps to the word-presentations; it is always ready to exchange one word for another till it finds the expression which is most handy for plastic representation.[1]

Now it is in this respect that the essential difference between the dream-work and schizophrenia becomes clear. In the latter, what becomes the subject of modification by the primary process are the words themselves in which the preconscious

1. I also ascribe to considerations of representability the fact which is insisted on and perhaps over-estimated by Silberer [1914] that some dreams admit of two simultaneous, and yet essentially different interpretations, one of which he calls the 'analytic' and the other the 'anagogic'. When this happens, we are invariably concerned with thoughts of a very abstract nature, which must have made their representation in the dream very difficult. We might compare it with the problem of representing in pictures a leading article from a political newspaper. In such cases, the dream-work must first replace the text that consists of abstract thoughts by one more concrete, connected with the former in some way – by comparison, symbolism, allegorical allusion, or best of all, genetically – so that the more concrete text then takes the place of the abstract one as material for the dream-work. The abstract thoughts yield the so-called anagogic interpretation, which, in our interpretative work, we discover more easily than the true analytic one. Otto Rank has justly remarked that certain dreams about their treatment, dreamt by patients in analysis, are the best models on which to form a view of these dreams which admit of more than one interpretation. [Freud added a paragraph on anagogic interpretations in 1919 to *The Interpretation of Dreams* (1900*a*), *P.F.L.*, **4**, 670–71.]

thought was expressed; in dreams, what are subject to this modification are not the words, but the thing-presentations to which the words have been taken back.[1] In dreams there is a topographical regression; in schizophrenia there is not. In dreams there is free communication between (*Pcs.*) word-cathexes and (*Ucs.*) thing-cathexes, while it is characteristic of schizophrenia that this communication is cut off. The impression this difference makes on one is lessened precisely by the dream-interpretations we carry out in psychoanalytic practice. For, owing to the fact that dream-interpretation traces the course taken by the dream-work, follows the paths which lead from the latent thoughts to the dream-elements, reveals the way in which verbal ambiguities have been exploited, and points out the verbal bridges between different groups of material – owing to all this, we get an impression now of a joke, now of schizophrenia, and are apt to forget that for a dream all operations with words are no more than a preparation for a regression to things.

The completion of the dream-process consists in the thought-content – regressively transformed and worked over into a wishful phantasy – becoming conscious as a sense-perception; while this is happening it undergoes secondary revision, to which every perceptual concept is subject. The dream-wish, as we say, is *hallucinated*, and, as a hallucination, meets with belief in the reality of its fulfilment. It is precisely round this concluding piece in the formation of dreams that the gravest uncertainties centre, and it is in order to clear them up that we are proposing to compare dreams with pathological states akin to them.

The formation of the wishful phantasy and its regression to hallucination are the most essential parts of the dream-work, but they do not belong exclusively to dreams. They are also found in two morbid states: in acute hallucinatory confusion (Meynert's 'amentia'),[2] and in the hallucinatory phase of schizophrenia. The hallucinatory delirium of amentia is a clearly

1. [Cf. 'The Unconscious' (p. 204 above).]

2. [In the rest of this paper the term 'amentia' should be understood as referring to this condition.]

recognizable wishful phantasy, often completely well-ordered like a perfect day-dream. One might speak quite generally of a 'hallucinatory wishful psychosis', and attribute it equally to dreams and amentia. There are even dreams which consist of nothing but undistorted wishful phantasies with a very rich content.[1] The hallucinatory phase of schizophrenia has been less thoroughly studied; it seems as a rule to be of a composite nature, but in its essence it might well correspond to a fresh attempt at restitution, designed to restore a libidinal cathexis to the ideas of objects.[2] I cannot extend the comparison to the other hallucinatory states in various pathological disorders, because in their case I have no experience of my own upon which to draw, and cannot utilize that of other observers.

Let us be clear that the hallucinatory wishful psychosis – in dreams or elsewhere – achieves two by no means identical results. It not only brings hidden or repressed wishes into consciousness; it also represents them, with the subject's entire belief, as fulfilled. The concurrence of these two results calls for explanation. It is quite impossible to maintain that unconscious wishes must necessarily be taken for realities when once they have become conscious; for, as we know, our judgement is very well able to distinguish realities from ideas and wishes, however intense they may be. On the other hand, it seems justifiable to assume that belief in reality is bound up with perception through the senses. When once a thought has followed the path to regression as far back as to the unconscious memory-traces of objects and thence to perception, we accept the perception of it as real.[3] So hallucination brings belief in reality with it. We now have to ask ourselves what determines the coming into being of a hallucination. The first answer would be regression, and this would replace the problem of the origin of hallucination by

1. [Cf. *The Interpretation of Dreams*, *P.F.L.*, **4**, 210 *n*. 2.]

2. In the paper on 'The Unconscious' [see pp. 209–10] we recognized the hypercathexis of word-presentations as a first attempt of this kind.

3. [This point was made by Breuer in his theoretical contribution to *Studies on Hysteria* (1895*d*), *P.F.L.*, **3**, 262–4 and 264 *n*. 1. He seems to attribute the idea to Meynert.]

that of the mechanism of regression. As regards dreams, this latter problem need not remain long unanswered. Regression of *Pcs.* dream-thoughts to mnemic images of things is clearly the result of the attraction which the *Ucs.* instinctual representatives – e.g. repressed memories of experiences – exercise upon the thoughts which have been put into words.[1] But we soon perceive that we are on a false scent. If the secret of hallucination is nothing else than that of regression, every regression of sufficient intensity would produce hallucination with belief in its reality. But we are quite familiar with situations in which a process of regressive reflection brings to consciousness very clear visual mnemic images, though we do not on that account for a single moment take them for real perceptions. Again, we could very well imagine the dream-work penetrating to mnemic images of this kind, making conscious to us what was previously unconscious, and holding up to us a wishful phantasy which rouses our longing, but which we should not regard as a real fulfilment of the wish. Hallucination must therefore be something more than the regressive revival of mnemic images that are in themselves *Ucs.*

Let us, furthermore, bear in mind the great practical importance of distinguishing perceptions from ideas, however intensely recalled. Our whole relation to the external world, to reality, depends on our ability to do so. We have put forward the fiction[2] that we did not always possess this ability and that at the beginning of our mental life we did in fact hallucinate the satisfying object when we felt the need for it. But in such a situation satisfaction did not occur, and this failure must very soon have moved us to create some contrivance with the help of which it was possible to distinguish such wishful perceptions from a real fulfilment and to avoid them for the future. In other words, we gave up hallucinatory satisfaction of our wishes at a very early period and set up a kind of 'reality-testing'.[3] The question now arises in what this reality-testing consisted, and

1. [*The Interpretation of Dreams*, *P.F.L.*, **4**, 694.]
2. [See Chapter VII (C) of *The Interpretation of Dreams*, ibid., **4**, 718 ff.]
3. [See Editor's Note, pp. 226–7.]

how the hallucinatory wishful psychosis of dreams and amentia and similar conditions succeeds in abolishing it and in re-establishing the old mode of satisfaction.

The answer can be given if we now proceed to define more precisely the third of our psychical systems, the system *Cs.*, which hitherto we have not sharply distinguished from the *Pcs.* In *The Interpretation of Dreams*[1] we were already led to a decision to regard conscious perception as the function of a special system, to which we ascribed certain curious properties, and to which we shall now have good grounds for attributing other characteristics as well. We may regard this system, which is there called the *Pcpt.*, as coinciding with the system *Cs.*, on whose activity becoming conscious usually depends. Nevertheless, even so, the fact of a thing's becoming conscious still does not wholly coincide with its belonging to a system, for we have learnt that it is possible to be aware of sensory mnemic images to which we cannot possibly allow a psychical location in the systems *Cs.* or *Pcpt.*

We must, however, put off discussing this difficulty till we can focus our interest upon the system *Cs.* itself.[2] In the present connection we may be allowed to assume that hallucination consists in a cathexis of the system *Cs.* (*Pcpt.*), which, however, is not effected – as normally – from without, but from within, and that a necessary condition for the occurrence of hallucination is that regression shall be carried far enough to reach this system itself and in so doing be able to pass over reality-testing.[3]

In an earlier passage[4] we ascribed to the still helpless organism a capacity for making a first orientation in the world by means of its perceptions, distinguishing 'external' and 'internal' according to their relation to its muscular action. A perception which is made to disappear by an action is recognized as external, as reality; where such an action makes no difference, the perception

1. [Chapter VII (B), *P.F.L.*, **4**, 681 ff.]
2. [Another probable reference to the missing paper on consciousness.]
3. I may add by way of supplement that any attempt to explain hallucination would have to start out from *negative* rather than positive hallucination.
4. 'Instincts and their Vicissitudes' [p. 115].

originates within the subject's own body – it is not real. It is of value to the individual to possess a means such as this of recognizing reality,[1] which at the same time helps him to deal with it, and he would be glad to be equipped with a similar power against the often merciless claims of his instincts. That is why he takes such pains to transpose outwards what becomes troublesome to him from within – that is, to *project* it.[2]

This function of orientating the individual in the world by discrimination between what is internal and what is external must now, after detailed dissection of the mental apparatus, be ascribed to the system *Cs.* (*Pcpt.*) alone. The *Cs.* must have at its disposal a motor innervation which determines whether the perception can be made to disappear or whether it proves resistant. Reality-testing need be nothing more than this contrivance.[3] We can say nothing more precise on this point for we know too little as yet of the nature and mode of operation of the system *Cs.* We shall place reality-testing among the major *institutions of the ego*, alongside the *censorships* which we have come to recognize between the psychical systems, and we shall expect that the analysis of the narcissistic disorders will help to bring other similar institutions to light. [Cf. p. 256.]

On the other hand, we can already learn from pathology the way in which reality-testing may be done away with or put out of action. We shall see this more clearly in the wishful psychosis of amentia than in that of dreams. Amentia is the reaction to a loss which reality affirms, but which the ego has to deny, since it finds it insupportable. Thereupon the ego breaks off its relation to reality; it withdraws the cathexis from the system of perceptions, *Cs.* – or rather, perhaps, it withdraws *a* cathexis,

1. [In German: '*Kennzeichen der Realität*'. Cf. '*Realitätszeichen*' ('indications of reality') in the 'Project' (1950*a*), Part I, Section 15, etc.]

2. [Cf. the further discussion of 'external' and 'internal' in the much later paper on 'Negation' (1925*h*), p. 439 below, and in Chapter I of *Civilization and its Discontents* (1930*a*), *P.F.L.*, **12**, 254–5.]

3. Cf. a later passage on the distinction between testing with regard to reality and testing with regard to immediacy. ['*Realitätsprüfung*' and '*Aktualitätsprüfung*'. No reference to the latter seems to occur anywhere else; and this may be one more reference to a missing paper.]

the special nature of which may be the subject of further enquiry. With this turning away from reality, reality-testing is got rid of, the (unrepressed, completely conscious) wishful phantasies are able to press forward into the system, and they are there regarded as a better reality. Such a withdrawal may be put on a par with the processes of repression. Amentia presents the interesting spectacle of a breach between the ego and one of its organs – one which had perhaps been its most faithful servant and had been bound up with it the most intimately.[1]

What is performed in amentia by this 'repression' is performed in dreams by voluntary renunciation. The state of sleep does not wish to know anything of the external world; it takes no interest in reality, or only so far as abandoning the state of sleep – waking up – is concerned. Hence it withdraws cathexis from the system *Cs.* as well as from the other systems, the *Pcs.* and the *Ucs.*, in so far as the cathexes[2] in them obey the wish to sleep. With the system *Cs.* thus uncathected, the possibility of reality-testing is abandoned; and the excitations which, independently of the state of sleep, have entered on the path of regression will find that path clear as far as the system *Cs.* where they will count as undisputed reality.[3]

As regards the hallucinatory psychosis of dementia praecox, we shall infer from our discussion that that psychosis cannot be among the initial symptoms of the affection. It becomes poss-

1. I may venture to suggest in this connection that the toxic hallucinoses, too, e.g. alcoholic delirium, are to be understood in an analogous fashion. Here the unbearable loss imposed by reality would be precisely the loss of alcohol. When the latter is supplied, the hallucinations cease.

2. [The German word here is '*Positionen*', 'military posts'. The use of the metaphor was no doubt suggested by the fact that '*Besetzung*' ('cathexis') can itself be used in the sense of 'military occupation'.]

3. Here the principle of the insusceptibility to excitation of uncathected systems [cf. p. 234] appears to be invalidated in the case of the system *Cs.* (*Pcpt.*). But it may be a question of only the *partial* removal of cathexis; and for the perceptual system in especial we must assume many conditions for excitation which are widely divergent from those of other systems. – We are not, of course, intending to disguise or gloss over the uncertain and tentative character of these metapsychological discussions. Only deeper investigation can lead to the achievement of a certain degree of probability.

ible only when the patient's ego is so far disintegrated that reality-testing no longer stands in the way of hallucination.

In what concerns the psychology of dream-processes we arrive at the result that all the essential characteristics of dreams are determined by the conditioning factor of sleep. Aristotle was entirely right, long ago, in his modest pronouncement that dreams are the mental activity of the sleeper.[1] We might expand this and say: they are a residue of mental activity, made possible by the fact that the narcissistic state of sleep has not been able to be completely established. This does not sound very different from what psychologists and philosophers have said all along, but it is based on quite different views about the structure and function of the mental apparatus. These views have this advantage over the earlier ones, that they have given us an understanding, too, of all the detailed characteristics of dreams.

Finally, let us once more glance at the significant light which the *topography* of the process of repression throws for us on the mechanism of mental disturbances. In dreams the withdrawal of cathexis (libido or interest) affects all systems equally; in the transference neuroses, the *Pcs.* cathexis is withdrawn; in schizophrenia, the cathexis of the *Ucs.*; in amentia, that of the *Cs.*

1. [Quoted near the beginning of *The Interpretation of Dreams* (1900*a*), *P.F.L.*, **4**, 59.]

MOURNING AND MELANCHOLIA
(1917 [1915])

EDITOR'S NOTE

TRAUER UND MELANCHOLIE

(A) German Editions:

1917 *Int. Z. ärztl. Psychoanal.*, **4** (6), 288–301.
1924 *Gesammelte Schriften*, **5**, 535–53.
1946 *Gesammelte Werke*, **10**, 428–46.

(B) English Translations:
'Mourning and Melancholia'

1925 *Collected Papers*, **4**, 152–70. (Tr. Joan Riviere.)
1957 *Standard Edition*, **14**, 237–58. (Translation, based on that of 1925, but very largely rewritten.)

The present edition is a reprint of the *Standard Edition* version, with some editorial modifications.

As we learn from Dr Ernest Jones (1955, 367–8), Freud had expounded the theme of the present paper to him in January 1914; and he spoke of it to the Vienna Psycho-Analytical Society on 30 December of that year. He wrote a first draft of the paper in February 1915. He submitted this to Abraham, who sent him some lengthy comments, which included the important suggestion that there was a connection between melancholia and the oral stage of libidinal development (pp. 258–9 below). (Cf. Abraham's letter of 31 March 1915, and Freud's of 4 May 1915; both included in Freud (1965*a*, 206 ff. and 211–12).) The final draft of the paper was finished on 4 May 1915, but, like its predecessor ('Metapsychological Supplement to the Theory of Dreams', 1917*d*), it was not published till two years later.

In very early days (probably in January 1895) Freud had sent Fliess an elaborate attempt at explaining melancholia (under which term he regularly included what are now usually described as states of depression) in purely neurological terms (Freud, 1950*a*, Draft G).

This attempt was not particularly fruitful, but it was soon replaced by a psychological approach to the subject. Only two years later we find one of the most remarkable instances of Freud's pre-vision. It occurs in a manuscript, also addressed to Fliess, and bearing the title 'Notes (III)'. This manuscript, dated 31 May 1897, is incidentally the one in which Freud first foreshadowed the Oedipus complex (Freud, 1950*a*, Draft N). The passage in question, whose meaning is so condensed as to be in places obscure, deserves to be quoted in full:

'Hostile impulses against parents (a wish that they should die) are also an integral constituent of neuroses. They come to light consciously as obsessional ideas. In paranoia what is worst in delusions of persecution (pathological distrust of rulers and monarchs) corresponds to these impulses. They are repressed at times when compassion for the parents is active – at times of their illness or death. On such occasions it is a manifestation of mourning to reproach oneself for their death (what is known as melancholia) or to punish oneself in a hysterical fashion (through the medium of the idea of retribution) with the same states [of illness] that they have had. The identification which occurs here is, as we can see, nothing other than a mode of thinking and does not relieve us of the necessity for looking for the motive.'

The further application to melancholia of the line of thought outlined in this passage seems to have been left completely on one side by Freud. Indeed he scarcely mentioned the condition again before the present paper, except for some remarks in a discussion on suicide at the Vienna Psycho-Analytical Society (1910*g*), when he stressed the importance of drawing a comparison between melancholia and normal states of mourning, but declared that the psychological problem involved was still insoluble.

What enabled Freud to reopen the subject was, of course, the introduction of the concepts of narcissism and of an ego ideal. The present paper may, indeed, be regarded as an extension of the one on narcissism which Freud had written a year earlier (1914*c*), p. 65 ff. above. Just as that paper had described the workings of the 'critical agency' in cases of paranoia (see above p. 89 f.), so this one sees the same agency in operation in melancholia.

But the implications of this paper were destined to be more important than the explanation of the mechanism of one particular pathological state, though those implications did not become immediately obvious. The material contained here led on to the further consideration of the 'critical agency' which is to be found in Chapter XI of *Group Psychology* (1921*c*); and this in turn led on to the hypothesis of the super-ego in *The Ego and the Id* (1923*b*), p. 367 below, and to a fresh assessment of the sense of guilt.

Along another line, this paper called for an examination of the whole question of the nature of identification. Freud seems to have been inclined at first to regard it as closely associated with, and perhaps dependent on, the oral or cannibalistic phase of libidinal development. Thus in *Totem and Taboo* (1912–13) he had written of the relation between the sons and the father of the primal horde that 'in the act of devouring him they accomplished their identification with him'. And again, in a passage added to the third edition of the *Three Essays*, published in 1915 but written some months before the present paper, he described the cannibalistic oral phase as 'the prototype of a process which, in the form of *identification*, is later to play such an important psychological part' (1905*d*), *P.F.L.*, **7**, 116–17. In the present paper (p. 258) he speaks of identification as 'a preliminary stage of object-choice . . . the first way in which the ego picks out an object' and adds that 'the ego wants to incorporate this object into itself, and, in accordance with the oral or cannibalistic phase of libidinal development at which it is, it wants to do so by devouring it'.[1] And indeed, though Abraham may have sug-

1. The term 'introjection' does not occur in this paper, though Freud had already used it, in a different connection, in the first of these metapsychological

gested the relevance of the oral phase to melancholia, Freud's own interest had already begun to turn to it, as is shown by the discussion of it in the 'Wolf Man' case history (1918*b*) which was written during the autumn of 1914 and in which a prominent part was played by that phase. (See *P.F.L.*, **9**, 347–9.) A few years later, in *Group Psychology* (1921*c*), where the subject of identification is taken up again, explicitly in continuation of the present discussion, a change in the earlier view – or perhaps only a clarification of it – seems to emerge. Identification, we there learn, is something that *precedes* object-cathexis and is distinct from it, though we are still told that 'it behaves like a derivative of the first, oral phase'. This view of identification is consistently emphasized in many of Freud's later writings, as, for instance, in Chapter III of *The Ego and the Id* (1923*b*), where he writes that identification with the parents 'is apparently not in the first instance the consequence or outcome of an object-cathexis; it is a direct and immediate identification and takes place earlier than any object-cathexis'. (See p. 370 below.)

What Freud seems later to have regarded as the most significant feature of this paper was, however, its account of the process by which in melancholia an object-cathexis is replaced by an identification. In Chapter III of *The Ego and the Id* (see pp. 367 ff. below), he argued that this process is not restricted to melancholia but is of quite general occurrence. These regressive identifications, he pointed out, were to a large extent the basis of what we describe as a person's 'character'. But, what was far more important, he suggested that the very earliest of these regressive identifications – those derived from the dissolution of the Oedipus complex – come to occupy a quite special position, and form, in fact, the nucleus of the super-ego.

papers (p. 133) above. When he returned to the topic of identification, in *Group Psychology* (*P.F.L.*, **12**, 134 ff.), he used the word 'introjection' at several points, and it reappears, though not very frequently, in his subsequent writings.

MOURNING AND MELANCHOLIA

DREAMS having served us as the prototype in normal life of narcissistic mental disorders, we will now try to throw some light on the nature of melancholia by comparing it with the normal affect of mourning.[1] This time, however, we must begin by making an admission, as a warning against any over-estimation of the value of our conclusions. Melancholia, whose definition fluctuates even in descriptive psychiatry, takes on various clinical forms the grouping together of which into a single unity does not seem to be established with certainty; and some of these forms suggest somatic rather than psychogenic affections. Our material, apart from such impressions as are open to every observer, is limited to a small number of cases whose psychogenic nature was indisputable. We shall, therefore, from the outset drop all claim to general validity for our conclusions, and we shall console ourselves by reflecting that, with the means of investigation at our disposal to-day, we could hardly discover anything that was not typical, if not of a whole class of disorders, at least of a small group of them.

The correlation of melancholia and mourning seems justified by the general picture of the two conditions.[2] Moreover, the exciting causes due to environmental influences are, so far as we can discern them at all, the same for both conditions. Mourning

1. [The German '*Trauer*', like the English 'mourning', can mean both the affect of grief and its outward manifestation. Throughout the present paper, the word has been rendered 'mourning'.]

2. Abraham (1912), to whom we owe the most important of the few analytic studies on this subject, also took this comparison as his starting point. [Freud himself had already made the comparison in 1910 and even earlier. (See Editor's Note, p. 248 above.)]

is regularly the reaction to the loss of a loved person, or to the loss of some abstraction which has taken the place of one, such as one's country, liberty, an ideal, and so on. In some people the same influences produce melancholia instead of mourning and we consequently suspect them of a pathological disposition. It is also well worth notice that, although mourning involves grave departures from the normal attitude to life, it never occurs to us to regard it as a pathological condition and to refer it to medical treatment. We rely on its being overcome after a certain lapse of time, and we look upon any interference with it as useless or even harmful.

The distinguishing mental features of melancholia are a profoundly painful dejection, cessation of interest in the outside world, loss of the capacity to love, inhibition of all activity, and a lowering of the self-regarding feelings to a degree that finds utterance in self-reproaches and self-revilings, and culminates in a delusional expectation of punishment. This picture becomes a little more intelligible when we consider that, with one exception, the same traits are met with in mourning. The disturbance of self-regard is absent in mourning; but otherwise the features are the same. Profound mourning, the reaction to the loss of someone who is loved, contains the same painful frame of mind, the same loss of interest in the outside world – in so far as it does not recall him – the same loss of capacity to adopt any new object of love (which would mean replacing him) and the same turning away from any activity that is not connected with thoughts of him. It is easy to see that this inhibition and circumscription of the ego is the expression of an exclusive devotion to mourning which leaves nothing over for other purposes or other interests. It is really only because we know so well how to explain it that this attitude does not seem to us pathological.

We should regard it as an appropriate comparison, too, to call the mood of mourning a 'painful' one. We shall probably see the justification for this when we are in a position to give a characterization of the economics of pain.[1]

1. [See footnote 1, p. 146 above.]

In what, now, does the work which mourning performs consist? I do not think there is anything far-fetched in presenting it in the following way. Reality-testing has shown that the loved object no longer exists, and it proceeds to demand that all libido shall be withdrawn from its attachments to that object. This demand arouses understandable opposition – it is a matter of general observation that people never willingly abandon a libidinal position, not even, indeed, when a substitute is already beckoning to them. This opposition can be so intense that a turning away from reality takes place and a clinging to the object through the medium of a hallucinatory wishful psychosis.[1] Normally, respect for reality gains the day. Nevertheless its orders cannot be obeyed at once. They are carried out bit by bit, at great expense of time and cathectic energy, and in the meantime the existence of the lost object is psychically prolonged. Each single one of the memories and expectations in which the libido is bound to the object is brought up and hypercathected, and detachment of the libido is accomplished in respect of it.[2] Why this compromise by which the command of reality is carried out piecemeal should be so extraordinarily painful is not at all easy to explain in terms of economics. It is remarkable that this painful unpleasure is taken as a matter of course by us. The fact is, however, that when the work of mourning is completed the ego becomes free and uninhibited again.[3]

Let us now apply to melancholia what we have learnt about mourning. In one set of cases it is evident that melancholia too may be the reaction to the loss of a loved object. Where the exciting causes are different one can recognize that there is a loss of a more ideal kind. The object has not perhaps actually died, but has been lost as an object of love (e.g. in the case of a betrothed girl who has been jilted). In yet other cases one feels

1. Cf. the preceding paper [pp. 237–8].

2. [This idea seems to be expressed already in *Studies on Hysteria* (1895*d*): a process similar to this one will be found described near the beginning of Freud's 'Discussion' of the case history of Fräulein Elisabeth von R. (*P.F.L.*, **3**, 233).]

3. [A discussion of the economics of this process will be found below on pp. 264–5].

justified in maintaining the belief that a loss of this kind has occurred, but one cannot see clearly what it is that has been lost, and it is all the more reasonable to suppose that the patient cannot consciously perceive what he has lost either. This, indeed, might be so even if the patient is aware of the loss which has given rise to his melancholia, but only in the sense that he knows *whom* he has lost but not *what* he has lost in him. This would suggest that melancholia is in some way related to an object-loss which is withdrawn from consciousness, in contradistinction to mourning, in which there is nothing about the loss that is unconscious.

In mourning we found that the inhibition and loss of interest are fully accounted for by the work of mourning in which the ego is absorbed. In melancholia, the unknown loss will result in a similar internal work and will therefore be responsible for the melancholic inhibition. The difference is that the inhibition of the melancholic seems puzzling to us because we cannot see what it is that is absorbing him so entirely. The melancholic displays something else besides which is lacking in mourning – an extraordinary diminution in his self-regard, an impoverishment of his ego on a grand scale. In mourning it is the world which has become poor and empty; in melancholia it is the ego itself. The patient represents his ego to us as worthless, incapable of any achievement and morally despicable; he reproaches himself, vilifies himself and expects to be cast out and punished. He abases himself before everyone and commiserates with his own relatives for being connected with anyone so unworthy. He is not of the opinion that a change has taken place in him, but extends his self-criticism back over the past; he declares that he was never any better. This picture of a delusion of (mainly moral) inferiority is completed by sleeplessness and refusal to take nourishment, and – what is psychologically very remarkable – by an overcoming of the instinct which compels every living thing to cling to life.

It would be equally fruitless from a scientific and a therapeutic point of view to contradict a patient who brings these accusations against his ego. He must surely be right in some way and be describing something that is as it seems to him to be. Indeed, we must at once confirm some of his statements without reservation. He really is as lacking in interest and as incapable of love and achievement as he says. But that, as we know, is secondary; it is the effect of the internal work which is consuming his ego – work which is unknown to us but which is comparable to the work of mourning. He also seems to us justified in certain other self-accusations; it is merely that he has a keener eye for the truth than other people who are not melancholic. When in his heightened self-criticism he describes himself as petty, egoistic, dishonest, lacking in independence, one whose sole aim has been to hide the weaknesses of his own nature, it may be, so far as we know, that he has come pretty near to understanding himself; we only wonder why a man has to be ill before he can be accessible to a truth of this kind. For there can be no doubt that if anyone holds and expresses to others an opinion of himself such as this (an opinion which Hamlet held both of himself and of everyone else[1]), he is ill, whether he is speaking the truth or whether he is being more or less unfair to himself. Nor is it difficult to see that there is no correspondence, so far as we can judge, between the degree of self-abasement and its real justification. A good, capable, conscientious woman will speak no better of herself after she develops melancholia than one who is in fact worthless; indeed, the former is perhaps more likely to fall ill of the disease than the latter, of whom we too should have nothing good to say. Finally, it must strike us that after all the melancholic does not behave in quite the same way as a person who is crushed by remorse and self-reproach in a normal fashion. Feelings of shame in front of other people, which would more than anything characterize this latter condition, are lacking in the melancholic, or at least they are not prominent in him. One might emphasize the presence in him of an almost opposite trait of insistent communicativeness which finds satisfaction in self-exposure.

The essential thing, therefore, is not whether the melan-

1. 'Use every man after his desert, and who shall scape whipping?' (Act II, Scene 2).

cholic's distressing self-denigration is correct, in the sense that his self-criticism agrees with the opinion of other people. The point must rather be that he is giving a correct description of his psychological situation. He has lost his self-respect and he must have good reason for this. It is true that we are then faced with a contradiction that presents a problem which is hard to solve. The analogy with mourning led us to conclude that he had suffered a loss in regard to an object; what he tells us points to a loss in regard to his ego.

Before going into this contradiction, let us dwell for a moment on the view which the melancholic's disorder affords of the constitution of the human ego. We see how in him one part of the ego sets itself over against the other, judges it critically, and, as it were, takes it as its object. Our suspicion that the critical agency which is here split off from the ego might also show its independence in other circumstances will be confirmed by every further observation. We shall really find grounds for distinguishing this agency from the rest of the ego. What we are here becoming acquainted with is the agency commonly called 'conscience'; we shall count it, along with the censorship of consciousness and reality-testing, among the major institutions of the ego,[1] and we shall come upon evidence to show that it can become diseased on its own account. In the clinical picture of melancholia, dissatisfaction with the ego on moral grounds is the most outstanding feature. The patient's self-evaluation concerns itself much less frequently with bodily infirmity, ugliness or weakness, or with social inferiority; of this category, it is only his fears and asseverations of becoming poor that occupy a prominent position.

There is one observation, not at all difficult to make, which leads to the explanation of the contradiction mentioned above [at the end of the last paragraph but one]. If one listens patiently to a melancholic's many and various self-accusations, one cannot in the end avoid the impression that often the most violent of them are hardly at all applicable to the patient himself, but that

1. [See above, p. 241.]

with insignificant modifications they do fit someone else, someone whom the patient loves or has loved or should love. Every time one examines the facts this conjecture is confirmed. So we find the key to the clinical picture: we perceive that the self-reproaches are reproaches against a loved object which have been shifted away from it on to the patient's own ego.

The woman who loudly pities her husband for being tied to such an incapable wife as herself is really accusing her *husband* of being incapable, in whatever sense she may mean this. There is no need to be greatly surprised that a few genuine self-reproaches are scattered among those that have been transposed back. These are allowed to obtrude themselves, since they help to mask the others and make recognition of the true state of affairs impossible. Moreover, they derive from the *pros* and *cons* of the conflict of love that has led to the loss of love. The behaviour of the patients, too, now becomes much more intelligible. Their complaints are really 'plaints' in the old sense of the word. They are not ashamed and do not hide themselves, since everything derogatory that they say about themselves is at bottom said about someone else. Moreover, they are far from evincing towards those around them the attitude of humility and submissiveness that would alone befit such worthless people. On the contrary, they make the greatest nuisance of themselves, and always seem as though they felt slighted and had been treated with great injustice. All this is possible only because the reactions expressed in their behaviour still proceed from a mental constellation of revolt, which has then, by a certain process, passed over into the crushed state of melancholia.

There is no difficulty in reconstructing this process. An object-choice, an attachment of the libido to a particular person, had at one time existed; then, owing to a *real slight or disappointment* coming from this loved person, the object-relationship was shattered. The result was not the normal one of a withdrawal of the libido from this object and a displacement of it on to a new one, but something different, for whose coming-about various conditions seem to be necessary. The object-cathexis proved to have little power of resistance and was brought to an end. But the free libido was not displaced on to another object; it was withdrawn into the ego. There, however, it was not employed in any unspecified way, but served to establish an *identification* of the ego with the abandoned object. Thus the shadow of the object fell upon the ego, and the latter could henceforth be judged by a special[1] agency, as though it were an object, the forsaken object. In this way an object-loss was transformed into an ego-loss and the conflict between the ego and the loved person into a cleavage between the critical activity of the ego and the ego as altered by identification.

One or two things may be directly inferred with regard to the preconditions and effects of a process such as this. On the one hand, a strong fixation to the loved object must have been present; on the other hand, in contradiction to this, the object-cathexis must have had little power of resistance. As Otto Rank has aptly remarked, this contradiction seems to imply that the object-choice has been effected on a narcissistic basis, so that the object-cathexis, when obstacles come in its way, can regress to narcissism. The narcissistic identification with the object then becomes a substitute for the erotic cathexis, the result of which is that in spite of the conflict with the loved person the love-relation need not be given up. This substitution of identification for object-love is an important mechanism in the narcissistic affections; Karl Landauer (1914) has lately been able to point to it in the process of recovery in a case of schizophrenia. It represents, of course, a *regression* from one type of object-choice to original narcissism. We have elsewhere shown that identification is a preliminary stage of object-choice, that it is the first way – and one that is expressed in an ambivalent fashion – in which the ego picks out an object. The ego wants to incorporate this object into itself, and, in accordance with the oral or cannibalistic phase of libidinal development in which it is, it wants to do so by devouring it.[2] Abraham is undoubtedly right in attrib-

1. [In the first (1917) edition only, this word does not occur.]
2. [See above, p. 136. Cf. also Editor's Note, pp. 249–50.]

uting to this connection the refusal of nourishment met with in severe forms of melancholia.[1]

The conclusion which our theory would require – namely, that the disposition to fall ill of melancholia (or some part of that disposition) lies in the predominance of the narcissistic type of object-choice – has unfortunately not yet been confirmed by observation. In the opening remarks of this paper, I admitted that the empirical material upon which this study is founded is insufficient for our needs. If we could assume an agreement between the results of observation and what we have inferred, we should not hesitate to include this regression from object-cathexis to the still narcissistic oral phase of the libido in our characterization of melancholia. Identifications with the object are by no means rare in the transference neuroses either; indeed, they are a well-known mechanism of symptom-formation, especially in hysteria. The difference, however, between narcissistic and hysterical identification may be seen in this: that, whereas in the former the object-cathexis is abandoned, in the latter it persists and manifests its influence, though this is usually confined to certain isolated actions and innervations. In any case, in the transference neuroses, too, identification is the expression of there being something in common, which may signify love. Narcissistic identification is the older of the two and it paves the way to an understanding of hysterical identification, which has been less thoroughly studied.[2]

Melancholia, therefore, borrows some of its features from mourning, and the others from the process of regression from narcissistic object-choice to narcissism. It is on the one hand, like mourning, a reaction to the real loss of a loved object; but over and above this, it is marked by a determinant which is absent in normal mourning or which, if it is present, transforms

1. [Abraham first drew Freud's attention to this in a private letter written on 31 March 1915. (Cf. Freud, 1965*a*.) See Jones's biography (1955, 368).]

2. [Identification was discussed later by Freud in his *Group Psychology* (1921*c*), *P.F.L.*, **12**, 134 ff. There is an early account of hysterical identification in *The Interpretation of Dreams* (1900*a*), *P.F.L.*, **4**, 232–3.]

the latter into pathological mourning. The loss of a love-object is an excellent opportunity for the ambivalence in love-relationships to make itself effective and come into the open.[1] Where there is a disposition to obsessional neurosis the conflict due to ambivalence gives a pathological cast to mourning and forces it to express itself in the form of self-reproaches to the effect that the mourner himself is to blame for the loss of the loved object, i.e. that he has willed it. These obsessional states of depression following upon the death of a loved person show us what the conflict due to ambivalence can achieve by itself when there is no regressive drawing-in of libido as well. In melancholia, the occasions which give rise to the illness extend for the most part beyond the clear case of a loss by death, and include all those situations of being slighted, neglected or disappointed, which can import opposed feelings of love and hate into the relationship or reinforce an already existing ambivalence. This conflict due to ambivalence, which sometimes arises more from real experiences, sometimes more from constitutional factors, must not be overlooked among the preconditions of melancholia. If the love for the object – a love which cannot be given up though the object itself is given up – takes refuge in narcissistic identification, then the hate comes into operation on this substitutive object, abusing it, debasing it, making it suffer and deriving sadistic satisfaction from its suffering. The self-tormenting in melancholia, which is without doubt enjoyable, signifies, just like the corresponding phenomenon in obsessional neurosis, a satisfaction of trends of sadism and hate[2] which relate to an object, and which have been turned round upon the subject's own self in the ways we have been discussing. In both disorders the patients usually still succeed, by the circuitous path of self-punishment, in taking revenge on the original object and in tormenting their loved one through their illness, having resorted to it in order to avoid the need to express

1. [Much of what follows is elaborated in Chapter V of *The Ego and the Id* (1923*b*), p. 389 ff. below.]

2. For the distinction between the two, see my paper on 'Instincts and their Vicissitudes' [pp. 136–7 above].

their hostility to him openly. After all, the person who has occasioned the patient's emotional disorder, and on whom his illness is centred, is usually to be found in his immediate environment. The melancholic's erotic cathexis in regard to his object has thus undergone a double vicissitude: part of it has regressed to identification, but the other part, under the influence of the conflict due to ambivalence, has been carried back to the stage of sadism which is nearer to that conflict.

It is this sadism alone that solves the riddle of the tendency to suicide which makes melancholia so interesting – and so dangerous. So immense is the ego's self-love, which we have come to recognize as the primal state from which instinctual life proceeds, and so vast is the amount of narcissistic libido which we see liberated in the fear that emerges at a threat to life, that we cannot conceive how that ego can consent to its own destruction. We have long known, it is true, that no neurotic harbours thoughts of suicide which he has not turned back upon himself from murderous impulses against others, but we have never been able to explain what interplay of forces can carry such a purpose through to execution. The analysis of melancholia now shows that the ego can kill itself only if, owing to the return of the object-cathexis, it can treat itself as an object – if it is able to direct against itself the hostility which relates to an object and which represents the ego's original reaction to objects in the external world.[1] Thus in regression from narcissistic object-choice the object has, it is true, been got rid of, but it has nevertheless proved more powerful than the ego itself. In the two opposed situations of being most intensely in love and of suicide the ego is overwhelmed by the object, though in totally different ways.[2]

As regards one particular striking feature of melancholia that we have mentioned [p. 256], the prominence of the fear of becoming poor, it seems plausible to suppose that it is derived

1. Cf. 'Instincts and their Vicissitudes' [p. 134 above].

2. [Later discussions of suicide will be found in Chapter V of *The Ego and the Id* (1923*b*), p. 394 ff. below, and in the last pages of 'The Economic Problem of Masochism' (1924*c*), pp. 425–6 below.]

from anal erotism which has been torn out of its context and altered in a regressive sense.

Melancholia confronts us with yet other problems, the answer to which in part eludes us. The fact that it passes off after a certain time has elapsed without leaving traces of any gross changes is a feature it shares with mourning. We found by way of explanation [p. 253] that in mourning time is needed for the command of reality-testing to be carried out in detail, and that when this work has been accomplished the ego will have succeeded in freeing its libido from the lost object. We may imagine that the ego is occupied with analogous work during the course of a melancholia; in neither case have we any insight into the economics of the course of events. The sleeplessness in melancholia testifies to the rigidity of the condition, the impossibility of effecting the general drawing-in of cathexes necessary for sleep. The complex of melancholia behaves like an open wound, drawing to itself cathectic energies – which in the transference neuroses we have called 'anticathexes' – from all directions, and emptying the ego until it is totally impoverished.[1] It can easily prove resistant to the ego's wish to sleep.

What is probably a somatic factor, and one which cannot be explained psychogenically, makes itself visible in the regular amelioration in the condition that takes place towards evening. These considerations bring up the question whether a loss in the ego irrespectively of the object – a purely narcissistic blow to the ego – may not suffice to produce the picture of melancholia and whether an impoverishment of ego-libido directly due to toxins may not be able to produce certain forms of the disease.

The most remarkable characteristic of melancholia, and the one in most need of explanation, is its tendency to change round into mania – a state which is the opposite of it in its symptoms. As we know, this does not happen to every melancholia. Some

1. [This analogy of the open wound appears already (illustrated by two diagrams) in the rather abstruse Section VI of Freud's early note on melancholia (Freud, 1950*a*, Draft G, probably written in January 1895). See Editor's Note, p. 248.]

cases run their course in periodic relapses, during the intervals between which signs of mania may be entirely absent or only very slight. Others show the regular alternation of melancholic and manic phases which has led to the hypothesis of a circular insanity. One would be tempted to regard these cases as non-psychogenic, if it were not for the fact that the psychoanalytic method has succeeded in arriving at a solution and effecting a therapeutic improvement in several cases precisely of this kind. It is not merely permissible, therefore, but incumbent upon us to extend an analytic explanation of melancholia to mania as well.

I cannot promise that this attempt will prove entirely satisfactory. It hardly carries us much beyond the possibility of taking one's initial bearings. We have two things to go upon: the first is a psychoanalytic impression, and the second what we may perhaps call a matter of general economic experience. The impression which several psychoanalytic investigators have already put into words is that the content of mania is no different from that of melancholia, that both disorders are wrestling with the same 'complex', but that probably in melancholia the ego has succumbed to the complex whereas in mania it has mastered it or pushed it aside. Our second pointer is afforded by the observation that all states such as joy, exultation or triumph, which give us the normal model for mania, depend on the same economic conditions. What has happened here is that, as a result of some influence, a large expenditure of psychical energy, long maintained or habitually occurring, has at last become unnecessary, so that it is available for numerous applications and possibilities of discharge – when, for instance, some poor wretch, by winning a large sum of money, is suddenly relieved from chronic worry about his daily bread, or when a long and arduous struggle is finally crowned with success, or when a man finds himself in a position to throw off at a single blow some oppressive compulsion, some false position which he has long had to keep up, and so on. All such situations are characterized by high spirits, by the signs of discharge of joyful emotion and by increased readiness for all kinds of action – in just the same way as in mania, and in complete contrast to the depression and inhibition of melancholia. We may venture to assert that mania is nothing other than a triumph of this sort, only that here again what the ego has surmounted and what it is triumphing over remain hidden from it. Alcoholic intoxication, which belongs to the same class of states, may (in so far as it is an elated one) be explained in the same way; here there is probably a suspension, produced by toxins, of expenditures of energy in repression. The popular view likes to assume that a person in a manic state of this kind finds such delight in movement and action because he is so 'cheerful'. This false connection must of course be put right. The fact is that the economic condition in the subject's mind referred to above has been fulfilled, and this is the reason why he is in such high spirits on the one hand and so uninhibited in action on the other.

If we put these two indications together,[1] what we find is this. In mania, the ego must have got over the loss of the object (or its mourning over the loss, or perhaps the object itself), and thereupon the whole quota of anticathexis which the painful suffering of melancholia had drawn to itself from the ego and 'bound' will have become available [p. 262]. Moreover, the manic subject plainly demonstrates his liberation from the object which was the cause of his suffering, by seeking like a ravenously hungry man for new object-cathexes.

This explanation certainly sounds plausible, but in the first place it is too indefinite, and, secondly, it gives rise to more new problems and doubts than we can answer. We will not evade a discussion of them, even though we cannot expect it to lead us to a clear understanding.

In the first place, normal mourning, too, overcomes the loss of the object, and it, too, while it lasts, absorbs all the energies of the ego. Why, then, after it has run its course, is there no hint in its case of the economic condition for a phase of triumph? I find it impossible to answer this objection straight away. It also draws our attention to the fact that we do not even know the

1. [The 'psychoanalytic impression' and the 'general economic experience'.]

economic means by which mourning carries out its task [p. 253]. Possibly, however, a conjecture will help us here. Each single one of the memories and situations of expectancy which demonstrate the libido's attachment to the lost object is met by the verdict of reality that the object no longer exists; and the ego, confronted as it were with the question whether it shall share this fate, is persuaded by the sum of the narcissistic satisfactions it derives from being alive to sever its attachment to the object that has been abolished. We may perhaps suppose that this work of severance is so slow and gradual that by the time it has been finished the expenditure of energy necessary for it is also dissipated.[1]

It is tempting to go on from this conjecture about the work of mourning and try to give an account of the work of melancholia. Here we are met at the outset by an uncertainty. So far we have hardly considered melancholia from the topographical point of view, nor asked ourselves in and between what psychical systems the work of melancholia goes on. What part of the mental processes of the disease still takes place in connection with the unconscious object-cathexes that have been given up, and what part in connection with their substitute, by identification, in the ego?

The quick and easy answer is that 'the unconscious (thing-) presentation[2] of the object has been abandoned by the libido'. In reality, however, this presentation is made up of innumerable single impressions (or unconscious traces of them), and this withdrawal of libido is not a process that can be accomplished in a moment, but must certainly, as in mourning, be one in which progress is long-drawn-out and gradual. Whether it begins simultaneously at several points or follows some sort of fixed sequence is not easy to decide; in analyses it often becomes evident that first one and then another memory is activated, and that the laments which always sound the same and are weari-

1. The economic standpoint has hitherto received little attention in psychoanalytic writings. I would mention as an exception a paper by Victor Tausk (1913) on motives for repression devalued by recompenses.

2. ['*Dingvorstellung*.' See above, p. 206 *n*.]

some in their monotony nevertheless take their rise each time in some different unconscious source. If the object does not possess this great significance for the ego – a significance reinforced by a thousand links – then, too, its loss will not be of a kind to cause either mourning or melancholia. This characteristic of detaching the libido bit by bit is therefore to be ascribed alike to mourning and to melancholia; it is probably supported by the same economic situation and serves the same purposes in both.

As we have seen, however [p. 259 f.], melancholia contains something more than normal mourning. In melancholia the relation to the object is no simple one; it is complicated by the conflict due to ambivalence. The ambivalence is either constitutional, i.e. is an element of every love-relation formed by this particular ego, or else it proceeds precisely from those experiences that involved the threat of losing the object. For this reason the exciting causes of melancholia have a much wider range than those of mourning, which is for the most part occasioned only by a real loss of the object, by its death. In melancholia, accordingly, countless separate struggles are carried on over the object, in which hate and love contend with each other; the one seeks to detach the libido from the object, the other to maintain this position of the libido against the assault. The location of these separate struggles cannot be assigned to any system but the *Ucs.*, the region of the memory-traces of *things* (as contrasted with *word*-cathexes). In mourning, too, the efforts to detach the libido are made in this same system; but in it nothing hinders these processes from proceeding along the normal path through the *Pcs.* to consciousness. This path is blocked for the work of melancholia, owing perhaps to a number of causes or a combination of them. Constitutional ambivalence belongs by its nature to the repressed; traumatic experiences in connection with the object may have activated other repressed material. Thus everything to do with these struggles due to ambivalence remains withdrawn from consciousness, until the outcome characteristic of melancholia has set in. This, as we know, consists in the threatened libidinal cathexis at length abandoning the object, only, however, to draw back to the place in the ego from which it had proceeded. So by taking flight into the ego love escapes extinction. After this regression of the libido the process can become conscious, and it is represented to consciousness as a conflict between one part of the ego and the critical agency.

What consciousness is aware of in the work of melancholia is thus not the essential part of it, nor is it even the part which we may credit with an influence in bringing the ailment to an end. We see that the ego debases itself and rages against itself, and we understand as little as the patient what this can lead to and how it can change. We can more readily attribute such a function to the *unconscious* part of the work, because it is not difficult to perceive an essential analogy between the work of melancholia and of mourning. Just as mourning impels the ego to give up the object by declaring the object to be dead and offering the ego the inducement of continuing to live [p. 265], so does each single struggle of ambivalence loosen the fixation of the libido to the object by disparaging it, denigrating it and even as it were killing it. It is possible for the process in the *Ucs.* to come to an end, either after the fury has spent itself or after the object has been abandoned as valueless. We cannot tell which of these two possibilities is the regular or more usual one in bringing melancholia to an end, nor what influence this termination has on the future course of the case. The ego may enjoy in this the satisfaction of knowing itself as the better of the two, as superior to the object.

Even if we accept this view of the work of melancholia, it still does not supply an explanation of the one point on which we were seeking light. It was our expectation that the economic condition for the emergence of mania after the melancholia has run its course is to be found in the ambivalence which dominates the latter affection; and in this we found support from analogies in various other fields. But there is one fact before which that expectation must bow. Of the three preconditions of melancholia – loss of the object, ambivalence, and regression of libido into the ego – the first two are also found in the obsessional self-reproaches arising after a death has occurred. In those cases it is unquestionably the ambivalence which is the motive force of the conflict, and observation shows that after the conflict has come to an end there is nothing left over in the nature of the triumph of a manic state of mind. We are thus led to the third factor as the only one responsible for the result. The accumulation of cathexis which is at first bound and then, after the work of melancholia is finished, becomes free and makes mania possible must be linked with regression of the libido to narcissism. The conflict within the ego, which melancholia substitutes for the struggle over the object, must act like a painful wound which calls for an extraordinarily high anticathexis. – But here once again, it will be well to call a halt and to postpone any further explanation of mania until we have gained some insight into the economic nature, first, of physical pain, and then of the mental pain which is analogous to it.[1] As we already know, the interdependence of the complicated problems of the mind forces us to break off every enquiry before it is completed – till the outcome of some other enquiry can come to its assistance.[2]

1. [See footnote 1, p. 146 above.]

2. [*Footnote added* 1925:] Cf. a continuation of this discussion of mania in *Group Psychology and the Analysis of the Ego* (1921*c*) [*P.F.L.*, **12**, 164–5].

BEYOND THE PLEASURE PRINCIPLE
(1920)

EDITOR'S NOTE

JENSEITS DES LUSTPRINZIPS

(A) German Editions:

1920 Leipzig, Vienna and Zurich: Internationaler Psychoanalytischer Verlag. Pp. 60.
1921 2nd ed. Same publishers. Pp. 64.
1923 3rd ed. Same publishers. Pp. 94.
1925 *Gesammelte Schriften*, **6**, 191–257.
1940 *Gesammelte Werke*, **13**, 3–69.

(B) English Translations:
Beyond the Pleasure Principle

1922 London and Vienna: International Psycho-Analytical Press. Pp. viii + 90. (Tr. C. J. M. Hubback; Pref. Ernest Jones.)
1924 New York: Boni and Liveright.
1942 London: Hogarth Press and Institute of Psycho-Analysis. (Re-issue of above.)
1950 Same publishers. Pp. vi + 97. (Tr. J. Strachey.)
1955 *Standard Edition*, **18**, 1–64. (A somewhat modified version of the translation published in 1950.)

Freud made a number of additions and alterations in the second edition, and a few in the third and *Gesammelte Schriften* editions. All those of importance are recorded in footnotes. The present edition is a reprint of the *Standard Edition* version, with some editorial modifications.

As is shown by his correspondence, Freud had begun working

on a first draft of *Beyond the Pleasure Principle* in March 1919, and he reported the draft as finished in the following May. During the same month he was completing his paper on 'The Uncanny' (1919*h*), which includes a paragraph setting out much of the gist of the present work in a few sentences. In this paragraph he refers to the 'compulsion to repeat' as a phenomenon exhibited in the behaviour of children and in psychoanalytic treatment; he suggests that this compulsion is something derived from the most intimate nature of the instincts; and he declares that it is powerful enough to disregard the pleasure principle. There is, however, no allusion to the 'death instincts'. He adds that he has already completed a detailed exposition of the subject. The paper on 'The Uncanny' containing this summary was published in the autumn of 1919. But Freud held back *Beyond the Pleasure Principle* for another year. In the early part of 1920 he was once more at work on it; he was still revising the work in May and June and it was finally completed by the middle of July 1920.

In the series of Freud's metapsychological writings, *Beyond the Pleasure Principle* may be regarded as introducing the final phase of his views. He had already drawn attention to the 'compulsion to repeat' as a clinical phenomenon, but here he attributes to it the characteristics of an instinct; here too for the first time he brings forward the new dichotomy between Eros and the death instincts which found its full elaboration in *The Ego and the Id* (1923*b*), p. 380 ff. below. In *Beyond the Pleasure Principle*, too, we can see signs of the new picture of the anatomical structure of the mind which was to dominate all Freud's later writings. Finally, the problem of destructiveness, which played an ever more prominent part in his theoretical works, makes its first explicit appearance. The derivation of various elements in the present discussion from his earlier metapsychological works – such as 'The Two Principles of Mental Functioning' (1911*b*), 'Narcissism' (1914*c*) and 'Instincts and their Vicissitudes' (1915*c*), see pp. 35, 65 and 113 above – will be obvious. But what is particularly remarkable is the closeness with which some of the earlier sections of the present work follow the 'Project for a Scientific Psychology' (1950*a*), drafted by Freud twenty-five years earlier, in 1895.

BEYOND THE PLEASURE PRINCIPLE

I

In the theory of psychoanalysis we have no hesitation in assuming that the course taken by mental events is automatically regulated by the pleasure principle. We believe, that is to say, that the course of those events is invariably set in motion by an unpleasurable tension, and that it takes a direction such that its final outcome coincides with a lowering of that tension – that is, with an avoidance of unpleasure or a production of pleasure. In taking that course into account in our consideration of the mental processes which are the subject of our study, we are introducing an 'economic' point of view into our work; and if, in describing those processes, we try to estimate this 'economic' factor in addition to the 'topographical' and 'dynamic' ones, we shall, I think, be giving the most complete description of them of which we can at present conceive, and one which deserves to be distinguished by the term 'metapsychological'.[1]

It is of no concern to us in this connection to enquire how far, with this hypothesis of the pleasure principle, we have approached or adopted any particular, historically established, philosophical system. We have arrived at these speculative assumptions in an attempt to describe and to account for the facts of daily observation in our field of study. Priority and originality are not among the aims that psychoanalytic work sets itself; and the impressions that underlie the hypothesis of the pleasure principle are so obvious that they can scarcely be overlooked. On the other hand we would readily express our gratitude to any philosophical or psychological theory which was able to inform us of the meaning of the feelings of pleasure and

1. [See Section IV of 'The Unconscious' (1915*e*), p. 183 ff. above.]

unpleasure which act so imperatively upon us. But on this point we are, alas, offered nothing to our purpose. This is the most obscure and inaccessible region of the mind, and, since we cannot avoid contact with it, the least rigid hypothesis, it seems to me, will be the best. We have decided to relate pleasure and unpleasure to the quantity of excitation that is present in the mind but is not in any way 'bound';[1] and to relate them in such a manner that unpleasure corresponds to an *increase* in the quantity of excitation and pleasure to a *diminution*. What we are implying by this is not a simple relation between the strength of the feelings of pleasure and unpleasure and the corresponding modifications in the quantity of excitation; least of all – in view of all we have been taught by psycho-physiology – are we suggesting any directly proportional ratio: the factor that determines the feeling is probably the amount of increase or diminution in the quantity of excitation *in a given period of time*. Experiment might possibly play a part here; but it is not advisable for us analysts to go into the problem further so long as our way is not pointed by quite definite observations.[2]

We cannot, however, remain indifferent to the discovery that an investigator of such penetration as G. T. Fechner held a view on the subject of pleasure and unpleasure which coincides in all essentials with the one that has been forced upon us by psychoanalytic work. Fechner's statement is to be found contained in a small work, *Einige Ideen zur Schöpfungs- und Entwicklungsgeschichte der Organismen*, 1873 (Part XI, Supplement, 94), and reads as follows: 'In so far as conscious impulses always have some relation to pleasure or unpleasure, pleasure and unpleasure too can be regarded as having a psycho-physical relation to conditions of stability and instability. This provides a basis for a

1. [The concepts of 'quantity' and of 'bound' excitation, which run through the whole of Freud's writings, found what is perhaps their most detailed discussion in the early 'Project' (1950*a* [1895]). See in particular the long discussion of the term 'bound' near the end of Section 1 of Part III of that work. See also p. 306 f. below.]

2. [This point is again mentioned below on p. 337 and further developed in 'The Economic Problem of Masochism' (1924*c*), p. 413 ff. below. See also Section 7 of Part I of the 'Project'.]

hypothesis into which I propose to enter in greater detail elsewhere. According to this hypothesis, every psycho-physical motion rising above the threshold of consciousness is attended by pleasure in proportion as, beyond a certain limit, it approximates to complete stability, and is attended by unpleasure in proportion as, beyond a certain limit, it deviates from complete stability; while between the two limits, which may be described as qualitative thresholds of pleasure and unpleasure, there is a certain margin of aesthetic indifference . . .'[1]

The facts which have caused us to believe in the dominance of the pleasure principle in mental life also find expression in the hypothesis that the mental apparatus endeavours to keep the quantity of excitation present in it as low as possible or at least to keep it constant. This latter hypothesis is only another way of stating the pleasure principle; for if the work of the mental apparatus is directed towards keeping the quantity of excitation low, then anything that is calculated to increase that quantity is bound to be felt as adverse to the functioning of the apparatus, that is as unpleasurable. The pleasure principle follows from the principle of constancy: actually the latter principle was inferred from the facts which forced us to adopt the pleasure principle.[2] Moreover, a more detailed discussion will show that the tendency which we thus attribute to the mental apparatus is subsumed as a special case under Fechner's principle of the 'tendency towards stability', to which he has brought the feelings of pleasure and unpleasure into relation.

It must be pointed out, however, that strictly speaking it is incorrect to talk of the dominance of the pleasure principle over the course of mental processes. If such a dominance existed, the

1. [Cf. 'Project', end of Section 8 of Part I. – 'Aesthetic' is here used in the old sense of 'relating to sensation or perception'.]

2. [The 'principle of constancy' dates back to the very beginning of Freud's psychological studies. The first published discussion of it of any length was by Breuer (in semi-physiological terms) towards the end of Section 2(A) of his theoretical part of the *Studies on Hysteria* (Breuer and Freud, 1895), *P.F.L.*, **3**, 272–8, 272 *n.* 1, and the Editor's Introduction, ibid., 37 ff. See also 'Instincts and their Vicissitudes' (1915*c*), p. 115 *n.* 1 and p. 117 f. above, as well as the Editor's Introduction to *The Interpretation of Dreams* (1900*a*), *P.F.L.*, **4**, 40–41.

immense majority of our mental processes would have to be accompanied by pleasure or to lead to pleasure, whereas universal experience completely contradicts any such conclusion. The most that can be said, therefore, is that there exists in the mind a strong *tendency* towards the pleasure principle, but that that tendency is opposed by certain other forces or circumstances, so that the final outcome cannot always be in harmony with the tendency towards pleasure. We may compare what Fechner (1873, 90) remarks on a similar point: 'Since however a tendency towards an aim does not imply that the aim is attained, and since in general the aim is attainable only by approximations. . . .'

If we turn now to the question of what circumstances are able to prevent the pleasure principle from being carried into effect, we find ourselves once more on secure and well-trodden ground and, in framing our answer, we have at our disposal a rich fund of analytic experience.

The first example of the pleasure principle being inhibited in this way is a familiar one which occurs with regularity. We know that the pleasure principle is proper to a *primary* method of working on the part of the mental apparatus, but that, from the point of view of the self-preservation of the organism among the difficulties of the external world, it is from the very outset inefficient and even highly dangerous. Under the influence of the ego's instincts of self-preservation, the pleasure principle is replaced by the *reality principle*.[1] This latter principle does not abandon the intention of ultimately obtaining pleasure, but it nevertheless demands and carries into effect the postponement of satisfaction, the abandonment of a number of possibilities of gaining satisfaction and the temporary toleration of unpleasure as a step on the long indirect road to pleasure. The pleasure principle long persists, however, as the method of working employed by the sexual instincts, which are so hard to 'educate', and, starting from those instincts, or in the ego itself, it often succeeds in overcoming the reality principle, to the detriment of the organism as a whole.

1. [See 'Formulations on the Two Principles of Mental Functioning', Freud 1911*b*, pp. 36–7 above.]

There can be no doubt, however, that the replacement of the pleasure principle by the reality principle can only be made responsible for a small number, and by no means the most intense, of unpleasurable experiences. Another occasion of the release of unpleasure, which occurs with no less regularity, is to be found in the conflicts and dissensions that take place in the mental apparatus while the ego is passing through its development into more highly composite organizations. Almost all the energy with which the apparatus is filled arises from its innate instinctual impulses. But these are not all allowed to reach the same phases of development. In the course of things it happens again and again that individual instincts or parts of instincts turn out to be incompatible in their aims or demands with the remaining ones, which are able to combine into the inclusive unity of the ego. The former are then split off from this unity by the process of repression, held back at lower levels of psychical development and cut off, to begin with, from the possibility of satisfaction. If they succeed subsequently, as can so easily happen with repressed sexual instincts, in struggling through, by roundabout paths, to a direct or to a substitutive satisfaction, that event, which would in other cases have been an opportunity for pleasure, is felt by the ego as unpleasure. As a consequence of the old conflict which ended in repression, a new breach has occurred in the pleasure principle at the very time when certain instincts were endeavouring, in accordance with the principle, to obtain fresh pleasure. The details of the process by which repression turns a possibility of pleasure into a source of unpleasure are not yet clearly understood or cannot be clearly represented; but there is no doubt that all neurotic unpleasure is of that kind – pleasure that cannot be felt as such.[1]

The two sources of unpleasure which I have just indicated are very far from covering the majority of our unpleasurable experiences. But as regards the remainder it can be asserted with

1. [*Footnote added* 1925:] No doubt the essential point is that pleasure and unpleasure, being conscious feelings, are attached to the ego. [This is made clearer in a discussion at the beginning of Chapter II of *Inhibitions, Symptoms and Anxiety* (1926*d*), *P.F.L.*, **10**, 242–3.]

some show of justification that their presence does not contradict the dominance of the pleasure principle. Most of the unpleasure that we experience is *perceptual* unpleasure. It may be perception of pressure by unsatisfied instincts; or it may be external perception which is either distressing in itself or which excites unpleasurable expectations in the mental apparatus – that is, which is recognized by it as a 'danger'. The reaction to these instinctual demands and threats of danger, a reaction which constitutes the proper activity of the mental apparatus, can then be directed in a correct manner by the pleasure principle or the reality principle by which the former is modified. This does not seem to necessitate any far-reaching limitation of the pleasure principle. Nevertheless the investigation of the mental reaction to external danger is precisely in a position to produce new material and raise fresh questions bearing upon our present problem.

II

A CONDITION has long been known and described which occurs after severe mechanical concussions, railway disasters and other accidents involving a risk to life; it has been given the name of 'traumatic neurosis'. The terrible war which has just ended gave rise to a great number of illnesses of this kind, but it at least put an end to the temptation to attribute the cause of the disorder to organic lesions of the nervous system brought about by mechanical force.[1] The symptomatic picture presented by traumatic neurosis approaches that of hysteria in the wealth of its similar motor symptoms, but surpasses it as a rule in its strongly marked signs of subjective ailment (in which it resembles hypochondria or melancholia) as well as in the evidence it gives of a far more comprehensive general enfeeblement and disturbance of the mental capacities. No complete[2] explanation has yet been reached either of war neuroses or of the traumatic neuroses of peace. In the case of the war neuroses, the fact that the same symptoms sometimes came about[3] without the intervention of any gross mechanical force seemed at once enlightening and bewildering. In the case of the ordinary traumatic neuroses two characteristics emerge prominently: first, that the chief weight in their causation seems to rest upon the factor of surprise, of fright; and secondly, that a wound or injury inflicted simultaneously works as a rule *against* the development of a neurosis. 'Fright', 'fear' and 'anxiety'[4] are improperly used as synonymous expressions; they are in fact capable of clear distinction in their relation to danger. 'Anxiety' describes a particular state of

1. Cf. the discussion on the psychoanalysis of war neuroses by Freud, Ferenczi, Abraham, Simmel and Jones (1919) [to which Freud provided the introduction (1919*d*). See also his posthumously published 'Report on the Electrical Treatment of War Neuroses' (1955*c* [1920]).]

2. ['Complete' was added in 1921.]

3. ['Could sometimes come about' in 1920.]

4. [In German, '*Schreck*', '*Furcht*' and '*Angst*'.]

expecting the danger or preparing for it, even though it may be an unknown one. 'Fear' requires a definite object of which to be afraid. 'Fright', however, is the name we give to the state a person gets into when he has run into danger without being prepared for it; it emphasizes the factor of surprise. I do not believe anxiety can produce a traumatic neurosis. There is something about anxiety that protects its subject against fright and so against fright-neuroses. We shall return to this point later [p. 303 f.].[1]

The study of dreams may be considered the most trustworthy method of investigating deep mental processes. Now dreams occurring in traumatic neuroses have the characteristic of repeatedly bringing the patient back into the situation of his accident, a situation from which he wakes up in another fright. This astonishes people far too little. They think the fact that the traumatic experience is constantly forcing itself upon the patient even in his sleep is a proof of the strength of that experience: the patient is, as one might say, fixated to his trauma. Fixations to the experience which started the illness have long been familiar to us in hysteria. Breuer and Freud declared in 1893[2] that 'hysterics suffer mainly from reminiscences'. In the war neuroses, too, observers like Ferenczi and Simmel have been able to explain certain motor symptoms by fixation to the moment at which the trauma occurred.

I am not aware, however, that patients suffering from traumatic neurosis are much occupied in their waking lives with memories of their accident. Perhaps they are more concerned with *not* thinking of it. Anyone who accepts it as something self-

1. [Freud is very far indeed from always carrying out the distinction he makes here. More often than not he uses the word '*Angst*' to denote a state of fear without any reference to the future. It seems not unlikely that in this passage he is beginning to adumbrate the distinction drawn in *Inhibitions, Symptoms and Anxiety* (1926*d*) between anxiety as a reaction to a traumatic situation – probably equivalent to what is here called *Schreck* – and anxiety as a warning signal of the approach of such an event. (Cf. *P.F.L.*, **10**, 243 ff. and 326–8.) See also his use of the phrase 'preparedness for anxiety' on p. 303.]

2. ['On the Psychical Mechanism of Hysterical Phenomena' (1893*a*), end of Section I, *P.F.L.*, **3**, 58.]

evident that their dreams should put them back at night into the situation that caused them to fall ill has misunderstood the nature of dreams. It would be more in harmony with their nature if they showed the patient pictures from his healthy past or of the cure for which he hopes. If we are not to be shaken in our belief in the wish-fulfilling tenor of dreams by the dreams of traumatic neurotics, we still have one resource open to us: we may argue that the function of dreaming, like so much else, is upset in this condition and diverted from its purposes, or we may be driven to reflect on the mysterious masochistic trends of the ego.[1]

At this point I propose to leave the dark and dismal subject of the traumatic neurosis and pass on to examine the method of working employed by the mental apparatus in one of its earliest *normal* activities – I mean in children's play.

The different theories of children's play have only recently been summarized and discussed from the psychoanalytic point of view by Pfeifer (1919), to whose paper I would refer my readers. These theories attempt to discover the motives which lead children to play, but they fail to bring into the foreground the *economic* motive, the consideration of the yield of pleasure involved. Without wishing to include the whole field covered by these phenomena, I have been able, through a chance opportunity which presented itself, to throw some light upon the first game played by a little boy of one and a half and invented by himself. It was more than a mere fleeting observation, for I lived under the same roof as the child and his parents for some weeks, and it was some time before I discovered the meaning of the puzzling activity which he constantly repeated.

The child was not at all precocious in his intellectual development. At the age of one and a half he could say only a few comprehensible words; he could also make use of a number of sounds which expressed a meaning intelligible to those around him. He was, however, on good terms with his parents and their

1. [The last 15 words of this sentence were added in 1921. For all this see *The Interpretation of Dreams* (1900*a*), *P.F.L.*, 4, 701 ff.]

one servant-girl, and tributes were paid to his being a 'good boy'. He did not disturb his parents at night, he conscientiously obeyed orders not to touch certain things or go into certain rooms, and above all he never cried when his mother left him for a few hours. At the same time, he was greatly attached to his mother, who had not only fed him herself but had also looked after him without any outside help. This good little boy, however, had an occasional disturbing habit of taking any small objects he could get hold of and throwing them away from him into a corner, under the bed, and so on, so that hunting for his toys and picking them up was often quite a business. As he did this he gave vent to a loud, long-drawn-out 'o-o-o-o', accompanied by an expression of interest and satisfaction. His mother and the writer of the present account were agreed in thinking that this was not a mere interjection but represented the German word '*fort*' ['gone']. I eventually realized that it was a game and that the only use he made of any of his toys was to play 'gone' with them. One day I made an observation which confirmed my view. The child had a wooden reel with a piece of string tied round it. It never occurred to him to pull it along the floor behind him, for instance, and play at its being a carriage. What he did was to hold the reel by the string and very skilfully throw it over the edge of his curtained cot, so that it disappeared into it, at the same time uttering his expressive 'o-o-o-o'. He then pulled the reel out of the cot again by the string and hailed its reappearance with a joyful '*da*' ['there']. This, then, was the complete game – disappearance and return. As a rule one only witnessed its first act, which was repeated untiringly as a game in itself, though there is no doubt that the greater pleasure was attached to the second act.[1]

1. A further observation subsequently confirmed this interpretation fully. One day the child's mother had been away for several hours and on her return was met with the words 'Baby o-o-o-o!' which was at first incomprehensible. It soon turned out, however, that during this long period of solitude the child had found a method of making *himself* disappear. He had discovered his reflection in a full-length mirror which did not quite reach to the ground, so that by crouching down he could make his mirror-image 'gone'. [A further reference to this story will be found in *The Interpretation of Dreams*, *P.F.L.*, **4**, 596 *n*.]

The interpretation of the game then became obvious. It was related to the child's great cultural achievement – the instinctual renunciation (that is, the renunciation of instinctual satisfaction) which he had made in allowing his mother to go away without protesting. He compensated himself for this, as it were, by himself staging the disappearance and return of the objects within his reach. It is of course a matter of indifference from the point of view of judging the effective nature of the game whether the child invented it himself or took it over on some outside suggestion. Our interest is directed to another point. The child cannot possibly have felt his mother's departure as something agreeable or even indifferent. How then does his repetition of this distressing experience as a game fit in with the pleasure principle? It may perhaps be said in reply that her departure had to be enacted as a necessary preliminary to her joyful return, and that it was in the latter that lay the true purpose of the game. But against this must be counted the observed fact that the first act, that of departure, was staged as a game in itself and far more frequently than the episode in its entirety, with its pleasurable ending.

No certain decision can be reached from the analysis of a single case like this. On an unprejudiced view one gets an impression that the child turned his experience into a game from another motive. At the outset he was in a *passive* situation – he was overpowered by the experience; but, by repeating it, unpleasurable though it was, as a game, he took on an *active* part. These efforts might be put down to an instinct for mastery that was acting independently of whether the memory was in itself pleasurable or not. But still another interpretation may be attempted. Throwing away the object so that it was 'gone' might satisfy an impulse of the child's, which was suppressed in his actual life, to revenge himself on his mother for going away from him. In that case it would have a defiant meaning: 'All right, then, go away! I don't need you. I'm sending you away myself.' A year later, the same boy whom I had observed at his first game used to take a toy, if he was angry with it, and throw it on the floor, exclaiming: 'Go to the fwont!' He had heard at that time that his absent father was 'at the front', and was far from regretting his absence; on the contrary he made it quite clear that he had no desire to be disturbed in his sole possession of his mother.[1] We know of other children who liked to express similar hostile impulses by throwing away objects instead of persons.[2] We are therefore left in doubt as to whether the impulse to work over in the mind some overpowering experience so as to make oneself master of it can find expression as a primary event, and independently of the pleasure principle. For, in the case we have been discussing, the child may, after all, only have been able to repeat his unpleasant experience in play because the repetition carried along with it a yield of pleasure of another sort but none the less a direct one.

Nor shall we be helped in our hesitation between these two views by further considering children's play. It is clear that in their play children repeat everything that has made a great impression on them in real life, and that in doing so they abreact the strength of the impression and, as one might put it, make themselves master of the situation. But on the other hand it is obvious that all their play is influenced by a wish that dominates them the whole time – the wish to be grown-up and to be able to do what grown-up people do. It can also be observed that the unpleasurable nature of an experience does not always unsuit it for play. If the doctor looks down a child's throat or carries out some small operation on him, we may be quite sure that these frightening experiences will be the subject of the next game; but we must not in that connection overlook the fact that there is a yield of pleasure from another source. As the child passes over from the passivity of the experience to the activity of the game, he hands on the disagreeable experience to one of his playmates and in this way revenges himself on a substitute.[3]

1. When this child was five and three-quarters, his mother died. Now that she was really 'gone' ('o-o-o'), the little boy showed no signs of grief. It is true that in the interval a second child had been born and had roused him to violent jealousy.

2. Cf. my note on a childhood memory of Goethe's (1917*b*) [*P.F.L.*, **14**, 323].

3. [Cf. 'Female Sexuality' (1931*b*), *P.F.L.*, **7**, 383–4.]

Nevertheless, it emerges from this discussion that there is no need to assume the existence of a special imitative instinct in order to provide a motive for play. Finally, a reminder may be added that the artistic play and artistic imitation carried out by adults, which, unlike children's, are aimed at an audience, do not spare the spectators (for instance, in tragedy) the most painful experiences and can yet be felt by them as highly enjoyable.[1] This is convincing proof that, even under the dominance of the pleasure principle, there are ways and means enough of making what is in itself unpleasurable into a subject to be recollected and worked over in the mind. The consideration of these cases and situations, which have a yield of pleasure as their final outcome, should be undertaken by some system of aesthetics with an economic approach to its subject-matter. They are of no use for *our* purposes, since they presuppose the existence and dominance of the pleasure principle; they give no evidence of the operation of tendencies *beyond* the pleasure principle, that is, of tendencies more primitive than it and independent of it.

1. [Freud had made a tentative study of this point in his posthumously published paper on 'Psychopathic Characters on the Stage' (1942*a*), *P.F.L.*, **14**, 119, which was probably written in 1905 or 1906.]

III

Twenty-five years of intense work have had as their result that the immediate aims of psychoanalytic technique are quite other to-day than they were at the outset. At first the analysing physician could do no more than discover the unconscious material that was concealed from the patient, put it together and, at the right moment, communicate it to him. Psychoanalysis was then first and foremost an art of interpreting. Since this did not solve the therapeutic problem, a further aim quickly came in view: to oblige the patient to confirm the analyst's construction from his own memory. In that endeavour the chief emphasis lay upon the patient's resistances: the art consisted now in uncovering these as quickly as possible, in pointing them out to the patient and in inducing him by human influence – this was where suggestion operating as 'transference' played its part – to abandon his resistances.

But it became ever clearer that the aim which had been set up – the aim that what was unconscious should become conscious – is not completely attainable by that method. The patient cannot remember the whole of what is repressed in him, and what he cannot remember may be precisely the essential part of it. Thus he acquires no sense of conviction of the correctness of the construction that has been communicated to him. He is obliged to *repeat* the repressed material as a contemporary experience instead of, as the physician would prefer to see, *remembering* it as something belonging to the past.[1] These reproductions, which emerge with such unwished-for exactitude, always have as their subject some portion of infantile sexual life – of the Oedipus complex, that is, and its derivatives; and they are

1. See my paper on 'Recollecting, Repeating and Working Through' (1914*g*). [An early reference will be found in this same paper to the 'compulsion to repeat', which is one of the principal topics discussed in the present work. (See also the Editor's Note above, p. 272.) – The term 'transference neurosis' in the special sense in which it is used a few lines lower down also appears in that paper.]

invariably acted out in the sphere of the transference, of the patient's relation to the physician. When things have reached this stage, it may be said that the earlier neurosis has now been replaced by a fresh, 'transference neurosis'. It has been the physician's endeavour to keep this transference neurosis within the narrowest limits: to force as much as possible into the channel of memory and to allow as little as possible to emerge as repetition. The ratio between what is remembered and what is reproduced varies from case to case. The physician cannot as a rule spare his patient this phase of the treatment. He must get him to re-experience some portion of his forgotten life, but must see to it, on the other hand, that the patient retains some degree of aloofness, which will enable him, in spite of everything, to recognize that what appears to be reality is in fact only a reflection of a forgotten past. If this can be successfully achieved, the patient's sense of conviction is won, together with the therapeutic success that is dependent on it.

In order to make it easier to understand this 'compulsion to repeat', which emerges during the psychoanalytic treatment of neurotics, we must above all get rid of the mistaken notion that what we are dealing with in our struggle against resistances is resistance on the part of the *unconscious*. The unconscious – that is to say, the 'repressed' – offers no resistance whatever to the efforts of the treatment. Indeed, it itself has no other endeavour than to break through the pressure weighing down on it and force its way either to consciousness or to a discharge through some real action. Resistance during treatment arises from the same higher strata and systems of the mind which originally carried out repression. But the fact that, as we know from experience, the motives of the resistances, and indeed the resistances themselves, are unconscious at first during the treatment, is a hint to us that we should correct a shortcoming in our terminology. We shall avoid a lack of clarity if we make our contrast not between the conscious and the unconscious but between the coherent *ego*[1] and the *repressed*. It is certain that

1. [Cf. a discussion of this in the Editor's Introduction to *The Ego and the Id* (1923*b*), below, p. 342 ff.]

much of the ego is itself unconscious, and notably what we may describe as its nucleus;[1] only a small part of it is covered by the term 'preconscious'.[2] Having replaced a purely descriptive terminology by one which is systematic or dynamic, we can say that the patient's resistance arises from his ego,[3] and we then at once perceive that the compulsion to repeat must be ascribed to the unconscious repressed. It seems probable that the compulsion can only express itself after the work of treatment has gone half-way to meet it and has loosened the repression.[4]

There is no doubt that the resistance of the conscious and preconscious ego operates under the sway of the pleasure principle: it seeks to avoid the unpleasure which would be produced by the liberation of the repressed. *Our* efforts, on the other hand, are directed towards procuring the toleration of that unpleasure by an appeal to the reality principle. But how is the compulsion to repeat – the manifestation of the power of the repressed – related to the pleasure principle? It is clear that the greater part of what is re-experienced under the compulsion to repeat must cause the ego unpleasure, since it brings to light activities of repressed instinctual impulses. That, however, is unpleasure of a kind we have already considered and does not contradict the pleasure principle: unpleasure for one system and simultaneously satisfaction for the other.[5] But we come now to a new and remarkable fact, namely that the compulsion to repeat also

1. [This statement is corrected in a footnote at the beginning of Chapter III of *The Ego and the Id*, below, p. 367.]

2. [In its present form this sentence dates from 1921. In the first edition (1920) it ran: 'It may be that much of the ego is itself unconscious; only a part of it, probably, is covered by the term "preconscious".']

3. [A fuller and somewhat different account of the sources of resistance will be found in Chapter XI of *Inhibitions, Symptoms and Anxiety* (1926*d*), *P.F.L.*, **10**, 316 ff.]

4. [*Footnote added* 1923:] I have argued elsewhere [1923*c*] that what thus comes to the help of the compulsion to repeat is the factor of 'suggestion' in the treatment – that is, the patient's submissiveness to the physician, which has its roots deep in his unconscious parental complex.

5. [Cf. Freud's allegorical use of the fairy tale of the 'Three Wishes' at the beginning of Lecture 14 of his *Introductory Lectures* (1916–17), *P.F.L.*, **1**, 253–4 and 256.]

recalls from the past experiences which include no possibility of pleasure, and which can never, even long ago, have brought satisfaction even to instinctual impulses which have since been repressed.

The early efflorescence of infantile sexual life is doomed to extinction because its wishes are incompatible with reality and with the inadequate stage of development which the child has reached. That efflorescence comes to an end in the most distressing circumstances and to the accompaniment of the most painful feelings. Loss of love and failure leave behind them a permanent injury to self-regard in the form of a narcissistic scar, which in my opinion, as well as in Marcinowski's (1918), contributes more than anything to the 'sense of inferiority' which is so common in neurotics. The child's sexual researches, on which limits are imposed by his physical development, lead to no satisfactory conclusion; hence such later complaints as 'I can't accomplish anything; I can't succeed in anything'. The tie of affection, which binds the child as a rule to the parent of the opposite sex, succumbs to disappointment, to a vain expectation of satisfaction or to jealousy over the birth of a new baby – unmistakable proof of the infidelity of the object of the child's affections. His own attempt to make a baby himself, carried out with tragic seriousness, fails shamefully. The lessening amount of affection he receives, the increasing demands of education, hard words and an occasional punishment – these show him at last the full extent to which he has been *scorned*. These are a few typical and constantly recurring instances of the ways in which the love characteristic of the age of childhood is brought to a conclusion.

Patients repeat all of these unwanted situations and painful emotions in the transference and revive them with the greatest ingenuity. They seek to bring about the interruption of the treatment while it is still incomplete; they contrive once more to feel themselves scorned, to oblige the physician to speak severely to them and treat them coldly; they discover appropriate objects for their jealousy; instead of the passionately desired baby of their childhood, they produce a plan or a promise of some grand present – which turns out as a rule to be no less unreal. None of these things can have produced pleasure in the past, and it might be supposed that they would cause less unpleasure to-day if they emerged as memories or dreams instead of taking the form of fresh experiences. They are of course the activities of instincts intended to lead to satisfaction; but no lesson has been learnt from the old experience of these activities having led instead only to unpleasure.[1] In spite of that, they are repeated, under pressure of a compulsion.

What psychoanalysis reveals in the transference phenomena of neurotics can also be observed in the lives of some normal people. The impression they give is of being pursued by a malignant fate or possessed by some 'daemonic' power; but psychoanalysis has always taken the view that their fate is for the most part arranged by themselves and determined by early infantile influences. The compulsion which is here in evidence differs in no way from the compulsion to repeat which we have found in neurotics, even though the people we are now considering have never shown any signs of dealing with a neurotic conflict by producing symptoms. Thus we have come across people all of whose human relationships have the same outcome: such as the benefactor who is abandoned in anger after a time by each of his *protégés*, however much they may otherwise differ from one another, and who thus seems doomed to taste all the bitterness of ingratitude; or the man whose friendships all end in betrayal by his friend; or the man who time after time in the course of his life raises someone else into a position of great private or public authority and then, after a certain interval, himself upsets that authority and replaces him by a new one; or, again, the lover each of whose love affairs with a woman passes through the same phases and reaches the same conclusion. This 'perpetual recurrence of the same thing' causes us no astonish-

1. [In the first edition the conclusion of this paragraph ran as follows: '. . . it might be supposed that they would cause less unpleasure to-day if they emerged as memories instead of taking the form of fresh experiences. But they are repeated under pressure of a compulsion.' The present form dates from 1921.]

ment when it relates to *active* behaviour on the part of the person concerned and when we can discern in him an essential character-trait which always remains the same and which is compelled to find expression in a repetition of the same experiences. We are much more impressed by cases where the subject appears to have a *passive* experience, over which he has no influence, but in which he meets with a repetition of the same fatality. There is the case, for instance, of the woman who married three successive husbands each of whom fell ill soon afterwards and had to be nursed by her on their death-beds.[1] The most moving poetic picture of a fate such as this is given by Tasso in his romantic epic *Gerusalemme Liberata*. Its hero, Tancred, unwittingly kills his beloved Clorinda in a duel while she is disguised in the armour of an enemy knight. After her burial he makes his way into a strange magic forest which strikes the Crusaders' army with terror. He slashes with his sword at a tall tree; but blood streams from the cut and the voice of Clorinda, whose soul is imprisoned in the tree, is heard complaining that he has wounded his beloved once again.

If we take into account observations such as these, based upon behaviour in the transference and upon the life-histories of men and women, we shall find courage to assume that there really does exist in the mind a compulsion to repeat which over-rides the pleasure principle. Now too we shall be inclined to relate to this compulsion the dreams which occur in traumatic neuroses and the impulse which leads children to play.

But it is to be noted that only in rare instances can we observe the pure effects of the compulsion to repeat, unsupported by other motives. In the case of children's play we have already laid stress on the other ways in which the emergence of the compulsion may be interpreted; the compulsion to repeat and instinctual satisfaction which is immediately pleasurable seem to converge here into an intimate partnership. The phenomena of transference are obviously exploited by the resistance which the ego maintains in its pertinacious insistence upon repression;

1. Cf. the apt remarks on this subject by C. G. Jung (1909).

the compulsion to repeat, which the treatment tries to bring into its service is, as it were, drawn over by the ego to *its* side (clinging as the ego does to the pleasure principle.)[1] A great deal of what might be described as the compulsion of destiny seems intelligible on a rational basis; so that we are under no necessity to call in a new and mysterious motive force to explain it.

The least dubious instance [of such a motive force] is perhaps that of traumatic dreams. But on maturer reflection we shall be forced to admit that even in the other instances the whole ground is not covered by the operation of the familiar motive forces. Enough is left unexplained to justify the hypothesis of a compulsion to repeat – something that seems more primitive, more elementary, more instinctual than the pleasure principle which it over-rides. But if a compulsion to repeat *does* operate in the mind, we should be glad to know something about it, to learn what function it corresponds to, under what conditions it can emerge and what its relation is to the pleasure principle – to which, after all, we have hitherto ascribed dominance over the course of the processes of excitation in mental life.

1. [Before 1923 the last clause read: 'the compulsion to repeat is as it were called to its help by the ego, clinging as it does to the pleasure principle.']

IV

WHAT follows is speculation, often far-fetched speculation, which the reader will consider or dismiss according to his individual predilection. It is further an attempt to follow out an idea consistently, out of curiosity to see where it will lead.

Psychoanalytic speculation takes as its point of departure the impression, derived from examining unconscious processes, that consciousness may be, not the most universal attribute of mental processes, but only a particular function of them. Speaking in metapsychological terms, it asserts that consciousness is a function of a particular system which it describes as *Cs.*[1] What consciousness yields consists essentially of perceptions of excitations coming from the external world and of feelings of pleasure and unpleasure which can only arise from within the mental apparatus; it is therefore possible to assign to the system *Pcpt.-Cs.*[2] a position in space. It must lie on the borderline between outside and inside; it must be turned towards the external world and must envelop the other psychical systems. It will be seen that there is nothing daringly new in these assumptions; we have merely adopted the views on localization held by cerebral anatomy, which locates the 'seat' of consciousness in the cerebral cortex – the outermost, enveloping layer of the central organ. Cerebral anatomy has no need to consider why, speaking anatomically, consciousness should be lodged on the surface of the brain instead of being safely housed somewhere in its inmost interior. Perhaps *we* shall be more successful in accounting for this situation in the case of our system *Pcpt.-Cs.*

Consciousness is not the only distinctive character which we ascribe to the processes in that system. On the basis of

1. [See *The Interpretation of Dreams* (1900*a*), *P.F.L.*, **4**, 770 ff., and 'The Unconscious' (1915*e*), Section II, p. 174 ff. above.]

2. [The system *Pcpt.* (the perceptual system) was first described by Freud in *The Interpretation of Dreams*, *P.F.L.*, **4**, 685 ff. In a later paper (1917*d*), p. 240 above, he argued that the system *Pcpt.* coincided with the system *Cs.*]

impressions derived from our psychoanalytic experience, we assume that all excitatory processes that occur in the *other* systems leave permanent traces behind in them which form the foundation of memory. Such memory-traces, then, have nothing to do with the fact of becoming conscious; indeed they are often most powerful and most enduring when the process which left them behind was one which never entered consciousness. We find it hard to believe, however, that permanent traces of excitation such as these are also left in the system *Pcpt.-Cs.* If they remained constantly conscious, they would very soon set limits to the system's aptitude for receiving fresh excitations.[1] If, on the other hand, they were unconscious, we should be faced with the problem of explaining the existence of unconscious processes in a system whose functioning was otherwise accompanied by the phenomenon of consciousness. We should, so to say, have altered nothing and gained nothing by our hypothesis relegating the process of becoming conscious to a special system. Though this consideration is not absolutely conclusive, it nevertheless leads us to suspect that becoming conscious and leaving behind a memory-trace are processes incompatible with each other within one and the same system. Thus we should be able to say that the excitatory process becomes conscious in the system *Cs.* but leaves no permanent trace behind there; but that the excitation is transmitted to the systems lying next within and that it is in *them* that its traces are left. I followed these same lines in the schematic picture which I included in the speculative section of my *Interpretation of Dreams.*[2] It must be borne in mind that little enough is known from other sources of the origin of consciousness; when, therefore, we lay down the proposition that *consciousness arises instead*

1. What follows is based throughout on Breuer's views in [the second section of his theoretical contribution to] *Studies on Hysteria* (Breuer and Freud, 1895). [*P.F.L.*, **3**, 267 ff. – Freud himself discussed the subject in *The Interpretation of Dreams*, *P.F.L.*, **4**, 689, and it had previously been fully considered in his 'Project' of 1895 (1950*a*), Part I, Section 3. He returned to the topic later in his paper on the 'Mystic Writing-Pad' (1925*a*), 430 ff. below.]

2. [*P.F.L.*, **4**, 687.]

of a memory-trace, the assertion deserves consideration, at all events on the ground of its being framed in fairly precise terms.

If this is so, then, the system *Cs.* is characterized by the peculiarity that in it (in contrast to what happens in the other psychical systems) excitatory processes do not leave behind any permanent change in its elements but expire, as it were, in the phenomenon of becoming conscious. An exception of this sort to the general rule requires to be explained by some factor that applies exclusively to that one system. Such a factor, which is absent in the other systems, might well be the exposed situation of the system *Cs.*, immediately abutting as it does on the external world.

Let us picture a living organism in its most simplified possible form as an undifferentiated vesicle of a substance that is susceptible to stimulation. Then the surface turned towards the external world will from its very situation be differentiated and will serve as an organ for receiving stimuli. Indeed embryology, in its capacity as a recapitulation of developmental history, actually shows us that the central nervous system originates from the ectoderm; the grey matter of the cortex remains a derivative of the primitive superficial layer of the organism and may have inherited some of its essential properties. It would be easy to suppose, then, that as a result of the ceaseless impact of external stimuli on the surface of the vesicle, its substance to a certain depth may have become permanently modified, so that excitatory processes run a different course in it from what they run in the deeper layers. A crust would thus be formed which would at last have been so thoroughly 'baked through' by stimulation that it would present the most favourable possible conditions for the reception of stimuli and become incapable of any further modification. In terms of the system *Cs.*, this would mean that its elements could undergo no further permanent modification from the passage of excitation, because they had already been modified in the respect in question to the greatest possible extent: now, however, they would have become capable of giving rise to consciousness. Various ideas may be formed which cannot at present be verified as to the nature of this modification of the substance and of the excitatory process. It may be supposed that, in passing from one element to another, an excitation has to overcome a resistance, and that the diminution of resistance thus effected is what lays down a permanent trace of the excitation, that is, a facilitation. In the system *Cs.*, then, resistance of this kind to passage from one element to another would no longer exist.[1] This picture can be brought into relation with Breuer's distinction between quiescent (or bound) and mobile cathectic energy in the elements of the psychical systems;[2] the elements of the system *Cs.* would carry no bound energy but only energy capable of free discharge. It seems best, however, to express oneself as cautiously as possible on these points. None the less, this speculation will have enabled us to bring the origin of consciousness into some sort of connection with the situation of the system *Cs.* and with the peculiarities that must be ascribed to the excitatory processes taking place in it.

But we have more to say of the living vesicle with its receptive cortical layer. This little fragment of living substance is suspended in the middle of an external world charged with the most powerful energies; and it would be killed by the stimulation emanating from these if it were not provided with a protective shield against stimuli. It acquires the shield in this way: its outermost surface ceases to have the structure proper to living matter, becomes to some degree inorganic and thenceforward functions as a special envelope or membrane resistant to stimuli. In consequence, the energies of the external world are able to pass into the next underlying layers, which have remained living, with only a fragment of their original intensity; and these layers can devote themselves, behind the protective shield, to the reception of the amounts of stimulus which have been allowed through it. By its death, the outer layer has saved all the deeper ones from a similar fate – unless, that is to say, stimuli

1. [This passage is foreshadowed in the later half of Section 3 of Part I of the 'Project'.]

2. Breuer and Freud, 1895. [See Section 2 of Breuer's theoretical contribution. (*P.F.L.*, **3**, 267 ff. and in particular 269 *n.* 1.) Cf. also footnote 1 on p. 276 above.]

reach it which are so strong that they break through the protective shield. *Protection against* stimuli is an almost more important function for the living organism than *reception of* stimuli. The protective shield is supplied with its own store of energy and must above all endeavour to preserve the special modes of transformation of energy operating in it against the effects threatened by the enormous energies at work in the external world – effects which tend towards a levelling out of them and hence towards destruction. The main purpose of the *reception* of stimuli is to discover the direction and nature of the external stimuli; and for that it is enough to take small specimens of the external world, to sample it in small quantities. In highly developed organisms the receptive cortical layer of the former vesicle has long been withdrawn into the depths of the interior of the body, though portions of it have been left behind on the surface immediately beneath the general shield against stimuli. These are the sense organs, which consist essentially of apparatus for the reception of certain specific effects of stimulation, but which also include special arrangements for further protection against excessive amounts of stimulation and for excluding unsuitable kinds of stimuli.[1] It is characteristic of them that they deal only with very small quantities of external stimulation and only take in *samples* of the external world. They may perhaps be compared with feelers which are all the time making tentative advances towards the external world and then drawing back from it.

At this point I shall venture to touch for a moment upon a subject which would merit the most exhaustive treatment. As a result of certain psychoanalytic discoveries, we are to-day in a position to embark on a discussion of the Kantian theorem that time and space are 'necessary forms of thought'. We have learnt that unconscious mental processes are in themselves 'timeless'.[2] This means in the first place that they are not ordered temporally, that time does not change them in any way and that the idea of time cannot be applied to them. These are negative

1. [Cf. 'Project', Part I, Sections 5 and 9.]
2. [See Section V of 'The Unconscious' (1915*e*), p. 191 above.]

characteristics which can only be clearly understood if a comparison is made with *conscious* mental processes. On the other hand, our abstract idea of time seems to be wholly derived from the method of working of the system *Pcpt.-Cs.* and to correspond to a perception on its own part of that method of working. This mode of functioning may perhaps constitute another way of providing a shield against stimuli. I know that these remarks must sound very obscure, but I must limit myself to these hints.[1]

We have pointed out how the living vesicle is provided with a shield against stimuli from the external world; and we had previously shown that the cortical layer next to that shield must be differentiated as an organ for receiving stimuli from without. This sensitive cortex, however, which is later to become the system *Cs.*, also receives excitations from *within*. The situation of the system between the outside and the inside and the difference between the conditions governing the reception of excitations in the two cases have a decisive effect on the functioning of the system and of the whole mental apparatus. Towards the outside it is shielded against stimuli, and the amounts of excitation impinging on it have only a reduced effect. Towards the inside there can be no such shield;[2] the excitations in the deeper layers extend into the system directly and in undiminished amount, in so far as certain of their characteristics give rise to feelings in the pleasure-unpleasure series. The excitations coming from within are, however, in their intensity and in other, qualitative, respects – in their amplitude, perhaps – more commensurate with the system's method of working than the stimuli which stream in from the external world.[3] This state of things produces two definite results. First, the feelings of pleasure and unpleasure (which are an index to what is happening in the interior of the apparatus) predominate over all external stimuli. And secondly, a particular way is adopted of dealing with any

1. [Freud recurs to the origin of the idea of time at the end of his paper on 'The Mystic Writing-Pad' (1925*a*), p. 434 below. The same paper contains a further discussion of the 'shield against stimuli'.]

2. [Cf. 'Project', beginning of Section 10 of Part I.]

3. [Cf. 'Project', later part of Section 4 of Part I.]

internal excitations which produce too great an increase of unpleasure: there is a tendency to treat them as though they were acting, not from the inside, but from the outside, so that it may be possible to bring the shield against stimuli into operation as a means of defence against them. This is the origin of *projection*, which is destined to play such a large part in the causation of pathological processes.

I have an impression that these last considerations have brought us to a better understanding of the dominance of the pleasure principle; but no light has yet been thrown on the cases that contradict that dominance. Let us therefore go a step further. We describe as 'traumatic' any excitations from outside which are powerful enough to break through the protective shield. It seems to me that the concept of trauma necessarily implies a connection of this kind with a breach in an otherwise efficacious barrier against stimuli. Such an event as an external trauma is bound to provoke a disturbance on a large scale in the functioning of the organism's energy and to set in motion every possible defensive measure. At the same time, the pleasure principle is for the moment put out of action. There is no longer any possibility of preventing the mental apparatus from being flooded with large amounts of stimulus, and another problem arises instead – the problem of mastering the amounts of stimulus which have broken in and of binding them, in the psychical sense, so that they can then be disposed of.

The specific unpleasure of physical pain is probably the result of the protective shield having been broken through in a limited area. There is then a continuous stream of excitations from the part of the periphery concerned to the central apparatus of the mind, such as could normally arise only from *within* the apparatus.[1] And how shall we expect the mind to react to this invasion? Cathectic energy is summoned from all sides to provide sufficiently high cathexes of energy in the environs of the breach. An 'anticathexis' on a grand scale is set up, for whose

1. Cf. 'Instincts and their Vicissitudes' (1915*c*) [p. 113 ff. above; and 'Project', Part I, Section 6. See also Addendum C of *Inhibitions, Symptoms and Anxiety* (1926*d*), *P.F.L.*, **10**, 329 ff.].

benefit all the other psychical systems are impoverished, so that the remaining psychical functions are extensively paralysed or reduced. We must endeavour to draw a lesson from examples such as this and use them as a basis for our metapsychological speculations. From the present case, then, we infer that a system which is itself highly cathected is capable of taking up an additional stream of fresh inflowing energy and of converting it into quiescent cathexis, that is of binding it psychically. The higher the system's own quiescent cathexis, the greater seems to be its 'binding' force; conversely, therefore, the lower its cathexis, the less capacity will it have for taking up inflowing energy[1] and the more violent must be the consequences of such a breach in the protective shield against stimuli. To this view it cannot be justly objected that the increase of cathexis round the breach can be explained far more simply as the direct result of the inflowing masses of excitation. If that were so, the mental apparatus would merely receive an increase in its cathexes of energy, and the paralysing character of pain and the impoverishment of all the other systems would remain unexplained. Nor do the very violent phenomena of discharge to which pain gives rise affect our explanation, for they occur in a reflex manner – that is, they follow without the intervention of the mental apparatus. The indefiniteness of all our discussions on what we describe as metapsychology is of course due to the fact that we know nothing of the nature of the excitatory process that takes place in the elements of the psychical systems, and that we do not feel justified in framing any hypothesis on the subject. We are consequently operating all the time with a large unknown factor, which we are obliged to carry over into every new formula. It may be reasonably supposed that this excitatory process can be carried out with energies that vary *quantitatively*; it may also seem probable that it has more than one *quality* (in the nature of amplitude, for instance). As a new factor we have taken into consideration Breuer's hypothesis that charges of energy occur in two forms [see p. 298]; so that we have to distinguish

1. [Cf. the 'principle of the insusceptibility to excitation of uncathected systems' in a footnote near the end of Freud, 1917*d*, p. 234 above.]

between two kinds of cathexis of the psychical systems or their elements – a freely flowing cathexis that presses on towards discharge and a quiescent cathexis. We may perhaps suspect that the 'binding' of the energy that streams into the mental apparatus consists in its change from a freely flowing into a quiescent state.

We may, I think, tentatively venture to regard the common traumatic neurosis as a consequence of an extensive breach being made in the protective shield against stimuli. This would seem to reinstate the old, naive theory of shock, in apparent contrast to the later and psychologically more ambitious theory which attributes aetiological importance not to the effects of mechanical violence but to fright and the threat to life. These opposing views are not, however, irreconcilable; nor is the psychoanalytic view of the traumatic neurosis identical with the shock theory in its crudest form. The latter regards the essence of the shock as being the direct damage to the molecular structure or even to the histological structure of the elements of the nervous system; whereas what *we* seek to understand are the effects produced on the organ of the mind by the breach in the shield against stimuli and by the problems that follow in its train. And we still attribute importance to the element of fright. It is caused by lack of any preparedness for anxiety,[1] including lack of hypercathexis of the systems that would be the first to receive the stimulus. Owing to their low cathexis those systems are not in a good position for binding the inflowing amounts of excitation and the consequences of the breach in the protective shield follow all the more easily. It will be seen, then, that preparedness for anxiety and the hypercathexis of the receptive systems constitute the last line of defence of the shield against stimuli. In the case of quite a number of traumas, the difference between systems that are unprepared and systems that are well prepared through being hypercathected may be a decisive factor in determining the outcome; though where the strength of a trauma exceeds a certain limit this factor will no doubt cease to carry weight. The fulfilment of wishes is, as we know, brought about

1. [Cf. footnote 1 on p. 282 above.]

in a hallucinatory manner by dreams, and under the dominance of the pleasure principle this has become their function. But it is not in the service of that principle that the dreams of patients suffering from traumatic neuroses lead them back with such regularity to the situation in which the trauma occurred. We may assume, rather, that dreams are here helping to carry out another task, which must be accomplished before the dominance of the pleasure principle can even begin. These dreams are endeavouring to master the stimulus retrospectively, by developing the anxiety whose omission was the cause of the traumatic neurosis. They thus afford us a view of a function of the mental apparatus which, though it does not contradict the pleasure principle, is nevertheless independent of it and seems to be more primitive than the purpose of gaining pleasure and avoiding unpleasure.

This would seem to be the place, then, at which to admit for the first time an exception to the proposition that dreams are fulfilments of wishes. Anxiety dreams, as I have shown repeatedly and in detail, offer no such exception. Nor do 'punishment dreams', for they merely replace the forbidden wish-fulfilment by the appropriate punishment for it; that is to say, they fulfil the wish of the sense of guilt which is the reaction to the repudiated impulse.[1] But it is impossible to classify as wish-fulfilments the dreams we have been discussing which occur in traumatic neuroses, or the dreams during psychoanalyses which bring to memory the psychical traumas of childhood. They arise, rather, in obedience to the compulsion to repeat, though it is true that in analysis that compulsion is supported by the wish (which is encouraged by 'suggestion')[2] to conjure up what has been forgotten and repressed. Thus it would seem that the function of dreams, which consists in setting aside any motives that might interrupt sleep, by fulfilling the wishes of the disturbing impulses, is not their *original* function. It would not be possible for them to perform that function until the whole of

1. [See *The Interpretation of Dreams* (1900*a*), *P.F.L.*, **4**, 710, and Section 9 of Freud's 'Remarks on the Theory and Practice of Dream-Interpretation' (1923*c*).]

2. [The clause in brackets was substituted in 1923 for the words 'which is not unconscious' which appeared in the earlier editions.]

mental life had accepted the dominance of the pleasure principle. If there is a 'beyond the pleasure principle', it is only consistent to grant that there was also a time before the purpose of dreams was the fulfilment of wishes. This would imply no denial of their later function. But if once this general rule has been broken, a further question arises. May not dreams which, with a view to the psychical binding of traumatic impressions, obey the compulsion to repeat – may not such dreams occur *outside* analysis as well? And the reply can only be a decided affirmative.

I have argued elsewhere[1] that 'war neuroses' (in so far as that term implies something more than a reference to the circumstances of the illness's onset) may very well be traumatic neuroses which have been facilitated by a conflict in the ego. The fact to which I have referred on page 281, that a gross physical injury caused simultaneously by the trauma diminishes the chances that a neurosis will develop, becomes intelligible if one bears in mind two facts which have been stressed by psychoanalytic research: firstly, that mechanical agitation must be recognized as one of the sources of sexual excitation,[2] and secondly, that painful and feverish illnesses exercise a powerful effect, so long as they last, on the distribution of libido. Thus, on the one hand, the mechanical violence of the trauma would liberate a quantity of sexual excitation which, owing to the lack of preparation for anxiety, would have a traumatic effect; but, on the other hand, the simultaneous physical injury, by calling for a narcissistic hypercathexis of the injured organ,[3] would bind the excess of excitation. It is also well known, though the libido theory has not yet made sufficient use of the fact, that such severe disorders in the distribution of libido as melancholia are temporarily brought to an end by intercurrent organic illness, and indeed that even a fully developed condition of dementia praecox is capable of a temporary remission in these same circumstances.

1. See my introduction (1919*d*) to *Psycho-Analysis and the War Neuroses*.

2. Cf. my remarks elsewhere (*Three Essays* [*P.F.L.*, **7**, 120–21]) on the effect of swinging and railway-travel.

3. See my paper on narcissism (1914*c*) [Beginning of Section II, p. 75 above].

V

THE fact that the cortical layer which receives stimuli is without any protective shield against excitations from within must have as its result that these latter transmissions of stimulus have a preponderance in economic importance and often occasion economic disturbances comparable with traumatic neuroses. The most abundant sources of this internal excitation are what are described as the organism's 'instincts' – the representatives of all the forces originating in the interior of the body and transmitted to the mental apparatus – at once the most important and the most obscure element of psychological research.

It will perhaps not be thought too rash to suppose that the impulses arising from the instincts do not belong to the type of *bound* nervous processes but of *freely mobile* processes which press towards discharge. The best part of what we know of these processes is derived from our study of the dream-work. We there discovered that the processes in the unconscious systems were fundamentally different from those in the preconscious (or conscious) systems. In the unconscious, cathexes can easily be completely transferred, displaced and condensed. Such treatment, however, could produce only invalid results if it were applied to preconscious material; and this accounts for the familiar peculiarities exhibited by manifest dreams after the preconscious residues of the preceding day have been worked over in accordance with the laws operating in the unconscious. I described the type of process found in the unconscious as the 'primary' psychical process, in contradistinction to the 'secondary' process which is the one obtaining in our normal waking life. Since all instinctual impulses have the unconscious systems as their point of impact, it is hardly an innovation to say that they obey the primary process. Again it is easy to identify the primary psychical process with Breuer's freely mobile cathexis and the secondary process with changes in his bound or tonic cathexis.[1] If so, it would be the task of the higher strata of the

1. Cf. my *Interpretation of Dreams*, Chapter VII [*P.F.L.*, 4, 745 ff. Cf. also

mental apparatus to bind the instinctual excitation reaching the primary process. A failure to effect this binding would provoke a disturbance analogous to a traumatic neurosis; and only after the binding has been accomplished would it be possible for the dominance of the pleasure principle (and of its modification, the reality principle) to proceed unhindered. Till then the other task of the mental apparatus, the task of mastering or binding excitations, would have precedence – not, indeed, in *opposition* to the pleasure principle, but independently of it and to some extent in disregard of it.

The manifestations of a compulsion to repeat (which we have described as occurring in the early activities of infantile mental life as well as among the events of psychoanalytic treatment) exhibit to a high degree an instinctual[1] character and, when they act in opposition to the pleasure principle, give the appearance of some 'daemonic' force at work. In the case of children's play we seemed to see that children repeat unpleasurable experiences for the additional reason that they can master a powerful impression far more thoroughly by being active than they could by merely experiencing it passively. Each fresh repetition seems to strengthen the mastery they are in search of. Nor can children have their *pleasurable* experiences repeated often enough, and they are inexorable in their insistence that the repetition shall be an identical one. This character trait disappears later on. If a joke is heard for a second time it produces almost no effect; a theatrical production never creates so great an impression the second time as the first; indeed, it is hardly possible to persuade an adult who has very much enjoyed reading a book to re-read it immediately. Novelty is always the condition of enjoyment. But children will never tire of asking an adult to repeat a game that he has shown them or played with them, till he is too exhausted to go on. And if a child has been told a nice story,

---

Breuer and Freud, 1895 (Section 2 of Breuer's theoretical contribution), *P.F.L.*, **3**, 267 ff.].

1. ['*Triebhaft*' here and at the beginning of the next paragraph. The word '*Trieb*' bears much more of a feeling of urgency than the English 'instinct'.]

he will insist on hearing it over and over again rather than a new one; and he will remorselessly stipulate that the repetition shall be an identical one and will correct any alterations of which the narrator may be guilty – though they may actually have been made in the hope of gaining fresh approval.[1] None of this contradicts the pleasure principle; repetition, the re-experiencing of something identical, is clearly in itself a source of pleasure. In the case of a person in analysis, on the contrary, the compulsion to repeat the events of his childhood in the transference evidently disregards the pleasure principle in *every* way. The patient behaves in a purely infantile fashion and thus shows us that the repressed memory-traces of his primaeval experiences are not present in him in a bound state and are indeed in a sense incapable of obeying the secondary process. It is to this fact of not being bound, moreover, that they owe their capacity for forming, in conjunction with the residues of the previous day, a wishful phantasy that emerges in a dream. This same compulsion to repeat frequently meets us as an obstacle to our treatment when at the end of an analysis we try to induce the patient to detach himself completely from his physician. It may be presumed, too, that when people unfamiliar with analysis feel an obscure fear – a dread of rousing something that, so they feel, is better left sleeping – what they are afraid of at bottom is the emergence of this compulsion with its hint of possession by some 'daemonic' power.

But how is the predicate of being 'instinctual'[2] related to the compulsion to repeat? At this point we cannot escape a suspicion that we may have come upon the track of a universal attribute of instincts and perhaps of organic life in general which has not hitherto been clearly recognized or at least not explicitly stressed.[3] *It seems, then, that an instinct is an urge inherent in organic life to restore an earlier state of things* which the living entity has been obliged to abandon under the pressure of external disturb-

1. [Cf. some remarks on this towards the end of the sixth section of Chapter VII of Freud's book on jokes (1905*c*), *P.F.L.*, **6**, 291.]

2. [See the last footnote but one.]

3. [The last six words added in 1921.]

ing forces; that is, it is a kind of organic elasticity, or, to put it another way, the expression of the inertia inherent in organic life.[1]

This view of instincts strikes us as strange because we have become used to see in them a factor impelling towards change and development, whereas we are now asked to recognize in them the precise contrary – an expression of the *conservative* nature of living substance. On the other hand we soon call to mind examples from animal life which seem to confirm the view that instincts are historically determined. Certain fishes, for instance, undertake laborious migrations at spawning-time in order to deposit their spawn in particular waters far removed from their customary haunts In the opinion of many biologists what they are doing is merely to seek out the localities in which their species formerly resided but which in the course of time they have exchanged for others. The same explanation is believed to apply to the migratory flights of birds of passage – but we are quickly relieved of the necessity for seeking for further examples by the reflection that the most impressive proofs of there being an organic compulsion to repeat lie in the phenomena of heredity and the facts of embryology. We see how the germ of a living animal is obliged in the course of its development to recapitulate (even if only in a transient and abbreviated fashion) the structures of all the forms from which it is sprung, instead of proceeding quickly by the shortest path to its final shape. This behaviour is only to a very slight degree attributable to mechanical causes, and the historical explanation cannot accordingly be neglected. So too the power of regenerating a lost organ by growing afresh a precisely similar one extends far up into the animal kingdom.

We shall be met by the plausible objection that it may very well be that, in addition to the conservative instincts which impel towards repetition, there may be others which push forward towards progress and the production of new forms. This argument must certainly not be overlooked, and it will be taken into

1. I have no doubt that similar notions as to the nature of 'instincts' have already been put forward repeatedly.

account at a later stage.[1] But for the moment it is tempting to pursue to its logical conclusion the hypothesis that all instincts tend towards the restoration of an earlier state of things. The outcome may give an impression of mysticism or of sham profundity; but we can feel quite innocent of having had any such purpose in view. We seek only for the sober results of research or of reflection based on it; and we have no wish to find in those results any quality other than certainty.[2]

Let us suppose, then, that all the organic instincts are conservative, are acquired historically and tend towards the restoration of an earlier state of things. It follows that the phenomena of organic development must be attributed to external disturbing and diverting influences. The elementary living entity would from its very beginning have had no wish to change; if conditions remained the same, it would do no more than constantly repeat the same course of life. In the last resort, what has left its mark on the development of organisms must be the history of the earth we live in and of its relation to the sun. Every modification which is thus imposed upon the course of the organism's life is accepted by the conservative organic instincts and stored up for further repetition. Those instincts are therefore bound to give a deceptive appearance of being forces tending towards change and progress, whilst in fact they are merely seeking to reach an ancient goal by paths alike old and new. Moreover it is possible to specify this final goal of all organic striving. It would be in contradiction to the conservative nature of the instincts if the goal of life were a state of things which had never yet been attained. On the contrary, it must be an *old* state of things, an initial state from which the living entity has at one time or other departed and to which it is striving to return by the circuitous paths along which its development leads. If we are to take it as a truth that knows no exception that everything

1. [The last half of this sentence was added in 1921.]

2. [*Footnote added* 1925:] The reader should not overlook the fact that what follows is the development of an extreme line of thought. Later on, when account is taken of the sexual instincts, it will be found that the necessary limitations and corrections are applied to it.

living dies for *internal* reasons – becomes inorganic once again – then we shall be compelled to say that '*the aim of all life is death*' and, looking backwards, that '*inanimate things existed before living ones*'.

The attributes of life were at some time evoked in inanimate matter by the action of a force of whose nature we can form no conception. It may perhaps have been a process similar in type to that which later caused the development of consciousness in a particular stratum of living matter. The tension which then arose in what had hitherto been an inanimate substance endeavoured to cancel itself out. In this way the first instinct came into being: the instinct to return to the inanimate state. It was still an easy matter at that time for a living substance to die; the course of its life was probably only a brief one, whose direction was determined by the chemical structure of the young life. For a long time, perhaps, living substance was thus being constantly created afresh and easily dying, till decisive external influences altered in such a way as to oblige the still surviving substance to diverge ever more widely from its original course of life and to make ever more complicated *détours* before reaching its aim of death. These circuitous paths to death, faithfully kept to by the conservative instincts, would thus present us to-day with the picture of the phenomena of life. If we firmly maintain the exclusively conservative nature of instincts, we cannot arrive at any other notions as to the origin and aim of life.

The implications in regard to the great groups of instincts which, as we believe, lie behind the phenomena of life in organisms must appear no less bewildering. The hypothesis of self-preservative instincts, such as we attribute to all living beings, stands in marked opposition to the idea that instinctual life as a whole serves to bring about death. Seen in this light, the theoretical importance of the instincts of self-preservation, of self-assertion and of mastery greatly diminishes. They are component instincts whose function it is to assure that the organism shall follow its own path to death, and to ward off any possible ways of returning to inorganic existence other than those which are immanent in the organism itself. We have no longer to reckon with the organism's puzzling determination (so hard to fit into any context) to maintain its own existence in the face of every obstacle. What we are left with is the fact that the organism wishes to die only in its own fashion. Thus these guardians of life, too, were originally the myrmidons of death. Hence arises the paradoxical situation that the living organism struggles most energetically against events (dangers, in fact) which might help it to attain its life's aim rapidly – by a kind of short-circuit. Such behaviour is, however, precisely what characterizes purely instinctual as contrasted with intelligent efforts.[1]

But let us pause for a moment and reflect. It cannot be so. The sexual instincts, to which the theory of the neuroses gives a quite special place, appear under a very different aspect.

The external pressure which provokes a constantly increasing extent of development has not imposed itself upon *every* organism. Many have succeeded in remaining up to the present time at their lowly level. Many, though not all, such creatures, which must resemble the earliest stages of the higher animals and plants, are, indeed, living to-day. In the same way, the whole path of development to natural death is not trodden by *all* the elementary entities which compose the complicated body of one of the higher organisms. Some of them, the germ-cells, probably retain the original structure of living matter and, after a certain time, with their full complement of inherited and freshly acquired instinctual dispositions, separate themselves from the organism as a whole. These two characteristics may be precisely what enables them to have an independent existence. Under favourable conditions, they begin to develop – that is, to repeat the performance to which they owe their existence; and in the end once again one portion of their substance pursues its development to a finish, while another portion harks back once again as a fresh residual germ to the beginning of the process of development. These germ-cells, therefore, work against the death of the living substance and succeed in winning for it what we can only regard as potential immortality, though that may

1. [In the editions before 1925 the following footnote appeared at this point. 'A correction of this extreme view of the self-preservative instincts follows.']

mean no more than a lengthening of the road to death. We must regard as in the highest degree significant the fact that this function of the germ-cell is reinforced, or only made possible, if it coalesces with another cell similar to itself and yet differing from it.

The instincts which watch over the destinies of these elementary organisms that survive the whole individual, which provide them with a safe shelter while they are defenceless against the stimuli of the external world, which bring about their meeting with other germ-cells, and so on – these constitute the group of the sexual instincts. They are conservative in the same sense as the other instincts in that they bring back earlier states of living substance; but they are conservative to a higher degree in that they are peculiarly resistant to external influences; and they are conservative too in another sense in that they preserve life itself for a comparatively long period.[1] They are the true life instincts. They operate against the purpose of the other instincts, which leads, by reason of their function, to death; and this fact indicates that there is an opposition between them and the other instincts, an opposition whose importance was long ago recognized by the theory of the neuroses. It is as though the life of the organism moved with a vacillating rhythm. One group of instincts rushes forward so as to reach the final aim of life as swiftly as possible; but when a particular stage in the advance has been reached, the other group jerks back to a certain point to make a fresh start and so prolong the journey. And even though it is certain that sexuality and the distinction between the sexes did not exist when life began, the possibility remains that the instincts which were later to be described as sexual may have been in operation from the very first, and it may not be true that it was only at a later time that they started upon their work of opposing the activities of the 'ego-instincts'.[2]

1. [*Footnote added* 1923:] Yet it is to them alone that we can attribute an internal impulse towards 'progress' and towards higher development! (See below [pp. 314–15].)

2. [*Footnote added* 1925:] It should be understood from the context that the term 'ego-instincts' is used here as a provisional description and derives from the earliest psychoanalytical terminology. [See below, pp. 323–4 and 334–5.]

Let us now hark back for a moment ourselves and consider whether there is any basis at all for these speculations. Is it really the case that, *apart from the sexual instincts*,[1] there are no instincts that do not seek to restore an earlier state of things? that there are none that aim at a state of things which has never yet been attained? I know of no certain example from the organic world that would contradict the characterization I have thus proposed. There is unquestionably no universal instinct towards higher development observable in the animal or plant world, even though it is undeniable that development does in fact occur in that direction. But on the one hand it is often merely a matter of opinion when we declare that one stage of development is higher than another, and on the other hand biology teaches us that higher development in one respect is very frequently balanced or outweighed by involution in another. Moreover there are plenty of animal forms from whose early stages we can infer that their development has, on the contrary, assumed a retrograde character. Both higher development and involution might well be the consequences of adaptation to the pressure of external forces; and in both cases the part played by instincts might be limited to the retention (in the form of an internal source of pleasure) of an obligatory modification.[2]

It may be difficult, too, for many of us, to abandon the belief that there is an instinct towards perfection at work in human beings, which has brought them to their present high level of intellectual achievement and ethical sublimation and which may be expected to watch over their development into supermen. I have no faith, however, in the existence of any such internal instinct and I cannot see how this benevolent illusion is to be preserved. The present development of human beings requires, as it seems to me, no different explanation from that of animals.

1. [These five words were italicized from 1921 onwards.]

2. Ferenczi (1913*a*, 137) has reached the same conclusion along different lines: 'If this thought is pursued to its logical conclusion, one must make oneself familiar with the idea of a tendency to perseveration or regression dominating organic life as well, while the tendency to further development, to adaptation, etc., would become active only as a result of external stimuli.'

What appears in a minority of human individuals as an untiring impulsion towards further perfection can easily be understood as a result of the instinctual repression upon which is based all that is most precious in human civilization. The repressed instinct never ceases to strive for complete satisfaction, which would consist in the repetition of a primary experience of satisfaction. No substitutive or reactive formations and no sublimations will suffice to remove the repressed instinct's persisting tension; and it is the difference in amount between the pleasure of satisfaction which is *demanded* and that which is actually *achieved* that provides the driving factor which will permit of no halting at any position attained, but, in the poet's words, '*ungebändigt immer vorwärts dringt*'.[1] The backward path that leads to complete satisfaction is as a rule obstructed by the resistances which maintain the repressions. So there is no alternative but to advance in the direction in which growth is still free – though with no prospect of bringing the process to a conclusion or of being able to reach the goal. The processes involved in the formation of a neurotic phobia, which is nothing else than an attempt at flight from the satisfaction of an instinct, present us with a model of the manner of origin of this suppositious 'instinct towards perfection' – an instinct which cannot possibly be attributed to *every* human being. The *dynamic* conditions for its development are, indeed, universally present; but it is only in rare cases that the *economic* situation appears to favour the production of the phenomenon.

I will add only a word to suggest that the efforts of Eros to combine organic substances into ever larger unities probably provide a substitute for this 'instinct towards perfection' whose existence we cannot admit. The phenomena that are attributed to it seem capable of explanation by these efforts of Eros taken in conjunction with the results of repression.[2]

1. ['Presses ever forward unsubdued.'] Mephistopheles in *Faust*, Part I [Scene 4].

2. [This paragraph, which was added in 1923, anticipates the account of Eros that is to follow in the next chapter, p. 323 ff.]

VI

THE upshot of our enquiry so far has been the drawing of a sharp distinction between the 'ego-instincts' and the sexual instincts, and the view that the former exercise pressure towards death and the latter towards a prolongation of life. But this conclusion is bound to be unsatisfactory in many respects even to ourselves. Moreover, it is actually only of the former group of instincts that we can predicate a conservative, or rather retrograde, character corresponding to a compulsion to repeat. For on our hypothesis the ego-instincts arise from the coming to life of inanimate matter and seek to restore the inanimate state; whereas as regards the sexual instincts, though it is true that they reproduce primitive states of the organism, what they are clearly aiming at by every possible means is the coalescence of two germ-cells which are differentiated in a particular way. If this union is not effected, the germ-cell dies along with all the other elements of the multicellular organism. It is only on this condition that the sexual function can prolong the cell's life and lend it the appearance of immortality. But what is the important event in the development of living substance which is being repeated in sexual reproduction, or in its fore-runner, the conjugation of two protista?[1] We cannot say; and we should consequently feel relieved if the whole structure of our argument turned out to be mistaken. The opposition between the ego or death instincts[2] and the sexual or life instincts would then cease to hold and the compulsion to repeat would no longer possess the importance we have ascribed to it.

Let us turn back, then, to one of the assumptions that we have already made, with the expectation that we shall be able to give it a categorical denial. We have drawn far-reaching conclusions

1. [In what follows Freud appears to use the terms 'protista' and 'protozoa' indifferently to signify unicellular organisms. The translation follows the original.]

2. [The first published appearance of the term.]

from the hypothesis that all living substance is bound to die from internal causes. We made this assumption thus carelessly because it does not seem to us to *be* an assumption. We are accustomed to think that such is the fact, and we are strengthened in our thought by the writings of our poets. Perhaps we have adopted the belief because there is some comfort in it. If we are to die ourselves, and first to lose in death those who are dearest to us, it is easier to submit to a remorseless law of nature, to the sublime *'Ανάγκη* [Necessity], than to a chance which might perhaps have been escaped. It may be, however, that this belief in the internal necessity of dying is only another of those illusions which we have created '*um die Schwere des Daseins zu ertragen*'.[1] It is certainly not a primaeval belief. The notion of 'natural death' is quite foreign to primitive races; they attribute every death that occurs among them to the influence of an enemy or of an evil spirit. We must therefore turn to biology in order to test the validity of the belief.

If we do so, we may be astonished to find how little agreement there is among biologists on the subject of natural death and in fact that the whole concept of death melts away under their hands. The fact that there is a fixed average duration of life at least among the higher animals naturally argues in favour of there being such a thing as death from natural causes. But this impression is countered when we consider that certain large animals and certain gigantic arboreal growths reach a very advanced age and one which cannot at present be computed. In the large-scale conception of Wilhelm Fliess [1906], all the phenomena of life exhibited by organisms – and also, no doubt, their death – are linked with the completion of fixed periods, which express the dependence of two kinds of living substance (one male and the other female) upon the solar year. When we see, however, how easily and how extensively the influence of external forces is able to modify the date of the appearance of vital phenomena (especially in the plant world) – to precipitate them or hold them back – doubts must be cast

1. ['To bear the burden of existence.' Schiller, *Die Braut von Messina*, **I**, 8.]

upon the rigidity of Fliess's formulas or at least upon whether the laws laid down by him are the sole determining factors.

The greatest interest attaches from our point of view to the treatment given to the subject of the duration of life and the death of organisms in the writings of Weismann (1882, 1884, 1892, etc.) It was he who introduced the division of living substance into mortal and immortal parts. The mortal part is the body in the narrower sense – the 'soma' – which alone is subject to natural death. The germ-cells, on the other hand, are potentially immortal, in so far as they are able, under certain favourable conditions, to develop into a new individual, or, in other words, to surround themselves with a new soma. (Weismann, 1884.)

What strikes us in this is the unexpected analogy with our own view, which was arrived at along such a different path. Weismann, regarding living substance morphologically, sees in it one portion which is destined to die – the soma, the body apart from the substance concerned with sex and inheritance – and an immortal portion – the germ-plasm, which is concerned with the survival of the species, with reproduction. We, on the other hand, dealing not with the living substance but with the forces operating in it, have been led to distinguish two kinds of instincts: those which seek to lead what is living to death, and others, the sexual instincts, which are perpetually attempting and achieving a renewal of life. This sounds like a dynamic corollary to Weismann's morphological theory.

But the appearance of a significant correspondence is dissipated as soon as we discover Weismann's views on the problem of death. For he only relates the distinction between the mortal soma and the immortal germ-plasm to *multicellular* organisms; in unicellular organisms the individual and the reproductive cell are still one and the same (Weismann, 1882, 38). Thus he considers that unicellular organisms are potentially immortal, and that death only makes its appearance with the multicellular metazoa. It is true that this death of the higher organisms is a natural one, a death from internal causes; but it is not founded on any primal characteristic of living substance (Weismann,

1884, 84) and cannot be regarded as an absolute necessity with its basis in the very nature of life (Weismann, 1882, 33). Death is rather a matter of expediency, a manifestation of adaptation to the external conditions of life; for, when once the cells of the body have been divided into soma and germ-plasm, an unlimited duration of individual life would become a quite pointless luxury. When this differentiation had been made in the multicellular organisms, death became possible and expedient. Since then, the soma of the higher organisms has died at fixed periods for internal reasons, while the protista have remained immortal. It is not the case, on the other hand, that reproduction was only introduced at the same time as death. On the contrary, it is a primal characteristic of living matter, like growth (from which it originated), and life has been continuous from its first beginning upon earth. (Weismann, 1884, 84 f.)

It will be seen at once that to concede in this way that higher organisms have a natural death is of very little help to us. For if death is a *late* acquisition of organisms, then there can be no question of there having been death instincts from the very beginning of life on this earth. Multicellular organisms may die for internal reasons, owing to defective differentiation or to imperfections in their metabolism, but the matter is of no interest from the point of view of our problem. An account of the origin of death such as this is moreover far less at variance with our habitual modes of thought than the strange assumption of 'death instincts'.

The discussion which followed upon Weismann's suggestions led, so far as I can see, to no conclusive results in any direction.[1] Some writers returned to the views of Goette (1883), who regarded death as a direct result of reproduction. Hartmann (1906, 29) does not regard the appearance of a 'dead body' – a dead portion of the living substance – as the criterion of death, but defines death as 'the termination of individual development'. In this sense protozoa too are mortal; in their case death always coincides with reproduction, but is to some extent obscured by

1. Cf. Hartmann (1906), Lipschütz (1914) and Doflein (1919).

it, since the whole substance of the parent animal may be transmitted directly into the young offspring.

Soon afterwards research was directed to the experimental testing on unicellular organisms of the alleged immortality of living substance. An American biologist, Woodruff, experimenting with a ciliate infusorian, the 'slipper-animalcule', which reproduces by fission into two individuals, persisted until the 3029th generation (at which point he broke off the experiment), isolating one of the part-products on each occasion and placing it in fresh water [Woodruff, 1914]. This remote descendant of the first slipper-animalcule was just as lively as its ancestor and showed no signs of ageing or degeneration. Thus, in so far as figures of this kind prove anything, the immortality of the protista seemed to be experimentally demonstrable.[1]

Other experimenters arrived at different results. Maupas [1888], Calkins [1902] and others, in contrast to Woodruff, found that after a certain number of divisions these infusoria become weaker, diminish in size, suffer the loss of some part of their organization and eventually die, unless certain recuperative measures are applied to them. If this is so, protozoa would appear to die after a phase of senescence exactly like the higher animals – thus completely contradicting Weismann's assertion that death is a late acquisition of living organisms.

From the aggregate of these experiments two facts emerge which seem to offer us a firm footing.

First: If two of the animalculae, at the moment before they show signs of senescence, are able to coalesce with each other, that is to 'conjugate' (soon after which they once more separate), they are saved from growing old and become 'rejuvenated'. Conjugation is no doubt the fore-runner of the sexual reproduction of higher creatures; it is as yet unconnected with propagation and is limited to the mixing of the substances of the two individuals. (Weismann's 'amphimixis'.) The recuperative effects of conjugation can, however, be replaced by certain stimulating agents, by alterations in the composition of the fluid

1. For this and what follows see Lipschütz (1914, 26 and 52 ff.).

which provides their nourishment, by raising their temperature or by shaking them. We are reminded of the celebrated experiment made by J. Loeb, in which, by means of certain chemical stimuli, he induced segmentation in sea-urchins' eggs – a process which can normally occur only after fertilization.[1]

Secondly: It is probable nevertheless that infusoria die a natural death as a result of their own vital processes. For the contradiction between Woodruff's findings and the others is due to his having provided each generation with fresh nutrient fluid. If he omitted to do so, he observed the same signs of senescence as the other experimenters. He concluded that the animalculae were injured by the products of metabolism which they extruded into the surrounding fluid. He was then able to prove conclusively that it was only the products of its *own* metabolism which had fatal results for the particular kind of animalcule. For the same animalculae which inevitably perished if they were crowded together in their own nutrient fluid flourished in a solution which was over-saturated with the waste products of a distantly related species. An infusorian, therefore, if it is left to itself, dies a natural death owing to its incomplete voidance of the products of its own metabolism. (It may be that the same incapacity is the ultimate cause of the death of all higher animals as well.)

At this point the question may well arise in our minds whether any object whatever is served by trying to solve the problem of natural death from a study of the protozoa. The primitive organization of these creatures may conceal from our eyes important conditions which, though in fact present in them too, only become *visible* in higher animals where they are able to find morphological expression. And if we abandon the morphological point of view and adopt the dynamic one, it becomes a matter of complete indifference to us whether natural death can be shown to occur in protozoa or not. The substance which is later recognized as being immortal has not yet become separated in them from the mortal one. The instinctual forces which

1. [The experiment was first carried out in 1899. Cf. Loeb (1909).]

seek to conduct life into death may also be operating in protozoa from the first, and yet their effects may be so completely concealed by the life-preserving forces that it may be very hard to find any direct evidence of their presence. We have seen, moreover, that the observations made by biologists allow us to assume that internal processes of this kind leading to death do occur also in protista. But even if protista turned out to be immortal in Weismann's sense, his assertion that death is a late acquisition would apply only to its *manifest* phenomena and would not make impossible the assumption of processes *tending* towards it.

Thus our expectation that biology would flatly contradict the recognition of death instincts has not been fulfilled. We are at liberty to continue concerning ourselves with their possibility, if we have other reasons for doing so. The striking similarity between Weismann's distinction of soma and germ-plasm and our separation of the death instincts from the life instincts persists and retains its significance.

We may pause for a moment over this pre-eminently dualistic view of instinctual life. According to E. Hering's theory, two kinds of processes are constantly at work in living substance, operating in contrary directions, one constructive or assimilatory and the other destructive or dissimilatory.[1] May we venture to recognize in these two directions taken by the vital processes the activity of our two instinctual impulses, the life instincts and the death instincts? There is something else, at any rate, that we cannot remain blind to. We have unwittingly steered our course into the harbour of Schopenhauer's philosophy. For him death is the 'true result and to that extent the purpose of life',[2] while the sexual instinct is the embodiment of the will to live.

Let us make a bold attempt at another step forward. It is generally considered that the union of a number of cells into a vital association – the multicellular character of organisms – has

1. [Cf. Hering (1878, 77 ff.). In Appendix A to 'The Unconscious' (1915*e*) another reference to Ewald Hering suggests that he may also have influenced Freud regarding his theory of the Unconscious. See p. 211 above.]

2. Schopenhauer (1851; *Sämtliche Werke*, ed. Hübscher, 1938, **5**, 236).

become a means of prolonging their life. One cell helps to preserve the life of another, and the community of cells can survive even if individual cells have to die. We have already heard that conjugation, too, the temporary coalescence of two unicellular organisms, has a life-preserving and rejuvenating effect on both of them. Accordingly, we might attempt to apply the libido theory which has been arrived at in psychoanalysis to the mutual relationship of cells. We might suppose that the life instincts or sexual instincts which are active in each cell take the other cells as their object, that they partly neutralize the death instincts (that is, the processes set up by them) in those cells and thus preserve their life; while the other cells do the same for *them*, and still others sacrifice themselves in the performance of this libidinal function. The germ-cells themselves would behave in a completely 'narcissistic' fashion – to use the phrase that we are accustomed to use in the theory of the neuroses to describe a whole individual who retains his libido in his ego and pays none of it out in object-cathexes. The germ-cells require their libido, the activity of their life instincts, for themselves, as a reserve against their later momentous constructive activity. (The cells of the malignant neoplasms which destroy the organism should also perhaps be described as narcissistic in this same sense: pathology is prepared to regard their germs as innate and to ascribe embryonic attributes to them.)[1] In this way the libido of our sexual instincts would coincide with the Eros of the poets and philosophers which holds all living things together.

Here then is an opportunity for looking back over the slow development of our libido theory. In the first instance the analysis of the transference neuroses forced upon our notice the opposition between the 'sexual instincts', which are directed towards an object, and certain other instincts, with which we were very insufficiently acquainted and which we described provisionally as the 'ego-instincts'.[2] A foremost place among these was necessarily given to the instincts serving the self-

1. [This sentence was added in 1921.]

2. [So, for instance, in the account of this opposition given in Freud's paper on psychogenic disturbances of vision (1910*i*), *P.F.L.*, **10**, 110–11.]

preservation of the individual. It was impossible to say what other distinctions were to be drawn among them. No knowledge would have been more valuable as a foundation for true psychological science than an approximate grasp of the common characteristics and possible distinctive features of the instincts. But in no region of psychology were we groping more in the dark. Everyone assumed the existence of as many instincts or 'basic instincts' as he chose, and juggled with them like the ancient Greek natural philosophers with their four elements – earth, air, fire and water. Psychoanalysis, which could not escape making *some* assumption about the instincts, kept at first to the popular division of instincts typified in the phrase 'hunger and love'. At least there was nothing arbitrary in this; and by its help the analysis of the psychoneuroses was carried forward quite a distance. The concept of 'sexuality', and at the same time of the sexual instinct, had, it is true, to be extended so as to cover many things which could not be classed under the reproductive function; and this caused no little hubbub in an austere, respectable or merely hypocritical world.

The next step was taken when psychoanalysis felt its way closer towards the psychological ego, which it had first come to know only as a repressive, censoring agency, capable of erecting protective structures and reactive formations. Critical and far-seeing minds had, it is true, long since objected to the concept of libido being restricted to the energy of the sexual instincts directed towards an object. But they failed to explain how they had arrived at their better knowledge or to derive from it anything of which analysis could make use. Advancing more cautiously, psychoanalysis observed the regularity with which libido is withdrawn from the object and directed on to the ego (the process of introversion); and, by studying the libidinal development of children in its earliest phases, came to the conclusion that the ego is the true and original reservoir of libido,[1] and that it is only from that reservoir that libido is

1. [This idea was fully stated by Freud in his paper on narcissism (1914*c*), Section 1, p. 67 ff. above. See, however, his later footnote, near the beginning

extended on to objects. The ego now found its position among sexual objects and was at once given the foremost place among them. Libido which was in this way lodged in the ego was described as 'narcissistic'.[1] This narcissistic libido was of course also a manifestation of the force of the sexual instinct in the analytical sense of those words, and it had necessarily to be identified with the 'self-preservative instincts' whose existence had been recognized from the first. Thus the original opposition between the ego-instincts and the sexual instincts proved to be inadequate. A portion of the ego-instincts was seen to be libidinal; sexual instincts – probably alongside others – operated in the ego. Nevertheless we are justified in saying that the old formula which lays it down that psychoneuroses are based on a conflict between ego-instincts and sexual instincts contains nothing that we need reject to-day. It is merely that the distinction between the two kinds of instinct, which was originally regarded as in some sort of way *qualitative*, must now be characterized differently – namely as being *topographical*. And in particular it is still true that the transference neuroses, the essential subject of psychoanalytic study, are the result of a conflict between the ego and the libidinal cathexis of objects.

But it is all the more necessary for us to lay stress upon the libidinal character of the self-preservative instincts now that we are venturing upon the further step of recognizing the sexual instinct as Eros, the preserver of all things, and of deriving the narcissistic libido of the ego from the stores of libido by means of which the cells of the soma are attached to one another. But we now find ourselves suddenly faced by another question. If the self-preservative instincts too are of a libidinal nature, are there perhaps no other instincts whatever but the libidinal ones? At all events there are none other visible. But in that case we shall after all be driven to agree with the critics who suspected from the first that psychoanalysis explains *everything* by sexuality, or with innovators like Jung who, making a hasty judge-

of Chapter III of *The Ego and the Id* (1923*b*), in which he corrects this statement and describes the *id* as 'the great reservoir of libido' (p. 369 *n*. 1 below).]

1. See my paper on narcissism (1914*c*) [Section 1, p. 67 above].

ment, have used the word 'libido' to mean instinctual force in general. Must not this be so?

It was not our *intention* at all events to produce such a result. Our argument had as its point of departure a sharp distinction between ego-instincts, which we equated with death instincts, and sexual instincts, which we equated with life instincts. (We were prepared at one stage [pp. 311–12] to include the so-called self-preservative instincts of the ego among the death instincts; but we subsequently [p. 325] corrected ourselves on this point and withdrew it.) Our views have from the very first been *dualistic*, and to-day they are even more definitely dualistic than before – now that we describe the opposition as being, not between ego-instincts and sexual instincts but between life instincts and death instincts. Jung's libido theory is on the contrary *monistic*; the fact that he has called his one instinctual force 'libido' is bound to cause confusion, but need not affect us otherwise.[1] We suspect that instincts other than the libidinal[2] self-preservative ones operate in the ego, and it ought to be possible for us to point to them. Unfortunately, however, the analysis of the ego has made so little headway that it is very difficult for us to do so. It is possible, indeed, that the libidinal instincts in the ego may be linked in a peculiar manner[3] with these other ego-instincts which are still strange to us. Even before we had any clear understanding of narcissism, psychoanalysts had a suspicion that the 'ego-instincts' had libidinal components attached to them. But these are very uncertain possibilities, to which our opponents will pay very little attention. The difficulty remains that psychoanalysis has not enabled us hitherto to point to any [ego-] instincts other than the libidinal ones. That, however, is no reason for our falling in with the conclusion that no others in fact exist.

In the obscurity that reigns at present in the theory of the instincts, it would be unwise to reject any idea that promises to

1. [The two preceding sentences were added in 1921.]
2. [The word 'libidinal' was added in 1921.]
3. [In the first edition only: '– by instinctual "confluence", to borrow a term used by Adler [1908] –'.]

throw light on it. We started out from the great opposition between the life and death instincts. Now object-love itself presents us with a second example of a similar polarity – that between love (or affection) and hate (or aggressiveness). If only we could succeed in relating these two polarities to each other and in deriving one from the other! From the very first we recognized the presence of a sadistic component in the sexual instinct.[1] As we know, it can make itself independent and can, in the form of a perversion, dominate an individual's entire sexual activity. It also emerges as a predominant component instinct in one of the 'pregenital organizations', as I have named them. But how can the sadistic instinct, whose aim it is to injure the object, be derived from Eros, the preserver of life? Is it not plausible to suppose that this sadism is in fact a death instinct which, under the influence of the narcissistic libido, has been forced away from the ego and has consequently only emerged in relation to the object? It now enters the service of the sexual function. During the oral stage of organization of the libido, the act of obtaining erotic mastery over an object coincides with that object's destruction; later, the sadistic instinct separates off, and finally, at the stage of genital primacy, it takes on, for the purposes of reproduction, the function of overpowering the sexual object to the extent necessary for carrying out the sexual act. It might indeed be said that the sadism which has been forced out of the ego has pointed the way for the libidinal components of the sexual instinct, and that these follow after it to the object. Wherever the original sadism has undergone no mitigation or intermixture, we find the familiar ambivalence of love and hate in erotic life.[2]

If such an assumption as this is permissible, then we have met the demand that we should produce an example of a death instinct – though, it is true, a displaced one. But this way of looking at things is very far from being easy to grasp and creates

1. This was already so in the first edition of *Three Essays on the Theory of Sexuality* in 1905 [*P.F.L.*, **7**, 70 ff.].

2. [This foreshadows Freud's discussion of instinctual 'fusion' in Chapter IV of *The Ego and the Id* (1923b), pp. 381–2 below.]

a positively mystical impression. It looks suspiciously as though we were trying to find a way out of a highly embarrassing situation at any price. We may recall, however, that there is nothing new in an assumption of this kind. We put one forward on an earlier occasion, before there was any question of an embarrassing situation. Clinical observations led us at that time to the view that masochism, the component instinct which is complementary to sadism, must be regarded as sadism that has been turned round upon the subject's own ego.[1] But there is no difference in principle between an instinct turning from an object to the ego and its turning from the ego to an object – which is the new point now under discussion. Masochism, the turning round of the instinct upon the subject's own ego, would in that case be a return to an earlier phase of the instinct's history, a regression. The account that was formerly given of masochism requires emendation as being too sweeping in one respect: there *might* be such a thing as primary masochism – a possibility which I had contested at that time.[2]

Let us, however, return to the self-preservative sexual instincts. The experiments upon protista have already shown us that conjugation – that is, the coalescence of two individuals which separate soon afterwards without any subsequent cell-division occurring – has a strengthening and rejuvenating effect upon both of them.[3] In later generations they show no signs of degenerating and seem able to put up a longer resistance to the

1. See my *Three Essays* (1905*d*) [*P.F.L.*, **7**, 71–2]; and 'Instincts and their Vicissitudes' (1915*c*) [p. 124 ff. above.].

2. A considerable portion of these speculations have been anticipated by Sabina Spielrein (1912) in an instructive and interesting paper which, however, is unfortunately not entirely clear to me. She there describes the sadistic components of the sexual instinct as 'destructive'. A. Stärcke (1914), again, has attempted to identify the concept of libido itself with the biological concept (assumed on theoretical grounds) of an impetus towards death. See also Rank (1907). All these discussions, like that in the text, give evidence of the demand for a clarification of the theory of the instincts such as has not yet been achieved. – [A later discussion of the destructive instinct by Freud himself occupies Chapter VI of *Civilization and its Discontents* (1930*a*), *P.F.L.*, **12**, 310 ff.]

3. See the account quoted above, p. 320, from Lipschütz (1914).

injurious effects of their own metabolism. This single observation may, I think, be taken as typical of the effect produced by sexual union as well. But how is it that the coalescence of two only slightly different cells can bring about this renewal of life? The experiment which replaces the conjugation of protozoa by the application of chemical or even of mechanical stimuli (cf. Lipschütz, 1914) enables us to give what is no doubt a conclusive reply to this question. The result is brought about by the influx of fresh amounts of stimulus. This tallies well with the hypothesis that the life process of the individual leads for internal reasons to an abolition of chemical tensions, that is to say, to death, whereas union with the living substance of a different individual increases those tensions, introducing what may be described as fresh *vital differences* which must then be 'lived off'. As regards this dissimilarity there must of course be one or more optima. The dominating tendency of mental life, and perhaps of nervous life in general, is the effort to reduce, to keep constant or to remove internal tension due to stimuli (the *Nirvana principle*, to borrow a term from Barbara Low [1920, 73]) – a tendency which finds expression in the pleasure principle;[1] and our recognition of that fact is one of our strongest reasons for believing in the existence of death instincts.

But we still feel our line of thought appreciably hampered by the fact that we cannot ascribe to the sexual instinct the characteristic of a compulsion to repeat which first put us on the track of the death instincts. The sphere of embryonic developmental processes is no doubt extremely rich in such phenomena of repetition; the two germ-cells that are involved in sexual reproduction and their life history are themselves only repetitions of the beginnings of organic life. But the essence of the processes to which sexual life is directed is the coalescence of two cell-bodies. That alone is what guarantees the immortality of the living substance in the higher organisms.

In other words, we need more information on the origin of sexual reproduction and of the sexual instincts in general. This

1. [Cf. p. 275 ff. The whole topic is further considered in 'The Economic Problem of Masochism' (1924*c*), p. 413 ff. below.]

is a problem which is calculated to daunt an outsider and which the specialists themselves have not yet been able to solve. We shall therefore give only the briefest summary of whatever seems relevant to our line of thought from among the many discordant assertions and opinions.

One of these views deprives the problem of reproduction of its mysterious fascination by representing it as a part manifestation of growth. (Cf. multiplication by fission, sprouting or gemmation.) The origin of reproduction by sexually differentiated germ-cells might be pictured along sober Darwinian lines by supposing that the advantage of amphimixis, arrived at on some occasion by the chance conjugation of two protista, was retained and further exploited in later development.[1] On this view 'sex' would not be anything very ancient; and the extraordinarily violent instincts whose aim it is to bring about sexual union would be repeating something that had once occurred by chance and had since become established as being advantageous.

The question arises here, as in the case of death [p. 321], whether we do right in ascribing to protista those characteristics alone which they actually exhibit, and whether it is correct to assume that forces and processes which become visible only in the higher organisms originated in those organisms for the first time. The view of sexuality we have just mentioned is of little help for our purposes. The objection may be raised against it that it postulates the existence of life instincts already operating in the simplest organisms; for otherwise conjugation, which works counter to the course of life and makes the task of ceasing to live more difficult, would not be retained and elaborated but would be avoided. If, therefore, we are not to abandon the hypothesis of death instincts, we must suppose them to be associated from the very first with life instincts. But it must be

1. Though Weismann (1892) denies this advantage as well: 'In no case does fertilization correspond to a rejuvenescence or renewal of life, nor is its occurrence necessary in order that life may endure: it is merely *an arrangement which renders possible the intermingling of two different hereditary tendencies.*' [English translation, 1893, 231.] He nevertheless believes that an intermingling of this kind leads to an increase in the variability of the organism concerned.

admitted that in that case we shall be working upon an equation with two unknown quantities.

Apart from this, science has so little to tell us about the origin of sexuality that we can liken the problem to a darkness into which not so much as a ray of a hypothesis has penetrated. In quite a different region, it is true, we *do* meet with such a hypothesis; but it is of so fantastic a kind – a myth rather than a scientific explanation – that I should not venture to produce it here, were it not that it fulfils precisely the one condition whose fulfilment we desire. For it traces the origin of an instinct to *a need to restore an earlier state of things*.

What I have in mind is, of course, the theory which Plato put into the mouth of Aristophanes in the *Symposium*, and which deals not only with the *origin* of the sexual instinct but also with the most important of its variations in relation to its object. 'The original human nature was not like the present, but different. In the first place, the sexes were originally three in number, not two as they are now; there was man, woman, and the union of the two. . . .' Everything about these primaeval men was double: they had four hands and four feet, two faces, two privy parts, and so on. Eventually Zeus decided to cut these men in two, 'like a sorb-apple which is halved for pickling'. After the division had been made, 'the two parts of man, each desiring his other half, came together, and threw their arms about one another eager to grow into one'.[1]

1. [Jowett's translation. *Footnote added* 1921:] I have to thank Professor Heinrich Gomperz, of Vienna, for the following discussion on the origin of the Platonic myth, which I give partly in his own words. It is to be remarked that what is essentially the same theory is already to be found in the Upanishads. For we find the following passage in the *Brihadâranyaka-upanishad*, 1, 4, 3 [Max-Müller's translation, 2, 85 f.], where the origin of the world from the Atman (the Self or Ego) is described: 'But he felt no delight. Therefore a man who is lonely feels no delight. He wished for a second. He was so large as man and wife together. He then made this his Self to fall in two, and then arose husband and wife. Therefore Yagñavalkya said: "We two are thus (each of us) like half a shell." Therefore the void which was there, is filled by the wife.'

The *Brihadâranyaka-upanishad* is the most ancient of all the Upanishads, and no competent authority dates it later than about the year 800 B.C. In contradiction to the prevailing opinion, I should hesitate to give an unqualified denial to the

Shall we follow the hint given us by the poet-philosopher, and venture upon the hypothesis that living substance at the time of its coming to life was torn apart into small particles, which have ever since endeavoured to reunite through the sexual instincts? that these instincts, in which the chemical affinity of inanimate matter persisted, gradually succeeded, as they developed through the kingdom of the protista, in overcoming the difficulties put in the way of that endeavour by an environment charged with dangerous stimuli – stimuli which compelled them to form a protective cortical layer? that these splintered fragments of living substance in this way attained a multicellular condition and finally transferred the instinct for reuniting, in the most highly concentrated form, to the germ-cells? – But here, I think, the moment has come for breaking off.

Not, however, without the addition of a few words of critical reflection. It may be asked whether and how far I am myself convinced of the truth of the hypotheses that have been set out in these pages. My answer would be that I am not convinced myself and that I do not seek to persuade other people to believe in them. Or, more precisely, that I do not know how far I believe in them. There is no reason, as it seems to me, why the emotional factor of conviction should enter into this question at all. It is surely possible to throw oneself into a line of thought and to follow it wherever it leads out of simple scientific curiosity, or, if the reader prefers, as an *advocatus diaboli*, who is not on that account himself sold to the devil. I do not dispute the fact that the third step in the theory of the instincts, which I have

possibility of Plato's myth being derived, even if it were only indirectly, from the Indian source, since a similar possibility cannot be excluded in the case of the doctrine of transmigration. But even if a derivation of this kind (through the Pythagoreans in the first instance) were established, the significance of the coincidence between the two trains of thought would scarcely be diminished. For Plato would not have adopted a story of this kind which had somehow reached him through some oriental tradition – to say nothing of giving it so important a place – unless it had struck him as containing an element of truth.

In a paper devoted to a systematic examination of this line of thought before the time of Plato, Ziegler (1913) traces it back to Babylonian origins.

[Freud had already alluded to Plato's myth in his *Three Essays*, *P.F.L.*, **7**, 46.]

taken here, cannot lay claim to the same degree of certainty as the two earlier ones – the extension of the concept of sexuality and the hypothesis of narcissism. These two innovations were a direct translation of observation into theory and were no more open to sources of error than is inevitable in all such cases. It is true that my assertion of the *regressive* character of instincts also rests upon observed material – namely on the facts of the compulsion to repeat. It may be, however, that I have overestimated their significance. And in any case it is impossible to pursue an idea of this kind except by repeatedly combining factual material with what is purely speculative and thus diverging widely from empirical observation. The more frequently this is done in the course of constructing a theory, the more untrustworthy, as we know, must be the final result. But the degree of uncertainty is not assignable. One may have made a lucky hit or one may have gone shamefully astray. I do not think a large part is played by what is called 'intuition' in work of this kind. From what I have seen of intuition, it seems to me to be the product of a kind of intellectual impartiality. Unfortunately, however, people are seldom impartial where ultimate things, the great problems of science and life, are concerned. Each of us is governed in such cases by deep-rooted internal prejudices, into whose hands our speculation unwittingly plays. Since we have such good grounds for being distrustful, our attitude towards the results of our own deliberations cannot well be other than one of cool benevolence. I hasten to add, however, that self-criticism such as this is far from binding one to any special tolerance towards dissentient opinions. It is perfectly legitimate to reject remorselessly theories which are contradicted by the very first steps in the analysis of observed facts, while yet being aware at the same time that the validity of one's own theory is only a provisional one.

We need not feel greatly disturbed in judging our speculation upon the life and death instincts by the fact that so many bewildering and obscure processes occur in it – such as one instinct being driven out by another or an instinct turning from the ego to an object, and so on. This is merely due to our being obliged to operate with the scientific terms, that is to say with the figurative language, peculiar to psychology (or, more precisely, to depth psychology). We could not otherwise describe the processes in question at all, and indeed we could not have become aware of them. The deficiencies in our description would probably vanish if we were already in a position to replace the psychological terms by physiological or chemical ones. It is true that they too are only part of a figurative language; but it is one with which we have long been familiar and which is perhaps a simpler one as well.

On the other hand it should be made quite clear that the uncertainty of our speculation has been greatly increased by the necessity for borrowing from the science of biology. Biology is truly a land of unlimited possibilities. We may expect it to give us the most surprising information and we cannot guess what answers it will return in a few dozen years to the questions we have put to it. They may be of a kind which will blow away the whole of our artificial structure of hypotheses. If so, it may be asked why I have embarked upon such a line of thought as the present one, and in particular why I have decided to make it public. Well – I cannot deny that some of the analogies, correlations and connections which it contains seemed to me to deserve consideration.[1]

1. I will add a few words to clarify our terminology, which has undergone some development in the course of the present work. We came to know what the 'sexual instincts' were from their relation to the sexes and to the reproductive function. We retained this name after we had been obliged by the findings of psychoanalysis to connect them less closely with reproduction. With the hypothesis of narcissistic libido and the extension of the concept of libido to the individual cells, the sexual instinct was transformed for us into Eros, which seeks to force together and hold together the portions of living substance. What are commonly called the sexual instincts are looked upon by us as the part of Eros which is directed towards objects. Our speculations have suggested that Eros operates from the beginning of life and appears as a 'life instinct' in opposition to the 'death instinct' which was brought into being by the coming to life of inorganic substance. These speculations seek to solve the riddle of life by supposing that these two instincts were struggling with each other from the very first. [*Added* 1921:] It is not so easy, perhaps, to follow the transformations through which the concept of the 'ego-instincts' has passed. To begin with we

applied that name to all the instinctual trends (of which we had no closer knowledge) which could be distinguished from the sexual instincts directed towards an object; and we opposed the ego-instincts to the sexual instincts of which the libido is the manifestation. Subsequently we came to closer grips with the analysis of the ego and recognized that a portion of the 'ego-instincts' is also of a libidinal character and has taken the subject's own ego as its object. These narcissistic self-preservative instincts had thenceforward to be counted among the libidinal sexual instincts. The opposition between the ego-instincts and the sexual instincts was transformed into one between the ego-instincts and the object-instincts, both of a libidinal nature. But in its place a fresh opposition appeared between the libidinal (ego- and object-) instincts and others, which must be presumed to be present in the ego and which may perhaps actually be observed in the destructive instincts. Our speculations have transformed this opposition into one between the life instincts (Eros) and the death instincts.

VII

IF IT is really the case that seeking to restore an earlier state of things is such a universal characteristic of instincts, we need not be surprised that so many processes take place in mental life independently of the pleasure principle. This characteristic would be shared by all the component instincts and in their case would aim at returning once more to a particular stage in the course of development. These are matters over which the pleasure principle has as yet no control; but it does not follow that any of them are necessarily opposed to it, and we have still to solve the problem of the relation of the instinctual processes of repetition to the dominance of the pleasure principle.

We have found that one of the earliest and most important functions of the mental apparatus is to 'bind' the instinctual impulses which impinge on it, to replace the primary process prevailing in them by the secondary process and convert their freely mobile cathectic energy into a mainly quiescent (tonic) cathexis. While this transformation is taking place no attention can be paid to the development of unpleasure; but this does not imply the suspension of the pleasure principle. On the contrary, the transformation occurs on *behalf* of the pleasure principle; the binding is a preparatory act which introduces and assures the dominance of the pleasure principle.

Let us make a sharper distinction than we have hitherto made between function and tendency. The pleasure principle, then, is a tendency operating in the service of a function whose business it is to free the mental apparatus entirely from excitation or to keep the amount of excitation in it constant or to keep it as low as possible. We cannot yet decide with certainty in favour of any of these ways of putting it; but it is clear that the function thus described would be concerned with the most universal endeavour of all living substance – namely to return to the quiescence of the inorganic world. We have all experienced how the greatest pleasure attainable by us, that of the sexual act, is associated with a momentary extinction of a highly intensified excitation. The binding of an instinctual impulse would be a preliminary function designed to prepare the excitation for its final elimination in the pleasure of discharge.

This raises the question of whether feelings of pleasure and unpleasure can be produced equally from bound and from unbound excitatory processes. And there seems to be no doubt whatever that the unbound or primary processes give rise to far more intense feelings in both directions than the bound or secondary ones. Moreover the primary processes are the earlier in time; at the beginning of mental life there are no others, and we may infer that if the pleasure principle had not already been operative in *them* it could never have been established for the later ones. We thus reach what is at bottom no very simple conclusion, namely that at the beginning of mental life the struggle for pleasure was far more intense than later but not so unrestricted: it had to submit to frequent interruptions. In later times the dominance of the pleasure principle is very much more secure, but it itself has no more escaped the process of taming than the other instincts in general. In any case, whatever it is that causes the appearance of feelings of pleasure and unpleasure in processes of excitation must be present in the secondary process just as it is in the primary one.

Here might be the starting-point for fresh investigations. Our consciousness communicates to us feelings from within not only of pleasure and unpleasure but also of a peculiar tension which in its turn can be either pleasurable or unpleasurable. Should the difference between these feelings enable us to distinguish between bound and unbound processes of energy? or is the feeling of tension to be related to the absolute magnitude, or perhaps to the level, of the cathexis, while the pleasure and unpleasure series indicates a change in the magnitude of the cathexis *within a given unit of time*?[1] Another striking fact is that the life instincts have so much more contact with our internal perception – emerging as breakers of the peace and constantly pro-

1. [Cf. above, p. 276. These questions had already been touched on by Freud in his 'Project', e.g. in Part I, Section 8 and Part III, Section 1.]

ducing tensions whose release is felt as pleasure – while the death instincts seem to do their work unobtrusively. The pleasure principle seems actually to serve the death instincts. It is true that it keeps watch upon stimuli from without, which are regarded as dangers by both kinds of instincts; but it is more especially on guard against increases of stimulation from within, which would make the task of living more difficult. This in turn raises a host of other questions to which we can at present find no answer. We must be patient and await fresh methods and occasions of research. We must be ready, too, to abandon a path that we have followed for a time, if it seems to be leading to no good end. Only believers, who demand that science shall be a substitute for the catechism they have given up, will blame an investigator for developing or even transforming his views. We may take comfort, too, for the slow advances of our scientific knowledge in the words of the poet:

> Was man nicht erfliegen kann, muss man erhinken.
>
> . . . .
>
> Die Schrift sagt, es ist keine Sünde zu hinken.[1]

1. ['What we cannot reach flying we must reach limping . . . The Book tells us it is no sin to limp.' The last lines of 'Die beiden Gulden', a version by Rückert of one of the *Maqâmât* of al-Hariri. Freud also quoted these lines in a letter to Fliess of 20 October 1895 (Freud, 1950*a*, Letter 32).]

THE EGO AND THE ID
(1923)

EDITOR'S INTRODUCTION

DAS ICH UND DAS ES

(A) German Editions:

1923 Leipzig, Vienna and Zurich: Internationaler Psychoanalytischer Verlag. Pp. 77.
1925 *Gesammelte Schriften*, **6**, 351–405.
1940 *Gesammelte Werke*, **13**, 237–89.

(B) English Translations:
The Ego and the Id

1927 London: Hogarth Press and Institute of Psycho-Analysis. Pp. 88. (Tr. Joan Riviere.)
1961 *Standard Edition*, **19**, 1–66. (A very considerably modified version of the translation published in 1927.)

The present edition is a reprint of the *Standard Edition* version, with some editorial modifications.

This book appeared in the third week of April 1923, though it had been in Freud's mind since at least the previous July (Jones, 1957, 104). On 26 September 1922, at the Seventh International Psycho-Analytical Congress, which was held in Berlin and was the last he ever attended, he read a short paper with the title 'Etwas vom Unbewussten [Some Remarks on the Unconscious]', in which he foreshadowed the contents of the book. The text of this paper was never published; an abstract, which may have been written by Freud himself, appeared in the autumn of that year (1922*f*).

The Ego and the Id is the last of Freud's major theoretical works. It offers a description of the mind and its workings which is at first sight new and even revolutionary; and indeed all psychoanalytic writings that date from after its publication bear the unmistakable imprint of its effects – at least in regard to their terminology. But, in spite of all its fresh insights and fresh syntheses, we can trace, as so often with Freud's apparent innovations, the seeds of his new ideas in earlier, and sometimes in far earlier, writings.

The forerunners of the present general picture of the mind had been successively the 'Project' of 1895 (Freud, 1950*a*), the seventh chapter of *The Interpretation of Dreams* (1900*a*) and the metapsychological papers of 1915. In all of these, the interrelated problems of mental functioning and mental structure were inevitably considered, though with varying stress upon the two aspects of the question. The historical accident that psychoanalysis had its origin in connection with the study of hysteria led at once to the hypothesis of repression (or, more generally, of defence) as a mental function, and this in turn to a topographical hypothesis – to a picture of the mind as including two portions, one repressed and the other repressing. The quality of 'consciousness' was evidently closely involved in these hypotheses; and it was easy to equate the repressed part of the mind with what was 'unconscious' and the repressing part with what was 'conscious'. Freud's earlier pictorial diagrams of the mind, in *The Interpretation of Dreams* (*P.F.L.*, **4**, 686–90) and in his letter to Fliess of 6 December 1896 (Freud, 1950*a*, Letter 52), were representations of this view of the position. And this apparently simple scheme underlay all of Freud's earlier theoretical ideas: functionally, a repressed force endeavouring to make its way into activity but held in check by a repressing force, and structurally, an 'unconscious' opposed by an 'ego'.

Nevertheless, complications soon became manifest. It was quickly seen that the word 'unconscious' was being used in two senses: the 'descriptive' sense (which merely attributed a particular *quality* to a mental state) and the 'dynamic' sense (which attributed a particular *function* to a mental state). This distinction was already stated, though not in these terms, in *The Interpretation of Dreams* (*P.F.L.*, **4**, 774–6). It was stated much more clearly in the English paper written for the Society for Psychical Research 1912*g*, pp. 52–3 above). But from the first another, more obscure notion was already involved (as was plainly shown by the pictorial diagrams) – the notion of 'systems' in the mind. This implied a topographical or structural division of the mind based on something more than function, a division into portions to which it was possible to attribute a number of differentiating characteristics and methods of operating. Some such idea was no doubt already implied in the phrase 'the unconscious', which appeared very early (e.g. in a footnote to the *Studies on Hysteria*, 1895*d*, *P.F.L.*, **3**, 134 *n.* 2). The concept of a 'system' became explicit in *The Interpretation of Dreams* (1900*a*), ibid., **4**, 684–6. From the terms in which it was there introduced, topographical imagery was at once suggested, though Freud gave a warning against taking this literally. There were a number of these 'systems' (mnemic, perceptual, and so on) and among them 'the unconscious' (ibid., 690 f.), which 'for simplicity's sake' was to be designated as 'the system *Ucs.*'. In these earlier passages all that was overtly meant by this unconscious system was the repressed, until we reach the final section of *The Interpretation of Dreams* (ibid., **4**, 771 ff.), where something with a much wider scope was indicated. Thereafter the question remained in abeyance until the S.P.R. paper (1912*g*) already referred to, where (besides the clear differentiation between the descriptive and dynamic uses of the term 'unconscious'), in the last sentences of the paper, a third, 'systematic', use was defined. It may be noted that in this passage (p. 57 above), it was only for this 'systematic' unconscious that Freud proposed to use the symbol '*Ucs.*'. All this seems very straightforward, but, oddly enough, the picture was blurred once more in the metapsychological paper on 'The Unconscious' (1915*e*). In Section II of that paper (p. 174 ff. above) there were no longer *three* uses of the term 'unconscious' but only two. The 'dynamic' use disappeared, and was presumably subsumed into the 'systematic' one,[1] which was still to be called the '*Ucs.*', though it now included the repressed. Finally, in Chapter I of the present work (as well as in Lecture 31 of the *New Introductory Lectures*, 1933*a*, *P.F.L.*, **2**, 88 ff.), Freud reverted to the threefold distinction and classification, though at the end of the chapter he applied the abbreviation '*Ucs.*', inadvertently perhaps, to all three kinds of 'unconscious' (p. 356).

But the question now arose whether, as applied to a *system*, the term 'unconscious' was at all appropriate. In the structural picture of the mind what had from the first been most clearly differentiated from 'the unconscious' had been 'the ego'. And it now began to appear that the ego itself ought partly to be described as 'unconscious'. This was pointed out in *Beyond the Pleasure Principle*, in a sentence which read in the first edition (1920*g*): 'It may be that much of the ego is itself unconscious[2]; only a part of it, probably, is covered by the term "preconscious".' In the second edition, a year later, this sentence was altered to: 'It is certain that much of the ego is itself unconscious . . .; only a small part of it is covered by the term "preconscious".'[3] And this discovery and the grounds for it were stated with still greater insistence in the first chapter of the present work.

It had thus become apparent that, alike as regards 'the unconscious' and as regards 'the ego', the criterion of consciousness was no longer helpful in building up a structural picture of the mind. Freud accordingly abandoned the use of consciousness in this capacity: 'being conscious' was henceforward to be regarded simply as a quality which might or might not be attached to a mental state. The old 'descriptive' sense of the term was in fact all that remained. The new terminology which he now introduced had a highly clarifying effect and so made further clinical

1. The two terms seem to be definitely equated in *Beyond the Pleasure Principle* (1920*g*), p. 290 above.

2. [I.e. not merely in the descriptive but also in the dynamic sense.]

3. Freud had actually already spoken in the opening sentence of his second paper on 'The Neuro-Psychoses of Defence' (1896*b*) of the psychical mechanism of defence as being 'unconscious'.

advances possible. But it did not in itself involve any fundamental changes in Freud's views on mental structure and functioning. Indeed, the three newly presented entities, the id, the ego and the super-ego, all had lengthy past histories (two of them under other names) and these will be worth examining.

The term '*das Es*',[1] as Freud himself explains below (p. 362), was derived in the first instance from Georg Groddeck, a physician practising at Baden-Baden, who had recently become attached to psychoanalysis and with whose wide-ranging ideas Freud felt much sympathy (Groddeck, 1923). Groddeck seems in turn to have derived '*das Es*' from his own teacher, Ernst Schweninger (1850–1924), a well-known German physician of an earlier generation. But, as Freud also points out, the use of the word certainly goes back to Nietzsche. In any case, the term was adapted by Freud to a different and more precise meaning than Groddeck's. It cleared up and in part replaced the ill-defined uses of the earlier terms 'the unconscious', 'the *Ucs.*' and 'the systematic unconscious'.[2]

The position in regard to '*das Ich*' is a good deal less clear. The term had of course been in familiar use before the days of Freud; but the precise sense which he himself attached to it in his earlier writings is not unambiguous. It seems possible to detect two main uses: one in which the term distinguishes a person's self as a whole (including, perhaps, his body) from other people, and the other in which it denotes a particular part of the mind characterized by special attributes and functions. It is in this second sense that the term was used in the elaborate account of the 'ego' in Freud's early 'Project' of 1895 (Freud, 1950*a*, Part I,

1. There was to begin with a good deal of discussion over the choice of an English equivalent. 'The id' was eventually decided upon in preference to 'the it', so as to be parallel with the long-established 'ego'.

2. The symbol '*Ucs.*' disappears after the present work, except for an occurrence in *Moses and Monotheism* (1939*a*), *P.F.L.*, **13**, 340, where oddly enough it is used in the 'descriptive' sense, and one in the *New Introductory Lectures* (1933*a*), *P.F.L.*, **2**, 104. Freud continued to use the term 'the unconscious', though with diminishing frequency, as a synonym for 'the id'.

Section 14); and it is in this same sense that it is used in the anatomy of the mind in *The Ego and the Id*. But in some of his intervening works, particularly in connection with narcissism, the 'ego' seems to correspond rather to the 'self'. It is not always easy, however, to draw a line between these two senses of the word.[1]

What is quite certain, however, is that, after the isolated attempt in the 'Project' of 1895 at a detailed analysis of the structure and functioning of the ego, Freud left the subject almost untouched for some fifteen years. His interest was concentrated on his investigations of the unconscious and its instincts, particularly the sexual ones, and in the part they played in normal and abnormal mental behaviour. The fact that repressive forces played an equally important part was, of course, never overlooked and was always insisted on; but the closer examination of them was left to the future. It was enough for the moment to give them the inclusive name of 'the ego'.

There were two indications of a change, both round about the year 1910. In a paper on psychogenic disturbances of vision (1910*i*), there comes what seems to be a first mention of 'ego-instincts' (*P.F.L.*, **10**, 110 and *n.* 1), which combine the functions of repression with those of self-preservation. The other and more important development was the hypothesis of narcissism which was first proposed in 1909 and which led the way to a detailed examination of the ego and its functions in a variety of connections – in the study on Leonardo (1910*c*), in the Schreber case history (1911*c*), in the paper on the two principles of mental functioning (1911*b*), in the paper on 'Narcissism' itself (1914*c*) and in the metapsychological paper on 'The Unconscious' (1915*e*). In this last work, however, a further development occurred: what had been described as the ego now became

1. In a few places in the *Standard Edition* where the sense seemed to demand it, '*das Ich*' has been translated by 'the self'. There is a passage in *Civilization and its Discontents* (1930*a*), in which Freud himself explicitly equates '*das Selbst*' and '*das Ich*' (*P.F.L.*, **12**, 253). And, in the course of a discussion of the moral responsibility for dreams (1925*i*), he makes a clear distinction between the two uses of the German word '*Ich*'. (*Standard Ed.*, **19**, 133.)

the 'system' *Cs.* (*Pcs.*).[1] It is this system which is the progenitor of the 'ego' as we have it in the new and corrected terminology, from which, as we have seen, the confusing connection with the quality of 'consciousness' has been removed.

The functions of the system *Cs.* (*Pcs.*), as enumerated in 'The Unconscious', p. 192 above, include such activities as censorship, reality-testing, and so on, all of which are now assigned to the 'ego'.[2] There is one particular function, however, whose examination was to lead to momentous results – the self-critical faculty. This and the correlated 'sense of guilt' attracted Freud's interest from early days, chiefly in connection with the obsessional neurosis. His theory that obsessions are 'transformed self-reproaches' for sexual pleasure enjoyed in childhood was fully explained in Section II of his second paper on 'The Neuro-Psychoses of Defence' (1896*b*) after being outlined somewhat earlier in his letters to Fliess. That the self-reproaches may be unconscious was already implied at this stage, and was stated specifically in the paper on 'Obsessive Actions and Religious Practices' (1907*b*). It was only with the concept of narcissism, however, that light could be thrown on the actual mechanism of these self-reproaches. In Section III of his paper on narcissism (1914*c*) Freud began by suggesting that the narcissism of infancy is replaced in the adult by devotion to an ideal ego set up within himself. He then put forward the notion that there may be 'a special psychical agency' whose task it is to watch the actual ego and measure it by the ideal ego or ego ideal – he seemed to use the terms indiscriminately (p. 89 above). So too in the *Introductory Lectures* (1916–17), *P.F.L.*, **1**, 479. He attributed a number of functions to this agency, including the normal conscience, the dream-censorship and certain paranoic delusions. In the paper on 'Mourning and Melancholia' (1917*e* [1915]) he further made

1. These abbreviations (like the '*Ucs.*') go back to *The Interpretation of Dreams* (1900*a*), *P.F.L.*, **4**, 691. Actually all of them are already used (in the 'systematic' sense) in the Fliess correspondence (Letter 64 and Draft N) on 31 May 1897 (Freud, 1950*a*).

2. Some remarks on the 'synthetic' function of the ego are to be found in the *New Introductory Lectures*, *P.F.L.*, **2**, 108–9 and 109 *n*. 1.

this agency responsible for pathological states of mourning (p. 256 above) and insisted more definitely that it is something apart from the rest of the ego, and this was made still more clear in *Group Psychology* (1921*c*). It must be noticed, however, that here the distinction between the 'ego ideal' itself and the 'agency' concerned with its enforcement had been dropped: the 'agency' was specifically called the 'ego ideal'. It is as an equivalent to the 'ego ideal' that '*das Über-Ich*'[1] makes its first appearance (p. 367 below), though its aspect as an enforcing or prohibiting agency predominates later. Indeed, after *The Ego and the Id* and the two or three shorter works immediately following it, the 'ego ideal' disappears almost completely as a technical term. It makes a brief re-emergence in a couple of sentences in the *New Introductory Lectures* (1933*a*), Lecture 31, *P.F.L.*, **2**, 96; but here we find a return to the original distinction, for 'an important function' attributed to the super-ego is to act as 'the verdict of the ego ideal by which the ego measures itself' – almost the exact terms in which the ego ideal was first introduced in the paper on narcissim (p. 88 above).

But this distinction may seem to be an artificial one when we turn to Freud's account of the genesis of the super-ego. This account (in Chapter III) is no doubt the part of the book second in importance only to the main thesis of the threefold division of the mind. The super-ego is there shown to be derived from a transformation of the child's earliest object-cathexes into identifications: it takes the place of the Oedipus complex. This mechanism (the replacement of an object-cathexis by an identification and the introjection of the former object) had been first applied by Freud (in his study of Leonardo, 1910*c*) to the explanation of one type of homosexuality, in which a boy replaces his love for his mother by identifying himself with her. He next applied the same notion to states of depression in 'Mourning and Melancholia' (1917*e*), pp. 257–8 above. Further and more elaborate discussions of these various kinds of identifications and

1. Jones (1957, 305 *n.*) remarks that the term had been used earlier by Münsterberg (1908), though, he adds, it was in a different sense and it is unlikely that Freud had come across the passage.

introjections were pursued in Chapters VII, VIII and XI of *Group Psychology* (1921*c*), but it was only in the present work that Freud arrived at his final views on the derivation of the super-ego from the child's earliest object-relations.

Having once established his new account of the anatomy of the mind, Freud was in a position to examine its implications, and this he already does in the later pages of the book – the relation between the divisions of the mind and the two classes of instincts, and the interrelations between the divisions of the mind themselves, with special reference to the sense of guilt. But many of these questions, and in particular the last one, were to form the subject of other writings which followed in rapid succession. See, for instance, 'The Economic Problem of Masochism' (1924*c*), p. 413 ff. below. 'The Dissolution of the Oedipus Complex' (1924*d*), *P.F.L.*, **7**, 315 ff., the two papers on neurosis and psychosis (1924*b* and 1924*e*), ibid., **10**, 213 ff. and 221 ff., and the one on the anatomical distinction between the sexes (1925*j*), ibid., **7**, 331 ff., as well as the still more important *Inhibitions, Symptoms and Anxiety* (1926*d*), ibid., **10**, 237 ff., published only a little later. Finally, a further long discussion of the super-ego, together with an interesting examination of the proper use of the terms 'super-ego', 'conscience', 'sense of guilt', 'need for punishment' and 'remorse' will be found in Chapters VII and VIII of *Civilization and its Discontents* (1930*a*), *P.F.L.*, **12**, 315 ff. and 327.

THE EGO AND THE ID
[PREFACE]

THE present discussions are a further development of some trains of thought which I opened up in *Beyond the Pleasure Principle* (1920*g*), and to which, as I remarked there [p. 333 above], my attitude was one of a kind of benevolent curiosity. In the following pages these thoughts are linked to various facts of analytic observation and an attempt is made to arrive at new conclusions from this conjunction; in the present work, however, there are no fresh borrowings from biology, and on that account it stands closer to psychoanalysis than does *Beyond the Pleasure Principle*. It is more in the nature of a synthesis than of a speculation and seems to have had an ambitious aim in view. I am conscious, however, that it does not go beyond the roughest outline and with that limitation I am perfectly content.

In these pages things are touched on which have not yet been the subject of psychoanalytic consideration, and it has not been possible to avoid trenching upon some theories which have been put forward by non-analysts or by former analysts on their retreat from analysis. I have elsewhere always been ready to acknowledge what I owe to other workers; but in this instance I feel burdened by no such debt of gratitude. If psychoanalysis has not hitherto shown its appreciation of certain things, this has never been because it overlooked their achievement or sought to deny their importance, but because it followed a particular path, which had not yet led so far. And finally, when it has reached them, things have a different look to it from what they have to others.

I

CONSCIOUSNESS AND WHAT IS UNCONSCIOUS

IN THIS introductory chapter there is nothing new to be said and it will not be possible to avoid repeating what has often been said before.

The division of the psychical into what is conscious and what is unconscious is the fundamental premiss of psychoanalysis; and it alone makes it possible for psychoanalysis to understand the pathological processes in mental life, which are as common as they are important, and to find a place for them in the framework of science. To put it once more, in a different way: psychoanalysis cannot situate the essence of the psychical in consciousness, but is obliged to regard consciousness as a quality of the psychical, which may be present in addition to other qualities or may be absent.

If I could suppose that everyone interested in psychology would read this book, I should also be prepared to find that at this point some of my readers would already stop short and would go no further; for here we have the first shibboleth of psychoanalysis. To most people who have been educated in philosophy the idea of anything psychical which is not also conscious is so inconceivable that it seems to them absurd and refutable simply by logic. I believe this is only because they have never studied the relevant phenomena of hypnosis and dreams, which – quite apart from pathological manifestations – necessitate this view. Their psychology of consciousness is incapable of solving the problems of dreams and hypnosis.

'Being conscious'[1] is in the first place a purely descriptive

1. ['*Bewusst sein*' (in two words) in the original. Similarly in Chapter II of *Lay Analysis* (1926*e*). '*Bewusstsein*' is the regular German word for 'consciousness', and printing it in two words emphasizes the fact that '*bewusst*' is in its form a

term, resting on perception of the most immediate and certain character. Experience goes on to show that a psychical element (for instance, an idea) is not as a rule conscious for a protracted length of time. On the contrary, a state of consciousness is characteristically very transitory; an idea that is conscious now is no longer so a moment later, although it can become so again under certain conditions that are easily brought about. In the interval the idea was – we do not know what. We can say that it was *latent*, and by this we mean that it was *capable of becoming conscious* at any time. Or, if we say that it was *unconscious*, we shall also be giving a correct description of it. Here 'unconscious' coincides with 'latent and capable of becoming conscious'. The philosophers would no doubt object: 'No, the term "unconscious" is not applicable here; so long as the idea was in a state of latency it was not anything psychical at all.' To contradict them at this point would lead to nothing more profitable than a verbal dispute.

But we have arrived at the term or concept of the unconscious along another path, by considering certain experiences in which mental *dynamics* play a part. We have found – that is, we have been obliged to assume – that very powerful mental processes or ideas exist (and here a quantitative or *economic* factor comes into question for the first time) which can produce all the effects in mental life that ordinary ideas do (including effects that can in their turn become conscious as ideas), though they themselves do not become conscious. It is unnecessary to repeat in detail here what has been explained so often before.[1] It is enough to say that at this point psychoanalytic theory steps in and asserts that the reason why such ideas cannot become conscious is that a certain force opposes them, that otherwise they could become conscious, and that it would then be apparent how little they

---

passive participle – 'being consciousised'. The English 'conscious' is capable of an active or a passive use; but in these discussions it is always to be taken as passive. Cf. a footnote at the end of the Editor's Note to Freud's metapsychological paper on 'The Unconscious', p. 165 above.]

1. [See, for instance, 'A Note on the Unconscious' (1912*g*), pp. 52 and 55 above.]

differ from other elements which are admittedly psychical. The fact that in the technique of psychoanalysis a means has been found by which the opposing force can be removed and the ideas in question made conscious renders this theory irrefutable. The state in which the ideas existed before being made conscious is called by us *repression*, and we assert that the force which instituted the repression and maintains it is perceived as *resistance* during the work of analysis.

Thus we obtain our concept of the unconscious from the theory of repression. The repressed is the prototype of the unconscious for us. We see, however, that we have two kinds of unconscious – the one which is latent but capable of becoming conscious, and the one which is repressed and which is not, in itself and without more ado, capable of becoming conscious. This piece of insight into psychical dynamics cannot fail to affect terminology and description. The latent, which is unconscious only descriptively, not in the dynamic sense, we call *preconscious*; we restrict the term *unconscious* to the dynamically unconscious repressed; so that now we have three terms, conscious (*Cs.*), preconscious (*Pcs.*), and unconscious (*Ucs.*), whose sense is no longer purely descriptive. The *Pcs.* is presumably a great deal closer to the *Cs.* than is the *Ucs.*, and since we have called the *Ucs.* psychical we shall with even less hesitation call the latent *Pcs.* psychical. But why do we not rather, instead of this, remain in agreement with the philosophers and, in a consistent way, distinguish the *Pcs.* as well as the *Ucs.* from the conscious psychical? The philosophers would then propose that the *Pcs.* and the *Ucs.* should be described as two species or stages of the 'psychoid', and harmony would be established. But endless difficulties in exposition would follow; and the one important fact, that these two kinds of 'psychoid' coincide in almost every other respect with what is admittedly psychical, would be forced into the background in the interests of a prejudice dating from a period in which these psychoids, or the most important part of them, were still unknown.

We can now play about comfortably with our three terms, *Cs.*, *Pcs.*, and *Ucs.*, so long as we do not forget that in the descriptive sense there are two kinds of unconscious, but in the dynamic sense only one.[1] For purposes of exposition this distinction can in some cases be ignored, but in others it is of course indispensable. At the same time, we have become more or less accustomed to this ambiguity of the unconscious and have managed pretty well with it. As far as I can see, it is impossible to avoid this ambiguity; the distinction between conscious and unconscious is in the last resort a question of perception, which must be answered 'yes' or 'no', and the act of perception itself tells us nothing of the reason why a thing is or is not perceived. No one has a right to complain because the actual phenomenon expresses the dynamic factor ambiguously.[2]

1. [Some comments on this sentence will be found in Appendix A (p. 402).]

2. This may be compared so far with my 'Note on the Unconscious in Psycho-Analysis' (1912*g*). [P. 50 ff. above. Cf. also Sections I and II of the metapsychological paper on 'The Unconscious' (1915*e*), p. 167 ff. above.] A new turn taken by criticisms of the unconscious deserves consideration at this point. Some investigators, who do not refuse to recognize the facts of psychoanalysis but who are unwilling to accept the unconscious, find a way out of the difficulty in the fact, which no one contests, that in consciousness (regarded as a phenomenon) it is possible to distinguish a great variety of gradations in intensity or clarity. Just as there are processes which are very vividly, glaringly, and tangibly conscious, so we also experience others which are only faintly, hardly even noticeably conscious; those that are most faintly conscious are, it is argued, the ones to which psychoanalysis wishes to apply the unsuitable name 'unconscious'. These too, however (the argument proceeds), are conscious or 'in consciousness', and can be made fully and intensely conscious if sufficient attention is paid to them.

In so far as it is possible to influence by arguments the decision of a question of this kind which depends either on convention or on emotional factors, we may make the following comments. The reference to gradations of clarity in consciousness is in no way conclusive and has no more evidential value than such analogous statements as: 'There are so very many gradations in illumination – from the most glaring and dazzling light to the dimmest glimmer – therefore there is no such thing as darkness at all'; or, 'There are varying degrees of vitality, therefore there is no such thing as death.' Such statements may in a certain way have a meaning, but for practical purposes they are worthless. This will be seen if one tries to draw particular conclusions from them, such as, 'there is therefore no need to strike a light', or, 'therefore all organisms are immortal'. Further, to include 'what is unnoticeable' under the concept of 'what is conscious' is simply to play havoc with the one and only piece of direct and certain knowledge that we have about the mind. And after all, a consciousness of which

In the further course of psychoanalytic work, however, even these distinctions have proved to be inadequate and, for practical purposes, insufficient. This has become clear in more ways than one; but the decisive instance is as follows. We have formed the idea that in each individual there is a coherent organization of mental processes; and we call this his *ego*. It is to this ego that consciousness is attached; the ego controls the approaches to motility – that is, to the discharge of excitations into the external world; it is the mental agency which supervises all its own constituent processes, and which goes to sleep at night, though even then it exercises the censorship on dreams. From this ego proceed the repressions, too, by means of which it is sought to exclude certain trends in the mind not merely from consciousness but also from other forms of effectiveness and activity. In analysis these trends which have been shut out stand in opposition to the ego, and the analysis is faced with the task of removing the resistances which the ego displays against concerning itself with the repressed. Now we find during analysis that, when we put certain tasks before the patient, he gets into difficulties; his associations fail when they should be coming near the repressed. We then tell him that he is dominated by a resistance; but he is quite unaware of the fact, and, even if he guesses from his unpleasurable feelings that a resistance is now at work in him, he does not know what it is or how to describe it. Since, however, there can be no question but that this resistance emanates from his ego and belongs to it, we find ourselves

one knows nothing seems to me a good deal more absurd than something mental that is unconscious. Finally, this attempt to equate what is unnoticed with what is unconscious is obviously made without taking into account the dynamic conditions involved, which were the decisive factors in forming the psychoanalytic view. For it ignores two facts: first, that it is exceedingly difficult and requires very great effort to concentrate enough attention on something unnoticed of this kind; and secondly, that when this has been achieved the thought which was previously unnoticed is not recognized by consciousness, but often seems entirely alien and opposed to it and is promptly disavowed by it. Thus, seeking refuge from the unconscious in what is scarcely noticed or unnoticed is after all only a derivative of the preconceived belief which regards the identity of the psychical and the conscious as settled once and for all.

in an unforeseen situation. We have come upon something in the ego itself which is also unconscious, which behaves exactly like the repressed – that is, which produces powerful effects without itself being conscious and which requires special work before it can be made conscious. From the point of view of analytic practice, the consequence of this discovery is that we land in endless obscurities and difficulties if we keep to our habitual forms of expression and try, for instance, to derive neuroses from a conflict between the conscious and the unconscious. We shall have to substitute for this antithesis another, taken from our insight into the structural conditions of the mind – the antithesis between the coherent ego and the repressed which is split off from it.[1]

For our conception of the unconscious, however, the consequences of our discovery are even more important. Dynamic considerations caused us to make our first correction; our insight into the structure of the mind leads to the second. We recognize that the *Ucs.* does not coincide with the repressed; it is still true that all that is repressed is *Ucs.*, but not all that is *Ucs.* is repressed. A part of the ego, too – and Heaven knows how important a part – may be *Ucs.*, undoubtedly is *Ucs.*[2] And this *Ucs.* belonging to the ego is not latent like the *Pcs.*; for if it were, it could not be activated without becoming *Cs.*, and the process of making it conscious would not encounter such great difficulties. When we find ourselves thus confronted by the necessity of postulating a third *Ucs.*, which is not repressed, we must admit that the characteristic of being unconscious begins to lose significance for us. It becomes a quality which can have many meanings, a quality which we are unable to make, as we should have hoped to do, the basis of far-reaching and inevitable conclusions. Nevertheless we must beware of ignoring this characteristic, for the property of being conscious or not is in the last resort our one beacon-light in the darkness of depth-psychology.

1. Cf. *Beyond the Pleasure Principle* (1920*g*) [p. 289 above].

2. [This had already been stated not only in *Beyond the Pleasure Principle* (loc. cit.) but earlier, in 'The Unconscious' (1915*e*), p. 197 above. Indeed, it was implied in a remark at the beginning of the second paper on 'The Neuro-Psychoses of Defence' (1896*b*).]

II

THE EGO AND THE ID

PATHOLOGICAL research has directed our interest too exclusively to the repressed. We should like to learn more about the ego, now that we know that it, too, can be unconscious in the proper sense of the word. Hitherto the only guide we have had during our investigations has been the distinguishing mark of being conscious or unconscious; we have finally come to see how ambiguous this can be.

Now all our knowledge is invariably bound up with consciousness. We can come to know even the *Ucs.* only by making it conscious. But stop, how is that possible? What does it mean when we say 'making something conscious'? How can that come about?

We already know the point from which we have to start in this connection. We have said that consciousness is the *surface* of the mental apparatus; that is, we have ascribed it as a function to a system which is spatially the first one reached from the external world – and spatially not only in the functional sense but, on this occasion, also in the sense of anatomical dissection.[1] Our investigations too must take this perceiving surface as a starting-point.

All perceptions which are received from without (sense-perceptions) and from within – what we call sensations and feelings – are *Cs.* from the start. But what about those internal processes which we may – roughly and inexactly – sum up under the name of thought-processes? They represent displacements of mental energy which are effected somewhere in the interior of the apparatus as this energy proceeds on its way towards action. Do they advance to the surface, which causes conscious-

1. *Beyond the Pleasure Principle* [p. 297 above].

ness to be generated? Or does consciousness make its way to them? This is clearly one of the difficulties that arise when one begins to take the spatial or 'topographical' idea of mental life seriously. Both these possibilities are equally unimaginable; there must be a third alternative.[1]

I have already, in another place,[2] suggested that the real difference between a *Ucs.* and a *Pcs.* idea (thought) consists in this: that the former is carried out on some material which remains unknown, whereas the latter (the *Pcs.*) is in addition brought into connection with *word-presentations*. This is the first attempt to indicate distinguishing marks for the two systems, the *Pcs.* and the *Ucs.*, other than their relation to consciousness. The question, 'How does a thing become conscious?' would thus be more advantageously stated: 'How does a thing become preconscious?' And the answer would be: 'Through becoming connected with the word-presentations corresponding to it.'

These word-presentations are residues of memories; they were at one time perceptions, and like all mnemic residues they can become conscious again. Before we concern ourselves further with their nature, it dawns upon us like a new discovery that only something which has once been a *Cs.* perception can become conscious, and that anything arising from within (apart from feelings) that seeks to become conscious must try to transform itself into external perceptions: this becomes possible by means of memory-traces.

We think of the mnemic residues as being contained in systems which are directly adjacent to the system *Pcpt.-Cs.*, so that the cathexes of those residues can readily extend from within on to the elements of the latter system.[3] We immediately think here of hallucinations, and of the fact that the most vivid memory is always distinguishable both from a hallucination and from an external perception[4] but it will also occur to us at once that

1. [This had been discussed at greater length in the second section of 'The Unconscious' (1915*e*), pp. 175–8 above.]
2. 'The Unconscious'[p. 206 ff. above].
3. [Cf. Chapter VII (B) of *The Interpretation of Dreams* (1900*a*), *P.F.L.*, **4**, 687.]
4. [This view had been expressed by Breuer in his theoretical contribution

when a memory is revived the cathexis remains in the mnemic system, whereas a hallucination, which is not distinguishable from a perception, can arise when the cathexis does not merely spread over from the memory-trace on to the *Pcpt.* element, but passes over to it *entirely*.

Verbal residues are derived primarily from auditory perceptions,[1] so that the system *Pcs.* has, as it were, a special sensory source. The visual components of word-presentations are secondary, acquired through reading, and may to begin with be left on one side; so may the motor images of words, which, except with deaf-mutes, play the part of auxiliary indications. In essence a word is after all the mnemic residue of a word that has been heard.

We must not be led, in the interests of simplification perhaps, to forget the importance of optical mnemic residues, when they are of *things*, or to deny that it is possible for thought-processes to become conscious through a reversion to visual residues, and that in many people this seems to be the favoured method. The study of dreams and of preconscious phantasies as shown in Varendonck's observations[2] can give us an idea of the special character of this visual thinking. We learn that what becomes conscious in it is as a rule only the concrete subject-matter of the thought, and that the relations between the various elements of this subject-matter, which is what specially characterizes thoughts, cannot be given visual expression. Thinking in pictures is, therefore, only a very incomplete form of becoming conscious. In some way, too, it stands nearer to unconscious processes than does thinking in words, and it is unquestionably older than the latter both ontogenetically and phylogenetically.

To return to our argument: if, therefore, this is the way in

---

to *Studies on Hysteria* (1895*d*), *P.F.L.*, **3**, 263.]

1. [Freud had arrived at this conclusion in his monograph on aphasia (1891*b*) on the basis of pathological findings. The point is represented in the diagram reproduced from that work in Appendix C to the paper on 'The Unconscious', p. 221 above.]

2. [Cf. Varendonck (1921), a book to which Freud contributed an introduction (1921*b*).]

which something that is in itself unconscious becomes preconscious, the question how we make something that is repressed (pre)conscious would be answered as follows. It is done by supplying *Pcs.* intermediate links through the work of analysis. Consciousness remains where it is, therefore; but, on the other hand, the *Ucs.* does not rise into the *Cs.*

Whereas the relation of *external* perceptions to the ego is quite perspicuous, that of *internal* perceptions to the ego requires special investigation. It gives rise once more to a doubt whether we are really right in referring the whole of consciousness to the single superficial system *Pcpt.-Cs.*

Internal perceptions yield sensations of processes arising in the most diverse and certainly also in the deepest strata of the mental apparatus. Very little is known about these sensations and feelings; those belonging to the pleasure-unpleasure series may still be regarded as the best examples of them. They are more primordial, more elementary, than perceptions arising externally and they can come about even when consciousness is clouded. I have elsewhere[1] expressed my views about their greater economic significance and the metapsychological reasons for this. These sensations are multilocular, like external perceptions; they may come from different places simultaneously and may thus have different or even opposite qualities.

Sensations of a pleasurable nature have not anything inherently impelling about them, whereas unpleasurable ones have it in the highest degree. The latter impel towards change, towards discharge, and that is why we interpret unpleasure as implying a heightening and pleasure a lowering of energic cathexis.[2] Let us call what becomes conscious as pleasure and unpleasure a quantitative and qualitative 'something' in the course of mental events; the question then is whether this 'something' can become conscious in the place where it is, or whether it must first be transmitted to the system *Pcpt.*

Clinical experience decides for the latter. It shows us that this 'something' behaves like a repressed impulse. It can exert driv-

1. [*Beyond the Pleasure Principle* (1920*g*), p. 300 above.]
2. [Ibid., 276.]

ing force without the ego noticing the compulsion. Not until there is resistance to the compulsion, a hold-up in the discharge-reaction, does the 'something' at once become conscious as unpleasure. In the same way that tensions arising from physical needs can remain unconscious, so also can pain – a thing intermediate between external and internal perception, which behaves like an internal perception even when its source is in the external world. It remains true, therefore, that sensations and feelings, too, only become conscious through reaching the system *Pcpt.*; if the way forward is barred, they do not come into being as sensations, although the 'something' that corresponds to them in the course of excitation is the same as if they did. We then come to speak, in a condensed and not entirely correct manner, of 'unconscious feelings', keeping up an analogy with unconscious ideas which is not altogether justifiable. Actually the difference is that, whereas with *Ucs. ideas* connecting links must be created before they can be brought into the *Cs.*, with *feelings*, which are themselves transmitted directly, this does not occur. In other words: the distinction between *Cs.* and *Pcs.* has no meaning where feelings are concerned; the *Pcs.* here drops out – and feelings are either conscious or unconscious. Even when they are attached to word-presentations, their becoming conscious is not due to that circumstance, but they become so directly.[1]

The part played by word-presentations now becomes perfectly clear. By their interposition internal thought-processes are made into perceptions. It is like a demonstration of the theorem that all knowledge has its origin in external perception. When a hypercathexis of the process of thinking takes place, thoughts are *actually* perceived – as if they came from without – and are consequently held to be true.

After this clarifying of the relations between external and internal perception and the superficial system *Pcpt.-Cs.*, we can go on to work out our idea of the ego. It starts out, as we see, from the system *Pcpt.*, which is its nucleus, and begins by

1. [Cf. 'The Unconscious' (1915*e*), pp. 180–81 above.]

embracing the *Pcs.*, which is adjacent to the mnemic residues. But, as we have learnt, the ego is also unconscious.

Now I think we shall gain a great deal by following the suggestion of a writer who, from personal motives, vainly asserts that he has nothing to do with the rigours of pure science. I am speaking of Georg Groddeck, who is never tired of insisting that what we call our ego behaves essentially passively in life, and that, as he expresses it, we are 'lived' by unknown and uncontrollable forces.[1] We have all had impressions of the same kind, even though they may not have overwhelmed us to the exclusion of all others, and we need feel no hesitation in finding a place for Groddeck's discovery in the structure of science. I propose to take it into account by calling the entity which starts out from the system *Pcpt.* and begins by being *Pcs.* the 'ego', and by following Groddeck in calling the other part of the mind, into which this entity extends and which behaves as though it were *Ucs.*, the 'id'.[2]

We shall soon see whether we can derive any advantage from this view for purposes either of description or of understanding. We shall now look upon an individual as a psychical id, unknown and unconscious, upon whose surface rests the ego, developed from its nucleus the *Pcpt.* system. If we make an effort to represent this pictorially, we may add that the ego does not completely envelop the id, but only does so to the extent to which the system *Pcpt.* forms its [the ego's] surface, more or less as the germinal disc rests upon the ovum. The ego is not sharply separated from the id; its lower portion merges into it.

But the repressed merges into the id as well, and is merely a part of it. The repressed is only cut off sharply from the ego by the resistances of repression; it can communicate with the ego through the id. We at once realize that almost all the lines of demarcation we have drawn at the instigation of pathology relate only to the superficial strata of the mental apparatus – the

1. Groddeck (1923).

2. [See Editor's Introduction, p. 345.] – Groddeck himself no doubt followed the example of Nietzsche, who habitually used this grammatical term for whatever in our nature is impersonal and, so to speak, subject to natural law.

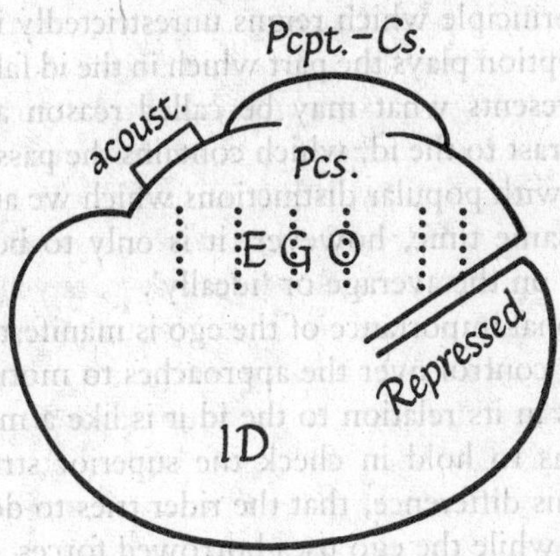

Fig. 1.

only ones known to us. The state of things which we have been describing can be represented diagrammatically (Fig. 1);[1] though it must be remarked that the form chosen has no pretensions to any special applicability, but is merely intended to serve for purposes of exposition.

We might add, perhaps, that the ego wears a 'cap of hearing'[2] – on one side only, as we learn from cerebral anatomy. It might be said to wear it awry.[3]

It is easy to see that the ego is that part of the id which has been modified by the direct influence of the external world through the medium of the *Pcpt.-Cs.*; in a sense it is an extension of the surface-differentiation. Moreover, the ego seeks to bring the influence of the external world to bear upon the id and its tendencies, and endeavours to substitute the reality principle for

1. [Compare the slightly different diagram near the end of Lecture 31 of the *New Introductory Lectures* (1933*a*) *P.F.L.*, **2**, 111. The entirely different one in *The Interpretation of Dreams* (1900*a*), *P.F.L.*, **4**, 690, and its predecessor in a letter to Fliess of 6 December 1896 (Freud, 1950*a*, Letter 52) are concerned with function as well as structure.]

2. ['*Hörkappe.*' I.e. the auditory lobe. Cf. footnote 1, p. 359 above.]

3. [Freud may here have had in mind 'Wernicke's area' (Wernicke, 1900), the higher auditory lobe of the brain concerned with the understanding of speech. Cf. p. 359 and *n*. 1 above.]

the pleasure principle which reigns unrestrictedly in the id. For the ego, perception plays the part which in the id falls to instinct. The ego represents what may be called reason and common sense, in contrast to the id, which contains the passions. All this falls into line with popular distinctions which we are all familiar with; at the same time, however, it is only to be regarded as holding good on the average or 'ideally'.

The functional importance of the ego is manifested in the fact that normally control over the approaches to motility devolves upon it. Thus in its relation to the id it is like a man on horseback, who has to hold in check the superior strength of the horse; with this difference, that the rider tries to do so with his own strength while the ego uses borrowed forces. The analogy may be carried a little further. Often a rider, if he is not to be parted from his horse, is obliged to guide it where it wants to go;[1] so in the same way the ego is in the habit of transforming the id's will into action as if it were its own.

Another factor, besides the influence of the system *Pcpt.*, seems to have played a part in bringing about the formation of the ego and its differentiation from the id. A person's own body, and above all its surface, is a place from which both external and internal perceptions may spring. It is *seen* like any other object, but to the *touch* it yields two kinds of sensations, one of which may be equivalent to an internal perception. Psycho-physiology has fully discussed the manner in which a person's own body attains its special position among other objects in the world of perception. Pain, too, seems to play a part in the process, and the way in which we gain new knowledge of our organs during painful illnesses is perhaps a model of the way by which in general we arrive at the idea of our body.

The ego is first and foremost a bodily ego; it is not merely a surface entity, but is itself the projection of a surface.[2] If we

1. [This analogy reappears in the *New Introductory Lectures* (1933*a*), *P.F.L.*, **2**, 109–10. A similar one appears as an association to one of Freud's dreams in *The Interpretation of Dreams* (1900*a*), *P.F.L.*, **4**, 326.]

2. [I.e. the ego is ultimately derived from bodily sensations, chiefly from those springing from the surface of the body. It may thus be regarded as a mental

wish to find an anatomical analogy for it we can best identify it with the 'cortical homunculus' of the anatomists, which stands on its head in the cortex, sticks up its heels, faces backwards and, as we know, has its speech-area on the left-hand side.

The relation of the ego to consciousness has been entered into repeatedly; yet there are some important facts in this connection which remain to be described here. Accustomed as we are to taking our social or ethical scale of values along with us wherever we go, we feel no surprise at hearing that the scene of the activities of the lower passions is in the unconscious; we expect, moreover, that the higher any mental function ranks in our scale of values the more easily it will find access to consciousness assured to it. Here, however, psychoanalytic experience disappoints us. On the one hand, we have evidence that even subtle and difficult intellectual operations which ordinarily require strenuous reflection can equally be carried out preconsciously and without coming into consciousness. Instances of this are quite incontestable; they may occur, for example, during the state of sleep, as is shown when someone finds, immediately after waking, that he knows the solution to a difficult mathematical or other problem with which he had been wrestling in vain the day before.[1]

There is another phenomenon, however, which is far stranger. In our analyses we discover that there are people in whom the faculties of self-criticism and conscience – mental activities, that is, that rank as extremely high ones – are unconscious and unconsciously produce effects of the greatest importance; the example of resistance remaining unconscious during analysis is therefore by no means unique. But this new discovery, which compels us, in spite of our better critical judgement,

projection of the surface of the body, besides, as we have seen above, representing the superficies of the mental apparatus – This footnote first appeared in the English translation of 1927, in which it was described as having been authorized by Freud. It does not appear in the German editions.]

1. I was quite recently told an instance of this which was, in fact, brought up as an objection against my description of the 'dream-work'. [Cf. *The Interpretation of Dreams*, *P.F.L.*, **4**, 131 f. and 718.]

to speak of an 'unconscious sense of guilt',[1] bewilders us far more than the other and sets us fresh problems, especially when we gradually come to see that in a great number of neuroses an unconscious sense of guilt of this kind plays a decisive economic part and puts the most powerful obstacles in the way of recovery.[2] If we come back once more to our scale of values, we shall have to say that not only what is lowest but also what is highest in the ego can be unconscious. It is as if we were thus supplied with a proof of what we have just asserted of the conscious ego: that it is first and foremost a body-ego.

1. [This phrase had already appeared in Freud's paper on 'Obsessive Actions and Religious Practices' (1907*b*), *P.F.L.*, **13**, 37. The notion was, however, foreshadowed much earlier, in Section II of the first paper on 'The Neuro-Psychoses of Defence' (1894*a*).]

2. [This is further discussed below, p. 390 ff.]

III

THE EGO AND THE SUPER-EGO (EGO IDEAL)

IF THE ego were merely the part of the id modified by the influence of the perceptual system, the representative in the mind of the real external world, we should have a simple state of things to deal with. But there is a further complication.

The considerations that led us to assume the existence of a grade in the ego, a differentiation within the ego, which may be called the 'ego ideal' or 'super-ego', have been stated elsewhere.[1] They still hold good.[2] The fact that this part of the ego is less firmly connected with consciousness is the novelty which calls for explanation.

At this point we must widen our range a little. We succeeded in explaining the painful disorder of melancholia by supposing that [in those suffering from it] an object which was lost has been set up again inside the ego – that is, that an object-cathexis has been replaced by an identification.[3] At that time, however, we did not appreciate the full significance of this process and did not know how common and how typical it is. Since then we

1. [See Editor's Introduction, pp. 347–8.] Cf. 'On Narcissism' (1914*c*), p. 88 ff. above, and *Group Psychology* [*P.F.L.*, **12**, 161 ff.].

2. Except that I seem to have been mistaken in ascribing the function of 'reality-testing' to this super-ego – a point which needs correction. [See *Group Psychology* (1921*c*), *P.F.L.*, **12**, 145, and the Editor's Note on p. 227 above.] It would fit in perfectly with the relations of the ego to the world of perception if reality-testing retained a task of the ego itself. Some earlier suggestions about a 'nucleus of the ego', never very definitely formulated, also require to be put right, since the system *Pcpt.-Cs.* alone can be regarded as the nucleus of the ego. [In *Beyond the Pleasure Principle* (1920*g*) Freud had spoken of the unconscious part of the ego as its nucleus (pp. 289–90 above); and in his later paper on 'Humour' (1927*d*), *P.F.L.*, **14**, 425, he referred to the super-ego as the nucleus of the ego.]

3. 'Mourning and Melancholia' (1917*e*) [pp. 257–8 above].

have come to understand that this kind of substitution has a great share in determining the form taken by the ego and that it makes an essential contribution towards building up what is called its 'character'.[1]

At the very beginning, in the individual's primitive oral phase, object-cathexis and identification are no doubt indistinguishable from each other.[2] We can only suppose that later on object-cathexes proceed from the id, which feels erotic trends as needs. The ego, which to begin with is still feeble, becomes aware of the object-cathexes, and either acquiesces in them or tries to fend them off by the process of repression.[3]

When it happens that a person has to give up a sexual object, there quite often ensues an alteration of his ego which can only be described as a setting up of the object inside the ego, as it occurs in melancholia; the exact nature of this substitution is as yet unknown to us. It may be that by this introjection, which is a kind of regression to the mechanism of the oral phase, the ego makes it easier for the object to be given up or renders that process possible. It may be that this identification is the sole condition under which the id can give up its objects. At any rate the process, especially in the early phases of development, is a very frequent one, and it makes it possible to suppose that the character of the ego is a precipitate of abandoned object-cathexes and that it contains the history of those object-choices. It must, of course, be admitted from the outset that there are varying degrees of capacity for resistance, which decide the extent to

1. [Some references to other passages in which Freud has discussed character-formation will be found in the Editor's Introduction to 'Character and Anal Erotism' (1908*b*), *P.F.L.*, **7**, 207 f.]

2. [Cf. Chapter VII of *Group Psychology* (1921*c*), *P.F.L.*, **12**, 134.]

3. An interesting parallel to the replacement of object-choice by identification is to be found in the belief of primitive peoples, and in the prohibitions based upon it, that the attributes of animals which are incorporated as nourishment persist as part of the character of those who eat them. As is well known, this belief is one of the roots of cannibalism and its effects have continued through the series of usages of the totem meal down to Holy Communion. [Cf. *Totem and Taboo* (1912–13).] The consequences ascribed by this belief to oral mastery of the object do in fact follow in the case of the later sexual object-choice.

which a person's character fends off or accepts the influences of the history of his erotic object-choices. In women who have had many experiences in love there seems to be no difficulty in finding vestiges of their object-cathexes in the traits of their character. We must also take into consideration cases of simultaneous object-cathexis and identification – cases, that is, in which the alteration in character occurs before the object has been given up. In such cases the alteration in character has been able to survive the object-relation and in a certain sense to conserve it.

From another point of view it may be said that this transformation of an erotic object-choice into an alteration of the ego is also a method by which the ego can obtain control over the id and deepen its relations with it – at the cost, it is true, of acquiescing to a large extent in the id's experiences. When the ego assumes the features of the object, it is forcing itself, so to speak, upon the id as a love-object and is trying to make good the id's loss by saying: 'Look, you can love me too – I am so like the object.'

The transformation of object-libido into narcissistic libido which thus takes place obviously implies an abandonment of sexual aims, a desexualization – a kind of sublimation, therefore. Indeed, the question arises, and deserves careful consideration, whether this is not the universal road to sublimation, whether all sublimation does not take place through the mediation of the ego, which begins by changing sexual object-libido into narcissistic libido and then, perhaps, goes on to give it another aim.[1] We shall later on have to consider whether other instinctual vicissitudes may not also result from this transformation, whether, for instance, it may not bring about a defusion of the various instincts that are fused together.[2]

1. Now that we have distinguished between the ego and the id, we must recognize the id as the great reservoir of libido indicated in my paper on narcissism (1914*c*) [p. 67 above]. The libido which flows into the ego owing to the identifications described above brings about its 'secondary narcissism'. [The point is elaborated below on p. 387.]

2. [Freud returns to this below, on pp. 386–7 and 396. The concept of the fusion and defusion of instincts is explained on pp. 381–2. The terms had been introduced already in an encyclopaedia article (1923*a*), *P.F.L.*, **15**.]

Although it is a digression from our aim, we cannot avoid giving our attention for a moment longer to the ego's object-identifications. If they obtain the upper hand and become too numerous, unduly powerful and incompatible with one another, a pathological outcome will not be far off. It may come to a disruption of the ego in consequence of the different identifications becoming cut off from one another by resistances; perhaps the secret of the cases of what is described as 'multiple personality' is that the different identifications seize hold of consciousness in turn. Even when things do not go so far as this, there remains the question of conflicts between the various identifications into which the ego comes apart, conflicts which cannot after all be described as entirely pathological.

But, whatever the character's later capacity for resisting the influences of abandoned object-cathexes may turn out to be, the effects of the first identifications made in earliest childhood will be general and lasting. This leads us back to the origin of the ego ideal; for behind it there lies hidden an individual's first and most important identification, his identification with the father in his own personal prehistory.[1] This is apparently not in the first instance the consequence or outcome of an object-cathexis; it is a direct and immediate identification and takes place earlier than any object-cathexis.[2] But the object-choices belonging to the first sexual period and relating to the father and mother seem normally to find their outcome in an identification of this kind, and would thus reinforce the primary one.

The whole subject, however, is so complicated that it will be necessary to go into it in greater detail. The intricacy of the

1. Perhaps it would be safer to say 'with the parents'; for before a child has arrived at definite knowledge of the difference between the sexes, the lack of a penis, it does not distinguish in value between its father and its mother. I recently came across the instance of a young married woman whose story showed that, after noticing the lack of a penis in herself, she had supposed it to be absent not in all women, but only in those whom she regarded as inferior, and had still supposed that her mother possessed one. [Cf. a footnote to 'The Infantile Genital Organization' (1923*e*), *P.F.L.*, **7**, 311 *n*. 2.] – In order to simplify my presentation I shall discuss only identification with the father.

2. [See *Group Psychology* (1921*c*), *P.F.L.*, **12**, 134.]

problem is due to two factors: the triangular character of the Oedipus situation and the constitutional bisexuality of each individual.

In its simplified form the case of a male child may be described as follows. At a very early age the little boy develops an object-cathexis for his mother, which originally related to the mother's breast and is the prototype of an object-choice on the anaclitic model;[1] the boy deals with his father by identifying himself with him. For a time these two relationships proceed side by side, until the boy's sexual wishes in regard to his mother become more intense and his father is perceived as an obstacle to them; from this the Oedipus complex originates.[2] His identification with his father then takes on a hostile colouring and changes into a wish to get rid of his father in order to take his place with his mother. Henceforward his relation to his father is ambivalent; it seems as if the ambivalence inherent in the identification from the beginning had become manifest. An ambivalent attitude to his father and an object-relation of a solely affectionate kind to his mother make up the content of the simple positive Oedipus complex in a boy.

Along with the demolition of the Oedipus complex, the boy's object-cathexis of his mother must be given up. Its place may be filled by one of two things: either an identification with his mother or an intensification of his identification with his father. We are accustomed to regard the latter outcome as the more normal; it permits the affectionate relation to the mother to be in a measure retained. In this way the dissolution of the Oedipus complex[3] would consolidate the masculinity in a boy's character. In a precisely analogous way,[4] the outcome of the Oedipus attitude in a little girl may be an intensification of her identification

1. [See the paper on narcissism (1914*c*), p. 81 ff. above.]

2. Cf. *Group Psychology* (1921*c*).

3. [Cf. the paper bearing this title (1924*d*) in which Freud discussed the question more fully. (*P.F.L.*, **7**, 315 ff.)]

4. [The idea that the outcome of the Oedipus complex was 'precisely analogous' in girls and boys was abandoned by Freud not long after this. See 'Some Psychical Consequences of the Anatomical Distinction between the Sexes' (1925*j*), *P.F.L.*, **7**, 331 ff.]

with her mother (or the setting up of such an identification for the first time) – a result which will fix the child's feminine character.

These identifications are not what we should have expected [from the previous account (p. 368)], since they do not introduce the abandoned object into the ego; but this alternative outcome may also occur, and is easier to observe in girls than in boys. Analysis very often shows that a little girl, after she has had to relinquish her father as a love-object, will bring her masculinity into prominence and identify herself with her father (that is, with the object which has been lost), instead of with her mother. This will clearly depend on whether the masculinity in her disposition – whatever that may consist in – is strong enough.

It would appear, therefore, that in both sexes the relative strength of the masculine and feminine sexual dispositions is what determines whether the outcome of the Oedipus situation shall be an identification with the father or with the mother. This is one of the ways in which bisexuality takes a hand in the subsequent vicissitudes of the Oedipus complex. The other way is even more important. For one gets an impression that the simple Oedipus complex is by no means its commonest form, but rather represents a simplification or schematization which, to be sure, is often enough justified for practical purposes. Closer study usually discloses the *more complete* Oedipus complex, which is twofold, positive and negative, and is due to the bisexuality originally present in children: that is to say, a boy has not merely an ambivalent attitude towards his father and an affectionate object-choice towards his mother, but at the same time he also behaves like a girl and displays an affectionate feminine attitude to his father and a corresponding jealousy and hostility towards his mother. It is this complicating element introduced by bisexuality that makes it so difficult to obtain a clear view of the facts in connection with the earliest object-choices and identifications, and still more difficult to describe them intelligibly. It may even be that the ambivalence displayed in the relations to the parents should be attributed entirely to bisexuality and that it is not, as I have represented above, developed out of identification in consequence of rivalry.[1]

In my opinion it is advisable in general, and quite especially where neurotics are concerned, to assume the existence of the complete Oedipus complex. Analytic experience then shows that in a number of cases one or the other constituent disappears, except for barely distinguishable traces; so that the result is a series with the normal positive Oedipus complex at one end and the inverted negative one at the other, while its intermediate members exhibit the complete form with one or other of its two components preponderating. At the dissolution of the Oedipus complex the four trends of which it consists will group themselves in such a way as to produce a father-identification and a mother-identification. The father-identification will preserve the object-relation to the mother which belonged to the positive complex and will at the same time replace the object-relation to the father which belonged to the inverted complex: and the same will be true, *mutatis mutandis*, of the mother-identification. The relative intensity of the two identifications in any individual will reflect the preponderance in him of one or other of the two sexual dispositions.

The broad general outcome of the sexual phase dominated by the Oedipus complex may, therefore, be taken to be the forming of a precipitate in the ego, consisting of these two identifications in some way united with each other. This modification of the ego retains its special position; it confronts the other contents of the ego as an ego ideal or super-ego.

The super-ego is, however, not simply a residue of the earliest object-choices of the id; it also represents an energetic reaction-

1. [Freud's belief in the importance of bisexuality went back a very long way. In the first edition of the *Three Essays* (1905*d*), for instance, he wrote: 'Without taking bisexuality into account I think it would scarcely be possible to arrive at an understanding of the sexual manifestations that are actually to be observed in men and women.' (*P.F.L.*, **7**, 142.) But still earlier we find a passage in a letter to Fliess (who influenced him greatly on this subject) which seems almost to foreshadow the present paragraph (Freud, 1950*a*, Letter 113, of 1 August 1899): 'Bisexuality! I am sure you are right about it. And I am accustoming myself to regarding every sexual act as an event between four individuals.']

formation against those choices. Its relation to the ego is not exhausted by the precept: 'You *ought to be* like this (like your father).' It also comprises the prohibition: 'You *may not be* like this (like your father) – that is, you may not do all that he does; some things are his prerogative.' This double aspect of the ego ideal derives from the fact that the ego ideal had the task of repressing the Oedipus complex; indeed, it is to that revolutionary event that it owes its existence. Clearly the repression of the Oedipus complex was no easy task. The child's parents, and especially his father, were perceived as the obstacle to a realization of his Oedipus wishes; so his infantile ego fortified itself for the carrying out of the repression by erecting this same obstacle within itself. It borrowed strength to do this, so to speak, from the father, and this loan was an extraordinarily momentous act. The super-ego retains the character of the father, while the more powerful the Oedipus complex was and the more rapidly it succumbed to repression (under the influence of authority, religious teaching, schooling and reading), the stricter will be the domination of the super-ego over the ego later on – in the form of conscience or perhaps of an unconscious sense of guilt. I shall presently [p. 389] bring forward a suggestion about the source of its power to dominate in this way – the source, that is, of its compulsive character which manifests itself in the form of a categorical imperative.

If we consider once more the origin of the super-ego as we have described it, we shall recognize that it is the outcome of two highly important factors, one of a biological and the other of a historical nature: namely, the lengthy duration in man of his childhood helplessness and dependence, and the fact of his Oedipus complex, the repression of which we have shown to be connected with the interruption of libidinal development by the latency period and so with the diphasic onset of man's sexual life.[1] According to one psychoanalytic hypothesis,[2] the last-

1. [In the German editions this sentence reads as follows: 'If we consider once more the origin of the super-ego as we have described it, we shall recognize that it is the outcome of two highly important biological factors: namely, the lengthy duration in man of his childhood helplessness and dependence, and the fact of

mentioned phenomenon, which seems to be peculiar to man, is a heritage of the cultural development necessitated by the glacial epoch. We see, then, that the differentiation of the super-ego from the ego is no matter of chance; it represents the most important characteristics of the development both of the individual and of the species; indeed, by giving permanent expression to the influence of the parents it perpetuates the existence of the factors to which it owes its origin.

Psychoanalysis has been reproached time after time with ignoring the higher, moral, supra-personal side of human nature. The reproach is doubly unjust, both historically and methodologically. For, in the first place, we have from the very beginning attributed the function of instigating repression to the moral and aesthetic trends in the ego, and secondly, there has been a general refusal to recognize that psychoanalytic research could not, like a philosophical system, produce a complete and ready-made theoretical structure, but had to find its way step by step along the path towards understanding the intricacies of the mind by making an analytic dissection of both normal and abnormal phenomena. So long as we had to concern ourselves with the study of what is repressed in mental life, there was no need for us to share in any agitated apprehensions as to the whereabouts of the higher side of man. But now that we have embarked upon the analysis of the ego we can give an answer to all those whose moral sense has been shocked and who have complained that there must surely be a higher nature in man: 'Very true,' we can say, 'and here we have that higher nature, in this ego ideal or super-ego, the representative of our relation to our parents. When we were little children we knew these

his Oedipus complex, which we have traced back to the interruption of libidinal development by the latency period and so to the diphasic origin of man's sexual life.' The slightly different version given in the text above was inserted by Freud's express orders in the English translation in 1927. For some reason the emendations were not included in the later German editions.]

2. [The idea was put forward by Ferenczi (1913*a*). Freud seems to accept it rather more definitely near the end of Chapter X of *Inhibitions, Symptoms and Anxiety* (1926*d*), *P.F.L.*, **10**, 314.]

higher natures, we admired them and feared them; and later we took them into ourselves.'

The ego ideal is therefore the heir of the Oedipus complex, and thus it is also the expression of the most powerful impulses and most important libidinal vicissitudes of the id. By setting up this ego ideal, the ego has mastered the Oedipus complex and at the same time placed itself in subjection to the id. Whereas the ego is essentially the representative of the external world, of reality, the super-ego stands in contrast to it as the representative of the internal world, of the id. Conflicts between the ego and the ideal will, as we are now prepared to find, ultimately reflect the contrast between what is real and what is psychical, between the external world and the internal world.

Through the forming of the ideal, what biology and the vicissitudes of the human species have created in the id and left behind in it is taken over by the ego and re-experienced in relation to itself as an individual. Owing to the way in which the ego ideal is formed, it has the most abundant links with the phylogenetic acquisition of each individual – his archaic heritage. What has belonged to the lowest part of the mental life of each of us is changed, through the formation of the ideal, into what is highest in the human mind by our scale of values. It would be vain, however, to attempt to localize the ego ideal, even in the sense in which we have localized the ego,[1] or to work it into any of the analogies with the help of which we have tried to picture the relation between the ego and the id.

It is easy to show that the ego ideal answers to everything that is expected of the higher nature of man. As a substitute for a longing for the father, it contains the germ from which all religions have evolved. The self-judgement which declares that the ego falls short of its ideal produces the religious sense of humility to which the believer appeals in his longing. As a child grows up, the role of father is carried on by teachers and others in authority; their injunctions and prohibitions remain powerful in

1. [The super-ego is accordingly not included in the diagram on p. 363. Nevertheless it is given a place in the later diagram in Lecture 31 of the *New Introductory Lectures* (1933*a*) *P.F.L.*, **2**, 111.]

the ego ideal and continue, in the form of conscience, to exercise the moral censorship. The tension between the demands of *conscience* and the actual performances of the ego is experienced as a *sense of guilt*. Social feelings rest on identifications with other people, on the basis of having the same ego ideal.

Religion, morality, and a social sense – the chief elements in the higher side of man[1] – were originally one and the same thing. According to the hypothesis which I put forward in *Totem and Taboo* [1912–13], they were acquired phylogenetically out of the father-complex: religion and moral restraint through the process of mastering the Oedipus complex itself, and social feeling through the necessity for overcoming the rivalry that then remained between the members of the younger generation. The male sex seems to have taken the lead in all these moral acquisitions; and they seem to have then been transmitted to women by cross-inheritance. Even to-day the social feelings arise in the individual as a superstructure built upon impulses of jealous rivalry against his brothers and sisters. Since the hostility cannot be satisfied, an identification with the former rival develops. The study of mild cases of homosexuality confirms the suspicion that in this instance, too, the identification is a substitute for an affectionate object-choice which has *taken* the place of the aggressive, hostile attitude.[2]

With the mention of phylogenesis, however, fresh problems arise, from which one is tempted to draw cautiously back. But there is no help for it, the attempt must be made – in spite of a fear that it will lay bare the inadequacy of our whole effort. The question is: which was it, the ego of primitive man or his id, that acquired religion and morality in those early days out of the father-complex? If it was his ego, why do we not speak simply of these things being inherited by the ego? If it was the id, how does that agree with the character of the id? Or are we wrong in carrying the differentiation between ego, super-ego, and id back into such early times? Or should we not honestly

1. I am at the moment putting science and art on one side.

2. Cf. *Group Psychology* (1921*c*) [*P.F.L.*, **12**, 151] and 'Some Neurotic Mechanisms in Jealousy, Paranoia and Homosexuality' (1922*b*) [*P.F.L.*, **10**, 206–7].

confess that our whole conception of the processes in the ego is of no help in understanding phylogenesis and cannot be applied to it?

Let us answer first what is easiest to answer. The differentiation between ego and id must be attributed not only to primitive man but even to much simpler organisms, for it is the inevitable expression of the influence of the external world. The super-ego, according to our hypothesis, actually originated from the experiences that led to totemism. The question whether it was the ego or the id that experienced and acquired these things soon comes to nothing. Reflection at once shows us that no external vicissitudes can be experienced or undergone by the id, except by way of the *ego*, which is the representative of the external world to the id. Nevertheless it is not possible to speak of direct inheritance in the *ego*. It is here that the gulf between an actual individual and the concept of a species becomes evident. Moreover, one must not take the difference between ego and id in too hard-and-fast a sense, nor forget that the ego is a specially differentiated part of the id [p. 363]. The experiences of the ego seem at first to be lost for inheritance; but, when they have been repeated often enough and with sufficient strength in many individuals in successive generations, they transform themselves, so to say, into experiences of the id, the impressions of which are preserved by heredity. Thus in the id, which is capable of being inherited, are harboured residues of the existences of countless egos; and, when the ego forms its super-ego out of the id, it may perhaps only be reviving shapes of former egos and be bringing them to resurrection.

The way in which the super-ego came into being explains how it is that the early conflicts of the ego with the object-cathexes of the id can be continued in conflicts with their heir, the super-ego. If the ego has not succeeded in properly mastering the Oedipus complex, the energic cathexis of the latter, springing from the id, will come into operation once more in the reaction-formation of the ego ideal. The abundant communication between the ideal and these *Ucs.* instinctual impulses solves the puzzle of how it is that the ideal itself can to a great extent remain unconscious and inaccessible to the ego. The struggle which once raged in the deepest strata of the mind, and was not brought to an end by rapid sublimation and identification, is now continued in a higher region, like the Battle of the Huns in Kaulbach's painting.[1]

1. [This was the battle, usually known as the Battle of Châlons, in which, in 451, Attila was defeated by the Romans and Visigoths. Wilhelm von Kaulbach (1805–74) made it the subject of one of his mural decorations, originally painted for the Neues Museum in Berlin. In this the dead warriors are represented as continuing their fight in the sky above the battlefield, in accordance with a legend that can be traced back to the sixth-century Neo-Platonist, Damascius.]

IV

THE TWO CLASSES OF INSTINCTS

We have already said that, if the differentiation we have made of the mind into an id, an ego, and a super-ego represents any advance in our knowledge, it ought to enable us to understand more thoroughly the dynamic relations within the mind and to describe them more clearly. We have also already concluded [pp. 363–4] that the ego is especially under the influence of perception, and that, speaking broadly, perceptions may be said to have the same significance for the ego as instincts have for the id. At the same time the ego is subject to the influence of the instincts, too, like the id, of which it is, as we know, only a specially modified part.

I have lately developed a view of the instincts[1] which I shall here hold to and take as the basis of my further discussions. According to this view we have to distinguish two classes of instincts, one of which, the *sexual instincts* or *Eros*, is by far the more conspicuous and accessible to study. It comprises not merely the uninhibited sexual instinct proper and the instinctual impulses of an aim-inhibited or sublimated nature derived from it, but also the self-preservative instinct, which must be assigned to the ego and which at the beginning of our analytic work we had good reason for contrasting with the sexual object-instincts. The second class of instincts was not so easy to point to; in the end we came to recognize sadism as its representative. On the basis of theoretical considerations, supported by biology, we put forward the hypothesis of a *death instinct*, the task of which is to lead organic life back into the inanimate state; on the other hand, we supposed that Eros, by bringing about a more and

1. *Beyond the Pleasure Principle* [(1920*g*), p. 275 ff. above].

more far-reaching combination of the particles into which living substance is dispersed, aims at complicating life and at the same time, of course, at preserving it. Acting in this way, both the instincts would be conservative in the strictest sense of the word, since both would be endeavouring to re-establish a state of things that was disturbed by the emergence of life. The emergence of life would thus be the cause of the continuance of life and also at the same time of the striving towards death; and life itself would be a conflict and compromise between these two trends. The problem of the origin of life would remain a cosmological one; and the problem of the goal and purpose of life would be answered *dualistically*.[1]

On this view, a special physiological process (of anabolism or catabolism) would be associated with each of the two classes of instincts; both kinds of instinct would be active in every particle of living substance, though in unequal proportions, so that some one substance might be the principal representative of Eros.

This hypothesis throws no light whatever upon the manner in which the two classes of instincts are fused, blended, and alloyed with each other; but that this takes place regularly and very extensively is an assumption indispensable to our conception. It appears that, as a result of the combination of unicellular organisms into multicellular forms of life, the death instinct of the single cell can successfully be neutralized and the destructive impulses be diverted on to the external world through the instrumentality of a special organ. This special organ would seem to be the muscular apparatus; and the death instinct would thus seem to express itself – though probably only in part – as an *instinct of destruction* directed against the external world and other organisms.[2]

Once we have admitted the idea of a fusion of the two classes of instincts with each other, the possibility of a – more or less

1. [Cf. footnote 2, p. 387 below.]
2. [Freud returns to this in 'The Economic Problem of Masochism', p. 418 below.]

complete – 'defusion' of them forces itself upon us.[1] The sadistic component of the sexual instinct would be a classical example of a serviceable instinctual fusion; and the *sadism* which has made itself independent as a perversion would be typical of a defusion, though not of one carried to extremes. From this point we obtain a view of a great domain of facts which has not before been considered in this light. We perceive that for purposes of discharge the *instinct of destruction* is habitually brought into the service of Eros; we suspect that the epileptic fit is a product and indication of an instinctual defusion;[2] and we come to understand that instinctual defusion and the marked emergence of the death instinct call for particular consideration among the effects of some severe neuroses – for instance, the obsessional neuroses. Making a swift generalization, we might conjecture that the essence of a regression of libido (e.g. from the genital to the sadistic-anal phase) lies in a defusion of instincts, just as, conversely, the advance from the earlier phase to the definitive genital one would be conditioned by an accession of erotic components.[3] The question also arises whether ordinary *ambivalence*, which is so often unusually strong in the constitutional disposition to neurosis, should not be regarded as the product of a defusion; ambivalence, however, is such a fundamental phenomenon that it more probably represents an instinctual fusion that has not been completed.

It is natural that we should turn with interest to enquire whether there may not be instructive connections to be traced between the structures we have assumed to exist – the ego, the super-ego and the id – on the one hand and the two classes of instincts on the other; and, further, whether the pleasure principle which dominates mental processes can be shown to have any constant relation both to the two classes of instincts and to these differentiations which we have drawn in the mind. But

1. [Cf. above, p. 369. What follows in regard to sadism is hinted at in *Beyond the Pleasure Principle*, p. 327 above.]

2. [Cf. Freud's later paper on Dostoevsky's fits (1928*b*), *P.F.L.*, **14**, 441 ff.]

3. [Freud recurs to this point in *Inhibitions, Symptoms and Anxiety* (1926*d*), *P.F.L.*, **10**, 268 f.]

before we discuss this, we must clear away a doubt which arises concerning the terms in which the problem itself is stated. There is, it is true, no doubt about the pleasure principle, and the differentiation within the ego has good clinical justification; but the distinction between the two classes of instincts does not seem sufficiently assured and it is possible that facts of clinical analysis may be found which will do away with its pretension.

One such fact there appears to be. For the opposition between the two classes of instincts we may put the polarity of love and hate [1] There is no difficulty in finding a representative of Eros; but we must be grateful that we can find a representative of the elusive death instinct in the instinct of destruction, to which hate points the way. Now, clinical observation shows not only that love is with unexpected regularity accompanied by hate (ambivalence), and not only that in human relationships hate is frequently a forerunner of love, but also that in a number of circumstances hate changes into love and love into hate. If this change is more than a mere succession in time – if, that is, one of them actually turns into the other – then clearly the ground is cut away from under a distinction so fundamental as that between erotic instincts and death instincts, one which presupposes physiological processes running in opposite directions.

Now the case in which someone first loves and then hates the same person (or the reverse), because that person has given him cause for doing so, has obviously nothing to do with our problem. Nor has the other case, in which feelings of love that have not yet become manifest express themselves to begin with by hostility and aggressive tendencies; for it may be that here the destructive component in the object-cathexis has hurried on ahead and is only later on joined by the erotic one. But we know of several instances in the psychology of the neuroses in which it is more plausible to suppose that a transformation does take place. In *paranoia persecutoria* the patient fends off an excessively

1. [For what follows, see the earlier discussion of the relation between love and hate in 'Instincts and their Vicissitudes' (1915*c*), pp. 134–8 above, as well as in *Civilization and its Discontents* (1930*a*), *P.F.L.*, **12**, 298 ff. and 308 ff.]

strong homosexual attachment to some particular person in a special way; and as a result this person whom he loved most becomes a persecutor, against whom the patient directs an often dangerous aggressiveness. Here we have a right to interpolate a previous phase which has transformed the love into hate. In the case of the origin of homosexuality, and of desexualized social feelings as well, analytic investigation has only recently taught us to recognize that violent feelings of rivalry are present which lead to aggressive inclinations, and that it is only after these have been surmounted that the formerly hated object becomes the loved one or gives rise to an identification.[1] The question arises whether in these instances we are to assume a direct transformation of hate into love. It is clear that here the changes are purely internal and an alteration in the behaviour of the object plays no part in them.

There is another possible mechanism, however, which we have come to know of by analytic investigation of the processes concerned in the change in paranoia. An ambivalent attitude is present from the outset and the transformation is effected by means of a reactive displacement of cathexis, energy being withdrawn from the erotic impulse and added to the hostile one.

Not quite the same thing but something like it happens when the hostile rivalry leading to homosexuality is overcome. The hostile attitude has no prospect of satisfaction; consequently – for economic reasons, that is – it is replaced by a loving attitude for which there is more prospect of satisfaction – that is, possibility of discharge. So we see that we are not obliged in any of these cases to assume a direct transformation of hate into love, which would be incompatible with the qualitative distinction between the two classes of instincts.

It will be noticed, however, that by introducing this other mechanism of changing love into hate, we have tacitly made another assumption which deserves to be stated explicitly. We have reckoned as though there existed in the mind – whether in the ego or in the id – a displaceable energy, which, indifferent

1. [See footnote 2, p. 377.]

in itself, can be added to a qualitatively differentiated erotic or destructive impulse, and augment its total cathexis. Without assuming the existence of a displaceable energy of this kind we can make no headway. The only question is where it comes from, what it belongs to, and what it signifies.

The problem of the quality of instinctual impulses and of its persistence throughout their various vicissitudes is still very obscure and has hardly been attacked up to the present. In the sexual component instincts, which are especially accessible to observation, it is possible to perceive a few processes which are in the same category as what we are discussing. We see, for instance, that some degree of communication exists between the component instincts, that an instinct deriving from one particular erotogenic source can make over its intensity to reinforce another component instinct originating from another source, that the satisfaction of one instinct can take the place of the satisfaction of another, and more facts of the same nature – which must encourage us to venture upon certain hypotheses.

In the present discussion, moreover, I am only putting forward a hypothesis; I have no proof to offer. It seems a plausible view that this displaceable and indifferent energy, which is no doubt active both in the ego and in the id, proceeds from the narcissistic store of libido – that it is desexualized Eros. (The erotic instincts appear to be altogether more plastic, more readily diverted and displaced than the destructive instincts.) From this we can easily go on to assume that this displaceable libido is employed in the service of the pleasure principle to obviate blockages and to facilitate discharge. In this connection it is easy to observe a certain indifference as to the path along which the discharge takes place, so long as it takes place somehow. We know this trait; it is characteristic of the cathectic processes in the id. It is found in erotic cathexis, where a peculiar indifference in regard to the object displays itself; and it is especially evident in the transferences arising in analysis, which develop inevitably, irrespective of the persons who are their object. Not long ago Rank [1913] published some good examples of the way in which neurotic acts of revenge can be directed against the wrong people. Such behaviour on the part of the unconscious reminds one of the comic story of the three village tailors, one of whom had to be hanged because the only village blacksmith had committed a capital offence.[1] Punishment must be exacted even if it does not fall upon the guilty. It was in studying the dream-work that we first came upon this kind of looseness in the displacements brought about by the primary process. In that case it was the objects that were thus relegated to a position of no more than secondary importance, just as in the case we are now discussing it is the paths of discharge. It would be characteristic of the ego to be more particular about the choice both of an object and of a path of discharge.

If this displaceable energy is desexualized libido, it may also be described as *sublimated* energy; for it would still retain the main purpose of Eros – that of uniting and binding – in so far as it helps towards establishing the unity, or tendency to unity, which is particularly characteristic of the ego. If thought-processes in the wider sense are to be included among these displacements, then the activity of thinking is also supplied from the sublimation of erotic motive forces.

Here we arrive again at the possibility which has already been discussed [p. 369] that sublimation may take place regularly through the mediation of the ego. The other case will be recollected, in which the ego deals with the first object-cathexes of the id (and certainly with later ones too) by taking over the libido from them into itself and binding it to the alteration of the ego produced by means of identification. The transformation [of erotic libido] into ego-libido of course involves an abandonment of sexual aims, a desexualization. In any case this throws light upon an important function of the ego in its relation to Eros. By thus getting hold of the libido from the object-cathexes, setting itself up as sole love-object, and desexualizing or sublimating the libido of the id, the ego is working in opposition to the purposes of Eros and placing itself at the service of

1. [The story was told by Freud in the last chapter of his book on jokes (1905*c*), *P.F.L.*, **6**, 267, and in Lecture 11 of the *Introductory Lectures* (1916–17), *P.F.L.*, **1**, 209.]

the opposing instinctual impulses. It has to acquiesce in some of the other object-cathexes of the id; it has, so to speak, to participate in them. We shall come back later to another possible consequence of this activity of the ego [p. 396].

This would seem to imply an important amplification of the theory of narcissism. At the very beginning, all the libido is accumulated in the id, while the ego is still in process of formation or is still feeble. The id sends part of this libido out into erotic object-cathexes, whereupon the ego, now grown stronger, tries to get hold of this object-libido and to force itself on the id as a love-object. The narcissism of the ego is thus a secondary one, which has been withdrawn from objects.[1]

Over and over again we find, when we are able to trace instinctual impulses back, that they reveal themselves as derivatives of Eros. If it were not for the considerations put forward in *Beyond the Pleasure Principle* [1920*g*], and ultimately for the sadistic constituents which have attached themselves to Eros, we should have difficulty in holding to our fundamental dualistic point of view.[2] But since we cannot escape that view, we are driven to conclude that the death instincts are by their nature mute and that the clamour of life proceeds for the most part from Eros.[3]

And from the struggle against Eros! It can hardly be doubted that the pleasure principle serves the id as a compass in its struggle against the libido – the force that introduces disturbances into the process of life. If it is true that Fechner's principle of constancy[4] governs life, which thus consists of a continuous descent towards death, it is the claims of Eros, of the sexual instincts, which, in the form of instinctual needs, hold up the falling level

1. [See Appendix B (p. 404) for a discussion of this.]

2. [The consistency with which Freud held to a dualistic classification of the instincts will be seen from his long footnote at the end of Chapter VI of *Beyond the Pleasure Principle* (1920*g*), pp. 334–5 above, and from the historical sketch in the Editor's Note to 'Instincts and their Vicissitudes' (1915*c*), pp. 110–12 above.]

3. In fact, on our view it is through the agency of Eros that the destructive instincts that are directed towards the external world have been diverted from the self.

4. [Cf. *Beyond the Pleasure Principle*, pp. 276–8 above]

and introduce fresh tensions. The id, guided by the pleasure principle – that is, by the perception of unpleasure – fends off these tensions in various ways. It does so in the first place by complying as swiftly as possible with the demands of the non-desexualized libido – by striving for the satisfaction of the directly sexual trends. But it does so in a far more comprehensive fashion in relation to one particular form of satisfaction in which all component demands converge – by discharge of the sexual substances, which are saturated vehicles, so to speak, of the erotic tensions.[1] The ejection of the sexual substances in the sexual act corresponds in a sense to the separation of soma and germ-plasm. This accounts for the likeness of the condition that follows complete sexual satisfaction to dying, and for the fact that death coincides with the act of copulation in some of the lower animals. These creatures die in the act of reproduction because, after Eros has been eliminated through the process of satisfaction, the death instinct has a free hand for accomplishing its purposes. Finally, as we have seen, the ego, by sublimating some of the libido for itself and its purposes, assists the id in its work of mastering the tensions.

1. [Freud's views on the part played by the 'sexual substances' will be found in Section 2 of the third of his *Three Essays* (1905*d*), *P.F.L.*, **7**, 133–8.]

V

THE DEPENDENT RELATIONSHIPS OF THE EGO

THE complexity of our subject-matter must be an excuse for the fact that none of the chapter-headings of this book quite correspond to their contents, and that in turning to new aspects of the topic we are constantly harking back to matters that have already been dealt with.

Thus we have said repeatedly that the ego is formed to a great extent out of identifications which take the place of abandoned cathexes by the id; that the first of these identifications always behave as a special agency in the ego and stand apart from the ego in the form of a super-ego, while later on, as it grows stronger, the ego may become more resistant to the influences of such identifications. The super-ego owes its special position in the ego, or in relation to the ego, to a factor which must be considered from two sides: on the one hand it was the first identification and one which took place while the ego was still feeble, and on the other hand it is the heir to the Oedipus complex and has thus introduced the most momentous objects into the ego. The super-ego's relation to the later alterations of the ego is roughly similar to that of the primary sexual phase of childhood to later sexual life after puberty. Although it is accessible to all later influences, it nevertheless preserves throughout life the character given to it by its derivation from the father-complex – namely, the capacity to stand apart from the ego and to master it. It is a memorial of the former weakness and dependence of the ego, and the mature ego remains subject to its domination. As the child was once under a compulsion to obey its parents, so the ego submits to the categorical imperative of its super-ego.

But the derivation of the super-ego from the first object-cathexes of the id, from the Oedipus complex, signifies even more for it. This derivation, as we have already shown [p. 376 ff.], brings it into relation with the phylogenetic acquisitions of the id and makes it a reincarnation of former ego-structures which have left their precipitates behind in the id. Thus the super-ego is always close to the id and can act as its representative *vis-à-vis* the ego. It reaches deep down into the id and for that reason is farther from consciousness than the ego is.[1]

We shall best appreciate these relations by turning to certain clinical facts, which have long since lost their novelty but which still await theoretical discussion.

There are certain people who behave in a quite peculiar fashion during the work of analysis. When one speaks hopefully to them or expresses satisfaction with the progress of the treatment, they show signs of discontent and their condition invariably becomes worse. One begins by regarding this as defiance and as an attempt to prove their superiority to the physician, but later one comes to take a deeper and juster view. One becomes convinced, not only that such people cannot endure any praise or appreciation, but that they react inversely to the progress of the treatment. Every partial solution that ought to result, and in other people does result, in an improvement or a temporary suspension of symptoms produces in them for the time being an exacerbation of their illness; they get worse during the treatment instead of getting better. They exhibit what is known as a 'negative therapeutic reaction'.

There is no doubt that there is something in these people that sets itself against their recovery, and its approach is dreaded as though it were a danger. We are accustomed to say that the need for illness has got the upper hand in them over the desire for recovery. If we analyse this resistance in the usual way – then, even after allowance has been made for an attitude of defiance towards the physician and for fixation to the various forms of gain from illness, the greater part of it is still left over; and this reveals itself as the most powerful of all obstacles to recovery, more powerful than the familiar ones of narcissistic inaccessi-

1. It may be said that the psychoanalytic or metapsychological ego stands on its head no less than the anatomical ego – the 'cortical homunculus' [p. 365].

bility, a negative attitude towards the physician and clinging to the gain from illness.

In the end we come to see that we are dealing with what may be called a 'moral' factor, a sense of guilt, which is finding its satisfaction in the illness and refuses to give up the punishment of suffering. We shall be right in regarding this disheartening explanation as final. But as far as the patient is concerned this sense of guilt is dumb; it does not tell him he is guilty; he does not feel guilty, he feels ill. This sense of guilt expresses itself only as a resistance to recovery which it is extremely difficult to overcome. It is also particularly difficult to convince the patient that this motive lies behind his continuing to be ill; he holds fast to the more obvious explanation that treatment by analysis is not the right remedy for his case.[1]

1. The battle with the obstacle of an unconscious sense of guilt is not made easy for the analyst. Nothing can be done against it directly, and nothing indirectly but the slow procedure of unmasking its unconscious repressed roots, and of thus gradually changing it into a *conscious* sense of guilt. One has a special opportunity for influencing it when this *Ucs.* sense of guilt is a 'borrowed' one – when it is the product of an identification with some other person who was once the object of an erotic cathexis. A sense of guilt that has been adopted in this way is often the sole remaining trace of the abandoned love-relation and not at all easy to recognize as such. (The likeness between this process and what happens in melancholia is unmistakable.) If one can unmask this former object-cathexis behind the *Ucs.* sense of guilt, the therapeutic success is often brilliant, but otherwise the outcome of one's efforts is by no means certain. It depends principally on the intensity of the sense of guilt; there is often no counteracting force of a similar order of strength which the treatment can oppose to it. Perhaps it may depend, too, on whether the personality of the analyst allows of the patient's putting him in the place of his ego ideal, and this involves a temptation for the analyst to play the part of prophet, saviour and redeemer to the patient. Since the rules of analysis are diametrically opposed to the physician's making use of his personality in any such manner, it must be honestly confessed that here we have another limitation to the effectiveness of analysis; after all, analysis does not set out to make pathological reactions impossible, but to give the patient's ego *freedom* to decide one way or the other. – [Freud returned to this topic in his paper on 'The Economic Problem of Masochism' (1924*c*), pp. 420–21 below, where he discussed the distinction between the unconscious sense of guilt and moral masochism. See also Chapters VII and VIII of *Civilization and its Discontents* (1930*a*), *P.F.L.*, **12**, 315 and 327.]

The description we have given applies to the most extreme instances of this state of affairs, but in a lesser measure this factor has to be reckoned with in very many cases, perhaps in all comparatively severe cases of neurosis. In fact it may be precisely this element in the situation, the attitude of the ego ideal, that determines the severity of a neurotic illness. We shall not hesitate, therefore, to discuss rather more fully the way in which the sense of guilt expresses itself under different conditions.

An interpretation of the normal, conscious sense of guilt (conscience) presents no difficulties; it is based on the tension between the ego and the ego ideal and is the expression of a condemnation of the ego by its critical agency. The feelings of inferiority so well known in neurotics are presumably not far removed from it. In two very familiar maladies the sense of guilt is over-strongly conscious; in them the ego ideal displays particular severity and often rages against the ego in a cruel fashion. The attitude of the ego ideal in these two conditions, obsessional neurosis and melancholia, presents, alongside of this similarity, differences that are no less significant.

In certain forms of obsessional neurosis the sense of guilt is over-noisy but cannot justify itself to the ego. Consequently the patient's ego rebels against the imputation of guilt and seeks the physician's support in repudiating it. It would be folly to acquiesce in this, for to do so would have no effect. Analysis eventually shows that the super-ego is being influenced by processes that have remained unknown to the ego. It is possible to discover the repressed impulses which are really at the bottom of the sense of guilt. Thus in this case the super-ego knew more than the ego about the unconscious id.

In melancholia the impression that the super-ego has obtained a hold upon consciousness is even stronger. But here the ego ventures no objection; it admits its guilt and submits to the punishment. We understand the difference. In obsessional neurosis what were in question were objectionable impulses which remained outside the ego, while in melancholia the object to which the super-ego's wrath applies has been taken into the ego through identification.

It is certainly not clear why the sense of guilt reaches such an extraordinary strength in these two neurotic disorders; but the main problem presented in this state of affairs lies in another direction. We shall postpone discussion of it until we have dealt with the other cases in which the sense of guilt remains unconscious. [See p. 394.]

It is essentially in hysteria and in states of a hysterical type that this is found. Here the mechanism by which the sense of guilt remains unconscious is easy to discover. The hysterical ego fends off a distressing perception with which the criticisms of its super-ego threaten it, in the same way in which it is in the habit of fending off an unendurable object-cathexis – by an act of repression. It is the ego, therefore, that is responsible for the sense of guilt remaining unconscious. We know that as a rule the ego carries out repressions in the service and at the behest of its super-ego; but this is a case in which it has turned the same weapon against its harsh taskmaster. In obsessional neurosis, as we know, the phenomena of reaction-formation predominate; but here [in hysteria] the ego succeeds only in keeping at a distance the material to which the sense of guilt refers.

One may go further and venture the hypothesis that a great part of the sense of guilt must normally remain unconscious, because the origin of conscience is intimately connected with the Oedipus complex, which belongs to the unconscious. If anyone were inclined to put forward the paradoxical proposition that the normal man is not only far more immoral than he believes but also far more moral than he knows, psychoanalysis, on whose findings the first half of the assertion rests, would have no objection to raise against the second half.[1]

It was a surprise to find that an increase in this *Ucs.* sense of guilt can turn people into criminals. But it is undoubtedly a fact. In many criminals, especially youthful ones, it is possible to detect a very powerful sense of guilt which existed before the crime, and is therefore not its result but its motive. It is as if it

1. This proposition is only apparently a paradox; it simply states that human nature has a far greater extent, both for good and for evil, than it thinks it has – i.e. than its ego is aware of through conscious perception.

was a relief to be able to fasten this unconscious sense of guilt on to something real and immediate.[1]

In all these situations the super-ego displays its independence of the conscious ego and its intimate relations with the unconscious id. Having regard, now, to the importance we have ascribed to preconscious verbal residues in the ego [p. 358 f.], the question arises whether it can be the case that the super-ego, in so far as it is *Ucs.*, consists in such word-presentations and, if it does not, what else it consists in. Our tentative answer will be that it is as impossible for the super-ego as for the ego to disclaim its origin from things heard; for it is a part of the ego and remains accessible to consciousness by way of these word-presentations (concepts, abstractions). But the *cathectic energy* does not reach these contents of the super-ego from auditory perception (instruction or reading) but from sources in the id.

The question which we put off answering [see p. 393] runs as follows: How is it that the super-ego manifests itself essentially as a sense of guilt (or rather, as criticism – for the sense of guilt is the perception in the ego answering to this criticism) and moreover develops such extraordinary harshness and severity towards the ego? If we turn to melancholia first, we find that the excessively strong super-ego which has obtained a hold upon consciousness rages against the ego with merciless violence, as if it had taken possession of the whole of the sadism available in the person concerned. Following our view of sadism, we should say that the destructive component had entrenched itself in the super-ego and turned against the ego. What is now holding sway in the super-ego is, as it were, a pure culture of the death instinct, and in fact it often enough succeeds in driving the ego into death, if the latter does not fend off its tyrant in time by the change round into mania.

The reproaches of conscience in certain forms of obsessional neurosis are as distressing and tormenting, but here the situation is less perspicuous. It is noteworthy that the obsessional neur-

1. [A full discussion of this (together with some other references) will be found in Part III of Freud's paper on 'Some Character-Types Met with in Psycho-Analytic Work' (1916*d*), *P.F.L.*, **14**, 317.]

otic, in contrast to the melancholic, never in fact takes the step of self-destruction; it is as though he were immune against the danger of suicide, and he is far better protected from it than the hysteric. We can see that what guarantees the safety of the ego is the fact that the object has been retained. In obsessional neurosis it has become possible, through a regression to the pre-genital organization, for the love-impulses to transform themselves into impulses of aggression against the object. Here again the instinct of destruction has been set free and it seeks to destroy the object, or at least it appears to have that intention. These purposes have not been adopted by the ego and it struggles against them with reaction-formations and precautionary measures; they remain in the id. The super-ego, however, behaves as if the ego were responsible for them and shows at the same time by the seriousness with which it chastises these destructive intentions that they are no mere semblance evoked by regression but an actual substitution of hate for love. Helpless in both directions, the ego defends itself vainly, alike against the instigations of the murderous id and against the reproaches of the punishing conscience. It succeeds in holding in check at least the most brutal actions of both sides; the first outcome is interminable self-torment, and eventually there follows a systematic torturing of the object, in so far as it is within reach.

The dangerous death instincts are dealt with in the individual in various ways: in part they are rendered harmless by being fused with erotic components, in part they are diverted towards the external world in the form of aggression, while to a large extent they undoubtedly continue their internal work unhindered. How is it then that in melancholia the super-ego can become a kind of gathering-place for the death instincts?

From the point of view of instinctual control, of morality, it may be said of the id that it is totally non-moral, of the ego that it strives to be moral, and of the super-ego that it can be super-moral and then become as cruel as only the id can be. It is remarkable that the more a man checks his aggressiveness towards the exterior the more severe – that is aggressive – he becomes in his ego ideal. The ordinary view sees the situation the other way round: the standard set up by the ego ideal seems to be the motive for the suppression of aggressiveness. The fact remains, however, as we have stated it: the more a man controls his aggressiveness, the more intense becomes his ideal's inclination to aggressiveness against his ego.[1] It is like a displacement, a turning round upon his own ego. But even ordinary normal morality has a harshly restraining, cruelly prohibiting quality. It is from this, indeed, that the conception arises of a higher being who deals out punishment inexorably.

I cannot go further in my consideration of these questions without introducing a fresh hypothesis. The super-ego arises, as we know, from an identification with the father taken as a model. Every such identification is in the nature of a desexualization or even of a sublimation. It now seems as though when a transformation of this kind takes place, an instinctual defusion occurs at the same time [p. 369]. After sublimation the erotic component no longer has the power to bind the whole of the destructiveness that was combined with it, and this is released in the form of an inclination to aggression and destruction. This defusion would be the source of the general character of harshness and cruelty exhibited by the ideal – its dictatorial 'Thou shalt'.

Let us again consider obsessional neurosis for a moment. The state of affairs is different here. The defusion of love into aggressiveness has not been effected by the work of the ego, but is the result of a regression which has come about in the id. But this process has extended beyond the id to the super-ego, which now increases its severity towards the innocent ego. It would seem, however, that in this case, no less than in that of melancholia, the ego, having gained control over the libido by means of identification, is punished for doing so by the super-ego through the instrumentality of the aggressiveness which was mixed with the libido.

1. [Freud returned to this paradox in Section B of 'Some Additional Notes on Dream-Interpretation as a Whole' (1925*i*), and in 'The Economic Problem of Masochism' (1924*c*), p. 425 below. He discussed it more fully in Chapter VII of *Civilization and its Discontents* (1930*a*), *P.F.L.*, **12**, 315 ff.]

Our ideas about the ego are beginning to clear, and its various relationships are gaining distinctness. We now see the ego in its strength and in its weaknesses. It is entrusted with important functions. By virtue of its relation to the perceptual system it gives mental processes an order in time and submits them to 'reality-testing'.[1] By interposing the processes of thinking, it secures a postponement of motor discharges and controls the access to motility.[2] This last power is, to be sure, a question more of form than of fact; in the matter of action the ego's position is like that of a constitutional monarch, without whose sanction no law can be passed but who hesitates long before imposing his veto on any measure put forward by Parliament. All the experiences of life that originate from without enrich the ego; the id, however, is its second external world, which it strives to bring into subjection to itself. It withdraws libido from the id and transforms the object-cathexes of the id into ego-structures. With the aid of the super-ego, in a manner that is still obscure to us, it draws upon the experiences of past ages stored in the id [p. 378].

There are two paths by which the contents of the id can penetrate into the ego. The one is direct, the other leads by way of the ego ideal; which of these two paths they take may, for some mental activities, be of decisive importance. The ego develops from perceiving instincts to controlling them, from obeying instincts to inhibiting them. In this achievement a large share is taken by the ego ideal, which indeed is partly a reaction-formation against the instinctual processes of the id. Psychoanalysis is an instrument to enable the ego to achieve a progressive conquest of the id.

From the other point of view, however, we see this same ego as a poor creature owing service to three masters and consequently menaced by three dangers: from the external world, from the libido of the id, and from the severity of the super-ego. Three kinds of anxiety correspond to these three dangers,

1. [Cf. 'The Unconscious' (1915*e*), p. 193 above.]
2. [Cf. 'Formulations on the Two Principles of Mental Functioning' (1911*b*), p. 38 above, and 'Negation' (1925*h*), p. 440 below.]

since anxiety is the expression of a retreat from danger. As a frontier-creature, the ego tries to mediate between the world and the id, to make the id pliable to the world and, by means of its muscular activity, to make the world fall in with the wishes of the id. In point of fact it behaves like the physician during an analytic treatment: it offers itself, with the attention it pays to the real world, as a libidinal object to the id, and aims at attaching the id's libido to itself. It is not only a helper to the id; it is also a submissive slave who courts his master's love. Whenever possible, it tries to remain on good terms with the id; it clothes the id's *Ucs.* commands with its *Pcs.* rationalizations; it pretends that the id is showing obedience to the admonitions of reality, even when in fact it is remaining obstinate and unyielding; it disguises the id's conflicts with reality and, if possible, its conflicts with the super-ego too. In its position midway between the id and reality, it only too often yields to the temptation to become sycophantic, opportunist and lying, like a politician who sees the truth but wants to keep his place in popular favour.

Towards the two classes of instincts the ego's attitude is not impartial. Through its work of identification and sublimation it gives the death instincts in the id assistance in gaining control over the libido, but in so doing it runs the risk of becoming the object of the death instincts and of itself perishing. In order to be able to help in this way it has had itself to become filled with libido; it thus itself becomes the representative of Eros and thenceforward desires to live and to be loved.

But since the ego's work of sublimation results in a defusion of the instincts and a liberation of the aggressive instincts in the super-ego, its struggle against the libido exposes it to the danger of maltreatment and death. In suffering under the attacks of the super-ego or perhaps even succumbing to them, the ego is meeting with a fate like that of the protista which are destroyed by the products of decomposition that they themselves have created.[1] From the economic point of view the morality that

1. [Freud had discussed these animalculae in *Beyond the Pleasure Principle*, p. 321 above. They would probably now be described as 'protozoa' rather than 'protista'.]

functions in the super-ego seems to be a similar product of decomposition.

Among the dependent relationships in which the ego stands, that to the super-ego is perhaps the most interesting.

The ego is the actual seat of anxiety.[1] Threatened by dangers from three directions, it develops the flight-reflex by withdrawing its own cathexis from the menacing perception or from the similarly regarded process in the id, and emitting it as anxiety. This primitive reaction is later replaced by the carrying-out of protective cathexes (the mechanism of the phobias). What it is that the ego fears from the external and from the libidinal danger cannot be specified; we know that the fear is of being overwhelmed or annihilated, but it cannot be grasped analytically.[2] The ego is simply obeying the warning of the pleasure principle. On the other hand, we can tell what is hidden behind the ego's dread of the super-ego, the fear of conscience.[3] The superior being, which turned into the ego ideal, once threatened castration, and this dread of castration is probably the nucleus round which the subsequent fear of conscience has gathered; it is this dread that persists as the fear of conscience.

The high-sounding phrase, 'every fear is ultimately the fear of death', has hardly any meaning, and at any rate cannot be justified.[4] It seems to me, on the contrary, perfectly correct to distinguish the fear of death from dread of an object (realistic

1. [What follows on the subject of anxiety must be read in connection with Freud's revised views as stated in *Inhibitions, Symptoms and Anxiety* (1926*d*), *P.F.L.*, **10**, 237 ff., where most of the points raised here are further discussed.]

2. [The notion of the ego being 'overwhelmed' (of an '*Überwältigung*') occurs very early in Freud's writings. See, for instance, a mention of it in Part II of his first paper on 'The Neuro-Psychoses of Defence' (1894*a*). But it plays a prominent part in his discussion of the mechanism of the neuroses in Draft K of 1 January 1896 in the Fliess correspondence (Freud, 1950*a*). There is an evident connection here with the 'traumatic situation' of *Inhibitions, Symptoms and Anxiety* (1926*d*), *P.F.L.*, **10**, 326–8. See also Essay III in *Moses and Monotheism* (1939*a*), *P.F.L.*, **13**, 321.]

3. ['*Gewissensangst*.' An Editor's footnote on the use of this word will be found in Chapter VII of *Inhibitions, Symptoms and Anxiety*, *P.F.L.*, **10**, 284*n*. 1.]

4. [Cf. Stekel (1908, 5).]

anxiety) and from neurotic libidinal anxiety. It presents a difficult problem to psychoanalysis, for death is an abstract concept with a negative content for which no unconscious correlative can be found. It would seem that the mechanism of the fear of death can only be that the ego relinquishes its narcissistic libidinal cathexis in a very large measure – that is, that it gives up itself, just as it gives up some *external* object in other cases in which it feels anxiety. I believe that the fear of death is something that occurs between the ego and the super-ego.

We know that the fear of death makes its appearance under two conditions (which, moreover, are entirely analogous to situations in which other kinds of anxiety develop), namely, as a reaction to an external danger and as an internal process, as for instance in melancholia. Once again a neurotic manifestation may help us to understand a normal one.

The fear of death in melancholia only admits of one explanation: that the ego gives itself up because it feels itself hated and persecuted by the super-ego, instead of loved. To the ego, therefore, living means the same as being loved – being loved by the super-ego, which here again appears as the representative of the id. The super-ego fulfils the same function of protecting and saving that was fulfilled in earlier days by the father and later by Providence or Destiny. But, when the ego finds itself in an excessive real danger which it believes itself unable to overcome by its own strength, it is bound to draw the same conclusion. It sees itself deserted by all protecting forces and lets itself die. Here, moreover, is once again the same situation as that which underlay the first great anxiety-state of birth[1] and the infantile anxiety of longing – the anxiety due to separation from the protecting mother.[2]

These considerations make it possible to regard the fear of death, like the fear of conscience, as a development of the fear of castration. The great significance which the sense of guilt has

1. [Some discussion of the appearance of this notion here will be found in the Editor's Introduction to *Inhibitions, Symptoms and Anxiety*, *P.F.L.*, **10**, 234–6.]

2. [This foreshadows the 'separation anxiety' discussed in *Inhibitions, Symptoms and Anxiety* (1926*d*), *P.F.L.*, **10**, 309.]

in the neuroses makes it conceivable that common neurotic anxiety is reinforced in severe cases by the generating of anxiety between the ego and the super-ego (fear of castration, of conscience, of death).

The id, to which we finally come back, has no means of showing the ego either love or hate. It cannot say what it wants; it has achieved no unified will. Eros and the death instinct struggle within it; we have seen with what weapons the one group of instincts defends itself against the other. It would be possible to picture the id as under the domination of the mute but powerful death instincts, which desire to be at peace and (prompted by the pleasure principle) to put Eros, the mischief-maker, to rest; but perhaps that might be to undervalue the part played by Eros.

APPENDIX A

THE DESCRIPTIVE AND THE DYNAMIC UNCONSCIOUS

A CURIOUS point arises out of two sentences which appear on pp. 353–4 above. The Editor's attention was drawn to it in a private communication from Dr Ernest Jones, who had come across it in the course of examining Freud's correspondence.

On 28 October 1923, a few months after this work appeared, Ferenczi wrote to Freud in these terms: '. . . Nevertheless I venture to put a question to you . . . since there is a passage in *The Ego and the Id* which, without your solution, I do not understand . . . On p. 13[1] I find the following: ". . . that in the descriptive sense there are two kinds of unconscious, but in the dynamic sense only one." Since, however, you write on p. 12[1] that the latent unconscious is unconscious only descriptively, not in the dynamic sense, I had thought that it was precisely the dynamic line of approach that called for the hypothesis of there being two sorts of *Ucs.*, while description knows only *Cs.* and *Ucs.*'

On close inspection, however, the two statements do not contradict each other: the fact that the latent unconscious is only descriptively unconscious does not in the least imply that it is the only thing that is descriptively unconscious. There is, indeed, a passage in Lecture 31 of Freud's *New Introductory Lectures* (1933*a*), written some ten years later than the present work, in which the whole of this argument is repeated in very similar terms. In that passage it is explained more than once that in the descriptive sense both the preconscious and the repressed are unconscious, but that in the dynamic sense the term is restricted to the repressed. (Cf. *P.F.L.*, **2**, 102–4.)

It seems likely that on reflection Freud realized that Ferenczi's

1. Of the German edition. The sentences are on pp. 353–4 here.

discovery was a mare's nest, for the passage was never altered in the later editions of the book.

A fuller discussion of the whole matter by James Strachey can be found in the *Standard Edition* (**19**, 60–62).

APPENDIX B

THE GREAT RESERVOIR OF LIBIDO

THERE is considerable difficulty over this matter, which is mentioned in the first footnote on p. 369 and discussed at greater length on p. 387.

The analogy seems to have made its first appearance in a new section added to the third edition of the *Three Essays* (1905*d*), which was published in 1915 but had been prepared by Freud in the autumn of 1914. The passage runs as follows (*P.F.L.*, **7**, 139–40): 'Narcissistic or ego libido seems to be the great reservoir from which the object-cathexes are sent out and into which they are withdrawn once more; the narcissistic libidinal cathexis of the ego is the original state of things, realized in earliest childhood, and is merely covered by the later extrusions of libido, but in essentials persists behind them.'

The same notion had, however, been expressed earlier in another favourite analogy of Freud's, which appears sometimes as an alternative and sometimes alongside the 'great reservoir'.[1] This earlier passage is in the paper on narcissism itself (1914*c*), which was written by Freud in the early part of the same year, 1914 (pp. 67–8 above): 'Thus we form the idea of there being an original libidinal cathexis of the ego, from which some is later given off to objects, but which fundamentally persists and is related to the object-cathexis much as the body of an amoeba is related to the pseudopodia which it puts out.'

The two analogies appear together in a semi-popular paper written at the end of 1916 for a Hungarian periodical ('A Difficulty in the Path of Psycho-Analysis', 1917*a*): 'The ego is a great reservoir from which the libido that is destined for objects

1. This analogy had appeared already in a rudimentary form in *Totem and Taboo*, which was first published early in 1913 (*P.F.L.*, **13**, 147).

flows out and into which it flows back from those objects . . . As an illustration of this state of things we may think of an amoeba, whose viscous substance puts out pseudopodia . . .'

The amoeba appears once more in Lecture 26 of the *Introductory Lectures* (1916–17), *P.F.L.*, **1**, 465–6 and 470, dating from 1917, and the reservoir in *Beyond the Pleasure Principle* (1920*g*), p. 324 above: 'Psychoanalysis . . . came to the conclusion that the ego is the true and original reservoir of libido, and that it is only from that reservoir that libido is extended on to objects.'

Freud included a very similar passage in an encyclopaedia article which he wrote in the summer of 1922 (1923*a*), and then almost immediately afterwards came the announcement of the id, and what appears like a drastic correction of the earlier statements: 'Now that we have distinguished between the ego and the id, we must recognize the id as the great reservoir of libido . . .' And again: 'At the very beginning, all the libido is accumulated in the id, while the ego is still in process of formation or is still feeble. The id sends part of this libido out into erotic object-cathexes, whereupon the ego, now grown stronger, tries to get hold of this object-libido and to force itself on the id as a love-object. The narcissism of the ego is thus a secondary one, which has been withdrawn from objects.' (Pp. 369 *n.* 1 and 387 above.)

This new position seems quite clearly intelligible, and it is therefore a little disturbing to come upon the following sentence, written only a year or so after *The Ego and the Id*, in the *Autobiographical Study* (1925*d* [1924]): 'All through the subject's life his ego remains the great reservoir of his libido, from which object-cathexes are sent out and into which the libido can stream back again from the objects.'[1]

The sentence, it is true, occurs in the course of a historical sketch of the development of psychoanalytic theory; but there is no indication of the change of view announced in *The Ego and the Id*. And, finally, we find this passage in one of Freud's very

1. An almost identical statement is made in Lecture 32 of the *New Introductory Lectures* (1933*a*), *P.F.L.*, **2**, 136. But see also ibid., **2**, 109: 'The object-cathexes spring from the instinctual demands of the id.'

last writings, in Chapter II of the *Outline of Psycho-Analysis* (1940*a*), written in 1938: 'It is hard to say anything of the behaviour of the libido in the id and in the super-ego. All that we know about it relates to the ego, in which at first the whole available quota of libido is stored up. We call this state the absolute primary narcissism. It lasts till the ego begins to cathect the ideas of objects with libido, to transform narcissistic libido into object-libido. Throughout the whole of life the ego remains the great reservoir, from which libidinal cathexes are sent out to objects and into which they are also once more withdrawn, just as an amoeba behaves with its pseudopodia.'

Do these later passages imply that Freud had retracted the opinions he expressed in the present work? It seems difficult to believe it, and there are two points that may help towards a reconciliation of the apparently conflicting views. The first is a very small one. The analogy of the 'reservoir' is from its very nature an ambiguous one: a reservoir can be regarded either as a water storage tank or as a source of water supply. There is no great difficulty in applying the image in both senses both to the ego and to the id, and it would certainly have clarified the various passages that have been quoted – and in particular the first footnote on p. 369 – if Freud had shown more precisely which picture was in his mind.

The second point is of greater importance. In the *New Introductory Lectures* (*P.F.L.*, **2**, 138), only a few pages after the passage referred to in the footnote above, in the course of a discussion of masochism, Freud writes: 'If it is true of the destructive instinct as well that the ego – but what we have in mind here is rather the id, the whole person – originally includes all the instinctual impulses . . .' The parenthesis points, of course, to a primitive state of things in which the id and the ego are still undifferentiated.[1] And there is a similar, but more definite, remark in the *Outline*, this time two paragraphs before the passage already quoted: 'We may picture an initial state as one in which the total available energy of Eros, which henceforward

1. This is, of course, a familiar view of Freud's.

we shall speak of as "libido", is present in the still undifferentiated ego-id . . .' If we take this as being the true essence of Freud's theory, the apparent contradiction in his expression of it is diminished. This 'ego-id' was originally the 'great reservoir of libido' in the sense of being a storage tank. After differentiation had occurred, the id would continue as a storage tank but, when it began sending out cathexes (whether to objects or to the now differentiated ego) it would in addition be a source of supply. But the same would be true of the ego as well, for it would be a storage tank of narcissistic libido as well as, on one view, a source of supply for object-cathexes.

This last point leads us, however, to a further question, on which it seems inevitable to suppose that Freud held different views at different times. In *The Ego and the Id* (p. 387) 'at the very beginning, all the libido is accumulated in the id'; then 'the id sends part of this libido out into erotic object-cathexes', which the ego tries to get control of by forcing itself on the id as a love-object: 'the narcissism of the ego is thus a secondary one.' But in the *Outline*, 'at first the whole available quota of libido is stored up in the ego', 'we call this state the absolute primary narcissism' and 'it lasts until the ego begins to cathect the ideas of objects with libido'. Two different processes seem to be envisaged in these two accounts. In the first the original object-cathexes are thought of as going out direct from the id, and only reaching the ego indirectly; in the second the whole of the libido is thought of as going from the id to the ego and only reaching the objects indirectly. The two processes do not seem incompatible, and it is possible that both may occur; but on this question Freud is silent.

THE ECONOMIC PROBLEM OF MASOCHISM
(1924)

EDITOR'S NOTE

DAS ÖKONOMISCHE PROBLEM DES MASOCHISMUS

(A) German Editions:

1924 *Int. Z. Psychoanal.*, **10** (2), 121–33.
1924 *Gesammelte Schriften*, **5**, 374–86.
1940 *Gesammelte Werke*, **13**, 371–83.

(B) English Translations:

'The Economic Problem in Masochism'

1924 *Collected Papers*, **2**, 255–68. (Tr. Joan Riviere.)
1961 *Standard Edition*, **19**, 155–70. (Translation, with a slightly changed title, based on that of 1924.)

The present edition is a reprint of the *Standard Edition* version, with some editorial modifications.

This paper was finished before the end of January 1924 (Jones, 1957, 114).

In this important work Freud gives his fullest account of the puzzling phenomenon of masochism. He had previously dealt with it, but always somewhat tentatively, in his *Three Essays on the Theory of Sexuality* (1905*d*), *P.F.L.*, **7**, 70–73,[1] in the metapsychological paper 'Instincts and their Vicissitudes' (1915*c*), pp. 124–7 above, and, at much greater length in '"A Child is Being Beaten"' (1919*e*), *P.F.L.*, **10**, 163 ff., which he himself described in a letter to Ferenczi as 'a paper on masochism'. In all these writings masochism is derived from a previous sadism;

1. Much of this was in fact only added to the book in 1915; a footnote added in 1924 gives the gist of the present paper.

no such thing as primary masochism is recognized. (See, for instance, p. 125 above, and *P.F.L.*, **10**, 180.) In *Beyond the Pleasure Principle* (1920*g*), however, after the introduction of the 'death instinct', we find a statement that 'there *might* be such a thing as primary masochism' (p. 328 above), and in the present paper the existence of a primary masochism is taken as certain.[1]

The existence of this primary masochism is here accounted for chiefly on the basis of the 'fusion' and 'defusion' of the two classes of instinct – a concept which had been examined at length in *The Ego and the Id* (1923*b*), published less than a year previously – while the apparently self-contradictory nature of an instinct which aims at unpleasure is dealt with in the interesting introductory discussion, which for the first time clearly distinguishes between the 'principle of constancy' and the 'pleasure principle'.

Freud's analysis shows that this primary or 'erotogenic' masochism leads to two derivative forms. One of these, which he terms 'feminine', is the form that Freud had already discussed in his paper on 'beating phantasies' (1919*e*). But the third form, 'moral masochism', gives him an opportunity of enlarging upon many points that had only been lightly touched on in *The Ego and the Id*, and of opening up fresh problems in connection with feelings of guilt and the operation of the conscience.

1. It should perhaps be mentioned that it was only in later writings, beginning with Chapter VI of *Civilization and its Discontents* (1930*a*), that Freud turned his attention more particularly to the *outward* operation of the death instinct – to aggressiveness and destructiveness, though it is discussed to some extent in the later part of the present paper. (Cf. *P.F.L.*, **12**, 310 ff.)

THE ECONOMIC PROBLEM OF MASOCHISM

The existence of a masochistic trend in the instinctual life of human beings may justly be described as mysterious from the economic point of view. For if mental processes are governed by the pleasure principle in such a way that their first aim is the avoidance of unpleasure and the obtaining of pleasure, masochism is incomprehensible. If pain and unpleasure can be not simply warnings but actually aims, the pleasure principle is paralysed – it is as though the watchman over our mental life were put out of action by a drug.

Thus masochism appears to us in the light of a great danger, which is in no way true of its counterpart, sadism. We are tempted to call the pleasure principle the watchman over our life rather than merely over our mental life. But in that case we are faced with the task of investigating the relationship of the pleasure principle to the two classes of instincts which we have distinguished – the death instincts and the erotic (libidinal) life instincts; and we cannot proceed further in our consideration of the problem of masochism till we have accomplished that task.

It will be remembered that we have taken the view that the principle which governs all mental processes is a special case of Fechner's 'tendency towards stability',[1] and have accordingly attributed to the mental apparatus the purpose of reducing to nothing, or at least of keeping as low as possible, the sums of excitation which flow in upon it. Barbara Low [1920, 73] has suggested the name of *Nirvana principle* for this supposed

1. *Beyond the Pleasure Principle* (1920*g*) [pp. 276–8 above].

tendency, and we have accepted the term.[1] But we have unhesitatingly identified the pleasure-unpleasure principle with this Nirvana principle. Every unpleasure ought thus to coincide with a heightening, and every pleasure with a lowering, of mental tension due to stimulus; the Nirvana principle (and the pleasure principle which is supposedly identical with it) would be entirely in the service of the death instincts, whose aim is to conduct the restlessness of life into the stability of the inorganic state, and it would have the function of giving warnings against the demands of the life instincts – the libido – which try to disturb the intended course of life. But such a view cannot be correct. It seems that in the series of feelings of tension we have a direct sense of the increase and decrease of amounts of stimulus, and it cannot be doubted that there are pleasurable tensions and unpleasurable relaxations of tension. The state of sexual excitation is the most striking example of a pleasurable increase of stimulus of this sort, but it is certainly not the only one.

Pleasure and unpleasure, therefore, cannot be referred to an increase or decrease of a quantity (which we describe as 'tension due to stimulus'), although they obviously have a great deal to do with that factor. It appears that they depend, not on this quantitative factor, but on some characteristic of it which we can only describe as a qualitative one. If we were able to say what this qualitative characteristic is, we should be much further advanced in psychology. Perhaps it is the *rhythm*, the temporal sequence of changes, rises and falls in the quantity of stimulus.[2] We do not know.

However this may be, we must perceive that the Nirvana principle, belonging as it does to the death instinct, has undergone a modification in living organisms through which it has

1. [*Beyond the Pleasure Principle*, p. 329 above. Freud had previously given this same principle the name of 'the principle of constancy'. A full discussion of the history of Freud's use of these concepts and of their relation to the pleasure principle will be found in an Editor's footnote to 'Instincts and their Vicissitudes' (1915*c*), pp. 117–18 above.]

2. [This possibility had already been raised in *Beyond the Pleasure Principle*, pp. 276 and 337 above.]

become the pleasure principle; and we shall henceforward avoid regarding the two principles as one. It is not difficult, if we care to follow up this line of thought, to guess what power was the source of the modification. It can only be the life instinct, the libido, which has thus, alongside of the death instinct, seized upon a share in the regulation of the processes of life. In this way we obtain a small but interesting set of connections. The *Nirvana* principle expresses the trend of the death instinct; the *pleasure* principle represents the demands of the libido; and the modification of the latter principle, the *reality* principle,[1] represents the influence of the external world.

None of these three principles is actually put out of action by another. As a rule they are able to tolerate one another, although conflicts are bound to arise occasionally from the fact of the differing aims that are set for each – in one case a quantitative reduction of the load of the stimulus, in another a qualitative characteristic of the stimulus, and, lastly [in the third case], a postponement of the discharge of the stimulus and a temporary acquiescence in the unpleasure due to tension.

The conclusion to be drawn from these considerations is that the description of the pleasure principle as the watchman over our life cannot be rejected.[2]

To return to masochism. Masochism comes under our observation in three forms: as a condition imposed on sexual excitation, as an expression of the feminine nature, and as a norm of behaviour.[3] We may, accordingly, distinguish an *erotogenic*, a *feminine* and a *moral* masochism. The first, the erotogenic, masochism – pleasure in pain – lies at the bottom of the other two forms as well. Its basis must be sought along biological and constitutional lines and it remains incomprehensible unless one decides to make certain assumptions about matters that are

1. [Cf. 'Formulations on the Two Principles of Mental Functioning' (1911*b*), p. 37 above.]

2. [Freud took up this discussion again in Chapter VIII of his *Outline* (1940*a* [1938]).]

3. [This last word is added in English in the original.]

extremely obscure. The third, and in some respects the most important, form assumed by masochism has only recently been recognized by psychoanalysis as a sense of guilt which is mostly unconscious; but it can already be completely explained and fitted into the rest of our knowledge. Feminine masochism, on the other hand, is the one that is most accessible to our observation and least problematical, and it can be surveyed in all its relations. We will begin our discussion with it.

We have sufficient acquaintance with this kind of masochism in men (to whom, owing to the material at my command, I shall restrict my remarks), derived from masochistic – and therefore often impotent – subjects whose phantasies either terminate in an act of masturbation or represent a sexual satisfaction in themselves.[1] The real-life performances of masochistic perverts tally completely with these phantasies, whether the performances are carried out as an end in themselves or serve to induce potency and to lead to the sexual act. In both cases – for the performances are, after all, only a carrying-out of the phantasies in play – the manifest content is of being gagged, bound, painfully beaten, whipped, in some way maltreated, forced into unconditional obedience, dirtied and debased. It is far more rare for mutilations to be included in the content, and then only subject to strict limitations. The obvious interpretation, and one easily arrived at, is that the masochist wants to be treated like a small and helpless child, but, particularly, like a naughty child. It is unnecessary to quote cases to illustrate this; for the material is very uniform and is accessible to any observer, even to non-analysts. But if one has an opportunity of studying cases in which the masochistic phantasies have been especially richly elaborated, one quickly discovers that they place the subject in a characteristically female situation; they signify, that is, being castrated, or copulated with, or giving birth to a baby. For this reason I have called this form of masochism, *a potiori* as it were [i.e. on the basis of its extreme examples], the feminine form,

1. [See Section VI of '"A Child is Being Beaten"' (1919*e*), *P.F.L.*, **10**, 182 ff.]

although so many of its features point to infantile life. This superimposed stratification of the infantile and the feminine will find a simple explanation later on. Being castrated – or being blinded, which stands for it – often leaves a negative trace of itself in phantasies, in the condition that no injury is to occur precisely to the genitals or the eyes. (Masochistic tortures, incidentally, rarely make such a serious impression as the cruelties of sadism, whether imagined or performed.) A sense of guilt, too, finds expression in the manifest content of masochistic phantasies; the subject assumes that he has committed some crime (the nature of which is left indefinite) which is to be expiated by all these painful and tormenting procedures. This looks like a superficial rationalization of the masochistic subject-matter, but behind it there lies a connection with infantile masturbation. On the other hand, this factor of guilt provides a transition to the third, moral, form of masochism.

This feminine masochism which we have been describing is entirely based on the primary, erotogenic masochism, on pleasure in pain. This cannot be explained without taking our discussion very far back.

In my *Three Essays on the Theory of Sexuality*, in the section on the sources of infantile sexuality, I put forward the proposition that 'in the case of a great number of internal processes sexual excitation arises as a concomitant effect, as soon as the intensity of those processes passes beyond certain quantitative limits'. Indeed, 'it may well be that nothing of considerable importance can occur in the organism without contributing some component to the excitation of the sexual instinct'.[1] In accordance with this, the excitation of pain and unpleasure would be bound to have the same result, too.[2] The occurrence of such a libidinal sympathetic excitation when there is tension due to pain and unpleasure would be an infantile physiological mechanism which ceases to operate later on. It would attain a varying degree of development in different sexual constitutions;

1. [*Three Essays* (1905*d*), *P.F.L.*, **7**, 124.]
2. [Ibid., **7**, 124.]

but in any case it would provide the physiological foundation on which the psychical structure of erotogenic masochism would afterwards be erected.

The inadequacy of this explanation is seen, however, in the fact that it throws no light on the regular and close connections of masochism with its counterpart in instinctual life, sadism. If we go back a little further, to our hypothesis of the two classes of instincts which we regard as operative in the living organism, we arrive at another derivation of masochism, which, however, is not in contradiction with the former one. In (multicellular) organisms the libido meets the instinct of death, or destruction, which is dominant in them and which seeks to disintegrate the cellular organism and to conduct each separate unicellular organism into a state of inorganic stability (relative though this may be). The libido has the task of making the destroying instinct innocuous, and it fulfils the task by diverting that instinct to a great extent outwards – soon with the help of a special organic system, the muscular apparatus – towards objects in the external world. The instinct is then called the destructive instinct, the instinct for mastery, or the will to power. A portion of the instinct is placed directly in the service of the sexual function, where it has an important part to play. This is sadism proper. Another portion does not share in this transposition outwards; it remains inside the organism and, with the help of the accompanying sexual excitation described above, becomes libidinally bound there. It is in this portion that we have to recognize the original, erotogenic masochism.[1]

We are without any physiological understanding of the ways and means by which this taming of the death instinct by the libido may be effected. So far as the psychoanalytic field of ideas is concerned, we can only assume that a very extensive fusion and amalgamation, in varying proportions, of the two classes of instincts takes place, so that we never have to deal with pure life instincts or pure death instincts but only with mixtures of

1. [For all of this see Chapter IV of *The Ego and the Id* (p. 381 above). Cf. also another account in Chapter VI of *Beyond the Pleasure Principle*, p. 323 above.]

them in different amounts. Corresponding to a fusion of instincts of this kind, there may, as a result of certain influences, be a *de*fusion of them. How large the portions of the death instincts are which refuse to be tamed in this way by being bound to admixtures of libido we cannot at present guess.

If one is prepared to overlook a little inexactitude, it may be said that the death instinct which is operative in the organism – primal sadism – is identical with masochism. After the main portion of it has been transposed outwards on to objects, there remains inside, as a residuum of it, the erotogenic masochism proper, which on the one hand has become a component of the libido and, on the other, still has the self as its object. This masochism would thus be evidence of, and a remainder from, the phase of development in which the coalescence, which is so important for life, between the death instinct and Eros took place. We shall not be surprised to hear that in certain circumstances the sadism, or instinct of destruction, which has been directed outwards, projected, can be once more introjected, turned inwards, and in this way regress to its earlier situation. If this happens, a secondary masochism is produced, which is added to the original masochism.

Erotogenic masochism accompanies the libido through all its developmental phases and derives from them its changing psychical coatings.[1] The fear of being eaten up by the totem animal (the father) originates from the primitive oral organization; the wish to be beaten by the father comes from the sadistic-anal phase which follows it; castration, although it is later disavowed, enters into the content of masochistic phantasies as a precipitate of the phallic stage of organization;[2] and from the final genital organization there arise, of course, the situations of being copulated with and of giving birth, which are characteristic of femaleness. The part played in masochism by the nates,

1. ['*Psychische Umkleidungen.*' The image is an old one of Freud's. It occurs several times, for instance, in the 'Dora' case history (1905*e*), *P.F.L.*, **8**, 120, 121 and 139 *n.* 2.]

2. See 'The Infantile Genital Organization' (1923*e*) [*P.F.L.*, **7**, 310 and *n.* 1, where a footnote discussing the use of the word 'disavowal' will also be found].

too, is easily understandable,[1] apart from its obvious basis in reality. The nates are the part of the body which is given erotogenic preference in the sadistic-anal phase, like the breast in the oral phase and the penis in the genital phase.

The third form of masochism, moral masochism,[2] is chiefly remarkable for having loosened its connection with what we recognize as sexuality. All other masochistic sufferings carry with them the condition that they shall emanate from the loved person and shall be endured at his command. This restriction has been dropped in moral masochism. The suffering itself is what matters; whether it is decreed by someone who is loved or by someone who is indifferent is of no importance. It may even be caused by impersonal powers or by circumstances; the true masochist always turns his cheek whenever he has a chance of receiving a blow. It is very tempting, in explaining this attitude, to leave the libido out of account and to confine oneself to assuming that in this case the destructive instinct has been turned inwards again and is now raging against the self; yet there must be some meaning in the fact that linguistic usage has not given up the connection between this norm of behaviour and erotism and calls these self-injurers masochists too.

Let us keep to a habit of our technique and consider first the extreme and unmistakably pathological form of this masochism. I have described elsewhere[3] how in analytic treatment we come across patients to whom, owing to their behaviour towards its therapeutic influence, we are obliged to ascribe an 'unconscious' sense of guilt. I pointed out the sign by which such people can be recognized (a 'negative therapeutic reaction') and I did not conceal the fact that the strength of such an impulse constitutes

1. [Cf. a reference to this at the end of Section 4 of the second of the *Three Essays* (1905*d*), *P.F.L.*, **7**, 111.]

2. [In a paragraph added in 1909 to *The Interpretation of Dreams* (1900*a*), Freud had proposed the term 'mental masochism' for people 'who find their pleasure, not in having *physical* pain inflicted on them, but in humiliation and mental torture'. (P.F.L., **4**, 243.)]

3. *The Ego and the Id* (1923*b*) [Chapter V, p. 390 f. above].

one of the most serious resistances and the greatest danger to the success of our medical or educative aims. The satisfaction of this unconscious sense of guilt is perhaps the most powerful bastion in the subject's (usually composite) gain from illness – in the sum of forces which struggle against his recovery and refuse to surrender his state of illness. The suffering entailed by neuroses is precisely the factor that makes them valuable to the masochistic trend. It is instructive, too, to find, contrary to all theory and expectation, that a neurosis which has defied every therapeutic effort may vanish if the subject becomes involved in the misery of an unhappy marriage, or loses all his money, or develops a dangerous organic disease. In such instances one form of suffering has been replaced by another; and we see that all that mattered was that it should be possible to maintain a certain amount of suffering.

Patients do not easily believe us when we tell them about the unconscious sense of guilt. They know only too well by what torments – the pangs of conscience – a conscious sense of guilt, a consciousness of guilt, expresses itself, and they therefore cannot admit that they could harbour exactly analogous impulses in themselves without being in the least aware of them. We may, I think, to some extent meet their objection if we give up the term 'unconscious sense of guilt', which is in any case psychologically incorrect,[1] and speak instead of a 'need for punishment', which covers the observed state of affairs just as aptly. We cannot, however, restrain ourselves from judging and localizing this unconscious sense of guilt in the same way as we do the conscious kind.

We have attributed the function of conscience to the super-ego and we have recognized the consciousness of guilt as an expression of a tension between the ego and the super-ego.[2] The ego reacts with feelings of anxiety (conscience anxiety)[3] to the

1. [Feelings cannot properly be described as 'unconscious'. See Chapter II of *The Ego and the Id*, p. 361 above.]

2. [Ibid., Chapter III, p. 377 above.]

3. ['*Gewissensangst.*' An Editor's footnote discussing this term will be found in Chapter VII of *Inhibitions, Symptoms and Anxiety* (1926*d*), *P.F.L.*, **10**, 284.]

perception that it has not come up to the demands made by its ideal, the super-ego. What we want to know is how the super-ego has come to play this demanding role and why the ego, in the case of a difference with its ideal, should have to be afraid.

We have said that the function of the ego is to unite and to reconcile the claims of the three agencies which it serves; and we may add that in doing so it also possesses in the super-ego a model which it can strive to follow. For this super-ego is as much a representative of the id as of the external world.[1] It came into being through the introjection into the ego of the first objects of the id's libidinal impulses – namely, the two parents. In this process the relation to those objects was desexualized; it was diverted from its direct sexual aims. Only in this way was it possible for the Oedipus complex to be surmounted. The super-ego retained essential features of the introjected persons – their strength, their severity, their inclination to supervise and to punish. As I have said elsewhere,[2] it is easily conceivable that, thanks to the defusion of instinct which occurs along with this introduction into the ego, the severity was increased. The super-ego – the conscience at work in the ego – may then become harsh, cruel and inexorable against the ego which is in its charge. Kant's Categorical Imperative is thus the direct heir of the Oedipus complex.[3]

But the same figures who continue to operate in the super-ego as the agency we know as conscience after they have ceased to be objects of the libidinal impulses of the id – these same figures also belong to the real external world. It is from there that they were drawn; their power, behind which lie hidden all the influences of the past and of tradition, was one of the most strongly-felt manifestations of reality. In virtue of this concurrence, the super-ego, the substitute for the Oedipus complex, becomes a representative of the real external world as well and thus also becomes a model for the endeavours of the ego.

In this way the Oedipus complex proves to be – as has already

1. [Cf. 'Neurosis and Psychosis' (1924*b*), *P.F.L.*, **10**, 216.]
2. *The Ego and the Id* [p. 396 above.].
3. [Cf. ibid., pp. 374 and 389.]

been conjectured in a historical sense[1] – the source of our individual ethical sense, our morality. The course of childhood development leads to an ever-increasing detachment from parents, and their personal significance for the super-ego recedes into the background. To the imagos[2] they leave behind there are then linked the influences of teachers and authorities, self-chosen models and publicly recognized heroes, whose figures need no longer be introjected by an ego which has become more resistant. The last figure in the series that began with the parents is the dark power of Destiny which only the fewest of us are able to look upon as impersonal. There is little to be said against the Dutch writer Multatuli[3] when he replaces the *Μοῖρα* [Destiny] of the Greeks by the divine pair '*Λόγος καὶ Ἀνάγκη*, [Reason and Necessity]';[4] but all who transfer the guidance of the world to Providence, to God, or to God and Nature, arouse a suspicion that they still look upon these ultimate and remotest powers as a parental couple, in a mythological sense, and believe themselves linked to them by libidinal ties. In *The Ego and the Id* [p. 400] I made an attempt to derive mankind's realistic fear of death, too, from the same parental view of fate. It seems very hard to free oneself from it.

After these preliminaries we can return to our consideration of moral masochism. We have said[5] that, by their behaviour during treatment and in life, the individuals in question give an

1. In Essay IV of *Totem and Taboo* (1912–13) [*P.F.L.*, **13**, 159.]

2. [The term 'imago' was not often used by Freud, especially in his later writings. Its first appearance seems to be in his technical paper on 'The Dynamics of Transference' (1912*b*), where he attributes it to Jung (1911, 164). In this latter passage Jung tells us that he partly chose the word from the title of a novel of the same name by the Swiss writer, Carl Spitteler (1845–1924); and we learn from Hanns Sachs (1945, 63) that the psychoanalytic periodical *Imago*, started by him and Rank in 1912, also owed its title to the same source.]

3. E. D. Dekker (1820–87). ['Multatuli' had long been a favourite of Freud's. He heads the list of 'ten good books' which he drew up in 1906. (Freud, 1906*f*.)]

4. ['Ἀνάγκη had been named by Freud at least as early as in the Leonardo paper (1910*c*). Λόγος, on the other hand, seems to appear for the first time here. Both are discussed, and more especially Λόγος, in the closing passage of *The Future of an Illusion* (1927*c*), *P.F.L.*, **12**, 239.]

5. [*The Ego and the Id*, p. 390 ff. above.]

impression of being morally inhibited to an excessive degree, of being under the domination of an especially sensitive conscience, although they are not conscious of any of this ultramorality. On closer inspection, we can see the difference there is between an unconscious extension of morality of this kind and moral masochism. In the former, the accent falls on the heightened sadism of the super-ego to which the ego submits; in the latter, it falls on the ego's own masochism which seeks punishment, whether from the super-ego or from the parental powers outside. We may be forgiven for having confused the two to begin with; for in both cases it is a question of a relationship between the ego and the super-ego (or powers that are equivalent to it), and in both cases what is involved is a need which is satisfied by punishment and suffering. It can hardly be an insignificant detail, then, that the sadism of the super-ego becomes for the most part glaringly conscious, whereas the masochistic trend of the ego remains as a rule concealed from the subject and has to be inferred from his behaviour.

The fact that moral masochism is unconscious leads us to an obvious clue. We were able to translate the expression 'unconscious sense of guilt' as meaning a need for punishment at the hands of a parental power. We now know that the wish, which so frequently appears in phantasies, to be beaten by the father stands very close to the other wish, to have a passive (feminine) sexual relation to him and is only a regressive distortion of it. If we insert this explanation into the content of moral masochism, its hidden meaning becomes clear to us. Conscience and morality have arisen through the overcoming, the desexualization, of the Oedipus complex; but through moral masochism morality becomes sexualized once more, the Oedipus complex is revived and the way is opened for a regression from morality to the Oedipus complex. This is to the advantage neither of morality nor of the person concerned. An individual may, it is true, have preserved the whole or some measure of ethical sense alongside of his masochism; but, alternatively, a large part of his conscience may have vanished into his masochism. Again, masochism creates a temptation to perform 'sinful' actions, which must then be expiated by the reproaches of the sadistic conscience (as is exemplified in so many Russian character-types) or by chastisement from the great parental power of Destiny. In order to provoke punishment from this last representative of the parents, the masochist must do what is inexpedient, must act against his own interests, must ruin the prospects which open out to him in the real world and must, perhaps, destroy his own real existence.

The turning back of sadism against the self regularly occurs where a *cultural suppression of the instincts* holds back a large part of the subject's destructive instinctual components from being exercised in life. We may suppose that this portion of the destructive instinct which has retreated appears in the ego as an intensification of masochism. The phenomena of conscience, however, lead us to infer that the destructiveness which returns from the external world is also taken up by the super-ego, without any such transformation, and increases its sadism against the ego. The sadism of the super-ego and the masochism of the ego supplement each other and unite to produce the same effects. It is only in this way, I think, that we can understand how the suppression of an instinct can – frequently or quite generally – result in a sense of guilt and how a person's conscience becomes more severe and more sensitive the more he refrains from aggression against others.[1] One might expect that if a man knows that he is in the habit of avoiding the commission of acts of aggression that are undesirable from a cultural standpoint he will for that reason have a good conscience and will watch over his ego less suspiciously. The situation is usually presented as though ethical requirements were the primary thing and the renunciation of instinct followed from them. This leaves the origin of the ethical sense unexplained. Actually, it seems to be the other way about. The first instinctual renunciation is enforced by external powers and it is only this which creates the ethical sense, which expresses itself in conscience and demands a further renunciation of instinct.[2]

1. [Cf. *The Ego and the Id*, p. 396 above.]
2. [The subjects discussed in this paragraph were enlarged upon by Freud in

Thus moral masochism becomes a classical piece of evidence for the existence of fusion of instinct. Its danger lies in the fact that it originates from the death instinct and corresponds to the part of that instinct which has escaped being turned outwards as an instinct of destruction. But since, on the other hand, it has the significance of an erotic component even the subject's destruction of himself cannot take place without libidinal satisfaction.[1]

Chapter VII of *Civilization and its Discontents* (1930*a*), *P.F.L.*, **12**, 315 ff.]

1. [Freud discussed masochism in relation to psychoanalytic treatment once more in Section VI of his paper on 'Analysis Terminable and Interminable' (1937*c*).]

A NOTE UPON THE 'MYSTIC WRITING-PAD'
(1925 [1924])

EDITOR'S NOTE

NOTIZ ÜBER DEN 'WUNDERBLOCK'

(A) German Editions:

1925 *Int. Z. Psychoanal.*, **11** (1), 1–5.
1925 *Gesammelte Schriften*. **6**, 415–20.
1948 *Gesammelte Werke*, **14**, 3–8.

(B) English Translations:
'A Note upon the "Mystic Writing-Pad"'

1940 *Int. J. Psycho-Analysis*, **21** (4), 469–74. (Tr. James Strachey.)
1950 *Collected Papers*, **5**, 175–80.
1961 *Standard Edition*, **19**, 225–32. (Slightly corrected reprint of the translation published in 1950, with some additional notes.)

The present edition is a reprint of the *Standard Edition* version, with some editorial modifications.

This paper was probably written in the autumn of 1924, for Freud reported in an unpublished letter to Abraham of 28 November of that year that he was revising it (Jones, 1957, 124–5). The curious little apparatus, which is the basis of this ingenious and illuminating discussion of the conscious, preconscious and perceptual-conscious systems, is still (1961) quite easily obtainable, at least in Great Britain, under the trade name of 'Printator'. The subject-matter of the paper will become much clearer if an actual specimen can be examined and dissected.

A NOTE UPON THE 'MYSTIC WRITING-PAD'

IF I distrust my memory – neurotics, as we know, do so to a remarkable extent, but normal people have every reason for doing so as well – I am able to supplement and guarantee its working by making a note in writing. In that case the surface upon which this note is preserved, the pocket-book or sheet of paper, is as it were a materialized portion of my mnemic apparatus, which I otherwise carry about with me invisible. I have only to bear in mind the place where this 'memory' has been deposited and I can then 'reproduce' it at any time I like, with the certainty that it will have remained unaltered and so have escaped the possible distortions to which it might have been subjected in my actual memory.

If I want to make full use of this technique for improving my mnemic function, I find that there are two different procedures open to me. On the one hand, I can choose a writing-surface which will preserve intact any note made upon it for an indefinite length of time – for instance, a sheet of paper which I can write upon in ink. I am then in possession of a 'permanent memory-trace'. The disadvantage of this procedure is that the receptive capacity of the writing-surface is soon exhausted. The sheet is filled with writing, there is no room on it for any more notes, and I find myself obliged to bring another sheet into use, that has not been written on. Moreover, the advantage of this procedure, the fact that it provides a 'permanent trace', may lose its value for me if after a time the note ceases to interest me and I no longer want to 'retain it in my memory'. The alternative procedure avoids both of these disadvantages. If, for instance, I write with a piece of chalk on a slate, I have a receptive surface which retains its receptive capacity for an unlimited time and the notes upon which can be destroyed as soon as they cease to interest me, without any need for throwing away the writing-surface itself. Here the disadvantage is that I cannot preserve a permanent trace. If I want to put some fresh notes on the slate, I must first wipe out the ones which cover it. Thus an unlimited receptive capacity and a retention of permanent traces seem to be mutually exclusive properties in the apparatus which we use as substitutes for our memory: either the receptive surface must be renewed or the note must be destroyed.

All the forms of auxiliary apparatus which we have invented for the improvement or intensification of our sensory functions are built on the same model as the sense organs themselves or portions of them: for instance, spectacles, photographic cameras, trumpets.[1] Measured by this standard, devices to aid our memory seem particularly imperfect, since our mental apparatus accomplishes precisely what they cannot: it has an unlimited receptive capacity for new perceptions and nevertheless lays down permanent – even though not unalterable – memory-traces of them. As long ago as in 1900 I gave expression in *The Interpretation of Dreams*[2] to a suspicion that this unusual capacity was to be divided between two different systems (or organs of the mental apparatus). According to this view, we possess a system *Pcpt.-Cs.*, which receives perceptions but retains no permanent trace of them, so that it can react like a clean sheet to every new perception; while the permanent traces of the excitations which have been received are preserved in 'mnemic systems' lying behind the perceptual system. Later, in *Beyond the Pleasure Principle* (1920*g*),[3] I added a remark to the effect that the inexplicable phenomenon of consciousness arises in the perceptual system *instead of* the permanent traces.

Now some time ago there came upon the market, under the

1. [This notion is expanded in Chapter III of *Civilization and its Discontents* (1930*a*), *P.F.L.*, **12**, 276–7.]

2. [*P.F.L.*, **4**, 689. As Freud mentions in *Beyond the Pleasure Principle* (1920*g*), p. 296 above, this distinction had already been drawn by Breuer in his theoretical section of *Studies on Hysteria* (1895*d*), *P.F.L.*, **3**, 263 *n.*]

3. [Pp. 296–7 above.]

name of the 'Mystic Writing-Pad', a small contrivance that promises to perform more than the sheet of paper or the slate. It claims to be nothing more than a writing-tablet from which notes can be erased by an easy movement of the hand. But if it is examined more closely it will be found that its construction shows a remarkable agreement with my hypothetical structure of our perceptual apparatus and that it can in fact provide both an ever-ready receptive surface and permanent traces of the notes that have been made upon it.

The Mystic Pad is a slab of dark brown resin or wax with a paper edging; over the slab is laid a thin transparent sheet, the top end of which is firmly secured to the slab while its bottom end rests on it without being fixed to it. This transparent sheet is the more interesting part of the little device. It itself consists of two layers, which can be detached from each other except at their two ends. The upper layer is a transparent piece of celluloid; the lower layer is made of thin translucent waxed paper. When the apparatus is not in use, the lower surface of the waxed paper adheres lightly to the upper surface of the wax slab.

To make use of the Mystic Pad, one writes upon the celluloid portion of the covering-sheet which rests on the wax slab. For this purpose no pencil or chalk is necessary, since the writing does not depend on material being deposited on the receptive surface. It is a return to the ancient method of writing on tablets of clay or wax: a pointed stilus scratches the surface, the depressions upon which constitute the 'writing'. In the case of the Mystic Pad this scratching is not effected directly, but through the medium of the covering-sheet. At the points which the stilus touches, it presses the lower surface of the waxed paper on to the wax slab, and the grooves are visible as dark writing upon the otherwise smooth whitish-grey surface of the celluloid. If one wishes to destroy what has been written, all that is necessary is to raise the double covering-sheet from the wax slab by a light pull, starting from the free lower end.[1] The close con-

1. [The method by which the covering-sheet is detached from the wax slab is slightly different in the current form of the device; but this does not affect the principle.]

tact between the waxed paper and the wax slab at the places which have been scratched (upon which the visibility of the writing depended) is thus brought to an end and it does not recur when the two surfaces come together once more. The Mystic Pad is now clear of writing and ready to receive fresh notes.

The small imperfections of the contrivance have, of course, no importance for us, since we are only concerned with its approximation to the structure of the perceptual apparatus of the mind.

If, while the Mystic Pad has writing on it, we cautiously raise the celluloid from the waxed paper, we can see the writing just as clearly on the surface of the latter, and the question may arise why there should be any necessity for the celluloid portion of the cover. Experiment will then show that the thin paper would be very easily crumpled or torn if one were to write directly upon it with the stilus. The layer of celluloid thus acts as a protective sheath for the waxed paper, to keep off injurious effects from without. The celluloid is a 'protective shield against stimuli'; the layer which actually receives the stimuli is the paper. I may at this point recall that in *Beyond the Pleasure Principle* [p. 298 ff.] I showed that the perceptual apparatus of our mind consists of two layers, of an external protective shield against stimuli whose task it is to diminish the strength of excitations coming in, and of a surface behind it which receives the stimuli, namely the system *Pcpt.-Cs.*

The analogy would not be of much value if it could not be pursued further than this. If we lift the entire covering-sheet – both the celluloid and the waxed paper – off the wax slab, the writing vanishes and, as I have already remarked, does not reappear again. The surface of the Mystic Pad is clear of writing and once more capable of receiving impressions. But it is easy to discover that the permanent trace of what was written is retained upon the wax slab itself and is legible in suitable lights. Thus the Pad provides not only a receptive surface that can be used over and over again, like a slate, but also permanent traces of what has been written, like an ordinary paper pad: it solves the problem of combining the two functions *by dividing them between two separate but interrelated component parts or systems.* But this is precisely the way in which, according to the hypothesis which I mentioned just now, our mental apparatus performs its perceptual function. The layer which receives the stimuli – the system *Pcpt.-Cs.* – forms no permanent traces; the foundations of memory come about in other, adjoining, systems.

We need not be disturbed by the fact that in the Mystic Pad no use is made of the permanent traces of the notes that have been received; it is enough that they are present. There must come a point at which the analogy between an auxiliary apparatus of this kind and the organ which is its prototype will cease to apply. It is true, too, that once the writing has been erased, the Mystic Pad cannot 'reproduce' it from within; it would be a mystic pad indeed if, like our memory, it could accomplish that. None the less, I do not think it is too far-fetched to compare the celluloid and waxed paper cover with the system *Pcpt.-Cs.* and its protective shield, the wax slab with the unconscious behind them, and the appearance and disappearance of the writing with the flickering-up and passing-away of consciousness in the process of perception.

But I must admit that I am inclined to press the comparison still further. On the Mystic Pad the writing vanishes every time the close contact is broken between the paper which receives the stimulus and the wax slab which preserves the impression. This agrees with a notion which I have long had about the method by which the perceptual apparatus of our mind functions, but which I have hitherto kept to myself.[1] My theory was that cathectic innervations are sent out and withdrawn in rapid periodic impulses from within into the completely pervious system *Pcpt.-Cs.* So long as that system is cathected in this manner, it receives perceptions (which are accompanied by consciousness) and passes the excitation on to the unconscious mnemic systems; but as soon as the cathexis is withdrawn, consciousness

1. [It had in fact been mentioned in *Beyond the Pleasure Principle*, p. 299 above. The notion reappears at the end of the paper on 'Negation' (1925*h*), below, pp. 440–41. It is already present in embryo at the end of Section 19 of Part I of the 'Project' of 1895 (Freud 1950*a*).]

is extinguished and the functioning of the system comes to a standstill.[1] It is as though the unconscious stretches out feelers, through the medium of the system *Pcpt.-Cs.*, towards the external world and hastily withdraws them as soon as they have sampled the excitations coming from it. Thus the interruptions, which in the case of the Mystic Pad have an external origin, were attributed by my hypothesis to the discontinuity in the current of innervation; and the actual breaking of contact which occurs in the Mystic Pad was replaced in my theory by the periodic non-excitability of the perceptual system. I further had a suspicion that this discontinuous method of functioning of the system *Pcpt.-Cs.* lies at the bottom of the origin of the concept of time.[2]

If we imagine one hand writing upon the surface of the Mystic Writing-Pad while another periodically raises its covering-sheet from the wax slab, we shall have a concrete representation of the way in which I tried to picture the functioning of the perceptual apparatus of our mind.

1. [This is in accordance with the 'principle of the insusceptibility to excitation of uncathected systems', which is discussed in an Editor's footnote to the metapsychological paper on dreams (1917*d*), pp. 234–5 above.]

2. [This also had been suggested in *Beyond the Pleasure Principle*, p. 300 above, and hinted at earlier, in 'The Unconscious' (1915*e*), p. 191 ff. above. It is restated in 'Negation' (1925*h*), pp. 440–41 below, where, however, Freud attributes the sending out of feelers to the ego.]

NEGATION
(1925)

EDITOR'S NOTE

DIE VERNEINUNG

(A) GERMAN EDITIONS:

1925 *Imago*, **11** (3), 217–21.
1928 *Gesammelte Schriften*, **11**, 3–7.
1948 *Gesammelte Werke*, **14**, 11–15.

(B) ENGLISH TRANSLATIONS:
'Negation'

1925 *Int. J. Psycho-Analysis*, **6** (4), 367–71. (Tr. Joan Riviere.)
1950 *Collected Papers*, **5**, 181–5. (Revision of above.)
1961 *Standard Edition*, **19**, 233–9. (Modified version of the translation published in 1950.)

The present edition is a reprint of the *Standard Edition* version, with some editorial modifications.

We are told by Ernest Jones (1957, 125) that this was written in July 1925. The subject had, however, evidently been in Freud's thoughts for some time, as is shown by the footnote added by him to the 'Dora' case history in 1923. (See p. 442 below.) The paper is one of his most succinct. Though primarily it deals with a special point of metapsychology, yet in its opening and closing passages it touches upon technique. It will be seen from the references in the footnotes that both of these aspects of the paper had a long previous history.

NEGATION

THE manner in which our patients bring forward their associations during the work of analysis gives us an opportunity for making some interesting observations. 'Now you'll think I mean to say something insulting, but really I've no such intention.' We realize that this is a repudiation, by projection, of an idea that has just come up. Or: 'You ask who this person in the dream can be. It's *not* my mother.' We emend this to: 'So it *is* his mother.' In our interpretation, we take the liberty of disregarding the negation and of picking out the subject-matter alone of the association. It is as though the patient had said: 'It's true that my mother came into my mind as I thought of this person, but I don't feel inclined to let the association count.'[1]

There is a very convenient method by which we can sometimes obtain a piece of information we want about unconscious repressed material. 'What', we ask, 'would you consider the most unlikely imaginable thing in that situation? What do you think was furthest from your mind at that time?' If the patient falls into the trap and says what he thinks is most incredible, he almost always makes the right admission. A neat counterpart to this experiment is often met with in an obsessional neurotic who has already been initiated into the meaning of his symptoms. 'I've got a new obsessive idea,' he says, 'and it occurred to me at once that it might mean so and so. But no; that can't be true, or it couldn't have occurred to me.' What he is rejecting, on grounds picked up from his treatment, is, of course, the correct meaning of the obsessive idea.

Thus the content of a repressed image or idea can make its

1. [Freud had drawn attention to this in (among other places) the 'Rat Man' analysis (1909*d*), *P.F.L.*, **9**, 64 *n*. 1.]

way into consciousness, on condition that it is *negated*.[1] Negation is a way of taking cognizance of what is repressed; indeed it is already a lifting of the repression, though not, of course, an acceptance of what is repressed. We can see how in this the intellectual function is separated from the affective process. With the help of negation only one consequence of the process of repression is undone – the fact, namely, of the ideational content of what is repressed not reaching consciousness. The outcome of this is a kind of intellectual acceptance of the repressed, while at the same time what is essential to the repression persists.[2] In the course of analytic work we often produce a further, very important and somewhat strange variant of this situation. We succeed in conquering the negation as well, and in bringing about a full intellectual acceptance of the repressed; but the repressive process itself is not yet removed by this.

Since to affirm or negate the content of thoughts is the task of the function of intellectual judgement, what we have just been saying has led us to the psychological origin of that function. To negate something in a judgement is, at bottom, to say: 'This is something which I should prefer to repress.' A negative judgement is the intellectual substitute for repression;[3] its 'no' is the hall-mark of repression, a certificate of origin – like, let us say, 'Made in Germany'.[4] With the help of the symbol of negation,

1. [The German '*verneinen*' is here translated by 'to negate' instead of by the more usual 'to deny', in order to avoid confusion with the German '*verleugnen*', which has also in the past been rendered by 'to deny'. In this edition 'to disavow' has in general been used for the latter German word. See the footnote on this point in 'The Infantile Genital Organization' (1923*e*), *P.F.L.*, **7**, 310 *n.* 1.]

2. The same process is at the root of the familiar superstition that boasting is dangerous. 'How nice not to have had one of my headaches for so long.' But this is in fact the first announcement of an attack, of whose approach the subject is already sensible, although he is as yet unwilling to believe it. [Freud's attention had first been drawn to this explanation by one of his earliest patients, Frau Cäcilie M. Cf. the long footnote on the subject in the first of Freud's case histories in *Studies on Hysteria* (1895*d*), *P.F.L.*, **3**, 134 *n.* 2.]

3. [This idea also occurs elsewhere. See, for instance, the paper on 'The Two Principles of Mental Functioning' (1911*b*), where further references are given (p. 38 and *n.* 2 above).]

4. [In English in the original.]

thinking frees itself from the restrictions of repression and enriches itself with material that is indispensable for its proper functioning.

The function of judgement is concerned in the main with two sorts of decisions. It affirms or disaffirms the possession by a thing of a particular attribute; and it asserts or disputes that a presentation has an existence in reality.[1] The attribute to be decided about may originally have been good or bad, useful or harmful. Expressed in the language of the oldest – the oral – instinctual impulses, the judgement is: 'I should like to eat this', or 'I should like to spit it out'; and, put more generally: 'I should like to take this into myself and to keep that out.' That is to say: 'It shall be inside me' or 'it shall be outside me'. As I have shown elsewhere, the original pleasure-ego wants to introject into itself everything that is good and to eject from itself everything that is bad. What is bad, what is alien to the ego and what is external are, to begin with, identical.[2]

The other sort of decision made by the function of judgement – as to the real existence of something of which there is a presentation (reality-testing) – is a concern of the definitive reality-ego, which develops out of the initial pleasure-ego. It is now no longer a question of whether what has been perceived (a thing) shall be taken into the ego or not, but of whether something which is in the ego as a presentation can be rediscovered in perception (reality) as well. It is, we see, once more a question of *external* and *internal*. What is unreal, merely a presentation and subjective, is only internal; what is real is also there *outside*. In this stage of development regard for the pleasure principle has been set aside. Experience has shown the subject that it is not only important whether a thing (an object of satisfaction for him) possesses the 'good' attribute and so deserves to be taken into his ego, but also whether it is there in the external world, so that he can get hold of it whenever he needs it. In order to

1. [This is explained in the next paragraph.]

2. See the discussion in 'Instincts and their Vicissitudes' (1915*c*) [p. 133 ff. above. – Freud took up this question again in the first chapter of *Civilization and its Discontents* (1930*a*), *P.F.L.*, **12**, 254–5.]

understand this step forward we must recollect that all presentations originate from perceptions and are repetitions of them. Thus originally the mere existence of a presentation was a guarantee of the reality of what was presented. The antithesis between subjective and objective does not exist from the first. It only comes into being from the fact that thinking possesses the capacity to bring before the mind once more something that has once been perceived, by reproducing it as a presentation without the external object having still to be there. The first and immediate aim, therefore, of reality-testing is, not to *find* an object in real perception which corresponds to the one presented, but to *refind* such an object, to convince oneself that it is still there.[1] Another capacity of the power of thinking offers a further contribution to the differentiation between what is subjective and what is objective. The reproduction of a perception as a presentation is not always a faithful one; it may be modified by omissions, or changed by the merging of various elements. In that case, reality-testing has to ascertain how far such distortions go. But it is evident that a precondition for the setting up of reality-testing is that objects shall have been lost which once brought real satisfaction.

Judging is the intellectual action which decides the choice of motor action, which puts an end to the postponement due to thought and which leads over from thinking to acting. This postponement due to thought has also been discussed by me elsewhere.[2] It is to be regarded as an experimental action, a

1. [Much of this is foreshadowed in *The Interpretation of Dreams* (1900*a*), *P.F.L.*, **4**, 718–21, and, more particularly, in the 1895 'Project' (Freud, 1950*a*; Section 16 of Part I). Here the 'object' to be refound is the mother's breast. Cf., too, a sentence which occurs in a similar connection in Essay III [5] of the *Three Essays* (1905*d*), *P.F.L.*, **7**, 145: 'The finding of an object is in fact a refinding of it.']

2. [Freud made this important point repeatedly. See, for instance, 'Formulations on the Two Principles of Mental Functioning' (1911*b*), p. 38 and *n.* 3 above, where earlier references are given. The concept is also mentioned in the later papers, 'The Unconscious' (1915*e*) and *The Ego and the Id* (1923*b*), pp. 190 and 397 above. It appears also in Lecture 32 of the *New Introductory Lectures* (1933*a*), *P.F.L.*, **2**, 122 and *n.* 1, as well as in Chapter VIII of the *Outline of Psycho-*

motor palpating, with small expenditure of discharge. Let us consider where the ego has used a similar kind of palpating before, at what place it learnt the technique which it now applies in its processes of thought. It happened at the sensory end of the mental apparatus, in connection with sense perceptions. For, on our hypothesis, perception is not a purely passive process. The ego periodically sends out small amounts of cathexes into the perceptual system, by means of which it samples the external stimuli, and then after every such tentative advance it draws back again.[1]

The study of judgement affords us, perhaps for the first time, an insight into the origin of an intellectual function from the interplay of the primary instinctual impulses. Judging is a continuation, along lines of expediency, of the original process by which the ego took things into itself or expelled them from itself, according to the pleasure principle. The polarity of judgement appears to correspond to the opposition of the two groups of instincts which we have supposed to exist. Affirmation – as a substitute for uniting – belongs to Eros; negation – the successor to expulsion – belongs to the instinct of destruction. The general wish to negate, the negativism which is displayed by some psychotics, is probably to be regarded as a sign of a defusion of instincts that has taken place through a withdrawal of the libidinal components.[2] But the performance of the function of judgement is not made possible until the creation of the symbol of negation has endowed thinking with a first measure of freedom from the consequences of repression and, with it, from the compulsion of the pleasure principle.

Analysis (1940*a* [1938]). Incidentally, the whole topic of judgement is discussed at great length, and on much the same lines as the present ones, in Sections 16, 17 and 18 of Part I of the 'Project' (1950*a*).]

1. [See *Beyond the Pleasure Principle* (1920*g*), p. 299 above, and 'A Note upon the "Mystic Writing-Pad"' (1925*a*), p. 434 above. It may be remarked that in this last passage Freud suggests not that the ego but that the *unconscious* 'stretches out feelers, through the medium of the system *Pcpt.-Cs.*, towards the external world'.]

2. [Cf. a remark in Chapter VI of the book on jokes (1905*c*), *P.F.L.*, **6**, 233 *n*. 2.]

This view of negation fits in very well with the fact that in analysis we never discover a 'no' in the unconscious and that recognition of the unconscious on the part of the ego is expressed in a negative formula. There is no stronger evidence that we have been successful in our effort to uncover the unconscious than when the patient reacts to it with the words 'I didn't think that', or 'I didn't (ever) think of that'.[1]

1. [Freud had made this point in almost the same words in a footnote added in 1923 to the 'Dora' analysis (1905*e*), *P.F.L.*, 8, 92 *n.* 1. He once more returned to it in his very late paper on 'Constructions in Analysis' (1937*d*).]

A DISTURBANCE OF MEMORY ON THE ACROPOLIS
(1936)

EDITOR'S NOTE

BRIEF AN ROMAIN ROLLAND (EINE ERINNERUNGSSTÖRUNG AUF DER AKROPOLIS)

(A) GERMAN EDITIONS:

1936 *Almanach 1937*, 9–21.
1950 *Gesammelte Werke*, **16**, 250–57.

(B) ENGLISH TRANSLATIONS:
'A Disturbance of Memory on the Acropolis'

1941 *Int. J. Psycho-Analysis*, **22** (2), 93–101. (Tr. James Strachey.)
1950 *Collected Papers*, **5**, 302–12. (Reprint of above.)
1964 *Standard Edition*, **22**, 237–48. (Corrected reprint of above.)

The present edition is a reprint of the *Standard Edition* version, with some editorial modifications.

Romain Rolland was born on 29 January 1866, and this paper was dedicated to him on the occasion of his seventieth birthday. Freud had the greatest admiration for him, as is proved not only by the present work, but by the message to Rolland on his sixtieth birthday (Freud, 1926*a*) and by the six or seven letters to him which have been published (Freud, 1960*a*), as well as by a passage at the beginning of *Civilization and its Discontents* (1930*a*). Freud had first corresponded with him in 1923, and had met him, for the only time, it seems, in 1924.

It has been impossible to trace any earlier publication of this paper in German, other than that in the *Almanach* noted above.

It should be borne in mind that any publications connected with Romain Rolland, as with many other authors, including Thomas Mann and of course all Jewish writers, were suppressed during this period by the Nazis.

A DISTURBANCE OF MEMORY ON THE ACROPOLIS

AN OPEN LETTER TO ROMAIN ROLLAND ON THE OCCASION OF HIS SEVENTIETH BIRTHDAY

My dear Friend,

I have been urgently pressed to make some written contribution to the celebration of your seventieth birthday and I have made long efforts to find something that might in any way be worthy of you and might give expression to my admiration for your love of the truth, for your courage in your beliefs and for your affection and good will towards humanity; or, again, something that might bear witness to my gratitude to you as a writer who has afforded me so many moments of exaltation and pleasure. But it was in vain. I am ten years older than you and my powers of production are at an end. All that I can find to offer you is the gift of an impoverished creature, who has 'seen better days'.

You know that the aim of my scientific work was to throw light upon unusual, abnormal or pathological manifestations of the mind – that is to say, to trace them back to the psychical forces operating behind them and to indicate the mechanisms at work. I began by attempting this upon myself and then went on to apply it to other people and finally, by a bold extension, to the human race as a whole. During the last few years, a phenomenon of this sort, which I myself had experienced a generation ago, in 1904, and which I had never understood, has kept on recurring to my mind.[1] I did not at first see why; but at last I determined to analyse the incident – and I now present you with the results of that enquiry. In the process, I shall have, of

1. [Freud had made a short allusion to the episode some ten years earlier, in Chapter V of *The Future of an Illusion* (1927*c*), *P.F.L.*, **12**, 206–7, but had not put forward the explanation.]

course, to ask you to give more attention to some events in my private life than they would otherwise deserve.

Every year, at that time, towards the end of August or the beginning of September, I used to set out with my younger brother on a holiday trip, which would last for some weeks and would take us to Rome or to some other region of Italy or to some part of the Mediterranean sea-board. My brother is ten years younger than I am, so he is the same age as you – a coincidence which has only now occurred to me. In that particular year my brother told me that his business affairs would not allow him to be away for long: a week would be the most that he could manage and we should have to shorten our trip. So we decided to travel by way of Trieste to the island of Corfu and there spend the few days of our holiday. At Trieste he called upon a business acquaintance who lived there, and I went with him. Our host enquired in a friendly way about our plans and, hearing that it was our intention to go to Corfu, advised us strongly against it: 'What makes you think of going there at this time of year? It would be too hot for you to do anything. You had far better go to Athens instead. The Lloyd boat sails this afternoon; it will give you three days there to see the town and will pick you up on its return voyage. That would be more agreeable and more worth while.'

As we walked away from this visit, we were both in remarkably depressed spirits. We discussed the plan that had been proposed, agreed that it was quite impracticable and saw nothing but difficulties in the way of carrying it out; we assumed, moreover, that we should not be allowed to land in Greece without passports. We spent the hours that elapsed before the Lloyd offices opened in wandering about the town in a discontented and irresolute frame of mind. But when the time came, we went up to the counter and booked our passages for Athens as though it were a matter of course, without bothering in the least about the supposed difficulties and indeed without having discussed with one another the reasons for our decision. Such behaviour, it must be confessed, was most strange. Later on we recognized that we had accepted the suggestion that we should go to Athens instead of Corfu instantly and most readily. But, if so, why had we spent the interval before the offices opened in such a gloomy state and foreseen nothing but obstacles and difficulties?

When, finally, on the afternoon after our arrival, I stood on the Acropolis and cast my eyes around upon the landscape, a surprising thought suddenly entered my mind: 'So all this really *does* exist, just as we learnt at school!' To describe the situation more accurately, the person who gave expression to the remark was divided, far more sharply than was usually noticeable, from another person who took cognizance of the remark; and both were astonished, though not by the same thing. The first behaved as though he were obliged, under the impact of an unequivocal observation, to believe in something the reality of which had hitherto seemed doubtful. If I may make a slight exaggeration, it was as if someone, walking beside Loch Ness, suddenly caught sight of the form of the famous Monster stranded upon the shore and found himself driven to the admission: 'So it really *does* exist – the sea-serpent we've never believed in!" The second person, on the other hand, was justifiably astonished, because he had been unaware that the real existence of Athens, the Acropolis, and the landscape around it had ever been objects of doubt. What he had been expecting was rather some expression of delight or admiration.

Now it would be easy to argue that this strange thought that occurred to me on the Acropolis only serves to emphasize the fact that seeing something with one's own eyes is after all quite a different thing from hearing or reading about it. But it would remain a very strange way of clothing an uninteresting commonplace. Or it would be possible to maintain that it was true that when I was a schoolboy I had *thought* I was convinced of the historical reality of the city of Athens and its history, but that the occurrence of this idea on the Acropolis had precisely shown that in my unconscious I had *not* believed in it, and that I was only now acquiring a conviction that 'reached down to the unconscious'. An explanation of this sort sounds very profound, but it is easier to assert than to prove; moreover, it is very much open to attack upon theoretical grounds. No. I believe that the two phenomena, the depression at Trieste and the idea on the Acropolis, were intimately connected. And the first of these is more easily intelligible and may help us towards an explanation of the second.

The experience at Trieste was, it will be noticed, also no more than an expression of incredulity: 'We're going to see Athens? Out of the question! – it will be far too difficult!' The accompanying depression corresponded to a regret that it *was* out of the question: it would have been so lovely. And now we know where we are. It is one of those cases of 'too good to be true'[1] that we come across so often. It is an example of the incredulity that arises so often when we are surprised by a piece of good news, when we hear we have won a prize, for instance, or drawn a winner, or when a girl learns that the man whom she has secretly loved has asked her parents for leave to pay his addresses to her.

When we have established the existence of a phenomenon, the next question is of course as to its cause. Incredulity of this kind is obviously an attempt to repudiate a piece of reality; but there is something strange about it. We should not be in the least astonished if an attempt of this kind were aimed at a piece of reality that threatened to bring unpleasure: the mechanism of our mind is, so to speak, planned to work along just such lines. But why should such incredulity arise in something which, on the contrary, promises to bring a high degree of pleasure? Truly paradoxical behaviour! But I recollect that on a previous occasion I dealt with the similar case of the people who, as I put it, are 'wrecked by success'.[2] As a rule people fall ill as a result of frustration, of the non-fulfilment of some vital necessity or desire. But with these people the opposite is the case; they fall ill, or even go entirely to pieces, because an overwhelmingly powerful wish of theirs has been fulfilled. But the contrast between the two situations is not so great as it seems at first.

1. [In English in the original.]

2. [Section II of 'Some Character-Types Met with in Psycho-Analytic Work' (1916*d*), *P.F.L.*, **14**, 299.]

What happens in the paradoxical case is merely that the place of the external frustration is taken by an internal one. The sufferer does not permit himself happiness: the internal frustration commands him to cling to the external one. But why? Because – so runs the answer in a number of cases – one cannot expect Fate to grant one anything so good. In fact, another instance of 'too good to be true', the expression of a pessimism of which a large portion seems to find a home in many of us. In another set of cases, just as in those who are wrecked by success, we find a sense of guilt or inferiority, which can be translated: 'I'm not worthy of such happiness, I don't deserve it.' But these two motives are essentially the same, for one is only a projection of the other. For, as has long been known, the Fate which we expect to treat us so badly is a materialization of our conscience, of the severe super-ego within us, itself a residue of the punitive agency of our childhood.[1]

This, I think, explains our behaviour in Trieste. We could not believe that we were to be given the joy of seeing Athens. The fact that the piece of reality that we were trying to repudiate was to begin with only a *possibility* determined the character of our immediate reactions. But when we were standing on the Acropolis the possibility had become an actuality, and the same disbelief found a different but far clearer expression. In an undistorted form this should have been: 'I could really not have imagined it possible that I should ever be granted the sight of Athens with my own eyes – as is now indubitably the case!' When I recall the passionate desire to travel and see the world by which I was dominated at school and later, and how long it was before that desire began to find its fulfilment, I am not surprised at its after-effect on the Acropolis; I was then forty-eight years old. I did not ask my younger brother whether he felt anything of the same sort. A certain amount of reserve surrounded the whole episode; and it was this which had already interfered with our exchanging thoughts at Trieste.

If I have rightly guessed the meaning of the thought that came

1. [Cf. *Civilization and its Discontents* (1930*a*), *P.F.L.*, **12**, 319.]

to me on the Acropolis and if it did in fact express my joyful astonishment at finding myself at that spot, the further question now arises why this meaning should have been subjected in the thought itself to such a distorted and distorting disguise.

The essential subject-matter of the thought, to be sure, was retained even in the distortion – that is, incredulity: 'By the evidence of my senses I am now standing on the Acropolis, but I cannot believe it.' This incredulity, however, this doubt of a piece of reality, was doubly displaced in its actual expression: first, it was shifted back into the past, and secondly it was transposed from my relation to the Acropolis on to the very existence of the Acropolis. And so something occurred which was equivalent to an assertion that at some time in the past I had doubted the real existence of the Acropolis – which, however, my memory rejected as being incorrect and, indeed, impossible.

The two distortions involve two independent problems. We can attempt to penetrate deeper into the process of transformation. Without for the moment particularizing as to how I have arrived at the idea, I will start from the presumption that the original factor must have been a sense of some feeling of the unbelievable and the unreal in the situation at the moment. The situation included myself, the Acropolis and my perception of it. I could not account for this doubt; I obviously could not attach the doubt to my sensory impressions of the Acropolis. But I remembered that in the past I had had a doubt about something which had to do with this precise locality, and I thus found the means for shifting the doubt into the past. In the process, however, the subject-matter of the doubt was changed. I did not simply recollect that in my early years I had doubted whether I myself would ever see the Acropolis, but I asserted that at that time I had disbelieved in the reality of the Acropolis itself. It is precisely this effect of the displacement that leads me to think that the actual situation on the Acropolis contained an element of doubt of reality. I have certainly not yet succeeded in making the process clear; so I will conclude by saying briefly that the whole psychical situation, which seems so confused and is so difficult to describe, can be satisfactorily cleared up by assuming that at the time I had (or might have had) a momentary feeling: '*What I see here is not real.*' Such a feeling is known as a 'feeling of derealization' ['*Entfremdungsgefühl*'].[1] I made an attempt to ward that feeling off, and I succeeded, at the cost of making a false pronouncement about the past.

These derealizations are remarkable phenomena which are still little understood. They are spoken of as 'sensations', but they are obviously complicated processes, attached to particular mental contents and bound up with decisions made about those contents. They arise very frequently in certain mental diseases, but they are not unknown among normal people, just as hallucinations occasionally occur in the healthy. Nevertheless they are certainly failures in functioning and, like dreams, which, in spite of their regular occurrence in healthy people, serve us as models of psychological disorder, they are abnormal structures. These phenomena are to be observed in two forms: the subject feels either that a piece of reality or that a piece of his own self is strange to him. In the latter case we speak of 'depersonalizations'; derealizations and depersonalizations are intimately connected. There is another set of phenomena which may be regarded as their positive counterparts – what are known as '*fausse reconnaissance*', '*déjà vu*', '*déjà raconté*' etc.,[2] illusions in which we seek to accept something as belonging to our ego, just as in the derealizations we are anxious to keep something out of us. A naïvely mystical and unpsychological attempt at explaining the phenomena of '*déjà vu*' endeavours to find evidence in it of a former existence of our mental self. Depersonalization leads us on to the extraordinary condition of '*double conscience*',[3] which is more correctly described as 'split person-

1. [The word has been rendered variously into English. Henderson and Gillespie, *Text-Book of Psychiatry* (10th ed., 1969), use the term 'derealization', and make the same distinction as Freud between it and 'depersonalization' (Freud's '*Depersonalisation*').]

2. [Freud discussed these phenomena twice at some length: in Chapter XII (D) of *The Psychopathology of Everyday Life* (1901*b*), *P.F.L.*, **5**, 328–32, and in a paper on '*Fausse Reconnaissance*' (1914*a*). Cf. also the Wolf Man's 'veil' (1918*b*), *P.F.L.*, **9**, 311 and 339 ff.]

3. [The French term: 'dual consciousness'.]

ality'. But all of this is so obscure and has been so little mastered scientifically that I must refrain from talking about it any more to you.

It will be enough for my purposes if I return to two general characteristics of the phenomena of derealization. The first is that they all serve the purpose of defence; they aim at keeping something away from the ego, at disavowing it. Now, new elements, which may give occasion for defensive measures, approach the ego from two directions – from the real external world and from the internal world of thoughts and impulses that emerge in the ego. It is possible that this alternative coincides with the choice between derealizations proper and depersonalizations. There are an extraordinarily large number of methods (or mechanisms, as we say) used by our ego in the discharge of its defensive functions. An investigation is at this moment being carried on close at hand which is devoted to the study of these methods of defence: my daughter, the child analyst, is writing a book upon them.[1] The most primitive and thoroughgoing of these methods, 'repression', was the starting-point of the whole of our deeper understanding of psychopathology. Between repression and what may be termed the normal method of fending off what is distressing or unbearable, by means of recognizing it, considering it, making a judgement upon it and taking appropriate action about it, there lie a whole series of more or less clearly pathological methods of behaviour on the part of the ego. May I stop for a moment to remind you of a marginal case of this kind of defence? You remember the famous lament of the Spanish Moors '*Ay de mi Alhama*' ['Alas for my Alhama'], which tells how King Boabdil[2] received the news of the fall of his city of Alhama. He feels that this loss means the end of his rule. But he will not 'let it be true', he determines to treat the news as '*non arrivé*'.[3] The verse runs:

1. [Anna Freud, *The Ego and the Mechanisms of Defence* (1936).]

2. [The last Moorish King of Granada at the end of the fifteenth century. Alhama, some twenty miles distant, was the key fortress to the capital.]

3. [Freud used the same phrase to describe the defensive process in Section I of his first paper on 'The Neuro-Psychoses of Defence' (1894*a*), and again in

'Cartas le fueron venidas
que Alhama era ganada:
las cartas echo en el fuego,
y al mensajero matara.'[1]

It is easy to guess that a further determinant of this behaviour of the king was his need to combat a feeling of powerlessness. By burning the letters and having the messenger killed he was still trying to show his absolute power.

The second general characteristic of the derealizations – their dependence upon the past, upon the ego's store of memories and upon earlier distressing experiences which have since perhaps fallen victim to repression – is not accepted without dispute. But precisely my own experience on the Acropolis, which actually culminated in a disturbance of memory and a falsification of the past, helps us to demonstrate this connection. It is not true that in my schooldays I ever doubted the real existence of Athens. I only doubted whether I should ever see Athens. It seemed to me beyond the realms of possibility that I should travel so far – that I should 'go such a long way'. This was linked up with the limitations and poverty of our conditions of life in my youth. My longing to travel was no doubt also the expression of a wish to escape from that pressure, like the force which drives so many adolescent children to run away from home. I had long seen clearly that a great part of the pleasure of travel lies in the fulfilment of these early wishes – that it is rooted, that is, in dissatisfaction with home and family. When first one catches sight of the sea, crosses the ocean and experiences as realities cities and lands which for so long had been distant, unattainable things of desire – one feels oneself like a hero who has performed deeds of improbable greatness. I might that day on the Acropolis have said to my brother: 'Do you still remember how, when we were young, we used day after day to walk along the same streets on our way to school, and how every Sunday

Chapter VI of *Inhibitions, Symptoms and Anxiety* (1926*d*), *P.F.L.*, **10**, 275 and *n.* 1.]

1. ['Letters had reached him telling that Alhama was taken. He threw the letters in the fire and killed the messenger.']

we used to go to the Prater or on some excursion we knew so well? And now, here we are in Athens, and standing on the Acropolis! We really *have* gone a long way!' So too, if I may compare such a small event with a greater one, Napoleon, during his coronation as Emperor in Notre Dame,[1] turned to one of his brothers – it must no doubt have been the eldest one, Joseph – and remarked: 'What would *Monsieur notre Père* have said to this, if he could have been here to-day?'

But here we come upon the solution of the little problem of why it was that already at Trieste we interfered with our enjoyment of the voyage to Athens. It must be that a sense of guilt was attached to the satisfaction in having gone such a long way: there was something about it that was wrong, that from earliest times had been forbidden. It was something to do with a child's criticism of his father, with the undervaluation which took the place of the overvaluation of earlier childhood. It seems as though the essence of success was to have got further than one's father, and as though to excel one's father was still something forbidden.

As an addition to this generally valid motive there was a special factor present in our particular case. The very theme of Athens and the Acropolis in itself contained evidence of the son's superiority. Our father had been in business, he had had no secondary education, and Athens could not have meant much to him. Thus what interfered with our enjoyment of the journey to Athens was a feeling of *filial piety*. And now you will no longer wonder that the recollection of this incident on the Acropolis should have troubled me so often since I myself have grown old and stand in need of forbearance and can travel no more.

I am ever sincerely yours,

SIGM. FREUD

January 1936

1. [The story is usually told of his assumption of the Iron Crown of Lombardy in Milan.]

SPLITTING OF THE EGO IN THE PROCESS OF DEFENCE
(1940 [1938])

EDITOR'S NOTE

DIE ICHSPALTUNG IM ABWEHRVORGANG

(A) German Editions:

1940 *Int. Z. Psychoanal. Imago*, **25** (3/4), 241–4.
1941 *Gesammelte Werke*, **17**, 59–62.

(B) English Translations:
'Splitting of the Ego in the Defensive Process'

1941 *Int. J. Psycho-Analysis*, **22** (1), 65–8. (Tr. James Strachey.)
1950 *Collected Papers*, **5**, 372–5. (Reprint of above.)
1964 *Standard Edition*, **23**, 271–8. (Translation, with a modified title, based on that of 1950, but considerably corrected.)

The present edition is a reprint of the *Standard Edition* version, with some editorial modifications.

The manuscript of this important unfinished paper, published posthumously, is dated 2 January 1938, and, according to Ernest Jones (1957, 255), it was 'written at Christmas, 1937'.

The paper carries further than before the investigation of the ego and its behaviour in difficult circumstances. Two inter-related topics are involved, both of which had latterly been occupying Freud's mind: the notion of the act of 'disavowal' ('*Verleugnung*') and the notion of that act's resulting in a 'splitting' of the ego. 'Disavowal' was usually discussed by Freud, as it is here, in connection with the castration complex. It emerged, for instance, in the paper on 'The Infantile Genital Organization' (1923*e*), *P.F.L.*, **7**, 310 *n.* 1, where an Editor's footnote gives a number of references to other appearances of the term. One of these is in the short study of 'Fetishism' (1927*e*), ibid., **7**, 352–3, to which the paper before us may be regarded as a sequel. For in that study the splitting of the ego consequent on disavowal was emphasized. (It had been hinted at already in 'Neurosis and Psychosis' (1924*b*); ibid., **10**, 217–18.)

Though the present paper was, for some unexplained reason, left unfinished by Freud, he took its subject up again a little later, in the last two or three pages of Chapter VIII of his *Outline of Psycho-Analysis* (1940*a* [1938]). He there, however, extends the application of the idea of a splitting of the ego beyond the cases of fetishism and of the psychoses to neuroses in general. Thus the topic links up with the wider question of the 'alteration of the ego' which is invariably brought about by the processes of defence. This, again, was something with which Freud had dealt recently – in his technical paper on 'Analysis Terminable and Interminable' (1937*c*, especially in Section V) – but which leads us back to very early times, to the second paper on the neuro-psychoses of defence (1896*b*), and to the even earlier Draft K of the Fliess correspondence (1950*a*).

SPLITTING OF THE EGO IN THE PROCESS OF DEFENCE

I FIND myself for a moment in the interesting position of not knowing whether what I have to say should be regarded as something long familiar and obvious or as something entirely new and puzzling. But I am inclined to think the latter.

I have at last been struck by the fact that the ego of a person whom we know as a patient in analysis must, dozens of years earlier, when it was young, have behaved in a remarkable manner in certain particular situations of pressure. We can assign in general and somewhat vague terms the conditions under which this comes about, by saying that it occurs under the influence of a psychical trauma. I prefer to select a single sharply defined special case, though it certainly does not cover all the possible modes of causation.

Let us suppose, then, that a child's ego is under the sway of a powerful instinctual demand which it is accustomed to satisfy and that it is suddenly frightened by an experience which teaches it that the continuance of this satisfaction will result in an almost intolerable real danger. It must now decide either to recognize the real danger, give way to it and renounce the instinctual satisfaction, or to disavow reality and make itself believe that there is no reason for fear, so that it may be able to retain the satisfaction. Thus there is a conflict between the demand by the instinct and the prohibition by reality. But in fact the child takes neither course, or rather he takes both simultaneously, which comes to the same thing. He replies to the conflict with two contrary reactions, both of which are valid and effective. On the one hand, with the help of certain mechanisms he rejects reality and refuses to accept any prohibition; on the other hand, in the same breath he recognizes the danger of reality, takes over the fear of that danger as a pathological symptom and tries subsequently to divest himself of the fear. It must be confessed that this is a very ingenious solution of the difficulty. Both of the parties to the dispute obtain their share: the instinct is allowed to retain its satisfaction and proper respect is shown to reality. But everything has to be paid for in one way or another, and this success is achieved at the price of a rift in the ego which never heals but which increases as time goes on. The two contrary reactions to the conflict persist as the centre-point of a splitting of the ego. The whole process seems so strange to us because we take for granted the synthetic nature of the processes of the ego.[1] But we are clearly at fault in this. The synthetic function of the ego, though it is of such extraordinary importance, is subject to particular conditions and is liable to a whole number of disturbances.

It will assist if I introduce an individual case history into this schematic disquisition. A little boy, while he was between three and four years of age, had become acquainted with the female genitals through being seduced by an older girl. After these relations had been broken off, he carried on the sexual stimulation set going in this way by zealously practising manual masturbation; but he was soon caught at it by his energetic nurse and was threatened with castration, the carrying out of which was, as usual, ascribed to his father. There were thus present in this case conditions calculated to produce a tremendous effect of fright. A threat of castration by itself need not produce a great impression. A child will refuse to believe in it, for he cannot easily imagine the possibility of losing such a highly prized part of his body. His [earlier] sight of the female genitals might have

1. [See, for instance, a passage in Lecture 31 of the *New Introductory Lectures* (1933*a*), *P.F.L.*, **2**, 108–9. Though Freud had stressed the synthetic tendency of the ego in his later writings, particularly in Chapter III of *Inhibitions, Symptoms and Anxiety* (1926*d*), *P.F.L.*, **10**, 249–52, and in *The Question of Lay Analysis* (1926*e*), the concept was implicit in his picture of the ego from the earliest times. During the Breuer period the term he almost invariably used for ideas that had to be repressed was 'incompatible' – i.e. that could not be synthesized by the ego.]

convinced our child of that possibility. But he drew no such conclusion from it, since his disinclination to doing so was too great and there was no motive present which could compel him to. On the contrary, whatever uneasiness he may have felt was calmed by the reflection that what was missing would yet make its appearance: she would grow one (a penis) later. Anyone who has observed enough small boys will be able to recollect having come across some such remark at the sight of a baby sister's genitals. But it is different if both factors are present together. In that case the threat revives the memory of the perception which had hitherto been regarded as harmless and finds in that memory a dreaded confirmation. The little boy now thinks he understands why the girl's genitals showed no sign of a penis and no longer ventures to doubt that his own genitals may meet with the same fate. Thenceforward he cannot help believing in the reality of the danger of castration.

The usual result of the fright of castration, the result that passes as the normal one, is that, either immediately or after some considerable struggle, the boy gives way to the threat and obeys the prohibition either wholly or at least in part (that is, by no longer touching his genitals with his hand). In other words, he gives up, in whole or in part, the satisfaction of the instinct. We are prepared to hear, however, that our present patient found another way out. He created a substitute for the penis which he missed in females – that is to say, a fetish. In so doing, it is true that he had disavowed reality, but he had saved his own penis. So long as he was not obliged to acknowledge that females have lost their penis, there was no need for him to believe the threat that had been made against him: he need have no fears for his own penis, so he could proceed with his masturbation undisturbed. This behaviour on the part of our patient strikes us forcibly as being a turning away from reality – a procedure which we should prefer to reserve for psychoses. And it is in fact not very different. Yet we will suspend our judgement, for upon closer inspection we shall discover a not unimportant distinction. The boy did not simply contradict his perceptions and hallucinate a penis where there was none to be seen; he effected no more than a displacement of value – he transferred the importance of the penis to another part of the body, a procedure in which he was assisted by the mechanism of regression (in a manner which need not here be explained). This displacement, it is true, related only to the female body; as regards his own penis nothing was changed.

This way of dealing with reality, which almost deserves to be described as artful, was decisive as regards the boy's practical behaviour. He continued with his masturbation as though it implied no danger to his penis; but at the same time, in complete contradiction to his apparent boldness or indifference, he developed a symptom which showed that he nevertheless did recognize the danger. He had been threatened with being castrated by his father, and immediately afterwards, simultaneously with the creation of his fetish, he developed an intense fear of his father punishing him, which it required the whole force of his masculinity to master and overcompensate. This fear of his father, too, was silent on the subject of castration: by the help of regression to an oral phase, it assumed the form of a fear of being eaten by his father. At this point it is impossible to forget a primitive fragment of Greek mythology which tells how Kronos, the old Father God, swallowed his children and sought to swallow his youngest son Zeus like the rest, and how Zeus was saved by the craft of his mother and later on castrated his father. But we must return to our case history and add that the boy produced yet another symptom, though it was a slight one, which he has retained to this day. This was an anxious susceptibility against either of his little toes being touched, as though, in all the to and fro between disavowal and acknowledgement, it was nevertheless castration that found the clearer expression . . .

* * * * *

APPENDIX

LIST OF WRITINGS BY FREUD DEALING MAINLY WITH GENERAL PSYCHOLOGICAL THEORY

[*The date at the beginning of each entry is that of the year during which the work in question was probably written. The date at the end is that of publication; and under that date fuller particulars of the work will be found in the* Bibliography and Author Index. *The items in square brackets were published posthumously.*]

[1895 'A Project for a Scientific Psychology' (1950a).]
[1896 Letters to Fliess of 1 January and 6 December (1950*a*).]
1899 *The Interpretation of Dreams*, Chapter VII (1900*a*).
1910–11 'Formulations on the Two Principles of Mental Functioning' (1911*b*).
1910 'Psycho-Analytic Notes on an Autobiographical Account of a Case of Paranoia (Dementia Paranoides)', Section III (1911*c*).
1912 'A Note on the Unconscious in Psycho-Analysis' (1912*g*).
1914 'On Narcissism: an Introduction' (1914*c*).
1915 'Instincts and their Vicissitudes' (1915*c*).
1915 'Repression' (1915*d*).
1915 'The Unconscious' (1915*e*).
1915 'A Metapsychological Supplement to the Theory of Dreams' (1917*d*).
1915 'Mourning and Melancholia' (1917*e*).
1915–17 *Introductory Lectures on Psycho-Analysis*, Lectures 22 and 26 (1916–17).
1920 *Beyond the Pleasure Principle* (1920*g*).
1921 *Group Psychology and the Analysis of the Ego*, Chapters VII and XI (1921*c*).
1922 'Two Encyclopaedia Articles: (B) The Libido Theory' (1923*a*).
1923 *The Ego and the Id* (1923*b*).
1924 'Neurosis and Psychosis' (1924*b*).
1924 'The Economic Problem of Masochism' (1924*c*).
1924 'The Loss of Reality in Neurosis and Psychosis' (1924*e*).

1925 'A Note upon the "Mystic Writing-Pad"' (1925*a*).
1925 'Negation' (1925*h*).
1927 'Fetishism' (1927*e*).
1929 *Civilization and its Discontents*, Chapters VI, VII and VIII (1930*a*).
1932 *New Introductory Lectures on Psycho-Analysis*, Lectures 31 and 32 (1933*a*).
[1938 *An Outline of Psycho-Analysis*, Chapters I, II, IV, VIII and IX (1940*a*).]
[1938 'Some Elementary Lessons in Psycho-Analysis' (1940*b*).]
[1938 'Splitting of the Ego in the Process of Defence' (1940*e*).]

BIBLIOGRAPHY AND AUTHOR INDEX

Titles of books and periodicals are in italics, titles of papers are in inverted commas. Abbreviations are in accordance with the *World List of Scientific Periodicals* (London, 1963–5). Further abbreviations used in this volume will be found in the List at the end of this bibliography. Numerals in bold type refer to volumes, ordinary numerals refer to pages. The figures in round brackets at the end of each entry indicate the page or pages of this volume on which the work in question is mentioned.

In the case of the Freud entries, only English translations are given. The initial dates are those of the German, or other, original publications. (The date of writing is added in square brackets where it differs from the latter.) The letters attached to the dates of publication are in accordance with the corresponding entries in the complete bibliography of Freud's writings included in Volume 24 of the *Standard Edition*. Details of the original publication, including the original German (or other) title, are given in the editorial introduction to each work included in the *Pelican Freud Library*.

For non-technical authors, and for technical authors where no specific work is mentioned, see the General Index.

ABRAHAM, K. (1908) 'Die psychosexuellen Differenzen der Hysterie und der Dementia praecox', *Zentbl. Nervenheilk.*, N.F., **19**, 521. (67, 201)

[*Trans.*: 'The Psycho-Sexual Differences Between Hysteria and Dementia Praecox', *Selected Papers*, London, 1927; New York, 1953, Chap. II.]

(1912) 'Ansätze zur psychoanalytischen Erforschung und Behandlung des manisch-depressiven Irreseins und verwandter Zustände', *Zentbl. Psychoanal.*, **2**, 302. (251)

[*Trans.*: 'Notes on the Psycho-Analytical Investigation and Treatment of Manic-Depressive Insanity and Allied Conditions', *Selected Papers*, London, 1927; New York, 1953, Chap. VI.]

ABRAHAM, K. (*cont.*)
(1965) With FREUD, S. *See* FREUD, S. (1965*a*)
ADLER, A. (1907) *Studie über Minderwertigkeit von Organen*, Berlin and Vienna. (93)
[*Trans.*: *Study of Organ-Inferiority and its Psychical Compensation*, New York, 1917.]
(1908) 'Der Aggressionstrieb im Leben und in der Neurose', *Fortschr. Med.*, **26**, 577. (326)
(1910) 'Der psychische Hermaphroditismus im Leben und in der Neurose', *Fortschr. Med.*, **28**, 486. (86)
ANDREAS-SALOMÉ, L., and FREUD, S. (1966) *See* FREUD, S. (1966*a*)
ARISTOTLE *De somniis* and *De divinatione per somnum*. (243)
[*Trans.* by W. S. Hett (in volume 'On the Soul', Loeb Classical Library), London and New York, 1935.]
AZAM, E. (1876) 'Amnésie périodique ou dédoublement de la vie', *Ann. méd. psychol.* (5ᵉ série), **16**, 5. (53)
(1887) *Hypnotisme, double conscience, et altérations de la personnalité*, Paris. (53)
BERNHEIM, H. (1886) *De la suggestion et de ses applications à la thérapeutique*, Paris. (2nd ed., 1887.) (177)
BINSWANGER, L. (1955) *See* FREUD, S. (1955*f*)
BLEULER, E. (1910) 'Vortrag über Ambivalenz' (Berne), Report in *Zentbl. Psychoanal.*, **1**, 266. (128)
(1911) *Dementia Praecox, oder Gruppe der Schizophrenien*, Leipzig and Vienna. (128, 204)
[*Trans.*: *Dementia Praecox, or the Group of Schizophrenias*, New York, 1950.]
(1912) *Das autistische Denken*, Leipzig and Vienna. (37)
[*Trans.*: 'Autistic Thinking', in D. Rapaport (ed.), *Organization and Pathology of Thought*, New York, 1951, Chap. 20.]
(1914) 'Die Kritiken der Schizophrenien', *Z. ges. Neurol. Psychiat.*, **22**, 19. (176)
BREUER, J., and FREUD, S. (1893) *See* FREUD, S. (1893*a*)
(1895) *See* FREUD, S. (1895*d*)
BUTLER, S. (1880) *Unconscious Memory*, London. (211)
CALKINS, G. N. (1902) 'Studies on the Life-History of Protozoa. I. The Life-Cycle of *Paramecium caudatum*', *Arch. Entw. Mech. Org.*, **15**, 139. (320)
DOFLEIN, F. (1919) *Das Problem des Todes und der Unsterblichkeit bei den Pflanzen und Tieren*, Jena. (319)

ELLIS, HAVELOCK (1898) 'Auto-Erotism: A Psychological Study', *Alien. & Neurol.*, **19**, 260. (65)

(1927) 'The Conception of Narcissism', *Psychoanal. Rev.*, **14**, 129; *Studies in the Psychology of Sex*, Vol. VII: *Eonism and Other Supplementary Studies*, Philadelphia, 1928, Chap. VI. (65)

FECHNER. G. T. (1873) *Einige Ideen zur Schöpfungs- und Entwicklungsgeschichte der Organismen*, Leipzig. (276–8, 387, 413)

FEDERN, P. (1913) 'Beiträge zur Analyse des Sadismus und Masochismus, I: Die Quellen des männlichen Sadismus', *Int. Z. ärztl. Psychoanal.*, **1**, 29. (130)

FERENCZI, S. (1909) 'Introjektion und Übertragung', *Jb. psychoanalyt. psychopath. Forsch.*, **1**, 422. (133)

[*Trans.*: 'Introjection and Transference', *First Contributions to Psycho-Analysis*, London, 1952, Chap. II.]

(1913*a*) 'Entwicklungsstufen des Wirklichkeitssinnes', *Int. Z. ärztl. Psychoanal.*, **1**, 124. (67, 314, 375)

[*Trans.*: 'Stages in the Development of the Sense of Reality', *First Contributions to Psycho-Analysis*, London, 1952, Chap. VIII.]

(1913*b*) Review of C. G. Jung's *Wandlungen und Symbole der Libido* (Leipzig and Vienna, 1912), *Int. Z. ärztl. Psychoanal.*, **1**, 391. (72)

et al. (1919) Contributions to a Symposium published as *Zur Psychoanalyse der Kriegsneurosen*, Leipzig and Vienna. (281)

[*Trans.*: *Psycho-Analysis and the War Neuroses*, London, Vienna and New York, 1921.]

FINKELNBURG, F. C. (1870) Niederrheinische Gesellschaft, Sitzung vom 21. März 1870 in Bonn, *Berlin klin. Wschr.*, **7**, 449, 460. (222)

FLIESS, W. (1906) *Der Ablauf des Lebens*, Vienna. (317)

FREUD, A. (1936) *Das Ich und die Abwehrmechanismen*, Vienna. (454)

[*Trans.*: *The Ego and the Mechanisms of Defence*, London, 1937; New York, 1946.]

FREUD, M. (1957) *Glory Reflected*, London. (23)

FREUD, S. (1888–9) Translation with Preface and Notes of H. Bernheim's *De la suggestion et de ses applications à la thérapeutique*, Paris, 1886, under the title *Die Suggestion und ihre Heilwirkung*, Vienna. (177)

[*Trans.*: Preface to the translation of Bernheim's *Suggestion*, *Standard Ed.*, **1**, 73.]

(1891*b*) *On Aphasia*, London and New York, 1953. (163, 169, 177, 207, 213–15, 216, 359)

(1893*a*) With BREUER, J., 'On the Psychical Mechanism of Hysterical

FREUD, S. (*cont.*)
Phenomena: Preliminary Communication', in *Studies on Hysteria*, *Standard Ed.*, **2**, 3; *P.F.L.*, **3**, 53. (141, 282)
(1893*c*) 'Some Points for a Comparative Study of Organic and Hysterical Motor Paralyses', *Standard Ed.*, **1**, 157. (115, 172)
(1893*h*) 'Lecture "On the Psychical Mechanism of Hysterical Phenomena"', *Standard Ed.*, **3**, 27. (115)
(1894*a*) 'The Neuro-Psychoses of Defence', *Standard Ed.*, **3**, 43. (35, 152, 366, 399, 454)
(1895*b* [1894]) 'On the Grounds for Detaching a Particular Syndrome from Neurasthenia under the Description "Anxiety Neurosis"', *Standard Ed.*, **3**, 87; *P.F.L.*, **10**, 31. (77, 110)
(1895*d*) With BREUER, J., *Studies on Hysteria*, London, 1956; *Standard Ed.*, **2**; *P.F.L.*, **3**. (142, 156, 164, 175, 188, 190, 238, 253, 277, 296, 298, 307, 343, 359, 430, 438)
(1896*b*) 'Further Remarks on the Neuro-Psychoses of Defence', *Standard Ed.*, **3**, 159. (154, 344, 347, 356, 460)
(1896*c*) 'The Aetiology of Hysteria', *Standard Ed.*, **3**, 189. (191)
(1900*a*) *The Interpretation of Dreams*, London and New York, 1955; *Standard Ed.*, **4–5**; *P.F.L.*, **4**. (32, 33, 35, 36, 39, 43, 92, 101, 103, 110, 115, 118, 148, 151, 164, 170, 172, 175, 176, 180, 186, 190, 191, 196, 204, 206, 207, 208, 225, 226, 231, 235, 236, 238, 243, 259, 277, 283, 284, 295, 296, 304, 342, 343, 347, 358, 363, 364, 365, 420, 430, 440)
(1901*b*) *The Psychopathology of Everyday Life*, *Standard Ed.*, **6**; *P.F.L.*, **5**. (184, 191, 453)
(1905*c*) *Jokes and their Relation to the Unconscious*, London, 1960; *Standard Ed.*, **8**; *P.F.L.*, **6**. (32, 35, 38, 39, 101, 150, 191, 207, 308, 386, 441)
(1905*d*) *Three Essays on the Theory of Sexuality*, London, 1962; *Standard Ed.*, **7**, 125; *P.F.L.*, **7**, 31. (62, 65, 69, 77, 81, 108, 110, 111, 118, 122, 123, 126, 132, 137, 150, 195, 249, 327, 328, 332, 373, 388, 404, 411, 417, 420, 440)
(1905*e* [1901]) 'Fragment of an Analysis of a Case of Hysteria', *Standard Ed.*, **7**, 3; *P.F.L.*, **8**, 29. (419, 442)
(1906*a* [1905]) 'My Views on the Part played by Sexuality in the Aetiology of the Neuroses', *Standard Ed.*, **7**, 271; *P.F.L.*, **10**, 71. (142)
(1906*f*) 'Contribution to a Questionnaire on Reading', *Standard Ed.*, **9**, 245. (423)

FREUD, S. (*cont.*)
(1907*b*) 'Obsessive Actions and Religious Practices', *Standard Ed.*, **9**, 116; *P.F.L.*, **13**, 27. (110, 347, 366)
(1908*a*) 'Hysterical Phantasies and their Relation to Bisexuality', *Standard Ed.*, **9**, 157; *P.F.L.*, **10**, 83. (39)
(1908*b*) 'Character and Anal Erotism', *Standard Ed.*, **9**, 169; *P.F.L.*, **7**, 205. (368)
(1908*e* [1907]) 'Creative Writers and Day-Dreaming', *Standard Ed.*, **9**, 143; *P.F.L.*, **14**, 129. (39, 42, 85)
(1909*a* [1908]) 'Some General Remarks on Hysterical Attacks', *Standard Ed.*, **9**, 229; *P.F.L.*, **10**, 95. (35)
(1909*b*) 'Analysis of a Phobia in a Five-Year-Old Boy', *Standard Ed.*, **10**, 3; *P.F.L.*, **8**, 165. (118, 119, 178)
(1909*d*) 'Notes upon a Case of Obsessional Neurosis', *Standard Ed.*, **10**, 155; *P.F.L.*, **9**, 31. (142, 157, 437)
(1910*a* [1909]) *Five Lectures on Psycho-Analysis*, *Standard Ed.*, **11**, 3; in *Two Short Accounts of Psycho-Analysis*, Penguin Books, Harmondsworth, 1962. (153)
(1910*c*) *Leonardo da Vinci and a Memory of his Childhood*, *Standard Ed.*, **11**, 59; *P.F.L.*, **14**, 143. (62, 84, 346, 348)
(1910*g*) 'Contribution to a Discussion on Suicide', *Standard Ed.*, **11**, 231. (248)
(1910*i*) 'The Psycho-Analytic View of Psychogenic Disturbance of Vision', *Standard Ed.*, **11**, 211; *P.F.L.*, **10**, 103. (111, 323, 346)
(1911*b*) 'Formulations on the Two Principles of Mental Functioning', *Standard Ed.*, **12**, 215; *P.F.L.*, **11**. (35 ff., 73, 101, 132, 190, 191, 197, 208, 226, 272, 278, 346, 397, 415, 438)
(1911*c* [1910]) 'Psycho-Analytic Notes on an Autobiographical Account of a Case of Paranoia (Dementia Paranoides)', *Standard Ed.*, **12**, 3; *P.F.L.*, **9**, 129. (31, 32, 62, 65, 66, 67, 73, 76, 81, 101, 103, 108, 111, 148, 209, 346)
(1912*b*) 'The Dynamics of Transference', *Standard Ed.*, **12**, 99. (66, 128, 423)
(1912*c*) 'Types of Onset of Neurosis', *Standard Ed.*, **12**, 229; *P.F.L.*, **10**, 115. (78, 201)
(1912*g*) 'A Note on the Unconscious in Psycho-Analysis', *Standard Ed.*, **12**, 257; *P.F.L.*, **11**, 45. (50 ff., 101, 164, 343, 352, 354)
(1912–13) *Totem and Taboo*, London, 1950; New York, 1952; *Standard Ed.*, **13**, 1; *P.F.L.*, **13**, 43. (62, 67, 96, 129, 210, 249, 368, 377, 404)
(1913*c*) 'On Beginning the Treatment', *Standard Ed.*, **12**, 123. (178)

FREUD, S. (*cont.*)

(1913*i*) 'The Disposition to Obsessional Neurosis', *Standard Ed.*, **12**, 313; *P.F.L.*, **10**, 129. (42, 137, 199)

(1914*a*) 'Fausse Reconnaissance ("déjà raconté") in Psycho-Analytic Treatment', *Standard Ed.*, **13**, 201. (453)

(1914*c*) 'On Narcissism: An Introduction', *Standard Ed.*, **14**, 69; *P.F.L.*, **11**, 59. (65 ff., 101, 109, 111, 114, 203, 249, 272, 305, 324, 325, 346, 347, 367, 369, 371, 404)

(1914*d*) 'On the History of the Psycho-Analytic Movement', *Standard Ed.*, **14**, 3; *P.F.L.*, **15**, 57. (62, 87, 132, 176)

(1914*g*) 'Remembering, Repeating and Working-Through (Further Recommendations on the Technique of Psycho-Analysis, II)', *Standard Ed.*, **12**, 147. (288)

(1915*b*) 'Thoughts for the Times on War and Death', *Standard Ed.*, **14**, 275; *P.F.L.*, **12**, 57. (126)

(1915*c*) 'Instincts and their Vicissitudes', *Standard Ed.*, **14**, 111; *P.F.L.*, **11**, 105. (41, 70, 78, 113 ff., 272, 277, 301, 328, 383, 387, 411, 414, 439)

(1915*d*) 'Repression', *Standard Ed.*. **14**, 143; *P.F.L.*, **11**, 139. (87, 145 ff., 191)

(1915*e*) 'The Unconscious', *Standard Ed.*, **14**, 161; *P.F.L.*, **11**. (38, 39, 167 ff., 275, 295, 299, 322, 343, 346, 354, 356, 358, 361, 397, 434, 440)

(1916*d*) 'Some Character-Types Met with in Psycho-Analytic Work', *Standard Ed.*, **14**, 311; *P.F.L.*, **14**, 291. 291. (394, 450)

(1916–17 [1915–17]) *Introductory Lectures on Psycho-Analysis*, New York, 1966; London, 1971; *Standard Ed.*, **15–16**; *P.F.L.*, **1**. (42, 43, 63, 68, 77 92, 112, 122, 123, 172, 181, 200, 230, 235, 290, 347, 386, 405)

(1917*a*) 'A Difficulty in the Path of Psycho-Analysis', *Standard Ed.*, **17**, 137. (404)

(1917*b*) 'A Childhood Recollection from *Dichtung und Wahrheit*', *Standard Ed.*, **17**, 147; *P.F.L.*, **14**, 321. 321. (286)

(1917*d* [1915]) 'A Metapsychological Supplement to the Theory of Dreams', *Standard Ed.*, **14**, 219; *P.F.L.*, **11**. (33, 229 ff., 247, 295, 302, 367, 434)

(1917*e* [1915]) 'Mourning and Melancholia', *Standard Ed.*, **14**, 239; *P.F.L.*, **11**, 245. (63, 206, 251 ff., 347, 348, 367)

(1918*b* [1914]) 'From the History of an Infantile Neurosis', *Standard Ed.*, **17**, 3; *P.F.L.*, **9**, 225. (126, 129, 155, 200, 250, 453)

FREUD, S. (*cont.*)

(1919*d*) Introduction to *Psycho-Analysis and the War Neuroses* (London and New York, 1921); *Standard Ed.*, **17**, 207. (281, 305)

(1919*e*) 'A Child is Being Beaten', *Standard Ed.*, **17**, 177; *P.F.L.*, **10**, 159. (87, 143, 411, 412, 416)

(1919*h*), 'The Uncanny' *Standard Ed.*, **17**, 219; *P.F.L.*, **14**, 335. (272)

(1920*a*) 'The Psychogenesis of a Case of Female Homosexuality', *Standard Ed.*, **18**, 147; *P.F.L.*, **9**, 367. (84)

(1920*g*) *Beyond the Pleasure Principle*, London, 1961; *Standard Ed.*, **18**, 7; *P.F.L.*, **11**. (109, 112, 115, 117, 122, 146, 191, 211, 234, 275 ff., 344, 350, 356, 360, 367, 380, 387, 405, 412, 413, 430, 432, 441)

(1921*b*) Introduction to Varendonck, *The Psychology of Day-Dreams*, London; *Standard Ed.*, **18**, 271. (359)

(1921*c*) *Group Psychology and the Analysis of the Ego*, London and New York, 1959, *Standard Ed.*, **18**, 69; *P.F.L.*, **12**, 91. (63, 88, 89, 93, 96, 226, 249, 250, 259, 268, 348, 349, 367, 368, 370, 371, 377)

(1922*b* [1921]) 'Some Neurotic Mechanisms in Jealousy, Paranoia and Homosexuality', *Standard Ed.*, **18**, 223; *P.F.L.*, **10**, 195. (377)

(1922*f*) 'Some Remarks on the Unconscious', *Standard Ed.*, **19**, 3. (341)

(1923*a* [1922]) 'Two Encyclopaedia Articles', *Standard Ed.*, **18**, 235; *P.F.L.*, **15**, 129. (369, 405)

(1923*b*) *The Ego and the Id*, London and New York, 1962; *Standard Ed.*, **19**, 3; *P.F.L.*, **11**. (49, 62, 63, 70, 89, 112, 165, 181, 197, 208, 227, 249, 250, 260, 261, 272, 325, 327, 350 ff., 403, 412, 420, 421, 440, 459)

(1923*c* [1922]) 'Remarks on the Theory and Practice of Dream-Interpretation', *Standard Ed.*, **19**, 109. (290, 304)

(1923*e*) 'The Infantile Genital Organization', *Standard Ed.*, **19**, 141; *P.F.L.*, **7**, 303. (370, 419, 438)

(1924*b* [1923]) 'Neurosis and Psychosis', *Standard Ed.*, **19**, 149; *P.F.L.*, **10**, 209. (227, 349, 422, 460)

(1924*c*) 'The Economic Problem of Masochism', *Standard Ed.*, **19**, 157; *P.F.L.*, **11**. (115, 118, 125, 276, 329, 349, 391, 396, 413 ff.)

(1924*d*) 'The Dissolution of the Oedipus Complex', *Standard Ed.*, **19**, 173; *P.F.L.*, **7**, 313. (349, 371)

(1924*e*) 'The Loss of Reality in Neurosis and Psychosis', *Standard Ed.*, **19**, 183; *P.F.L.*, **10**, 219. (227, 349)

(1925*a* [1924]) 'A Note upon the "Mystic Writing-Pad"', *Standard Ed.*, **19**, 227; *P.F.L.*, **11**. (193, 227, 234, 296, 300, 429 ff., 441)

FREUD, S. (*cont.*)

(1925*d* [1924]) *An Autobiographical Study*, *Standard Ed.*, **20**, 3; *P.F.L.*, **15**, 183. (14, 142, 405)

(1925*h*) 'Negation', *Standard Ed.*, **19**, 235; *P.F.L.*, **11**, 435. (38, 39, 115, 227, 241, 397, 433, 434, 437 ff.)

(1925*i*) 'Some Additional Notes upon Dream-Interpretation as a Whole', *Standard Ed.*, **19**, 125. (346, 396)

(1925*j*) 'Some Psychical Consequences of the Anatomical Distinction between the Sexes', *Standard Ed.*, **19**, 243; *P.F.L.*, **7**, 323. (84, 349, 371)

(1926*a*) 'To Romain Rolland', *Standard Ed.*, **20**, 279. (444)

(1926*d* [1925]) *Inhibitions, Symptoms and Anxiety*, London, 1960; *Standard Ed.*, **20**, 77; *P.F.L.*, **10**, 227. (142, 143, 146, 153, 181, 186, 189, 279, 282, 290, 301, 349, 375, 382, 399, 400, 421, 455, 462)

(1926*e*) *The Question of Lay Analysis*, London, 1947; *Standard Ed.*, **20**, 179; *P.F.L.*, **15**, 277. (172, 351, 462)

(1926*g*) 'Translation with Footnotes of I. Levine's *The Unconscious* (Part I, Section 13: "Samuel Butler")', London, 1923, under the title *Das Unbewusste*, Vienna. (211)

(1927*a*) 'Postscript to *The Question of Lay Analysis*', *Standard Ed.*, **20**, 251; *P.F.L.*, **15**, 355. (14)

(1927*c*) *The Future of an Illusion*, London, 1962; *Standard Ed.*, **21**, 3; *P.F.L.*, **12**, 179. (423, 447)

(1927*d*) 'Humour', *Standard Ed.*, **21**, 159; *P.F.L.*, **14**, 425. (367)

(1927*e*) 'Fetishism', *Standard Ed.*, **21**, 149; *P.F.L.*, **7**, 345. (143, 227, 460)

(1928*b*) 'Dostoevsky and Parricide', *Standard Ed.*, **21**, 175; *P.F.L.*, **14**, 435. (382)

(1930*a* [1929]) *Civilization and its Discontents*, New York and London, 1963; *Standard Ed.*, **21**, 59; *P.F.L.*, **12**, 243. (112, 115, 241, 328, 346, 349, 383, 391, 396, 412, 426, 430, 439, 444, 451)

(1931*b*) 'Female Sexuality', *Standard Ed.*, **21**, 223; *P.F.L.*, **7**, 367. (84, 286)

(1933*a* [1932]) *New Introductory Lectures on Psycho-Analysis*, New York, 1966; London, 1971; *Standard Ed.*, **22**; *P.F.L.*, **2**. (49, 84, 112, 143, 165, 191, 344, 345, 347, 348, 363, 364, 376, 402, 405, 406, 440, 462)

(1935*a*) Postscript (1935) to *An Autobiographical Study*, new edition, London and New York; *Standard Ed.*, **20**, 71; *P.F.L.*, **15**. (14)

(1936*a*) 'A Disturbance of Memory on the Acropolis', *Standard Ed.*, **22**, 239; *P.F.L.*, **11**, 443. (447 ff.)

FREUD, S. (*cont.*)
(1937*c*) 'Analysis Terminable and Interminable', *Standard Ed.*, **23**, 211. (147, 460)
(1937*d*) 'Constructions in Analysis', *Standard Ed.*, **23**, 257. (442)
(1939*a* [1934–38]) *Moses and Monotheism*, *Standard Ed.*, **23**, 3; *P.F.L.*, **13**, 237. (345, 399)
(1940*a* [1938]) *An Outline of Psycho-Analysis*, New York, 1968; London, 1969; *Standard Ed.*, **23**, 141; *P.F.L.*, **15**. (112, 118, 193, 227, 406, 415, 440, 460)
(1940*b* [1938]) 'Some Elementary Lessons in Psycho-Analysis', *Standard Ed.*, **23**, 281. (162, 170)
(1940*e* [1938]) 'Splitting of the Ego in the Process of Defence', *Standard Ed.*, **23**, 273: *P.F.L.*, **11**, 457. (461 ff.)
(1942*a* [1905–6]) 'Psychopathic Characters on the Stage', *Standard Ed.*, **7**, 305; *P.F.L.*, **14**, 119. (287)
(1950*a* [1887–1902]) *The Origins of Psycho-Analysis*, London and New York, 1954. (Partly, including 'A Project for a Scientific Psychology', in *Standard Ed.*, **1**, 175.) (32, 101, 110, 115, 117, 122, 143, 146, 154, 163, 176, 184, 186, 197, 208, 226, 241, 248, 262, 273, 276, 296, 338, 342, 345, 347, 363, 373, 399, 433, 441, 460)
(1955*c* [1920]) 'Memorandum on the Electrical Treatment of War Neurotics', *Standard Ed.*, **17**, 211. (281)
(1955*f* [1909–38]). Letters and Extracts from Letters to Ludwig Binswanger, in L. Binswanger's *Sigmund Freud: Reminiscences of a Friendship*, New York and London, 1957. (102)
(1960*a*) *Letters 1873–1939* (ed. E. L. Freud) (trans. T. and J. Stern), New York, 1960; London, 1961. (25, 102, 191, 444)
(1963*a* [1909–39]) *Psycho-Analysis and Faith. The Letters of Sigmund Freud and Oskar Pfister* (ed. H. Meng and E. L. Freud) (trans. E. Mosbacher), London and New York, 1963. (25)
(1965*a* [1907–26]) *A Psycho-Analytic Dialogue. The Letters of Sigmund Freud and Karl Abraham* (ed. H. C. Abraham and E. L. Freud) (trans. B. Marsh and H. C. Abraham), London and New York, 1965. (25, 102, 247, 259)
(1966*a* [1912–36]) *Sigmund Freud and Lou Andreas-Salomé: Letters* (ed. E. Pfeiffer) (trans. W. and E. Robson-Scott), London and New York, 1972. (25, 103)
(1968*a* [1927–39]) *The Letters of Sigmund Freud and Arnold Zweig* (ed. E. L. Freud) (trans. W. and E. Robson-Scott), London and New York, 1970. (25)

FREUD, S. (*cont.*)

(1970*a* [1919–35]) *Sigmund Freud as a Consultant. Recollections of a Pioneer in Psychoanalysis* (Letters from Freud to Edoardo Weiss, including a Memoir and Commentaries by Weiss, with Foreword and Introduction by M. Grotjahn), New York, 1970. (25, 87)

(1974*a* [1906–23]) *The Freud/Jung Letters* (ed. W. McGuire) (trans. R. Manheim and R. F. C. Hull), London and Princeton, N.J., 1974. (25)

GOETTE, A. (1883) *Über den Ursprung des Todes*, Hamburg. (319)

GRIESINGER, W. (1845) *Pathologie und Therapie der psychischen Krankheiten*, Stuttgart. (35)

GRODDECK, G. (1923) *Das Buch vom Es*, Vienna. (345, 362)
[*Trans.*: *The Book of the It*, New York, 1950.]

HARTMANN, M. (1906) *Tod und Fortpflanzung*, Munich. (319)

HENDERSON, D. K., and GILLESPIE, R. D. (1969) *A Text-Book of Psychiatry* (10th ed.), London. (453)

HERBART, J. F. (1824–5) *Psychologie als Wissenschaft neu gegründet auf Erfahrung, Metaphysik und Mathematik*, Königsberg. (141–2, 162)

HERING, E. (1870) 'Über das Gedächtnis als eine allgemeine Funktion der organisierten Materie.' Lecture to the Imperial Academy of Sciences, Vienna, 30 May. (211–12)
[*Trans.* Included in S. Butler's *Unconscious Memory*, London, 1880.]

(1878) *Zur Lehre vom Lichtsinne*, Vienna. (322)

JACKSON, J. HUGHLINGS (1878) 'On Affections of Speech from Disease of the Brain', *Brain*, **1**, 304. (215)

JANET, P. (1909) *Les névroses*, Paris. (35, 52, 73)

JEKELS, L. (1913) 'Einige Bemerkungen zur Trieblehre', *Int. Z. ärztl. Psychoanal.*, **1**, 439. (130)

JONES, E. (1953) *Sigmund Freud: Life and Work*, Vol. 1, London and New York. (Page references are to the English edition.) (142, 162, 211)

(1955) *Sigmund Freud: Life and Work*, Vol. 2, London and New York. (Page references are to the English edition.) (47, 61, 63, 102, 148, 247, 259)

(1957) *Sigmund Freud: Life and Work*, Vol. 3, London and New York. (Page references are to the English edition.) (112, 341, 348, 411, 428, 436, 459)

JUNG, C. G. (1909) 'Die Bedeutung des Vaters für das Schicksal des Einzelnen', *Jb. psychoanalyt. psychopath. Forsch.*, **1**, 155. (293)
[*Trans.*: 'The Significance of the Father in the Destiny of the Indi-

JUNG, C. G. (*cont.*)
vidual', *Collected Papers on Analytical Psychology*, London, 1916 (2nd ed., London, 1917; New York, 1920), Chap. III.]
(1911–12) 'Wandlungen und Symbole der Libido', *Jb. psychoanalyt. psychopath. Forsch.*, **3**, 120 and **4**, 162; in book form, Leipzig and Vienna, 1912. (72, 423)
[*Trans.*: *Psychology of the Unconscious*, New York, 1916; London, 1917.]
(1913) 'Versuch einer Darstellung der psychoanalytischen Theorie', *Jb. psychoanalyt. psychopath. Forsch.*, **5**, 307; in book form, Leipzig and Vienna, 1913. (73)
[*Trans.*: *The Theory of Psycho-Analysis*, New York, 1915.]
(1974) With FREUD, S. *See* FREUD, S. (1974*a*)

KANT, I. (1781) *Kritik der reinen Vernunft*, Riga. (2nd ed., 1787.) (173, 299, 422)

KRIS, E. (1956) 'Freud in the History of Science', *The Listener*, **55**, No. 1416 (17 May), 631. (211)

LANDAUER, K. (1914) 'Spontanheilung einer Katatonie', *Int. Z. ärztl. Psychoanal.*, **2**, 441. (258)

LEVINE, I. (1923) *The Unconscious*, London. (211)

LIPSCHÜTZ, A. (1914) *Warum wir sterben*, Stuttgart. (319, 320, 328, 329)

LOEB, J. (1909) *Die chemische Entwicklungserregung des tierischen Eies: künstliche Parthenogenese*, Paris. (321)

LOW, B. (1920) *Psycho-Analysis*, London and New York. (329, 413)

MARCINOWSKI, J. (1918) 'Erotische Quellen der Minderwertigkeitsgefühle', *Z. SexWiss., Bonn*, **4**, 313. (291)

MAUPAS, E. (1888) 'Recherches expérimentales sur la multiplication des infusoires ciliés', *Arch. Zool. exp. gén.* (Sér. 2), **6**, 165. (320)

MILL, J. S. (1843) *A System of Logic*, London. (222)
(1865) *An Examination of Sir William Hamilton's Philosophy*, London. (222)

'MULTATULI' [E. D. DEKKER] (1906) *Multatuli-Briefe* (2 vols.), Frankfurt. (423)

MÜNSTERBERG, H. (1908) *Philosophie der Werte: Grundzüge einer Weltanschauung*, Leipzig. (348)

NÄCKE, P. (1899) 'Kritisches zum Kapitel der normalen und pathologischen Sexualität', *Arch. Psychiat. Nervenkrankh.*, **32**, 356. (65)

PFEIFER, S. (1919) 'Äusserungen infantil-erotischer Triebe im Spiele', *Imago*, **5**, 243. (283)

PFISTER, O., and FREUD, S. (1963) *See* FREUD, S. (1963*a*)

Plato *Symposium*. (331)
[*Trans*. by B. Jowett, in *Dialogues*, Vol. 2, Oxford, 1871.]

Rank, O. (1907) *Der Künstler, Ansätze zu einer Sexualpsychologie*, Leipzig and Vienna. (42, 328)

(1910) 'Schopenhauer über den Wahnsinn', *Zentbl. Psychoanal*., **1**, 69. (35)

(1911) 'Ein Beitrag zum Narzissismus', *Jb. psychoanalyt. psychopath. Forsch*., **3**, 401. (62, 65)

(1913) 'Der "Familienroman" in der Psychologie des Attentäters', *Int. Z. ärztl. Psychoanal*., **1**, 565. (385)

Reitler, R. (1913) 'Zur Genital- und Sekret-Symbolik'. *Int. Z. ärztl. Psychoanal*., **1**, 492. (206)

Sachs, H. (1945) *Freud, Master and Friend*, Cambridge (Mass.) and London. (Page reference is to the English edition.) (48, 423)

Schopenhauer, A. (1819) *Die Welt als Wille und Vorstellung*, Leipzig. (2nd ed., Leipzig, 1844.) In *Sämtliche Werke* (ed. Hübscher) (2nd ed.), Vols. 2–3, Wiesbaden, 1949. (35)

(1851) 'Über die anscheinende Absichtlichkeit im Schicksale des Einzelnen', *Parerga und Paralipomena* (Essay IV), Vol. 1, Leipzig. (2nd ed., Berlin, 1862.) In *Sämtliche Werke* (ed. Hübscher), Leipzig, 1938, Vol. 5, 213. (322)

Silberer, H. (1909) 'Bericht über eine Methode, gewisse symbolische Halluzinations-Erscheinungen hervorzurufen und zu beobachten', *Jb. psychoanalyt. psychopath. Forsch*., **1**, 513. (91–2)

(1912) 'Symbolik des Erwachens und Schwellensymbolik überhaupt', *Jb. psychoanalyt. psychopath. Forsch*., **3**, 621. (91–2)

(1914) *Probleme der Mystik und ihrer Symbolik*, Leipzig and Vienna. (236)
[*Trans*.: *Problems of Mysticism and its Symbolism*, New York, 1917.]

Spamer, C. (1876) 'Über Aphasie und Asymbolie nebst Versuch einer Theorie der Sprachbildung', *Arch. Psychiat. Nervenkrankh*., **6**, 496. (222)

Spielrein, S. (1912) 'Die Destruktion als Ursache des Werdens', *Jb. psychoanalyt. psychopath. Forsch*., **4**, 465. (328)

Stärcke, A. (1914) Introduction to Dutch translation of Freud's '"Civilized" Sexual Morality and Modern Nervous Illness', Leyden. (328)

Stekel, W. (1908) *Nervöse Angstzustände und ihre Behandlung*, Berlin and Vienna. (399)

STOUT, G. F. (1938) *A Manual of Psychology* (5th ed.), London. (1st ed., 1899.) (217)

TAUSK, V. (1913) 'Entwertung des Verdrängungsmotivs durch Rekompense', *Int. Z. ärztl. Psychoanal.*, **1**, 230. (265)

[*Trans.*: 'Compensation as a Means of Discounting the Motive of Repression', *Int. J. Psycho-Analysis*, **5** (1924), 130.]

(1919) 'Über die Entstehung des "Beeinflussungsapparates" in der Schizophrenie', *Int. Z. ärztl. Psychoanal.*, **5**, 1. (203)

[*Trans.*: 'On the Origin of the "Influencing Machine" in Schizophrenia', in *The Psycho-Analytic Reader* (ed. R. Fliess), New York, 1948; London, 1950.]

TROTTER, W. (1916) *Instincts of the Herd in Peace and War*, London. (88)

VARENDONCK, J. (1921) *The Psychology of Day-Dreams*, London and New York. (359)

WEISMANN, A. (1882) *Über die Dauer des Lebens*, Jena. (318, 319)

(1884) *Über Leben und Tod*, Jena. (318, 319)

(1892) *Das Keimplasma*, Jena. (318, 330)

[*Trans.*: *The Germ-Plasm*, London, 1893.]

WEISS, E., and FREUD, S. (1970) *See* FREUD, S. (1970*a*)

WERNICKE, C. (1900) *Grundriss der Psychiatrie*, Leipzig. (363)

WOODRUFF, L. L. (1914) 'A Five-Year Pedigreed Race of *Paramecium* without Conjugation', *Proc. Soc. exp. Biol.*, **9**, 129. (320)

ZIEGLER, K. (1913) 'Menschen- und Weltenwerden', *Neue Jb. klass. Altert.*, **31**, 529. (332)

ZWEIG, A., and FREUD, S. (1968) *See* FREUD, S. (1968*a*)

LIST OF ABBREVIATIONS

Gesammelte Schriften	=	Freud, *Gesammelte Schriften* (12 vols.), Vienna, 1924–34.
Gesammelte Werke	=	Freud, *Gesammelte Werke* (18 vols.), Vols. 1–17 London, 1940–52, Vol. 18 Frankfurt am Main, 1968. From 1960 the whole edition published by S. Fischer Verlag, Frankfurt am Main.
Almanach 1937	=	*Almanach für das Jahr 1937*, Vienna, Internationaler Psychoanalytischer Verlag, 1936.
S.K.S.N.	=	Freud, *Sammlung kleiner Schriften zur Neurosenlehre* (5 vols.), Vienna, 1906–22.
Collected Papers	=	Freud, *Collected Papers* (5 vols.), London, 1924–50.
Standard Edition	=	*The Standard Edition of the Complete Psychological Works of Sigmund Freud* (24 vols.), Hogarth Press and The Institute of Psycho-Analysis, London, 1953–74.
P.F.L.	=	*Pelican Freud Library* (15 vols.), Penguin Books, Harmondsworth, from 1973.

GENERAL INDEX

This index includes the names of non-technical authors. It also includes the names of technical authors where no reference is made in the text to specific works. For references to specific technical works, the Bibliography should be consulted.

THE PELICAN FREUD LIBRARY

Based on James Strachey's Standard Edition, this collection of fifteen volumes is the first full paperback edition of Freud's works in English. The first eleven volumes have been edited by Angela Richards, and subsequent volumes by Albert Dickson.

1 INTRODUCTORY LECTURES ON PSYCHOANALYSIS
2 NEW INTRODUCTORY LECTURES ON PSYCHOANALYSIS
3 STUDIES ON HYSTERIA (by Josef Breuer and Sigmund Freud)
4 THE INTERPRETATION OF DREAMS
5 THE PSYCHOPATHOLOGY OF EVERYDAY LIFE
6 JOKES AND THEIR RELATION TO THE UNCONSCIOUS
7 ON SEXUALITY (including *Three Essays on the Theory of Sexuality* and shorter clinical and theoretical papers)
8 CASE HISTORIES I ('Dora' and 'Little Hans')
9 CASE HISTORIES II ('The Rat Man', Schreber, 'The Wolf Man', A Case of Female Homosexuality)
10 PSYCHOPATHOLOGY (including *Inhibitions, Symptoms and Anxiety* and shorter works on Hysteria, Anxiety Neurosis, Obsessional Neurosis, Paranoia and Perversions)
11 METAPSYCHOLOGY – The Theory of Psychoanalysis (including *Beyond the Pleasure Principle*, *The Ego and the Id*, and papers on the Unconscious, Narcissism, the theory of the instincts, Mourning and Melancholia, Masochism, the theory of mental functioning)
12 CIVILIZATION, SOCIETY AND RELIGION (including *Group Psychology*, *The Future of an Illusion*, *Civilization and its Discontents* and shorter works)
13 THE ORIGINS OF RELIGION (including *Totem and Taboo*, *Moses and Monotheism* and shorter works)
14 ART AND LITERATURE (including writings on Dostoyevsky, Goethe, E. T. A. Hoffmann, Ibsen, Jensen, Leonardo, Michelangelo, Shakespeare, Stefan Zweig and the case of the 17th-century painter Christoph Haizmann)
15 THE HISTORY OF PSYCHOANALYSIS AND EXPOSITORY WORKS (including 'On the History of the Psychoanalytic Movement', *An Autobiographical Study*, *The Question of Lay Analysis*, *An Outline of Psychoanalysis* and shorter works)